Law, Society, Policy

Series Editor: **Rosie Harding**,
University of Birmingham

Law, Society, Policy offers an outlet for high quality, socio-legal research monographs and edited collections with the potential for policy impact.

Also available in the series:

Adult Social Care Law and Policy
by **Jean McHale** and **Laura Noszlopy**

Mental Capacity Law, Sexual Relationships, and Intimacy
edited by **Beverley Clough** and **Laura Pritchard-Jones**

Children's Voices, Family Disputes and Child-Inclusive Mediation
by **Anne Barlow** and **Jan Ewing**

Observing Justice
by **Judith Townend** and **Lucy Welsh**

Egalitarian Digital Privacy
by **Tsachi Keren-Paz**

Fragile Rights
by **Anne Revillard**

Polygamy, Policy and Postcolonialism in English Marriage Law
by **Zainab Naqvi**

Intersex Embodiment
by **Fae Garland** and **Mitchell Travis**

Unsettling Apologies
edited by **Melanie Judge** and **Dee Smythe**

Death, Family and the Law
by **Edward Kirton-Darling**

Deprivation of Liberty in the Shadows of the Institution
by **Lucy Series**

Women, Precarious Work and Care
by **Emily Grabham**

Pandemic Legalities
edited by **Dave Cowan** and **Ann Mumford**

Find out more at:

bristoluniversitypress.co.uk/law-society-policy

Law, Society, Policy

Series Editor: **Rosie Harding**,
University of Birmingham

Find out more at:

bristoluniversitypress.co.uk/law-society-policy

FUTURE DIRECTIONS IN SURROGACY LAW

Law and Policy Reform in the UK and Beyond

Edited by
Kirsty Horsey, Zaina Mahmoud and
Katherine Wade

BRISTOL
UNIVERSITY
PRESS

First published in Great Britain in 2025 by

Bristol University Press
University of Bristol
1–9 Old Park Hill
Bristol
BS2 8BB
UK
t: +44 (0)117 374 6645
e: bup-info@bristol.ac.uk

Details of international sales and distribution partners are available at bristoluniversitypress.co.uk

British Library Cataloguing in Publication Data
A catalogue record for this book is available from the British Library

ISBN 978-1-5292-3876-1 hardcover
ISBN 978-1-5292-3877-8 ePub
ISBN 978-1-5292-3878-5 ePdf

Cover design: Andrew Corbett
Front cover image: iStock/kamisoka
Bristol University Press uses environmentally responsible print partners.
Printed and bound in Great Britain by CPI Group (UK) Ltd, Croydon, CR0 4YY

FSC
www.fsc.org
MIX
Paper | Supporting responsible forestry
FSC® C013604

Contents

Series Editor's Preface

The Law, Society, Policy series publishes high-quality, socio-legal research monographs and edited collections with the potential for policy impact. Cutting across the traditional divides of legal scholarship, Law, Society, Policy offers an interdisciplinary, policy-engaged approach to socio-legal research that explores law in its social and political contexts with a particular focus on the place of law in everyday life.

The series seeks to take an explicitly society-first view of socio-legal studies, with a focus on the ways that law shapes social life, and the constitutive nature of law and society. International in scope, engaging with domestic, international and global legal and regulatory frameworks, texts in the Law, Society, Policy series engage with the full range of socio-legal topics and themes.

List of Abbreviations

ACART	Advisory Committee on Assisted Reproductive Technology (New Zealand)
AHRRA	Assisted Human Reproduction Regulatory Authority (Ireland)
ART	assisted reproductive techniques
CAFCASS	Children and Family Court Advisory and Support Service
CAHR	Commission on Assisted Human Reproduction (Ireland)
CHIP	Child Identity Protection Network
DHSC	Department of Health and Social Care
ECART	Ethics Committee on Assisted Reproductive Technology (New Zealand)
ECHR	European Convention on Human Rights
ECtHR	European Court of Human Rights
FCDO	Foreign Commonwealth and Development Office
HCCH	Hague Conference on Private International Law
HFEA	Human Fertilisation and Embryology Authority (regulator of the fertility and embryology sector in the UK)
HFE Act	Human Fertilisation and Embryology Act 1990 or 2008
IP	intended parent
IVF	in vitro fertilisation
NECAHR	National Ethics Committee on Assisted Human Reproduction (New Zealand)
NGO	non-governmental organisation
NICE	National Institute for Health and Clinical Excellence
NZLC	New Zealand Law Commission
PROGAR	Project Group on Assisted Reproduction
RSA	proposed new regulated surrogacy agreement
RSO	proposed new regulated surrogacy organisation
RSS	proposed new regulated surrogacy statement

SAA	Surrogacy Arrangements Act 1985
SR	proposed new surrogacy register
UNCRC	United Nations Convention on the Rights of the Child 1989
UNICEF	United Nations International Children's Emergency Fund

Glossary

Commercial surrogacy	A form of surrogacy typified by profit-making intermediaries (brokers, agencies and so on), enforceable arrangements and compensated surrogates.
Compensated surrogacy	A system of surrogacy that allows for payments to surrogates over and above out-of-pocket expenses.
Domestic surrogacy	A surrogacy arrangement between UK-based IPs and a UK-based surrogate.
Gestational surrogacy	Where a woman carries a child genetically unrelated to herself on behalf of others, following the transfer of an embryo created using IVF. The embryo could be created using gametes from both IPs, or one IP plus a donor or, in rare cases, from donation of both egg and sperm.
Intended parent	A person who uses a surrogacy arrangement to have a child, and who intends to raise that child from birth. Intended parents may or may not be genetically related to the child.
International surrogacy	A surrogacy arrangement undertaken across international borders (sometimes referred to as cross-border surrogacy).
Parental order	A court order removing legal parenthood from the surrogate (and her spouse/partner where appropriate) and granting it to the intended parent(s).
Surrogate	A woman who agrees to carry and give birth to a child that will be raised by its intended parent(s).

Surrogacy expenses Out-of-pocket expenses incurred by a surrogate in preparation for, during or connected to the surrogacy process.

Traditional surrogacy Where a woman carries a child genetically related to herself on behalf of others. This could be following the transfer of an embryo created using her egg, or via her insemination in either a clinical setting or at home.

Notes on Contributors

Alan Brown is Senior Lecturer in Private Law at the University of Glasgow. His research interests are primarily in the field of family law, focusing on the construction of the family and parenthood within the law, particularly in the context of assisted reproduction, surrogacy and non-traditional families. His monograph, *What is the Family of Law? – The Influence of the Nuclear Family*, involves a discursive and theoretical analysis of the definition and construction of 'family' within the law.

Natalie Gamble is a UK surrogacy lawyer who founded the UK's first fertility law firm NGA Law and non-profit surrogacy agency Brilliant Beginnings. She and her team have moved the law forward through 21 reported surrogacy cases (to date). She has given expert advice to government departments and international organisations, and is a regular voice at global conferences, in Parliament and the media. She is co-chair of the Academy of Assisted Reproduction and Adoption Attorneys International Committee, chairs the UK and Ireland LGBT Family Law Institute, is a member of the Law, Policy and Ethics Special Interest Group of the British Fertility Society, and is the UK representative on the International Advisory Board of Growing Families.

Kirsty Horsey is Professor in Law at the University of Kent. Her research focuses on the socio-legal implications of families created by assisted reproduction, particularly surrogacy. Since 2015, she has been involved in campaigning for surrogacy law reform, initially as the academic member of the SurrogacyUK Working Group on Legal Reform. She sits on the Ethics Committee of SurrogacyUK and is a member of the Advisory Board of My Surrogacy Journey and the Law, Policy and Ethics Special Interest Group of the British Fertility Society. She is a co-investigator on the Children's Voices in Surrogacy Law project.

Marianna Iliadou is Lecturer in Law at the University of Sussex. She conducts research at the intersection of medical law, family law, and human rights. Marianna's research includes, among other topics, domestic and international surrogacy practices within and beyond Europe, medically assisted reproduction and legal parenthood, and the human rights and reproductive justice frameworks.

Zaina Mahmoud is Lecturer in Law at the School of Law and Social Justice, University of Liverpool, with a keen interest in (assisted) reproduction and gestation. Her socio-legal empirical doctoral thesis compared surrogacy regulation in the UK and California. She is a co-investigator on the Children's Voices in Surrogacy Law project. Her published work related to legal and regulatory issues in surrogacy may be found in various leading academic publications, as well as various edited collections.

Lottie Park-Morton is Senior Lecturer in Law at the University of Gloucestershire. She researches in family and medical law, with a particular interest in surrogacy and legal parenthood. Her PhD, defended December 2024, was a doctrinal examination of domestic surrogacy laws from a child rights perspective.

Linder Pott has helped to create families as a surrogate and has represented the voices of surrogates throughout the Law Commissions' consultation on surrogacy law reform. She has previously sat on SurrogacyUK's Ethics Committee and Board of Directors and is now Chair of the Board of Trustees of the SurrogacyUK Foundation, the UK's first surrogacy charity.

Brian Tobin is Associate Professor in Law at the University of Galway, Republic of Ireland, specialising in Child and Family Law, with a focus on non-traditional families. He has given oral evidence on the intersection between the law, surrogacy and AHR techniques to parliamentary committees in Ireland and the UK. His book, *The Legal Recognition of Same-Sex Relationships: Emerging Families in Ireland and Beyond*, was published by Hart in Spring 2023.

Katherine Wade is Lecturer in Family Law at Bristol Law School. She researches issues in family law and medical law from a children's rights perspective. Her current research is focused on surrogacy and donor conception. She is Principal Investigator on the Children's Voices in Surrogacy Law project.

Alan White is a parent through surrogacy and Chair of SurrogacyUK's Board of Directors. As Chair, he is overseeing SurrogacyUK's sustainability, resilience and organisational development in preparation for regulated status if the Law Commissions' proposals become law. Alan is also a founding Trustee of the SurrogacyUK Foundation.

Debra Wilson is Professor of Law at the University of Canterbury, Aotearoa New Zealand, and a member of the Governmental Advisory Committee on Assisted Reproductive Technology (ACART). She was also a member of the New Zealand Law Commission Expert Advisory Group on Surrogacy Law Reform. Her research spans criminal and medical law, especially surrogacy.

1

Introduction: Future Directions in Surrogacy Law – Law and Policy Reform in the UK and Beyond

Kirsty Horsey, Zaina Mahmoud and Katherine Wade

Surrogacy, a pre-conception arrangement in which a woman ('the surrogate'), becomes pregnant, carries and gives birth to child(ren) on behalf of the 'intended parent(s)' (IPs) is a form of assisted reproduction used by couples or individuals who are medically or socially unable to have a child.[1] Surrogacy arrangements fall into one of two types. The first, 'gestational surrogacy', requires clinic involvement and IVF using the IPs' gametes, donor gametes, or a combination of both, and the surrogate subsequently carries a genetically unrelated foetus. The alternative, 'traditional surrogacy', does not necessarily require clinic involvement, with pregnancy often established via self-insemination of the surrogate's own egg with an intended father's sperm.[2]

In the UK, surrogacy has been regulated for 40 years and is practised on what is defined as an 'altruistic' basis. Unlike in some jurisdictions, commercial aspects of surrogacy, such as the involvement of for-profit

---

[1] See the broad definition of 'infertility' adopted by the American Society for Reproductive Medicine, which includes a larger group of individuals/couples seeking to build families, irrespective of sexual orientation or relationship status, and aims to maximise both inclusion and access to care, well summarised in Sigal Klipstein, 'Family building is a basic human right' (22 January 2024) *BioNews* 1223. Throughout this collection we use female pronouns when referring to surrogates, though we are aware that not all surrogates are women.

[2] See *Glossary* in the Law Commission of England and Wales and Scottish Law Commission's joint consultation on surrogacy (Law Commission and Scottish Law Commission: Joint Consultation Paper, *Building Families Through Surrogacy: a New Law* (Law Com Consultation Paper No 244, Scot Law Com Discussion Paper No 167, 6 June 2019), xvi; xx.

agencies or intermediaries facilitating or negotiating arrangements are prohibited.[3] All surrogacy agreements are unenforceable,[4] as is advertising for or as a surrogate.[5] Legal parenthood rests with the surrogate at birth (and her spouse/civil partner of either sex, if she has one),[6] but can be transferred to IPs via a 'parental order', a bespoke court order granted when certain conditions are met, including that the surrogate should have received no more than 'reasonable expenses' in connection with the arrangement.[7] Despite being vanishingly rare, many IPs perceive there to be a high risk in domestic surrogacy arrangements that the surrogate will change her mind and seek to keep the baby. Others feel there is a danger they may not obtain a parental order if they make a mistake in relation to 'reasonable expenses' (despite the law not actually prohibiting payments to surrogates) or they 'fail' the post-birth welfare of the child assessment conducted by the court-appointed officer of the Children and Family Court Advisory and Support Service (CAFCASS).[8] Indeed, domestic cases reveal how surrogacy law remains 'hazy' to many,[9] and is 'contradictory and confusing'.[10] This is also reflected in the results of several surveys to which surrogates and IPs have responded.[11]

The emergence of cross-border or international surrogacy arrangements in the early 21st century – and the domestic courts' attempts to deal

---

3 Surrogacy Arrangements Act 1985, s2.

4 ibid, s1A.

5 ibid, s3.

6 Human Fertilisation and Embryology (HFE) Act 2008, s33.

7 ibid, ss54 (couples) and 54A (single applicants). Most orders are granted by a local family court, though some applications (including all international surrogacy cases) go to the Family Division of the High Court. There are some differences between court processes in England & Wales and Scotland (see Law Commissions, n2, chapter 6).

8 The court appoints a 'parental order reporter' to surrogacy cases upon receipt of a parental order application. Their job is to report to the court on the suitability of the IPs' arrangements and ability to provide for the child's welfare, and whether the ss54/54A HFE Act 2008 criteria are met.

9 Kirsty Horsey and Sally Sheldon, 'Still Hazy After All These Years: the Law Regulating Surrogacy' (2012) 20(4) *Medical Law Review* 67.

10 Amel Alghrani and Danielle Griffiths, 'The Regulation of Surrogacy in the United Kingdom: the Case for Reform' (2017) 29 *Child and Family Law Quarterly* 165, 166.

11 See, inter alia: Kirsty Horsey, 'Surrogacy in the UK: Myth Busting and Reform' Report of the Surrogacy UK Working Group on Surrogacy Law Reform (Surrogacy UK, November 2015); Kirsty Horsey, 'Surrogacy in the UK: Further Evidence for Reform' Report of the Surrogacy UK Working Group on Surrogacy Law Reform (Surrogacy UK, December 2018); Kirsty Horsey, Mimi Arian-Schad, Nicholas Macklon and Kamal Ahuja, 'UK Surrogates' Characteristics, Experiences, and Views on Surrogacy Law Reform' (2022) 36 *International Journal of Law, Policy and the Family* ebac030; Kirsty Horsey, Mimi Arian-Schad, Nicholas Macklon and Kamal Ahuja, 'UK Intended Parents' Characteristics,

with these – led to a situation in which existing regulation of surrogacy is 'no longer fit for purpose' – if it ever was.[12] Drivers for international surrogacy arrangements are indubitably fuelled by the inadequacies of domestic law. Confusions related to acceptable payments/expenses and the uncertainty felt by IPs (both that they will successfully have a child and/or become legal parents) result in some seeking overseas arrangements, especially in jurisdictions where surrogacy contracts are enforceable.[13] International surrogacy arrangements are typically commercial, with payments made to agencies, other professionals, brokers and surrogates. As the court's primary obligation is to consider the lifelong welfare of the child,[14] commercial payments are usually retrospectively judicially authorised when considering whether a parental order should be granted, as the child will (usually) by that time be living with and being cared for by the IPs. This creates a contradiction within law and practice relating to surrogacy: the law formally prohibits commercial activity in domestic surrogacy arrangements yet 'allows' it when IPs undertake surrogacy overseas.[15]

'Pull factors' towards international surrogacy include the recognition of IPs as parents on birth certificates from birth, or the promise of citizenship for the child, which expedites the ability to obtain a child's passport, enabling the family to travel home. Nevertheless, there is considerable variability in how surrogacy is practised globally. It is important for IPs to distinguish between destinations where there is poor practice (including but not limited to infringements on surrogates' autonomy, as well as more dangerous medical practices including the transfer of multiple embryos) from those where surrogacy is regulated, safe and practised ethically.[16] However, this tends to

---

Experiences, and Views on Surrogacy Law Reform' (2023) 37 *International Journal of Law, Policy and the Family* ebad004.

12 All-Party Parliamentary Group on Surrogacy, 'Report on understandings of the law and practice of surrogacy' (October 2020), available at www.andrewpercy.org/storage/app/media/appgs/Surrogacy%20APPG%204.pdf (last accessed 26 June 2024), p3.

13 See Vasanti Jadva, Helen Prosser and Natalie Gamble, (2018) 'Cross-border and Domestic Surrogacy in the UK Context: an Exploration of Practical and Legal Decision-making' 24(2) *Human Fertility* 93 and Claire Fenton-Glynn (2022) 'International Surrogacy Arrangements: a Survey' (Cambridge Family Law, April 2022), available at www.family.law.cam.ac.uk/sites/www.law.cam.ac.uk/files/images/www.family.law.cam.ac.uk/documents/surrogacy/international_surrogacy_arrangements_-_a_survey_april_2022.pdf (last accessed 26 February 2024); see also Horsey (2018), n11.

14 Human Fertilisation and Embryology (Parental Order) Regulations 2010.

15 It should be noted that the terms 'altruistic' and 'commercial', when used to describe surrogacy are not only contested but have different meanings in different contexts.

16 Lavanya Fischer, Natalie Gamble, Kirsty Horsey, Emily Jackson, Denise Seidelman and Richard Vaughn, 'Surrogacy Needs to be Regulated, not Prohibited' (2024) *British Medical*

come at increased financial cost. For example, where regulated, safe, and ethical surrogacy takes place in the US, IPs can expect to pay more than £250,000 for one surrogacy journey.

Overview of UK surrogacy and its regulation

The first birth following IVF was reported in 1978, raising concerns that developments in reproductive medicine – particularly those involving third parties in the reproductive process – could threaten the sanctity of the nuclear family.[17] In 1982, a government committee of inquiry was established, chaired by moral philosopher Mary Warnock, to consider all aspects of fertility treatments (including surrogacy) and related science, and to recommend regulation. The Warnock Report was published in 1984, recommending regulation of human fertilisation and embryology based on an assumed 'common moral position' on the importance of promoting the nuclear family.[18] The committee had little positive to say about surrogacy, remarking that 'a woman [who] deliberately allows herself to become pregnant with the intention of giving up the child to which she will give birth … is the wrong way to approach pregnancy'.[19] It was swayed by arguments against surrogacy, including the danger of exploitation (without explanation or evidence for this) and moral objections to a practice which it viewed as persons being used as a means to another's end.[20] The majority of the committee recommended that surrogacy agencies (both commercial and non-profit) be prohibited, that all surrogacy agreements should be void and unenforceable,[21] and that participants in surrogacy arrangements other than the parties themselves should be criminalised (private parties involved

Journal 386:e079542; Kirsty Horsey, 'The Future of Surrogacy: a Review of Current Global Trends and National Landscapes' (2023) 48(5) *Reproductive BioMedicine Online* 103764.

17 Committee of Inquiry into Human Fertilisation and Embryology, Report Cmnd 9314 (1984) (London: HMSO) ('Warnock Report'), para 2.02.

18 ibid, 3.

19 ibid, para 8.11. Michael Freeman called this a 'moralistic, paternalistic' stance ('Is Surrogacy Exploitative?' in Sheila McLean (ed.), *Legal Issues in Human Reproduction* (Dartmouth 1989) 166). Writing several years later, Mary Warnock acknowledged that this position was wrong, and based on incorrect assumptions she had made about surrogacy (Mary Warnock, 'Foreword: the Need for Full Reform of the Law on Surrogacy' (2016) 4(3) *Journal of Medical Law and Ethics* 155).

20 Warnock Report, ibid, paras 8.17–8.19. A good discussion of the Warnock Committee majority's response to surrogacy, the social context in which it arose and the assumptions it rested upon, is seen in Zaina Mahmoud, 'Surrogates Across the Atlantic: Comparing the Impact of Legal and Health Regulatory Frameworks on Surrogates' Autonomy, Health, and Wellbeing' (unpublished PhD, University of Exeter 2023), s2.1.1.

21 Warnock Report, ibid, para 8.19.

would avoid the 'taint of criminality').[22] It also recommended that the legal principle *mater est quam gestatio demonstrat* (by birth, motherhood is demonstrated) be enshrined in law, whether a surrogacy arrangement was traditional or gestational, meaning that IPs would have to adopt any resulting child.[23] A dissenting minority contended that surrogacy was the only option for some infertile couples, and that demand would not cease, arguing that surrogacy should therefore not be prohibited, but rather be regulated and overseen by licensed surrogacy agencies.[24]

Around the same time, *Re C* (known as the 'Baby Cotton' case)[25] caused much public debate. Kim Cotton, a British woman, acted as a traditional surrogate for an anonymous Swedish couple in an arrangement organised by an American agency based in London, for £6,500. After the birth, she left the baby girl in the care of the hospital until she was collected by the couple. The child was subsequently made a ward of court, until the court was convinced that she should be raised by the couple. This was not the first domestic surrogacy case, but was the first to receive widespread media attention, described as veering on 'moral panic'.[26] The first reported domestic surrogacy cases in the late 1970s and early 1980s evidenced severe judicial disapproval of surrogacy.[27] Soon after the Warnock Report's publication and the negative public response to *Re C*, the Surrogacy Arrangements Act (SAA) 1985 was hastily passed. Intended as an immediate, necessary, and short-term response,[28] rather than a comprehensive solution, the SAA 1985 aimed to discourage the practice of surrogacy.[29] The short Act comprises only five

---

[22] ibid, para 8.18: 'We do not envisage that this legislation would render private persons entering into surrogacy arrangements liable to criminal prosecution, as we are anxious to avoid children being born to mothers subject to the taint of criminality'.

[23] ibid, para 8.20. At the time, adoption was the only way to formally transfer legal parenthood from one party to another.

[24] ibid, 'Expression of Dissent A: Surrogacy'.

[25] *Re C (A minor) (Wardship: surrogacy)* [1985] FLR 846.

[26] Mahmoud, n20.

[27] Surrogacy arrangements were inter alia described as 'immoral', 'unnatural', 'sordid', and 'a kind of baby-farming operation of a wholly distasteful and lamentable kind' – see especially Ormrod LJ in *A v C* [1985] FLR 445. The state was concerned for child welfare, even where no dispute arose (see Kim Cotton, 'The UK's Antiquated Laws on Surrogacy: a Personal and Professional Perspective' (2016) 4(3) *Journal of Medical Law and Ethics* 229).

[28] The government said that it intended to introduce 'comprehensive legislation as soon as practicable': *Hansard* HC Deb, vol 77, 15 April 1985: Surrogacy Arrangements Bill.

[29] Or, as put by Margaret Brazier, the expectation was that surrogacy would 'wither on the vine' (Surrogacy: Review for Health Ministers of Current Arrangements for Payments and Regulation, Report of the Review Team Cm 4068 (1998) (HMSO) ('the Brazier Report') para 2.23 and Margaret Brazier, 'Regulating the Reproduction Business?' *Medical Law Review* 166 (1999), 180).

sections, including criminal provisions, aimed to secure this discouragement and protect (presumed vulnerable) women and children.[30]

Five years after the SAA, the Human Fertilisation and Embryology (HFE) Act 1990 defined the legal parents of children born following assisted conception procedures, including surrogacy. As this legislation passed through Parliament, a late amendment established parental orders, allowing the transfer of legal parenthood from the surrogate (and her spouse/partner, where appropriate) to IPs, without recourse to adoption.[31] The amendment was moved by Michael Jopling MP, after he was approached by constituents who objected to adopting their biological child following a gestational surrogacy arrangement.[32] Initially, parental orders could only be granted to heterosexual married couples, but eligibility criteria were later updated to include same-sex and unmarried couples, and still later to include single individuals, and are now contained in the HFE Act 2008.[33]

In 1997, the government commissioned a further inquiry into surrogacy, chaired by Professor Margaret Brazier.[34] This considered the issue of payments to surrogates, which were reportedly becoming increasingly high.[35] The resulting report recommended repeal of existing surrogacy provisions and their replacement with a bespoke Surrogacy Act, under which 'surrogacy should remain an option of last resort available only to couples where the intending mother's condition renders pregnancy impossible or highly dangerous to her'.[36] It recommended that only receipted 'justifiable expenses' should be allowed, including maternity

[30] Emily Jackson, *Regulating Reproduction: Law, Technology and Autonomy* (Hart Publishing 2001) 262.

[31] In the 2015 survey referred to above (n11), only four of the 110 surrogate respondents said the law should regard them as the legal mother at birth; 76 said surrogates should not be able to change their mind about handing the baby to the IPs.

[32] *Hansard* HC Deb, vol 170, cols 944–945, 2 April 1990.

[33] In ss54 (couples) and 54A (single applicants).

[34] The Brazier Report, n29.

[35] Expenses payments in the UK are still not high. 2015 survey responses showed that most UK surrogates (68.2%) reported receiving £10,000–£15,000, with none receiving over £20,000. The IPs in the survey reported paying £0 to £25,000 to surrogates with the average payment being £10,859 (Horsey (2015) n11, 20; 23). In 2018, 58.4% reported receiving £10,000–£15,000, with none receiving over £20,000, though there had been a small increase in surrogates reporting receiving £15,001–£20,000, from 4.7% in 2015 to 14.6% in 2018 (Horsey (2018) n11, 35). Upon review of court documents, the Law Commissions found that 'the median payment made by the intended parents to surrogates in domestic surrogacy arrangements was £14,795.54. The mean payment was £13,535.18' (Law Commissions, n2, para 12.30). See also Horsey, Chapter 3, this volume.

[36] Brazier Report, n29, para 8.9.

clothing, healthy food, travel expenses, counselling, insurances and the costs of medical tests and procedures.[37] However, these recommendations were never acted upon.[38]

Notwithstanding the limitations of the law, what has emerged is a practice of surrogacy founded on 'altruistic' values, encouraged by prohibitions on commercialism and the misconception that surrogates may receive only reasonable expenses if legal parenthood is to be achieved. Surrogacy organisations have emerged in this context to offer support on a not-for-profit basis. This involves guiding surrogates and IPs through arrangements, based on experience and good practice.[39] Additionally, an experienced 'independent' surrogacy community offers support via various social media platforms.[40] In this context, the number of surrogate births has gradually increased over time, reflecting scientific advances and increasing social acceptance of non-traditional families, and societal tendencies towards delayed parenthood.[41] That said, surrogacy remains an uncommon way to have children. Family court data, published quarterly by the Ministry of Justice, show that around 450–500 parental orders are granted annually.[42] In practice, the process of obtaining an order can take many months. If the child resides with the IPs during this time, as is typical, then unless and until the order is made the people caring for the child may not be

[37] ibid, paras 5.24–5.25.

[38] It has been observed that the opportunity to fully re-examine the law relating to surrogacy was missed in the context of a wider Department of Health review of the HFE Act 1990 in 2005–2007, despite a recommendation to do so by the House of Commons Science and Technology Committee (Kirsty Horsey, 'Swept Under the Carpet: Why Surrogacy Law Needs Urgent Review' in N. Priaulx and A. Wrigley (eds) *Ethics, Law and Society: Vol. 5* (Ashgate 2013)). The consultation on the Act merely asked whether changes to surrogacy law were needed and, if so, whether they should follow the Brazier Report's recommendations (Department of Health, *Review of the Human Fertilisation and Embryology Act: a Public Consultation* (HMSO 2005)). There was no consideration of the then emerging international commercial surrogacy market, or issues that this might generate.

[39] See Kim Cotton, n27; Natalie Smith, 'Mapping out a Future for the UK's Law on Surrogacy' (2016) 4(3) *JMLE* 237; Natalie Gamble and Helen Prosser 'Modern Surrogacy Practice and the Need for Reform' (2016) 4(3) *Journal of Medical Law and Ethics* 257. Also see Pott and White, Chapter 2, this volume.

[40] While some of this is good, and often a cheaper option than joining an organisation, or easier for some to become involved with, some 'independent' surrogacy generates concerns.

[41] Law Commissions, n2, para 1.9; Kirsty Horsey et al, 'First Clinical report of 179 Surrogacy Cases in the UK: Implications for Policy and Practice' (2022) 45(4) *Reproductive BioMedicine Online* 831.

[42] This includes orders relating to children born via surrogacy overseas. There has been a gradual increase in the number of parental orders being granted each year from 117 orders in 2011, to 423 in 2020, 435 in 2021, 448 in 2022 and 513 in 2023 (*Ministry of Justice Family Court Statistics Quarterly*, June 2024).

legally responsible and have no decision-making authority,[43] while the surrogate (and potentially her partner) technically remains financially and legally responsible.

Very few disputes – for example, where a surrogate changed her mind and decided to keep the baby she carried – have been documented in the UK.[44] Very rarely does a worrying case emerge, for example concerning a surrogate's bodily autonomy or the behaviour of either party.[45] Where they occur, it appears that better regulation and/or support and guidance for the participants might have prevented the situation.[46] Given the nature of the relationship between surrogates and IPs and the support available in the UK, it is unsurprising that studies show altruism as being the primary motivation for surrogates.[47] Further, evidence shows that the majority of

[43] Unless they have been granted parental responsibility via a child arrangements order or the surrogate does not have a spouse/civil partner and one of the IPs is registered on the birth certificate at birth.

[44] Gamble and Prosser (n39) identified only five reported dispute cases, though not all were because the surrogate changed her mind. Since that publication some cases have arisen where surrogates have refused consent to a parental order, though without wishing to keep the child: see *Re AB (Surrogacy Consent)* [2016] EWHC 2643 (Fam); *Re C (Surrogacy: Consent)* [2023] EWCA Civ 16; and *Re Z (Surrogacy: Step-parent Adoption)* [2024] EWFC 2 (relating to the same arrangement as *Re C* [2023]. Some anti-surrogacy organisations claim to see many cases of 'surrogacy regret', without providing evidence of such. Their campaigns tend to be against *all* surrogacy and rely heavily on examples stemming from overseas commercial surrogacy practices. They reflect similar views to radical feminists from the 1980s, especially from North America, who claimed all surrogacy was inherently exploitative and commodifies children and women's reproductive capacity (for example, Andrea Dworkin, *Right Wing Women* (The Women's Press 1983), Gena Corea, *The Mother Machine: Reproductive Technologies from Artificial Insemination to Artificial Wombs* (The Women's Press 1988)). The Pope has also declared surrogacy a threat to human dignity: see Angela Giuffrida, 'Vatican Calls Gender Fluidity and Surrogacy Threats to Human Dignity' *The Guardian* 8 April 2024.

[45] Although a handful of reported surrogacy cases raise this type of concern, the tendency is that such reports come from places where surrogacy is/has been practised in less than optimum circumstances, including with little or no regulation to keep participants safe and/or ensure parties' informed consent. The Thai 'Baby Gammy' case is one prominent example (discussed in Ainsley Newson and Sascha Callaghan, 'Surrogacy, Motherhood and Baby Gammy' *BioNews* 766, 11 August 2014), as are reports from Crete in 2023 and Cambodia in 2024 about situations where women had been trafficked and kept confined to be surrogates (Katia Neofytou, 'Eight Arrested in Crete Over Surrogacy and IVF Fraud' *BioNews* 1204, 29 August 2023; Blair Sowry, 'Police discover 20 Filipino surrogates in Cambodia' *BioNews* 1260, 14 October 2024).

[46] *Re Z (Surrogacy: Step-parent Adoption)* [2024] EWFC 2.

[47] Vasanti Jadva, 'Surrogates and Intended Parents in the UK' (2016) 3 *Journal of Medical Law and Ethics* 215; Mahmoud, n20. Also see Horsey, Chapter 3 and Mahmoud, Chapter 8, this volume.

surrogates in the UK stay in touch with the families they helped create, and demonstrates a high level of openness between IPs and their children about the method of their conception.[48]

Calls for reform

Since 2010, there have been increasing calls for surrogacy laws to be reformed – not only from academics but also from legal practitioners, the judiciary, and those with lived experience. In particular, the phenomenon of international surrogacy heightened and renewed interest in how surrogacy is and should be regulated in the UK (and elsewhere),[49] due to concerns about unsafe and unethical practices in some (largely unregulated) jurisdictions, and the unreserved commercialism of others, including various US states. One argument for reform is that better domestic laws, which facilitate ethical surrogacy arrangements and protect the interests of all involved, especially the child, will result in fewer IPs travelling to access surrogacy overseas.[50] Some commentators suggest that international regulation might be appropriate,[51] though it is also acknowledged that this would be difficult to achieve.[52]

48 Horsey, n11, 20; 22. Also see Jadva, ibid and Horsey, Chapter 3, this volume.

49 Horsey and Sheldon, n9, 67; Emily Jackson, 'UK Law and International Commercial Surrogacy: "the Very Antithesis of Sensible"' (2016) 3 *Journal of Medical Law and Ethics* 197; Emily Jackson, Jenni Millbank, Isabel Karpin and Anita Stuhmcke, 'Learning from Cross-Border Reproduction' 25(1) *Medical Law Review* 23, Jadva et al, n13.

50 Jackson et al, ibid; Ezra Kneebone, Kiri Beilby and Karin Hammarberg, 'Experiences of Surrogates and Intended Parents of Surrogacy Arrangements: a Systematic Review' 45(4) *Reproductive BioMedicine Online* 815; Fischer et al, n16; Law Commission and Scottish Law Commission, *Building Families Through Surrogacy: a New Law: Volume II: Full Report* (Law Com No 411, Scot Law Com No 262, 29 March 2023), para 16.9.

51 Colin Rogerson, 'The Prospect of an International Regime for Surrogacy Arrangements' (2016) 3 *Journal of Medical Law and Ethics* 275. See also the work of the Permanent Bureau of The Hague Convention on Private International Law (HCCH) Parentage and Surrogacy Project – www.hcch.net/en/projects/legislative-projects/parentage-surrogacy. However, universal agreement is unlikely to be achieved – see Horsey, n16.

52 Horsey, ibid. Nevertheless, there have been attempts to create international best practice guidelines, in the form of the 'Verona Principles' ('Principles for the Protection of the Rights of the Child born through Surrogacy', published by the International Social Service, available at https://bettercarenetwork.org/sites/default/files/2021-03/VeronaPrinciples_25February2021.pdf) and also by the organisation Surrogacy360 ('Recommended Principles and Standards for Engaging in International Commercial Surrogacy Arrangements', available at https://surrogacy360.org/considering-surrogacy/principles-and-standards/). Both involved input from international collaborators from a variety of disciplines and jurisdictions.

Problems with existing UK law

Many aspects of the existing law on surrogacy are either outdated or unsustainable. The legislative formula assigning legal parenthood following assisted reproduction does not work if IPs are unable to carry – rather than to conceive – a child: it utterly fails to recognise the social and familial reality intended when surrogacy is used.[53] Instead, the law opted for an inefficient post-birth transfer of parenthood, resting on a set of eligibility criteria, several of which have been effectively erased by case law. For example, a series of cases beginning with *X (A Child) (Surrogacy: Time Limit)*[54] have eradicated the six-month statutory timeframe within which applications must be made.[55] Not only have IPs since regularly been allowed to apply 'out of time', but in 2022 a parental order was granted in respect of an *adult*, to secure his identity as the legal child of his parents.[56]

The fact that at least one IP must be genetically related to the child to be able to apply for an order creates a barrier for a minority of people seeking parenthood via surrogacy.[57] This includes single people or couples who require 'double donation' (donation of both sperm and egg) or a donated embryo, due to infertility or a choice not to become a genetic parent. This is particularly notable, since parenthood provisions in other parts of the HFE Act 2008 surrounding donor conception deprioritise the genetic link, raising questions as to whether this is a tenable distinction.[58]

As already mentioned, courts routinely retrospectively authorise payments that may be viewed as exceeding 'reasonable expenses', where it is in the best interest of the child to grant a parental order.[59] This is largely to do with

[53] Kirsty Horsey, 'Unconsidered Inconsistencies: Parenthood and Assisted Conception' in K. Horsey and H. Biggs, (eds), *Human Fertilisation and Embryology: Reproducing Regulation* (Routledge-Cavendish 2007).

[54] [2014] EWHC 3135 (Fam). Sir James Munby, then President of the Family Division of the High Court, asked: 'Can Parliament really have intended that the gate should be barred forever if the application for a parental order is lodged even one day late? I cannot think so... [G]iven the transcendental importance of a parental order, with its consequences stretching many, many decades into the future, can it sensibly be thought that Parliament intended the difference between six months and six months and one day to be determinative and one day's delay to be fatal? I assume that Parliament intended a sensible result' (at [54]).

[55] Under s54(3) HFE Act 2008.

[56] *X v Z (Parental Order: Adult)* [2022] EWFC 26.

[57] ss54(1)(b) and 54A(1)(b) HFE Act 2008.

[58] Kirsty Horsey, (2010) 'Challenging Presumptions: Legal Parenthood and Surrogacy Arrangements' (2010) 4(22) *Child and Family Law Quarterly* 449; Alghrani and Griffiths, n10, 176.

[59] See, for example, *Re X and Y (Children)* [2011] EWHC 3147 (Fam); *Re D and L (Surrogacy)* [2012] EWHC 2631 (Fam); *Re W* [2013] EWHC 3570 (Fam) as just some of the many examples.

recognising the status quo and avoiding disruption in a child's settled life with his or her parents. As some judges have identified, in the best interests of the children concerned, there is little else they could do.[60] It is axiomatic that the refusal to grant an order on this basis would merely place the child into further uncertainty regarding their family life, identity, and the legal status of those bringing them up. Enforced return to the surrogate is not an option, leaving only the possibility of adoption or a 'lives with' child arrangements order under s8 of the Children Act 1989.

Parental orders cannot be granted without the surrogate's consent even if it is considered unreasonably withheld and where this is not in the child's best interest.[61] If a court finds, despite a withholding of consent, that it would be in the child's best interests to be with the IPs, a 'lives with' order might still be made.[62] The HFE Act 2008 allows for an exception to the consent requirement where a surrogate cannot be found or lacks capacity.[63] For example, in *Re D and L*, an order was granted, despite the absence of consent (the surrogate could not be found).[64] This case illustrates the jeopardy faced by some IPs, and highlights the surrogate's clear intention not to be involved with the child.[65]

International developments in surrogacy

European developments

In addition to domestic developments, surrogacy has been the subject of debate at an international level. There have been a number of high-profile rulings from the European Court of Human Rights (ECtHR) in recent years.[66] These cases have arisen when IPs use surrogacy abroad, due to bans

60 See, for example, Hedley J in *Re X and Y* [2008] at [24]; Theis J in *Re P-M* [2013] EWHC 2328 (Fam) at [19].

61 s54(6) HFE Act 2008. Not being able to override this has led to situations whereby a court is unable to prioritise children's best interests – see *Re AB (Surrogacy Consent)* [2016] EWHC 2643 (Fam); *Re N (Adoption – Surrogacy)* [2024] EWFC 41. This is not the case in adoption orders, where the birth mother's consent can be dispensed with (s52 Adoption and Children Act 2002).

62 See *Re N* [2007] EWCA Civ 1053 (a deception case, preceding *Re N*, ibid); but compare *CW v NT and another* [2011] EWHC 33. Such an order also confers parental responsibility.

63 s54(7).

64 *Re D and L (Minors) (Surrogacy)* [2012] EWHC 2631 (Fam). See also *RS v T (Surrogacy: Service, Consent and Payments)* [2015] EWFC 22; *Re QR (Parental Order: Dispensing with Consent: Proportionality)* [2023] EWHC 3196 (Fam).

65 Though this is not always the case. In a recent example a parental order was overturned because the surrogate had not given *unconditional* consent, and wanted to ensure ongoing contact with the child was maintained (*Re C (Surrogacy: Consent)* [2023] EWCA Civ 16).

66 Attempts to develop Council of Europe guidelines have failed. In 2016 the Parliamentary Assembly to the Council of Europe rejected a draft recommendation on surrogacy.

or restrictions in their home country, then encountering legal obstacles relating to parentage and/or citizenship of the children upon their return.[67] The ECtHR has held that in cases where a genetic link between one IP and the child exists, non-recognition of the parent–child relationship violates children's right to identity under the right to private life limb of Article 8 of the European Convention on Human Rights (ECHR).[68] However, there is no violation in cases where no genetic link exists.[69] A 2019 ECtHR advisory opinion dealt with the issues of parenthood for non-genetically related female partners of a man who has a genetic link with a child born through international surrogacy. It stated that where the legal parent–child relationship with an intended father is recognised in domestic law, the law must provide a possibility for the legal recognition of a parent–child relationship with an intended mother who is designated in the foreign birth certificate as the 'legal mother'.[70] However, states have discretion over how to achieve this, whether through registration of the foreign birth certificate or adoption, for example.[71] The means of recognition chosen by the state must be implemented promptly and effectively, in accordance with the child's best interests.[72]

The European Parliament has historically taken a negative view of surrogacy. For example, in 2015 it passed a resolution stating that it '[c]ondemns the practice of surrogacy, which undermines the human dignity of the woman since her body and its reproductive functions are used as a

---

See Children's Rights Related to Surrogacy (Committee on Social Affairs, Health and Sustainable Development of the Parliamentary Assembly, 21 September 2016). See also Iliadou, Chapter 9, this volume.

67 See, for example, *D and Others v Belgium* App no 29176/13 (ECtHR, 8 July 2014); *Foulon and Bouvet v France* App nos 9063/14 and 10410/14 (ECtHR, 21 July 2016); *Laborie v France* App no 44024/13 (ECtHR, 19 January 2017); *C and E v France* App nos 1462/18 and 17348/18 (ECtHR, 19 November 2019); *K.K. and Others v Denmark* App no 25212/21 (ECtHR, 6 December 2022).

68 *Mennesson v France* App no 65192/11 (ECtHR, 26 June 2014) and *Labassee v France* App no 65941/11 (ECtHR, 26 June 2014).

69 *Paradiso and Campanelli v Italy* App no 25358/12, (ECtHR, 24 January 2017) and *Valdis Fjölnisdóttir and Others v Iceland* App no 71552/17 (ECtHR, 18 May 2021).

70 Advisory opinion concerning the recognition in domestic law of a legal parent–child relationship between a child born through a gestational surrogacy arrangement abroad and the intended mother (ECtHR, 10 April 2019) (Advisory Opinion) paras 37–47. This is based on the child's best interests and the fact that the margin of appreciation is restricted, since a 'particularly important facet of an individual's identity was at stake'. See further Lydia Bracken, 'The ECtHR's First Advisory Opinion: Implications for Cross-Border Surrogacy Involving Male Intended Parents' (2021) 21(1) *Medical Law International* 3 and Alice Margaria, 'Parenthood and Cross-Border Surrogacy: What Is 'New'? The ECtHR's First Advisory Opinion' (2020) 28(2) *Medical Law Review* 412.

71 Advisory Opinion, ibid, para 55.

72 ibid.

commodity'.[73] In its 2021 Human Rights and Democracy in the World Annual Report, the European Parliament focused on commercial surrogacy, stating that it '[c]ondemns the commercial practice of surrogacy, a global phenomenon that exposes women worldwide to exploitation and human trafficking while targeting financially and socially vulnerable women in particular'.[74] More recently, while not endorsing surrogacy, the European Parliament voted in support of draft European Commission legislation[75] to facilitate legal parenthood in one EU country being recognised in other EU countries and the introduction of a European Certificate of Parenthood.[76] While member states do not have to change their own laws on parenthood, a determination of parenthood from states that permit surrogacy, for example, must be recognised.[77]

The Hague Conference on Private International Law

There have also been efforts by the Hague Conference on Private International Law to develop binding norms on surrogacy at an international level.[78] A group of experts was established in 2015 to explore the feasibility of advancing work on private international law issues on parentage, including parentage in international surrogacy agreements, followed by a working group from 2023 onwards, whose mandate is to 'explore provisions for, if possible, one new instrument on these matters', taking into account the final

[73] European Parliament resolution of 17 December 2015 on the Annual Report on Human Rights and Democracy in the World 2014 and the European Union's policy on the matter (2015/2229(INI)), para 115.

[74] European Parliament, 'Human Rights and Democracy in the World and the European Union's Policy on the Matter – Annual Report 2021' (2021/2181(INI)), para 60.

[75] European Commission, Proposal for a Council regulation on jurisdiction, applicable law, recognition of decisions and acceptance of authentic instruments in matters of parenthood and on the creation of a European Certificate of Parenthood (7 December 2022), available at https://commission.europa.eu/document/928ae98d-d85f-4c3d-ac50-ba13ed981897_en (last accessed 16 March 2024).

[76] M. Vass, 'European Parliament Press Release, Recognition of Parenthood in the EU: No Discrimination Against Children's Rights', 8 November 2023, available at www.europarl.europa.eu/news/en/press-room/20231031IPR08715/recognition-of-parenthood-in-the-eu-no-discrimination-against-children-s-rights (last accessed 16 March 2024).

[77] Exceptions based on public policy grounds would be permitted, but only in exceptional circumstances.

[78] For proposed models see Katarina Trimmings and Paul Beaumont (eds), *International Surrogacy Arrangements: Legal Regulation at the International Level* (Bloomsbury 2013) and Richard Blauwhoff and Lisette Frohn, 'International Commercial Surrogacy Arrangements: the Interests of the Child as a Concern of Both Human Rights and Private International Law', in Fundamental Rights' in *International and European Law: Public and Private Law Perspectives* (Asser Institute 2016) 211.

report of the expert group.[79] This report recommended that is generally feasible to develop a binding multilateral convention for the recognition of parentage in cross-jurisdictional cases, but that rules on legal parentage as a result of international surrogacy should be included in an optional protocol.[80] The optional protocol was recommended in order to 'respect the policy concerns of many States as well as the various approaches to surrogacy globally'.[81] Due to varying approaches to surrogacy, with some states prohibiting and some permitting it, agreement on a set of principles for inclusion in a convention on parentage is challenging.[82]

International children's rights

There have also been developments from international bodies concerned with children's rights. Since surrogacy is a means of conceiving children, there are often arguments made relating to how surrogacy might impact their health, identity, and best interests, more generally.[83] The UN Committee on the Rights of the Child monitors the implementation of the United Nations Convention on the Rights of the Child 1989 (UNCRC). It has not released specific guidance on surrogacy, but the Special Rapporteur on the Sale and Sexual Exploitation of Children released a 2018 thematic report on the sale and exploitation of children.[84] This called for the creation of safeguards to prevent the sale of children in commercial surrogacy, which could include a ban or strict regulation.[85] Such regulation should ensure that

---

[79] Working Group on Parentage/Surrogacy: Report of the First Meeting (13–17 November 2023) (rel. Doc. No 1 of November 2023) para 2.

[80] Conclusion Nos 3–10, Parentage/Surrogacy Experts' Group: Final Report 'The Feasibility of One or More Private International Law Instruments on Legal Parentage' (Prel. Doc. No 1, November 2022) (Hague Experts Group Report).

[81] ibid, Conclusion No 8.

[82] For example, while the experts believed that an *a priori* model for establishing parentage would better protect human rights, they recognised that such models imply acceptance of surrogacy. Therefore, states that ban surrogacy may prefer an *a posterior* model (ibid, Conclusion No 10).

[83] See John Tobin, 'The *Convention on the Rights of the Child:* the Rights and Best Interests of Children Conceived Through Assisted Reproduction' (Victorian Law Reform Commission, 2004), Paula Gerber and Katie O'Byrne, 'Souls in the House of Tomorrow: the Rights of Children Born via Surrogacy' in Paula Gerber and Katie O'Byrne (eds), *Surrogacy, Law and Human Rights* (Ashgate 2016) and Katherine Wade, 'The Regulation of Surrogacy: a Children's Rights Perspective' (2017) 29(2) *Child and Family Law Quarterly* 113.

[84] Report of the Special Rapporteur on the Sale and Sexual Exploitation of Children, including Child Prostitution, Child Pornography and Other Child Sexual Abuse Material' (2018) A/HRC/37/60 (Thematic Report).

[85] ibid, para 77.

surrogates retain parentage and parental responsibility on the birth of the child, that all payments are made prior to any transfer of the child, and that enforceable surrogacy contracts are impermissible.[86] It also recommended that altruistic surrogacy should only involve reasonable, itemised expenses and that surrogates retain parentage and parental responsibility at birth.[87] These recommendations were reiterated and expanded upon in a 2019 report, which grounded the recommendations in the principles of the prohibition on the sale of children, the best interests principle under Article 3 UNCRC, the non-discrimination principle under Article 2, right to health under Article 24, and rights to identity under Articles 7 and 8.[88] The report also stressed the need to collect data on surrogacy arrangements,[89] and suggested that the views of children born through surrogacy should influence legal reform, where possible.[90]

There have been calls from other bodies that take a children's rights-based perspective on surrogacy, drawing on the UNCRC. Notably, in 2019 the International Social Service, a Geneva-based NGO, developed the Verona Principles, after an extended period of worldwide consultation.[91] These have been given formal support from the UN Committee on the Rights of the Child[92] and the former UN Special Rapporteur.[93] The principles are shaped by the UNCRC, namely: human dignity, the child as an independent rights holder, the non-discrimination principle, the right to health and the best interests of the child.[94] Some of the core principles include ensuring that the surrogate's consent is obtained with regard to the IP's parentage,[95] that states should prohibit any remuneration or consideration where linked

86 ibid. This is to ensure surrogacy does not fall into the definition of the sale of children which is defined in Article 2 of the Optional Protocol to the CRC on the Sale of Children, Child Prostitution and Child Pornography A/RES/54/263 of 25 May 2000 as: 'Sale of children means any act or transaction whereby a child is transferred by any person or group of persons to another for remuneration or any other consideration'.

87 ibid. It also recommended best interests of the child determinations regarding parentage/parental responsibility decisions, monitoring of financial aspects of arrangements, regulation of intermediaries, protection of identity rights and access to origin information and international cooperation to avoid statelessness.

88 Sale and Sexual Exploitation of Children, including Child Prostitution, Child Pornography and Other Child Sexual Abuse Material, (2019) A/74/162, paras 99–101.

89 ibid, para 102.

90 ibid, para 99.

91 Verona Principles, n52, 2.

92 ibid, 3.

93 Maud de Boer-Buquicchio (2012–2020). Verona Principles, ibid, 4.

94 ibid, Principles 1–6.

95 ibid, Principle 7. The Principles accept both pre-birth and post-birth transfer of parentage with the surrogate's consent.

to the determination of parentage,[96] and that children have access to identity information.[97] The Child Identity Protection Network (CHIP), an international NGO formed in 2020, has also released statements on children's rights protection relating specifically to identity in surrogacy. Its 2023 briefing note identifies three priority issues: the need to ensure that adoption procedures are not used for surrogacy, the requirements for free and informed consent of the surrogate and effective regulation of surrogacy intermediaries.[98] This builds on the CHIP and UNICEF briefing note that recommended that states parties to the UNCRC and Optional Protocol on the Sale of Children ensure the preservation of identity information of surrogate-born children, collect data on surrogate births, prohibit the sale and trafficking of children, undertake post-birth best interests determinations regarding parentage and ensure mechanisms are in place to prevent statelessness.[99]

The contribution of this edited collection

In 2016, the Law Commission of England and Wales consulted on its 13th programme of law reform, asking whether it should review surrogacy law. Perhaps given that the current regulatory framework had been described as 'an ill-considered and largely irrelevant panic measure',[100] this prompted the highest number of responses, and surrogacy became one of the Commission's selected projects.[101] A Department of Health and Social Care (DHSC)-funded project was initiated, in which the Law Commission of England and Wales and the Scottish Law Commission[102] (the Law Commissions) held

96 The Principles also set out that 'unregulated, excessive or lump sum payments' and/or reimbursement for 'pain and suffering' should be prohibited and that certain intermediary activities are also not permitted, if these lead to the creation/control of surrogacy markets/networks, facilitate the transfer of the child for remuneration/other consideration and/or intermediaries receive excessive remuneration for their services compared to comparable work (ibid, Principles 14.8 and 14.11).

97 ibid, Principle 11. This includes access as an adult.

98 Child Identity Protection (CHIP), Child Identity Protection Briefing Note: Surrogacy in 2023: Priority Issues Relating to Children's Rights, 2023.

99 CHIP and UNICEF Briefing Note: Key Considerations – Children's Rights and Surrogacy (2022), available at www.unicef.org/media/115331/file (last accessed 16 March 2024). They also recommend that states that permit surrogacy should prohibit agencies facilitating foreign parents from states that prohibit surrogacy in a surrogacy arrangement in their own state.

100 Michael Freeman, 'Is Surrogacy Exploitative?' in Sheila A.M. McLean (ed.), *Legal Issues in Human Reproduction* (Gower 1989) 165.

101 Law Commissions, n2, paras 1.39, 2.42.

102 The Scottish Law Commission contributed to this project as part of its 10th Programme of Law Reform.

a public consultation on surrogacy between June and October 2019. The editors of this collection received funding from the SLS Small Research Grant fund to hold a conference on the 2019 consultation and to consider future directions in surrogacy law. This was a full-day conference held at the Institute of Advanced Legal Studies in London on 30 November 2022, attracting over 100 attendees ranging from judges, policy makers and regulators to surrogates, parents through surrogacy and children with experience of surrogacy. Many of the authors in this collection spoke to the topic of their chapters at this conference, in the context of the Law Commissions' preliminary recommendations.

On 29 March 2023, the Law Commissions released their recommendations in their final report: 'Building Families Through Surrogacy: a New Law', alongside a draft Surrogacy Bill.[103] This makes detailed recommendations for surrogacy regulation, notably in relation to legal parenthood, regulation and governance of surrogacy, including the creation of 'regulated surrogacy organisations' as 'gatekeepers' to surrogacy, permitted and prohibited payments, and storage and disclosure of information about surrogacy arrangements. The proposals have inevitably reignited academic, public, and political discussion of surrogacy law.

This original edited collection provides an opportunity to critically analyse the law and make suggestions for improvement and new proposals for reform, with the knowledge of the Law Commissions' final recommendations. It explores the regulatory landscape of surrogacy in the UK, in the context of its development over the last four decades and law reform recommendations that seek to provide a legitimate and safe 'pathway' through surrogacy in the best interests of children, surrogates and parents created through surrogacy. It contributes to contemporary debate: the authors are academic experts in the field of surrogacy, leading practitioners or those with first-hand lived experience. The chapters each illustrate different perspectives, addressing a wide range of issues/themes that have long been identified as requiring reform, including expenses/payments in surrogacy, protecting origin information of children, acquisition of legal parenthood, enforceability of surrogacy arrangements and what to do about transnational/cross-border surrogacy arrangements (using experience from overseas jurisdictions where appropriate). They explore whether the Law Commissions' recommendations

[103] Law Commissions, n50. Notably, the publication of the final report was delayed several times, not only due to the COVID-19 pandemic, but also because of a resurgence of anti-surrogacy voices, as well as complex and contentious dilemmas that the practice continues to raise for policy makers (Professors Nicholas Hopkins and Gillian Black, 'Building Families Through Surrogacy: the Law Commissions and Surrogacy Law Reform' (presented at 'Future Directions in Surrogacy Law' conference, London, 30 November 2022).

and draft Surrogacy Bill will provide effective reform, the extent to which they provide guidance for other jurisdictions, and whether they appropriately balance the interests of all involved.

It is not the case that the authors support the proposed reforms wholesale, without amendment. However, we have not included a chapter which makes arguments against the practice of surrogacy *per se*. The reason for this deliberate omission is threefold: first, the work arises from and is inspired by a law reform project that has been already undertaken; second, the Law Commissions were clear at the launch of their consultation and in their final report that surrogacy is already legal and that their recommendations start from this premise;[104] third, the editors and the contributors of this collection support surrogacy when it is performed ethically and believe it would be a retrograde step to ban it in the UK given the consequences this would have. Effective regulation is a better option than prohibition, which would drive more IPs overseas or into unregulated independent surrogacy arrangements with little to no safeguards.

Detailed synopsis

In Part I the authors provide a snapshot of surrogacy from the perspectives of those involved, including non-profit organisations, surrogates, and lawyers. Part II analyses specific issues that are the subject of debate related to surrogate-born children, payments, and the intersection of law and health policy. The authors in Part II critique fundamental regulatory aspects that shape how surrogacy is perceived, specifically issues of identity and payment. In Part III, international perspectives are discussed, both comparatively in terms of the healthcare surrogates receive, and from other jurisdictions that are also in the process of law reform or have recently regulated surrogacy.

Part I: Perspectives on the surrogacy landscape

In Chapter 2, Pott and White give a unique insight into how some surrogacy arrangements take place in practice in the UK. Drawing on their experiences as a surrogate and a parent through surrogacy alongside their roles in SurrogacyUK, the authors explore personal stories of surrogates and IPs, and set out their views on the biggest challenges for surrogacy regulation and how the Law Commissions' proposals address these. Horsey builds on these insights in Chapter 3, which draws on data collected from interviews with UK-based surrogates. The chapter provides original insights into the participants' motivations, experiences, perspectives on the existing law,

[104] Law Commissions, n50, para 1.7.

and views on the proposed legal reforms in relation to expenses and legal parenthood in particular.

In Chapter 4, Gamble provides another unique insight into the practice of surrogacy. Drawing on her experience at Natalie Gamble Associates, a leading surrogacy law firm, she outlines the reasons IPs seek surrogacy arrangements abroad. She also sets out the ethical concerns regarding some practices in the international context, particularly relating to a lack of safeguards where unregulated surrogacy takes place. She argues that, in the context of international surrogacy, it is children who are detrimentally affected, as they are sometimes deprived of parentage and citizenship, which is a significant concern due to the paramountcy of the welfare of the child principle in English family law. Gamble argues that, instead of a stance that seeks to encourage IPs to undertake domestic surrogacy, UK policy should accept that 'global surrogacy' is a reality. In this regard, she argues that the legal framework should focus on encouraging – as far as possible – informed consent by all parties in surrogacy, adequate support for those involved and protection of the welfare of the child.

Part II: Specific issues in the Law Commissions' recommendations

In Chapter 5, Park-Morton explores the issue of 'double donation'. Under s54(1)(b) or s54A(1)(b) of the HFE Act 2008, a parental order can only be granted where there is a genetic link with one of the IPs in the case of a couple, or with the single IP where there is a single applicant. This chapter explores the reasons for the Law Commissions' recommendation to retain the requirement for a genetic link in all legally recognised surrogacy arrangements. Park-Morton argues that this position undermines the role of non-genetic IPs on the child's identity. Drawing on Article 8 of both the UNCRC and the European Convention on Human Rights, along with the court's use of the concept of identity in parental order cases, she argues that identity rights of surrogate-born children necessitate recognition of the relationship between children and IPs, irrespective of genetic link.

In Chapter 6, Brown considers the regulation of payments within surrogacy arrangements in the UK. The background context is the approach taken to payments from IPs to the surrogate within both the recent law reform project and the current legal regime. After outlining well-known critiques of the current law, the chapter evaluates the approach to payments adopted by the Law Commissions. Thereafter, it takes a wider perspective, considering how a reformed legal regime could approach the issue of payments to surrogates and whether such 'ambiguity' is inherent to regulating payments. Brown contends that the regime for payments requires a 'clear regulatory rationale', and the chapter sets out some potential underlying bases for this. The chapter then explores whether it is possible to resolve the ambiguities of the current legal regime, and the equivocations of the law reform process, or whether these ambiguities will remain in *any* system regulating payments to surrogates.

Wade's chapter, Chapter 7, examines the proposed surrogacy register, a new system for storage of and access to origin information for children born through surrogacy. This chapter analyses the information that would be collected, the age/circumstances where access to information would be permitted, birth certificate notification of surrogacy conception, access to information by children of the surrogate and information sharing between children born of the same surrogate. Wade argues that, while many of the recommendations evidence a children's rights-based approach, there is a lack of clarity regarding the information that it is envisaged would be collected and that further measures could have been taken to disincentive the use of anonymous gamete donors/surrogates in the context of international surrogacy. She also notes that a lack of congruence with recent proposals in the context of gamete donation must be addressed to ensure parity in the enjoyment of children's rights of access to origin information in assisted reproduction.

Part III: International impacts and perspectives

Part III explores surrogacy in various international contexts. In Chapter 8, Mahmoud compares the impact of existing legal and health regulatory frameworks on surrogates' experiences of obstetric care provision in Britain and in California, drawing on empirical work conducted between 2018 and 2021. The chapter argues that surrogates' experiences are emblematic of wider issues with obstetric care provision and suggests potential solutions for both jurisdictions.

In Chapter 9, Iliadou explores developments regarding surrogacy at the ECtHR. The chapter identifies emerging themes from case law, which indicate a clear preference for genetic connection, alongside a vague application of the child's best interests. She argues that this apparent European standard serves as a basis to assess the compatibility of the Law Commissions' proposals with the ECHR. She concludes that this standard is very low, due to surrogacy being unlawful in the states referred to the court and concludes that a different application of the Convention's standards would be more appropriate in the UK context.

Insight from the Irish context is provided by Tobin in Chapter 10. He explores Ireland's Health (Assisted Human Reproduction) Act 2024, which regulates domestic, altruistic, gestational surrogacy arrangements in Ireland, as well as international surrogacy arrangements. This chapter analyses both approaches in the context of significant international developments in the areas of surrogacy regulation and law reform, including the proposals of the Law Commissions and international instruments from the UN Special

Rapporteur on the Sale and Exploitation of Children, and the International Social Service.

In Chapter 11, Wilson provides insights into surrogacy in Aotearoa New Zealand, one of only three jurisdictions in the world that requires pre-approval of domestic surrogacy arrangements involving fertility clinics by an ethics committee. She argues that, while this process adds additional time and cost to surrogacy arrangements, having an independent committee that considers the interests and needs of all parties involved in the arrangement may increase the likelihood of positive outcomes. She then explores the current reviews underway in New Zealand and analyses potential recommendations for change. She notes how her analysis may provide an alternative approach to the regulation of surrogacy for other countries reviewing their surrogacy laws.

Conclusion

In 2008, Dawn Primarolo MP, the minister responsible for driving the HFE Act 2008 through Parliament stated: 'discussions about surrogacy should be dealt with elsewhere and not by amending [the 2007 Bill], because the issues involved are complex and the debate [on surrogacy] has not been properly considered due to its late emergence as an issue'.[105] Considering the Law Commissions' report and recommendations, it is now the time and place for those discussions to begin, in public and in Parliament. Hopefully, the Surrogacy Bill (which was published when the previous Conservative government was in place) will be laid before Parliament, and parliamentarians will be given ample time for full and thorough debate. This collection brings together different voices on surrogacy law at a pivotal time for surrogacy law reform, and it is hoped that the contributions can inform forthcoming public and parliamentary debate, with a view to shaping a new future for surrogacy law and policy in the UK, and beyond.

[105] *Hansard* Public Bill Committee, col 249, 12 June 2008.

PART I

Perspectives on the Surrogacy Landscape

2

From Wilful Neglect to Progressive Support: Surrogacy Law and Its Human Impact

Linder Pott and Alan White

This chapter, written by the chairs of SurrogacyUK, the UK's largest non-profit surrogacy support organisation and its sister charity the SurrogacyUK Foundation, gives an organisational perspective on surrogacy.[1] Both authors have personal experience of surrogacy and, drawing on the testimony of others, offer grassroots understanding of many issues surrogacy raises. The chapter considers the need for – and potential impact of – law reform through the lens of lived experience. It offers a personal, rather than academic, account of the issues and day-to-day effects of the existing law on those who seek to become (or who have become) parents through surrogacy in the UK, or who act as surrogates.

In this chapter we share our experience of the impact that surrogacy law has had on people involved in surrogacy journeys and people excluded from them, and the stories of individuals[2] and organisations that have both campaigned for legal reform and had to evolve with it. Using case studies, we explore and consider the lived experience of surrogates, their partners,

1 SurrogacyUK was established in 2002. The SurrogacyUK Foundation (Charity No 1205088), the UK's first surrogacy charity, was launched in 2024 to 'advance the education of the public about surrogacy and, in particular, approaches to surrogacy that are ethical and safeguard the interests of all parties' (https://surrogacyukfoundation.org/ (last accessed 3 July 2024)).

2 Except where surnames are given, pseudonyms are used throughout the chapter and some quotes are paraphrased for sense and to protect anonymity.

intended parents (IPs) and those involved in SurrogacyUK in over 20 years of support for surrogacy teams.

'Surrogacy is not illegal in the UK'

Everyone involved in domestic surrogacy will be familiar with this kind of statement. For years we have read it in official surrogacy guidance or used it when explaining to friends, family and healthcare workers that the child we are carrying – or intend to parent – will be born within a well-established legal framework. We have an urge to reassure people that we are not doing anything illegal. But why?

Perhaps it is due to the dramatic roots of today's surrogacy laws? Baby Cotton's birth in the 1980s to Kim Cotton – the UK's 'first' surrogate – caught lawmakers off guard.[3] It led to a legislative scramble to formalise a legal framework for surrogacy through the Warnock Report in 1984 and the subsequent Surrogacy Arrangements Act (SAA) 1985.[4] Social attitudes towards family and conception were very different in the 1980s and *Re C* added fuel to a fiery debate, illustrated by the Reverend Ian Paisley MP's contribution to a November 1984 parliamentary debate on the Warnock Report:

> The committee also holds that the embryo should have some status in law, yet it maintains that the human embryo may be sold. I thought that the House had repudiated slavery long ago. To buy and sell the living body of a human being is slavery and is barbaric. For Warnock to say that the embryo should have a special status and then to say that it is a saleable commodity is at best contradictory and at worst hypocritical [...] I am glad that the recommendation of the committee is to ban surrogate parenthood. I do not see why a rich couple should be able to hire the womb of a poor person and pay for what they want. That is totally immoral, and the House needs to reject it out of hand.[5]

Perhaps we feel the need to assert surrogacy's legality because, four decades later, it remains relatively uncommon. In 2023, 513 parental orders were issued in England and Wales, including for surrogate children born overseas.[6] That is a tiny proportion of the 605,479 live births in England and Wales in

---

3 *Re C (A minor) (Wardship: surrogacy)* [1985] FLR 846.

4 See Chapter 1, this volume.

5 *Hansard* HC Deb, vol 68, col 555, 23 November 1984.

6 Ministry of Justice, 'Family Court Tables: January to March 2024' (27 June 2024), available at www.gov.uk/government/statistics/family-court-statistics-quarterly-january-to-march-2024 (last accessed 2 July 2024).

that year.[7] Public awareness of the legality of surrogacy is also low: a 2022 survey found that only 26% of respondents were 'aware that surrogacy is legal throughout the UK, despite the fact that surrogacy has been regulated and permitted by UK law for almost 40 years'.[8] This suggests that, if IPs explain their family plan to a stranger, there is a three in four chance that they will be received with at least a suspicion of illegality. Societal awareness, understanding and acceptance of surrogacy – though certainly better than it once was – has a long way to go.

Or perhaps our tendency to affirm 'legality' is rooted in the legal hurdles that surrogates and IPs face to create and grow families and to establish legal parenthood? The state normally only intervenes in parenthood and family life where there's a risk to children (as defined by the Children Act 1989), and most people's experience of parenthood doesn't begin with a visit from the Children and Family Court Advisory and Support Service (CAFCASS) and a court order. But for those seeking to be legally recognised as parents following a surrogacy arrangement, this is a legal requirement.[9]

For these reasons and more, the creation of surrogacy families too often starts with this negative framing. While the SAA 1985 did not prohibit surrogacy, it was not *permissive* legislation. Surrogacy was accommodated, in the hope that its use would decline over time.[10] Commercial aspects of the practice were criminalised. Later, the Human Fertilisation and Embryology (HFE) Act 1990 established a legal framework for parenthood following surrogacy arrangements. It allowed IPs who had children through surrogacy to become legal parents through the 'parental order' process. Rather than recognising legal parenthood from birth (as in routes to parenthood via assisted conception, such as IVF) this process was modelled on adoption and enabled legal parenthood to be transferred from the surrogate (and their husband if they were married)[11] to IPs, under certain conditions. It reflected and cemented some prevailing inequalities, making legal parenthood

---

7 Office for National Statistics, 'Births in England and Wales: 2022 (Refreshed Populations)' (23 February 2024), available at www.ons.gov.uk/peoplepopulationandcommunity/birthsdeathsandmarriages/livebirths/bulletins/birthsummarytablesenglandandwales/2022refreshedpopulations (last accessed 2 July 2024).

8 Ipsos, 'Two-thirds of People Believe the NHS Should Provide Fertility Treatment' (22 June 2022), available at www.ipsos.com/en-uk/two-thirds-people-believe-nhs-should-provide-fertility-treatment (last accessed 2 July 2024).

9 This association between surrogacy, risk and legality is also embedded in the presentation of surrogacy data: to find the statistics for children born through surrogacy in the Ministry of Justice's 'Family Court Tables' (n6) we must scroll through statistics about children in local authority care, supervision or emergency protection.

10 Kirsty Horsey, 'Not Withered on the Vine: the Need for Surrogacy Law Reform' (2016) 4(3) *Journal of Medical Law and Ethics* 181, 185. See also Chapter 1, this volume.

11 Later extended to civil partners.

following surrogacy accessible only to married, heterosexual couples. Of course, this would not – and did not – stop other people from *using* surrogacy and creating their much-wanted families: it just put those families on a different – lesser – legal footing. And, as we explore, it accommodated surrogacy only begrudgingly, from a position of wilful neglect, rather than of support or celebration.

Surrogacy: a self-supporting community

Over the decades that followed the early legislation, *support* for surrogacy as a route to parenthood was provided not by the law, but instead by the UK's surrogacy community, through informal groups and a small number of non-profit organisations, largely established by surrogates and IPs themselves. They provide opportunities for parties to meet, provide peer-to-peer support and shared experiences of surrogacy journeys. Some organisations offer an active 'matching' service between IPs and surrogates.[12] To varying degrees these groups and organisations have also campaigned for improvements in healthcare provision for surrogacy teams and for improvements in the legal framework for surrogacy.

Natalie Smith is one such campaigner. Between 2014 and 2017 Natalie was a board member of SurrogacyUK. As chair of its Working Group on Law Reform she was instrumental in the campaign that led to the Law Commissions' 2023 proposals.[13] Reflecting on the early development of surrogacy law in the UK, Natalie recognises some positives, explaining that: 'What those laws and restrictions did from the start, is create a really strong culture of surrogacy in the UK that is values-based, relationship-based and self-regulated'. At SurrogacyUK we have supported surrogates, IPs and surrogacy 'teams' through the highs and lows of surrogacy since 2002. Today, we have over 1,000 members and – by the end of 2024 – will have supported the birth of over 500 surrogate children. Since SurrogacyUK was established, legal changes have made legal parenthood through surrogacy accessible to same-sex and unmarried couples in enduring relationships and, more recently, to single people. It was not until the HFE Act 2008 that legally recognised parenthood through surrogacy became available to same-sex and unmarried couples, and not until 2019 that it became available to single people, and only then after a human rights challenge.[14]

12 SurrogacyUK does not.

13 See Natalie Smith, 'Mapping Out a Future for the UK's Law on Surrogacy' (2016) 4(3) *Journal of Medical Law and Ethics* 237.

14 Human Fertilisation and Embryology Act 2008 (Remedial) Order 2018.

Single parenthood through surrogacy

In 2014 David Watkins, a single gay man, set out to become a dad. David had explored adoption and had friends who had adopted, but having a biological connection to his child was important to him. In partnership with a close female friend, he started a co-parenting journey. They created embryos in Finland: IVF is more affordable there and people born through donor conception have similar rights to access information about their origins to those in the UK. A successful embryo transfer resulted in a pregnancy, but David and his friend's co-parenting journey ended in a miscarriage two months later. They both agreed not to continue to pursue this pathway to parenthood. David's desire to be a father did not wane and, following further research, he approached SurrogacyUK in 2018.

Many SurrogacyUK members come to surrogacy as IPs after long, emotional and sometimes traumatic journeys through fertility challenges and IVF or – for our LGBTQI+ members – through reconciling their sexuality or gender identity with parenthood. While things have changed so much for the better in our 20-year history, there are still societal challenges to gay parenthood and (especially) to trans identity. People are often worn down by their journey – and almost always anxious – when they approach surrogacy organisations. Joining one can be an uplifting experience: our members talk about their relief at finding rooms full of people with shared experience, whether that is a willingness to talk about (in)fertility or gay parenting.

David's initial approach to SurrogacyUK was, regrettably, not an entirely uplifting experience. The law, as it stood then, blocked his path to parenthood not because he was gay, but because he was single. Single people at that time were ineligible for parental orders (and SurrogacyUK policy is to only support journeys for those who are eligible). David was single by choice. Other IPs are single because they have lost someone or following separation. The law therefore shone a light on people's relationship status, an experience that David describes as 'othering'. He had experienced prejudice as a gay man, but prejudice against him as a *single* man was unexpected. He was aware of attitudes in the wider social media context that opposed surrogacy (even more so when it involves single men) and so at times felt defined (negatively) by strangers by virtue of a combination of his gender and relationship status, commenting: 'Society has low expectations of men as caregivers in general, and – in the eyes of some – single people haven't even proven their ability to have a relationship, let alone children!' However, in 2016 the case of *Z* was heard in the High Court.[15] Z was conceived using a donor egg and

[15] *Re Z (A Child) (No 2)* [2016] EWHC 1191 (Fam). See also Rosalind English, 'Father Should Be Allowed to Apply for Parental Responsibility Following Surrogacy' *UK Human*

carried, in the US, by a gestational surrogate. Z's father (a British citizen) returned to the UK and found himself ineligible for a parental order (though his parenthood had been recognised in the US). The government conceded that the exclusion of single people from the parental order provisions in the HFE Act 2008 was incompatible with Z's 'right to private and family life and to non-discrimination under the European Convention on Human Rights 1950'.[16]

As a result, the Act was amended through a 2018 remedial order allowing single people to pursue surrogacy with the confidence that their future legal parenthood could be established.[17] The change came into force in January 2019 and David became eligible for a parental order and a member of SurrogacyUK. He describes feeling very accepted within the SurrogacyUK community, although being the only solo male IP at the time meant that for some aspects of the journey there really was no template to follow. Several hurdles on his journey to parenthood remained. First, because surrogacy is illegal in Finland, the Finnish clinic would not transfer David's remaining embryos to the UK unless the intended mother (his friend) was going to carry the baby. As their co-parenting relationship had ended, David decided to pursue other paths.

At several points in his journey, David faced challenge and stigma. A receptionist at one clinic laughed in disbelief when he said he would like to create embryos as a single man. During the initial search for a clinic, he felt at times like he was treated like a sperm donor rather than a father-to-be. He found information and advice – including from SurrogacyUK – framed towards couples and needing recalibration to accommodate his circumstances. This reinforced David's sense that there was something wrong, or strange, in being single and choosing to pursue parenthood. He feels that regulatory change in 2018 *preceded* a change in societal attitudes towards single parenthood by choice; a change that is, arguably, ongoing.[18]

Rights Blog 25 May 2016 (https://ukhumanrightsblog.com/2016/05/25/father-should-be-allowed-to-apply-for-parental-responsibility-following-surrogacy/ (last accessed 28 February 2024)).

16 As recognised in the Joint Committee on Human Rights' *Proposal for a Draft Human Fertilisation and Embryology Act 2008 (Remedial) Order 2018*, para 2 (https://publications.parliament.uk/pa/jt201719/jtselect/jtrights/645/64503.htm (last accessed 28 February 2024)).

17 Human Fertilisation and Embryology Act 2008 (Remedial) Order 2018.

18 Attitudes to single motherhood, including through assisted conception, could be considered at least a decade ahead. In 2008 an amendment to the HFE Act, with respect to clinics' undertaking of welfare of the child assessments, removed a reference to 'the need of that child for a father' and replaced it with 'the need of that child for supportive parenting'. Some clinics had, even prior to that change, begun treating single women. See Ellie Lee, Jan Macvarish and Sally Sheldon, 'Assessing Child Welfare Under the Human Fertilisation and Embryology Act 2008: a Case Study in Medicalisation?' (2014)

More surprisingly, clinics and organisations were slow to respond to the law change and David (and a few other single IPs and their surrogates) had to help them be inclusive. Groups set up to support single parents did not understand how to support parents who were single 'by design', as David explains:

> I tried to join organisations for single parents but that was a complete fail because they had absolutely no understanding of single fathers who *wanted to be* single fathers so none of their resources were suitable for me. They were all for people who had been in relationships, had children, and *become* single dads or mums.

David was offered help by a surrogate soon after the law change. He is now a single father to a baby boy and provides support to other single men who want to pursue solo parenthood through surrogacy. He has been happy to adopt a public profile through his journey but has had to distance himself from the trolling and vilification encountered on social media as a result. He is one example of many who have pushed the surrogacy agenda, and the treatment of surrogacy teams, forward. But, he acknowledges, 'some people just want to have a kid – and that's fight enough'.

The role of the surrogate partner

The Law Commissions' 2023 report proposes a 'new pathway to legal parenthood' that will allow IPs to hold legal parenthood from birth.[19] Eligibility for the pathway will require IPs to pursue domestic surrogacy, for surrogates and IPs to undertake several steps prior to conception including receiving independent legal advice and implications counselling, and to use a 'regulated surrogacy organisation' (RSO, to be established under the proposed reforms) which will undertake a welfare assessment of the prospective child. The existing parental order route will remain in place for those who do not meet the eligibility criteria for the new pathway, including those who do not work with an RSO, and for all international surrogacy journeys.

One key impact of the proposed reform will be to make a significant and beneficial difference to the status of surrogates' partners – one party who often goes unconsidered by those discussing law reform. Under

---

36(4) *Sociology of Health & Illness* 500. More concerningly, there is a tendency among anti-surrogacy campaigners (especially on social media) to paint intended single fathers by choice as somehow predatory or as potential child abusers.

[19] Law Commission and Scottish Law Commission, *Building Families Through Surrogacy: a New Law: Volume II: Full Report* (Law Com No 411, Scot Law Com No 262, 29 March 2023), chapter 2.

current law, surrogates have legal parenthood at birth and, if they are married or in a civil partnership, their spouse or partner is, by default, the 'father' or second parent on the birth certificate.[20] Most people involved in surrogacy are deeply uncomfortable with this because of the practical implications (which we consider here), notwithstanding the patriarchal implications of the law.[21] Surrogates make an empowered choice about what to do with their body when considering a surrogacy journey, but then the law says that they require their partner's (normally a man) 'permission' to do so.

If the Law Commissions' proposals become law, then, under both the new pathway and existing parental order route, the requirement for surrogates' partners to consent to the transfer of legal parenthood will be removed. This is a significant step forward and will ease some risks that surrogacy teams can face. Occasionally, surrogates' relationships with their partners break down during surrogacy journeys, or journeys start when surrogates are already separated but divorce proceedings are incomplete. The consequences of surrogates' separation can be serious where that happens during a pregnancy. Ongoing communication between parties is required to ensure that the surrogate partner is willing to consent to the parental order, and the welfare of the surrogate child can become bound up in difficult and personal separation or divorce matters.

The proposed law reform will remove this outdated requirement and remove a source of anxiety for surrogate partners. In SurrogacyUK our surrogates' partners are regarded as key people in surrogacy journeys. In most cases, they are involved and supportive but legal parenthood of – and responsibility for – surrogate babies is an unwanted burden for them. There may, however, be unintended consequences that come with such reform. The current law, for all its faults, has created a culture (at least in SurrogacyUK) of engagement and support from surrogate partners. The legal responsibility currently demanded of them does encourage participation

---

20 HFE Act 2008, ss33, 35 and 42.

21 For discussion and evidence on these points see, inter alia: Kirsty Horsey, 'Surrogacy in the UK: Myth Busting and Reform: Report of the Surrogacy UK Working Group on Surrogacy Law Reform' (Surrogacy UK, November 2015); Kirsty Horsey, 'Surrogacy in the UK: Further Evidence for Reform', Second Report of the Surrogacy UK Working Group on Surrogacy Law Reform (December 2018); Kirsty Horsey, Mimi Arian-Schad, Nicholas Macklon and Kamal Ahuja, 'UK Surrogates' Characteristics, Experiences, and Views on Surrogacy Law Reform' (2022) 36 *International Journal of Law, Policy and the Family* ebac030; Kirsty Horsey, Mimi Arian-Schad, Nicholas Macklon and Kamal Ahuja, 'UK Intended Parents' Characteristics, Experiences, and Views on Surrogacy Law Reform' (2023) 37 *International Journal of Law, Policy and the Family* ebad004. See also Horsey, Chapter 3, this volume.

in their partners' journeys, providing emotional support and being active members in surrogacy teams. As we prepare for a law change that we see as generally positive, we will make every effort to ensure that there are no unforeseen negative consequences.

The problems with parental orders

The parental order process has been central to UK surrogacy law for over 30 years. For domestic surrogacy journeys, parental order applications are made by IPs to their local family court, which coordinates engagement between them, the surrogate and CAFCASS, who have a responsibility to assess the welfare of the surrogate-born child and satisfy themselves that only reasonable expenses have been paid. Applications for parental orders for international surrogacy journeys follow a similar process but are heard by the High Court. The Law Commissions' proposed new pathway will offer surrogates and IPs an alternative to the parental order process that many currently find challenging and/or an unnecessary hurdle.

Jessica is a parent through surrogacy. Medically unable to sustain a pregnancy herself, she joined SurrogacyUK with her partner, Steven. She found the community supportive and described her friends in the community as 'people who just get it' adding: 'People outside just don't understand it, they can't, it's very unique'.

The couple joined SurrogacyUK in 2020, met Lauren, a surrogate, in 2021 and began their gestational surrogacy journey using embryos created from their own gametes. After a first transfer which resulted in miscarriage, Lauren became pregnant a second time and later gave birth to Jessica and Steven's daughter. Reflecting on their relationship as a team, Jessica says: 'We're really lucky it's been good. We're really fortunate in our journey and our relationship with Lauren. We will stay in contact and I hope she feels the same way'. But Jessica's reflections on the parental order process, and the denial of legal parenthood from birth, shines a light on the human impact of the current law:

> There are emotional and psychological ramifications [of not being the legal parent] and the practicalities of it makes life very difficult. [Our daughter] is completely ours biologically but having a birth certificate that says you are not the mother isn't very nice. If we wanted to get a passport, we'd have to get permission. It's things like that: you *can* do them, but they make life harder.

Practical challenges were also experienced by Leanne, a parent through surrogacy: 'Due to not being on our son's original birth certificate it has been more complicated, time consuming and upsetting to apply for a passport and tax-free childcare. It's a painful reminder that I couldn't carry him myself. I'm not treated like his mother which is painfully unfair'.

In SurrogacyUK's experience, parental orders generally take between six and nine months for courts to process, with a lot of regional variation in terms of timescale and experience and frequent delays. In Jessica's view:

> The parental order is quite a milestone, even though you know they are yours, it feels like they are really, really yours. The christening, we could have done before, but it doesn't feel appropriate until things are in place. The CAFCASS process has been hard, it is unsettling that you could get a court reporter who wants to be difficult then it could be really damaging. I found it stressful, as parents you want your child to be legally yours.

The parental order process deprives parents-through-surrogacy of some of the 'rites of passage' of parenthood. Christenings and other traditional ceremonies are either delayed (voluntarily) or compromised by IPs' sense that their parenthood is incomplete without legal recognition. Birth registrations are compromised because (in the view of surrogacy teams) they register the 'wrong' parent(s). Julie, a mum through surrogacy, found the experience challenging:

> When we registered our son's birth it hit home for me that I had no parental rights and was not considered to be my child's mother. The registrar's question – 'who is mum?' – had to be answered with our surrogate's name, and her information was entered on the birth certificate. After a difficult journey to become parents, at a time when I was trying to adjust to my new identity as a mother – in the context of having had my child through surrogacy and not having been pregnant with him – this felt painful.

Many *surrogates* feel the same. Chrissy, for example, said:

> Sitting there with myself and my husband being called the baby's mum and dad and having to answer all the questions as though that was the case was uncomfortable and a lie. We were never his parents. His parents were sat right next to us, and they should have had the joy of registering their baby's birth, which I had experienced when I did this for my own children. It is such an exciting experience when you have a baby, officially giving them a name that you have chosen and making them an 'official' little person. It felt it should have been his parents having that amazing experience.

As is often the case in surrogacy, the experience and reflections of intended mothers and mothers-through-surrogacy – who have often endured years of fertility challenges, attempted IVF and miscarriage or child-loss – focus hearts and minds on the inadequacy of existing law and the parental order process. There are also significant child welfare issues at stake. Legally, until a parental order is granted to IPs, responsibility for making decisions about the child's healthcare lies with the surrogate (and potentially their spouse/partner). This applies from birth onwards and across acute, primary care and community healthcare settings. Letters, signed by surrogates, can help when healthcare professionals are prepared to exercise judgement in matters of consent, but their acceptance is not assured. Both surrogates and IPs worry about the consequences, as Emma, a surrogate, explained:

> My third surro-baby needed surgery, before the parental order was granted. This meant I had to consent to the operation. Initially the hospital was adamant that I would need to attend a pre-op appointment in person, a five hour round trip. I had to fight with the hospital to be allowed to attend – and to sign the consent forms – virtually. It felt so wrong to be the person signing to consent for the operation. It's a decision that her parents should have been able to make.

Chrissy, a surrogate, agreed, explaining: 'I shouldn't be making decisions for a child who isn't even with me, their parents should be making those decisions. They know their child and what is right and best for them'. John, a parent through surrogacy, explained this from the IPs' perspective:

> Our surrogate and her husband have full lives and three children of their own, they had no desire to be legally responsible for another child, especially one that did not live with them. We all worried about our son getting ill during this period and a doctor or hospital seeking permission from our surrogate before commencing treatment.

Across the SurrogacyUK community, both surrogates and IPs are frustrated by the current law. Rosie is an experienced surrogate and has campaigned for reform:

> It annoys me when I when I think of surrogacy law, the way it is now: I feel annoyed, and disrespected. The law is disrespectful to everyone. It's disrespectful to me to think that I would want to keep the baby when I've made such an important decision. It's disrespectful to the parents to not be the parents from the birth and it's disrespectful to the baby who deserves to have their true parentage recognised from birth. That's what annoys me and that is what has always been my fighting point.

IPs can find the parental order process invasive and uncomfortable. Eddy, a parent through surrogacy, said that:

> I wholeheartedly agree that there need to be checks and balances and it always seemed like an administrative exercise. Knowing that we would meet all the conditions to qualify for a PO meant I wasn't worried when it came to applying [...] Having said that, it was strange to go through the process after several months of *being* parents to our son. Just the concept that strangers would have any role in 'assessing' and 'deciding' when it comes to your child's welfare and future does make you feel a bit uneasy and even resentful, especially as you've done nothing wrong to invite that scrutiny into your lives.

CAFCASS officers are often inexperienced in handling parental orders (they remain relatively uncommon) and experiences with CAFCASS can vary across the country, and even within teams (IPs and surrogates may be interviewed separately by officers from their local family court where they live in different jurisdictions). This experience, shared by Nicola, is not uncommon:

> Our experience with CAFCASS was extremely positive but our surrogate, Sarah, was deeply uncomfortable that during her CAFCASS appointment she was repeatedly asked if she was ready to 'give up her baby' and told that any stage, right up to the court day she could 'change her mind and keep her baby'. She was very upset by this lack of awareness and understanding, despite her repeatedly saying 'he is not my baby, he has never been my baby' the same language continues to be used.[22]

Eddy's experience was more positive, but also emphasises training and development needs in CAFCASS teams:

> Our CAFCASS officer was very friendly but inexperienced in the process and, as was the case when we registered our son's birth, at times we ended up directing the professional as to what needed to happen! Her report, whilst very positive and complimentary about us and our family, was very clearly written in the style of a social services report – it was odd to read about our son in that kind of context and language. The fact that the report highlights that your child is happy

[22] See also discussion of language/terminology used by healthcare and other professionals in Mahmoud, Chapter 9 and Horsey, Chapter 3, this volume.

> and well cared for reminds you that you're being assessed, and that the professional is there to check on these things. These are checks that parents of a newborn who didn't have to pursue a surrogacy journey wouldn't be subjected to.

Eddy's view reflects a frustration that SurrogacyUK hears a lot from members and the wider surrogacy community: children born through surrogacy are the result of carefully planned pregnancies between consenting parties but are subject to the kind of state 'invasiveness' normally reserved for cases of family breakdown or – at the extreme – neglect and abuse. Eddy, like most members of the community, is positive about the prospect of a new surrogacy pathway: 'I would certainly pursue the proposed new pathway if it was available for a future surrogacy journey. I think it offers increased protection to all parties and would allow teams to enjoy their journeys safe in the knowledge that legalities are all resolved in advance'. Again, however, there is some concern about potential 'unintended consequences'. Some surrogates see the parental order process as a way for them to 'secure' a relationship with IPs and surrogate-born children post-birth or, simply, as a welcome element of surrogacy journeys. Georgie, an independent surrogate, was

> quite happy with [the existing pathway] and so were my IPs. We saw registering the birth and the PO process as another lovely thing we could do together! I wouldn't match with IPs who wanted to follow the new pathway and wouldn't be a surrogate if that was the only option.

Georgie's view *is not* shared by most surrogates in SurrogacyUK, who welcome the new pathway, but illustrates the variety of views held in the community.

The right to object

Under existing law, surrogates (and their spouse/partner where relevant) must consent to the making of a parental order and, therefore, have the potential to influence the designation of legal parenthood simply by withholding that consent. Except in cases where the surrogate 'cannot be found or is incapable of giving agreement',[23] if consent is denied, the parental order cannot be granted. Under existing law, consent cannot be given until six weeks after birth[24] and must be given within six months of birth to be

[23] HFE Act 2008, ss54(7), 54A(6).

[24] ibid.

valid.[25] There are several reasons why a surrogate might refuse consent. This may be because of a breakdown in the surrogacy team's relationship; because of concern about the child's welfare; because they are owed expenses by the IPs and have no other recourse under existing law to 'force' a resolution of financial disputes.[26]

Under the Law Commissions' proposed pathway, surrogates' (informed) consent will be given at the point that the surrogacy agreement is made, but they will have the right to withdraw that consent until six weeks after birth.[27] If she withdraws consent before birth, the IPs must apply for a parental order (in effect the arrangement would default to the existing pathway). If the surrogate withdraws her consent *after* birth, parenthood will not default to her: if *she* wanted to obtain legal parenthood, *she* must use the existing parental order process.[28]

The proposals were drafted with the best interests of surrogate-born children at their heart. For example, regarding the first reason given above, it is uncommon for surrogacy teams' relationships to breakdown to the extent that consent is refused, but the Law Commissions' consultation considered one such case, *Re AB (Surrogacy Consent)*,[29] in which a surrogate declined to give consent for a parental order following relationship breakdown. In this case: 'the "catalyst" for the breakdown appears to have been that the surrogate felt that the IPs had not shown sufficient concern for her wellbeing after she had been told, at her 12-week scan, that the continuation of pregnancy could put her health at risk'.[30] In her judgment on that case, finding that it was not possible to override the refusal of consent, Theis J stated:

> The result is that these children are left in a legal limbo, where, contrary to what was agreed by the parties at the time of the arrangement, the

---

25 HFE Act 2008, ss54(3), 54A(2). Though this is what the law *says*, it is not the case that applications made after six months will fail. Since the judgment in *Re X (A Child) (Surrogacy: Time Limit)* [2015] FAM 186, where it was stated that parliament could not possibly have intended legal parenthood to be unavailable if the six-month deadline was not met (at [55]), there have been several cases where parental orders have been granted 'late', including, in one case, in respect of an *adult* born through surrogacy (*X v Z (Parental Order Adult)* [2022] EWFC 26).

26 Despite these reasons, it should be noted that refusal of consent is very rare. Note, also, we are not talking here about the surrogate seeking to keep the baby, as this is *extremely* rare and something SurrogacyUK has in fact never encountered.

27 Law Commissions, n19, para 4.106.

28 ibid, para 4.118.

29 [2016] EWHC 2643 (Fam).

30 Law Commission and Scottish Law Commission: Joint Consultation Paper, *Building Families Through Surrogacy: a New Law* (Law Com Consultation Paper No 244, Scot Law Com Discussion Paper No 167, 6 June 2019), para 5.66.

> respondents will remain their legal parents even though they are not biologically related to them and they expressly wish to play no part in the children's lives.[31]

Under the proposals, legal parenthood in that case would be decided by the court.

The same principles around withdrawal of consent will apply where a surrogate has concerns about the child's welfare. Under the existing process, welfare assessments are made by CAFCASS during the parental order process. In the new pathway – as we explore later – they will be undertaken in advance of conception by an RSO as a first safeguard in the process.[32] If a surrogate becomes pregnant and, subsequently, concerns arise about the potential future welfare of the child, they can withdraw consent. If they do, the arrangement reverts to the parental order process and the responsibility for welfare assessment reverts to CAFCASS. If concerns arise after birth, the surrogate can raise those concerns with social services. As the Law Commissions say, at that point 'concerns about safeguarding, which is imperative and must be taken seriously, would be better met through other routes, including existing child protection systems'.[33] Finally, in relation to the third scenario outlined above, the Law Commissions' proposals allow for the financial terms of surrogacy agreements to be enforced in a civil court, offering 'a clear means of resolving financial disputes and keep[ing] these separate from legal parental status'.[34] Critically, the proposals distinguish between parental and financial considerations, allowing those to be determined independently and removing the potential for financial disputes to affect the resolution of the child's parentage.

SurrogacyUK fully supports the recommendations above and recognise them as a balanced compromise between divergent views across the surrogacy community. In a survey we conducted among SurrogacyUK's surrogates in preparing our response to the Law Commissions' initial proposals, 93% said that they *did not* think they should have a right to refuse a parental order. Rosie, who we met earlier, sums up the general view:

> As surrogates, we make a decision to do this thing and we should commit to it and commit to the whole process. You have the baby

[31] At [8]. In June 2024, following a change of heart from the surrogate, a parental order relating to the twins in this case was finally granted (case as yet unreported).

[32] Law Commissions, n19, paras 2.23, 4.39, 17.1.

[33] ibid, para 4.74.

[34] ibid, para 12.216 (see also para 12.195).

for the IPs. If you change your mind, you *should* have to go through some kind of lengthy and difficult process to overturn that decision.

Surrogate expenses: black and white and grey

The issue of expenses is challenging for everyone involved in surrogacy. The spectrum of views reflects the wide variety of approaches to surrogacy internationally. Definitions are contested and can overlap. In the UK context, some would prefer the system of altruistic surrogacy (in which only pregnancy-related expenses are reimbursed) to be maintained, while others would prefer that to be replaced by either a *compensatory* system (in which surrogates are paid a fee for the work they do in carrying a child) or a fully *commercial* approach (a full 'for profit' system allowing agencies and brokers to make money from surrogacy too).

SurrogacyUK is rooted firmly in the UK's altruistic model (it is important to note that not all UK surrogacy organisations share our view) and many surrogates join SurrogacyUK in part because our values align with that model. To illustrate the sensitivity around expenses: some SurrogacyUK surrogates are concerned that the Law Commissions' report specifically refers to *payments* rather than expenses 'to highlight that we are not simply trying to capture (and then permit) payments that have been accepted as "expenses" under the current law'.[35] Our surrogates challenge any notion that they are paid and – with our support – cost their pregnancy expenses carefully and seek to be reimbursed for only what we advise as 'allowable'.[36] We advise surrogates to keep receipts, and our agreements stipulate that expenses should be paid in ten equal instalments over the course of a pregnancy, with the first payment at the point of a positive test. SurrogacyUK has processes in place to 'balance' payments in the case that expenses are unused at the end of a pregnancy (which can happen in the case of miscarriage, for example) or – as is more often the case – complications during pregnancy or birth mean that additional expenses need to be recovered by a surrogate.

As an organisation we are especially cautious, aware that in order to obtain a parental order, CAFCASS needs to be satisfied that 'no money or other benefit (other than for expenses reasonably incurred) has been given or received by either of the applicants'.[37] However, there is a grey area around what constitutes an allowable expense, as the Law Commissions identified

35 ibid, para 12.2.

36 Notably, the Law Commissions do also use the language of 'costs', saying this 'more accurately reflects the idea that the money paid should not leave the surrogate financially better off' (ibid).

37 HFE Act 2008, s54(8).

in their consultation document, '[t]he meaning of "expenses reasonably incurred" is not defined by the HFEA 2008' and, in practice, parental orders are granted 'even where the payments exceed expenses'.[38]

The flexibility demonstrated by courts – intended to avoid criminalisation that might impact children's welfare – has generated a wide interpretation of 'reasonable expenses' by both organisations and independent parties in surrogacy. The Law Commissions' proposals intend to address this – for both the existing and new pathways – by listing the types of acceptable payments and specifically excluding others (including compensatory payments) and stipulating that expenses must be paid as they are accrued, rather than evenly apportioned over a pregnancy (though a 'float' can be provided).[39]

For SurrogacyUK, the list of allowable expenses is close to the list we currently use but other organisations, and people undertaking surrogacy independently, may find the list restrictive if they have, in practice, made, received, condoned or encouraged compensatory payments to surrogates. The Law Commissions are clear on their rationale for prohibiting such payments, linking them to the increased potential for exploitation (though acknowledging that their approach can only minimise, not eradicate, this potential).[40]

Whilst at SurrogacyUK we do not envisage any negative impact on the number of surrogates applying for membership, other organisations – such as Brilliant Beginnings – think the proposals are a retrograde step:

> The new requirement for IPs to account for every penny they pay their surrogate against a narrow permitted expenses list, and potential criminal offences for those who pay more, is a significant step backwards. We are deeply concerned that this will worsen the existing shortage of UK surrogates, giving even more parents no choice but to go overseas.[41]

If Brilliant Beginnings is right, the proposed reforms could jeopardise one of the Commissions' own stated goals: to 'encourage intended parents in the UK who wish to enter into surrogacy agreements to do so in the UK, rather than overseas'.[42] However, it might be argued that by offering clarity,

---

38 Law Commissions, n30, paras 14.8, 14.12.

39 Law Commissions, n19, paras 12.19–12.22.

40 ibid, paras 12.9–12.12.

41 Brilliant Beginnings, 'The Law Commission Final Surrogacy Law Reform Report: Key Takeaways and Our Response' (2023) https://brilliantbeginnings.co.uk/law-commission-final-report-surrogacy-law-reform-takeaways-response/ (last accessed 3 July 2024).

42 Law Commissions, n19, para 16.9.

the proposed reforms will address the anxiety surrogates and IPs currently experience around expenses. Despite the flexibility of the courts, parties in surrogacy journeys generally approach the parental order process with trepidation and a fear of 'getting it wrong' and jeopardising the order itself.

This is where the support of surrogacy organisations is invaluable. All organisations will need to adapt their processes to accommodate new regulations. SurrogacyUK is rethinking processes and protocols relating to expenses to ensure that the required evidence can be provided under either surrogacy pathway. Inevitably, there will be an impact in terms of administration and resources. Sarah Jones, SurrogacyUK's chief executive officer, explains:

> The proposals are going to change the way that we oversee surrogate expenses and it's going to increase the complexity of that. We will still ask surrogates to work out their overall expenses because that is really key information that IPs need upon starting the journey. But we're having discussions about how frequently we will need to review surrogates' expenses and we will have various check-in points throughout the pregnancy to check in on them and to adjust them.

SurrogacyUK's view is that the Law Commissions have struck a sensible balance in their definition of expenses, and one that aligns well with our current practice, but which will nonetheless place an additional administrative burden on us and our members. Our experience is that surrogates are motivated by helping others to experience parenthood. They want to be compensated for out-of-pocket expenses relating to pregnancy, but – despite strong, feminist, arguments that would justify their receipt of payment for the 'work' of carrying other people's children – they do not want to receive compensatory payments.

Implications counselling and legal advice

SurrogacyUK is also preparing for additional responsibilities that the proposed new pathway will require of RSOs. Two of these will make existing practices in fertility clinics, currently applicable to gestational surrogacy journeys only, applicable to all journeys under the new pathway. The first is the requirement that all parties receive implications counselling provided by 'a counsellor who is a member of the British Infertility Counselling Association or an equivalent body recognised by the HFEA' before embarking on a surrogacy journey.[43] Clinics are already required to offer similar counselling. SurrogacyUK

[43] ibid, para 8.67.

has always provided 'advisory' and 'agreement' sessions to members and encouraged discussion within surrogacy teams around the implications of surrogacy, including discussion of issues pertinent to pregnancy such as pre-natal testing and 'red lines' regarding termination, for example. We also require that surrogacy teams stipulate expectations around ongoing contact between IPs, surrogates and children born through surrogacy in their agreements.[44] This recommendation within the proposed reforms is a welcome extension of existing good practice.

The Law Commissions also propose that it should be a requirement (of access to the new pathway) that 'both the surrogate and the intended parents take independent legal advice about entering into the surrogacy agreement'.[45] Concerned that unnecessary legal costs could be incurred by members, SurrogacyUK is pleased that, alongside this

> there would not be any need for the parties to use solicitors to negotiate or draft the surrogacy agreement. As happens at present, the agreement can be prepared using templates provided by surrogacy organisations. This agreement will not be legally binding: the legal consequences of the new pathway will arise entirely from the statutory regime. Thus, while they would be free to do so, there would be no need to use solicitors, and thus no additional costs incurred, at this stage.[46]

We are keen to avoid additional legal costs for our members, or to jeopardise our altruistic, friendship-first ethos by introducing transactional and contractual elements to surrogacy journeys. We recognise, though, the importance of legally-binding elements of future surrogacy agreements – namely around expenses – being robust and achieving the Commissions' intention of providing recourse through the courts if surrogates' expenses are not paid.

The welfare of the child

The final significant legal changes that we consider here both relate to the welfare of children born through surrogacy. First, under the proposed new pathway, RSOs will be required to undertake statutorily required screening of IPs and a 'welfare of the child' assessment before a surrogacy team enters

[44] In 2023 we repackaged and enhanced our existing practice and now provide implications counselling, from BICA-qualified counsellors to members of traditional surrogacy teams prior to making a surrogacy agreement.

[45] Law Commissions, n19, para 8.106.

[46] ibid, para 8.103

an agreement.[47] Welfare assessments are currently undertaken (in England and Wales) by CAFCASS officers within the parental order process and, in IVF (and therefore gestational surrogacy), by fertility clinics in advance of treatment in a form-based process. Since January 2024, SurrogacyUK has undertaken welfare of the child assessments, based on our own enhancement of current practice in fertility clinics, exploring surrogacy teams' intentions around informing surrogate-born children about their origins (which we regard as critical to the best interests of the child). We will be interested to see guidance that emerges from the HFEA around welfare of the child assessments, should the proposals become law. The existing form-based approach required in clinics could be considered weak; the current CAFCASS process could be considered invasive, and we would be interested in co-producing guidance if the opportunity arose.

Second, the proposed introduction of a surrogacy register will give people born through surrogacy the right to information about their origins when they come of age.[48] This proposal has been overwhelmingly well received by the surrogacy community. While some people may be dissuaded from becoming a surrogate due to this transparency, SurrogacyUK believes this is a beneficial consequence of the proposal. Children and young people with experience of surrogacy also agree with this change. Concurrent with the Law Commissions' work, UK academics have made a pioneering effort to engage children born through surrogacy, and the children of surrogates, in research on surrogacy law. In their preliminary findings, based on primary research with a group of 25 young people aged 8–17 with experience of surrogacy: 22 (88%) agreed that that children born through surrogacy should 'know they were born this way' and 21 (84%) agreed that surrogate-born children should 'know the identity of their surrogate'.[49]

In adopting and implementing the Law Commissions' proposals, the surrogacy community has the potential to counter concerns around the wellbeing of children born through surrogacy that are often raised by those who oppose surrogacy. While SurrogacyUK disagrees with any suggestion that surrogate-born children are subject to greater risk of harm than other children, we understand that surrogate-born children have, as well as their

[47] ibid, paras 8.1, 8.166 and recommendation 25.

[48] Age definitions vary between England & Wales and Scotland: for details see Law Commissions, ibid, chapter 13. See discussion of the proposed surrogacy register by Wade, Chapter 7, this volume.

[49] Katherine Wade, Kirsty Horsey and Zaina Mahmoud, 'Children's Voices in Surrogacy Law – Phase One Preliminary Report' (2023) https://childrensvoices.bristol.ac.uk/files/2023/10/CVSL-PHASE-ONE-Preliminary-Report-2023.pdf (last accessed 24 February 2024).

parents, an additional important person in their lives (their surrogate and possibly a gamete donor).

We have an opportunity to make surrogacy not just an acceptable form of family-building, but a positive role-model for it. The creation of families through surrogacy can and should be focussed, from before conception, on children's welfare, take a thoughtful but positive approach to consideration of children's origins, and celebrate the special relationships that exist in surrogacy families.

Surrogacy organisations: changing, and driving change

If the proposed reforms are passed into law, UK surrogacy organisations will need to make material changes to the way that they administer surrogacy journeys. SurrogacyUK will do this very willingly – we have campaigned for many of these changes since 2014 – and we are used to adapting. For example, we recently updated our processes to accommodate revised HFEA guidelines allowing HIV-positive people to use their own gametes in fertility treatment, IVF and gestational surrogacy. The biggest change for us – in terms of the volume and constitution of our membership – was the impact of the HFE Act 2008, which made parental orders accessible to same-sex and unmarried couples.

Martin is a married gay man and a father through surrogacy. His desire to become a parent was ignited when he and his partner realised that, due to the 2008 Act, they had the opportunity to experience parenthood in its entirety, through conception, pregnancy and birth and leading to legal parenthood. The change in law had a profound impact on his aspirations and life plan. Martin remembers attending a SurrogacyUK conference in 2013, with his partner, and being overwhelmed by the number of gay couples seeking to access parenthood through surrogacy. The uptake of membership by gay couples (who, today, comprise about half of SurrogacyUK's IP membership) is testament to the desire that people in the LGBTQI+ community have to become parents. Our experience is borne out by fertility clinics: a 2022 study found that 38% of surrogacy-related IVF treatments over an eight-year period at one UK clinic were for same-sex male IPs.[50]

The 2008 law change came too late for many gay men. Martin remembers the 'bittersweetness' with which many of his older friends received the news of his surrogacy plans. A sense of inequality for gay people and more broadly with the perception and treatment of all surrogates and IPs, drove Martin's engagement with SurrogacyUK and a determination to improve surrogacy

[50] Kirsty Horsey et al, 'First Clinical Report of 179 Surrogacy Cases in the UK: Implications for Policy and Practice' (2022) 45(4) *Reproductive BioMedicine Online* 831.

law, access and equality. He describes the surrogacy community's drive for law reform as 'an amazing example of civil society coming together'.

In 2014 SurrogacyUK convened surrogates, IPs, families through surrogacy, surrogacy organisations, lawyers, academics, healthcare professionals and MPs and began a letter-writing and engagement campaign to raise awareness of the need for surrogacy law reform among parliamentarians and policy makers. We also established a Working Group on Law Reform which, in 2015, published a landmark paper containing primary research and data and making the case for law reform.[51] Notably, Dame Mary Warnock – the chair of the Warnock Committee whose 1984 Report led to the Surrogacy Arrangements Act 1985 – co-authored a foreword that urged the government to 'reconsider surrogacy, to facilitate further research into how it is conducted and what compensations are paid, to bring the law into line with modern social realities'.[52] Natalie Smith remembers how widely drawn the data for the 2015 report was:

> In addition to SurrogacyUK members we worked really hard to make sure that we got people from outside the organisation to complete the survey. COTS and Brilliant Beginnings pushed it out to their members and we shared it on independent Facebook groups too. The research was 'organisation agnostic' and was the widest that had been undertaken into how surrogacy was actually practised.

That report, and the campaign that accompanied it, led to a 2016 debate about surrogacy in the House of Lords. The debate was notable for the change in tone – a marked contrast to the 1984 parliamentary debates mentioned earlier. It demonstrated evolving social attitudes towards assisted reproduction, modern family life and surrogacy and highlighted the need for reform. In the words of Lady Barker, who initiated the debate:

> We have shown the world that, in this field of assisted reproduction, it is possible to make laws that reflect the realities of modern life while protecting the best interests of children. Surrogacy is, and will remain, a matter of intense importance to a very few people, many of whom are often misunderstood. I submit that this is an area in which there will never be a widespread, popular clamour for change in the law. It is a matter which needs detailed consideration. It is one in which Members of your Lordships' House, even those who disagree in principle, should be involved in lengthy debate. Above all, it needs

51 Horsey (2015), n21.

52 ibid, 5.

> the Government to put their shoulder behind law reform which, in the interests of children, is now urgent.[53]

In late 2017 a review of surrogacy law was accepted into the Law Commission of England and Wales' 13th Programme of Law Reform,[54] leading to the joint project with the Scottish Law Commission[55] from which they ultimately reported in 2023. However, the surrogacy community did not have to wait until then to see improvements in conditions for surrogacy in the UK. In 2018, the Department of Health and Social Care (DHSC) published two pieces of guidance for the UK surrogacy community, co-produced in a collaboration between the DHSC, representatives from the surrogacy community and related organisations including CAFCASS.[56] The DHSC guidance provides separate information setting out both the process and legalities of surrogacy for surrogates and IPs,[57] and advice for healthcare practitioners involved in providing care to surrogate teams.[58]

Martin remembers that, in early meetings with the Department of Health,[59] healthcare professionals would claim expertise on surrogacy having delivered just a few surrogate births, far beneath any kind of threshold for statistical significance:

> I knew, going into these conversations, that we knew much more about surrogacy than anyone else around the room did because by then we were the largest surrogacy organisation. We were the nexus. We were where people came to meet IPs or surrogates and we were across

53 *Hansard* HL Deb, vol 777, col 1319, 14 December 2016.

54 Law Commission of England and Wales, '13th Programme of Law Reform' launched 14 December 2017 (https://lawcom.gov.uk/project/13th-programme-of-law-reform/ (last accessed 28 February 2024)).

55 Scottish Law Commission, 'Tenth Programme of Law Reform' (www.scotlawcom.gov.uk/law-reform/previous-programmes-of-law-reform/tenth-programme-of-law-reform-consultation/ (last accessed 28 February 2024)).

56 DHSC, 'Having a Child Through Surrogacy' 28 February 2018 (updated April 2024), all documents available at www.gov.uk/government/publications/having-a-child-through-surrogacy (last accessed 2 July 2024). This had been one of the recommendations in the SurrogacyUK Working Group's 2015 Report (Horsey, n21). The guidance credits SurrogacyUK, COTS, the Royal College of Midwives and the Royal College of Nursing and thanks the British Fertility Society, Royal College of Obstetricians and Gynaecologists, the HFEA, the British Association of Social Worker's Project Group on Assisted Reproduction (PROGAR) and CAFCASS.

57 DHSC, 'The Surrogacy Pathway: Surrogacy and the Legal Process for Intended Parents and Surrogates in England and Wales' (updated 25 April 2024).

58 DHSC, 'Care in Surrogacy: Guidance for the Care of Surrogates and Intended Parents in Surrogate Births in England and Wales' (updated 25 April 2024).

59 Since 2018, the Department of Health and Social Care.

> the country in terms of the hospitals and clinics that our members dealt with.

There was a chronic lack of reliable data to inform decision-making, and, despite their best intentions, policy makers lacked an evidence base and policy developments risked being informed by the loudest voices, rather than the greater good. As a result of the co-production and the deep and meaningful engagement between the DHSC and the surrogacy community, the guidance considered and addressed the *practice* and lived experience of surrogacy, rather than hearsay, assumptions and narrow datasets. The guidance marked the first time that a function of the British state had provided something that was *supportive* of surrogacy, rather than simply tolerant of it. To the best of our knowledge that 2018 guidance was the first of its kind anywhere in the world: it is still maintained and updated by the DHSC in collaboration with SurrogacyUK and other community representatives.

Also in 2018, the SurrogacyUK Working Group on Law Reform published an update to its 2015 report that provided additional survey data and made 14 further recommendations for consideration by the Law Commissions, the majority of which were addressed in their 2023 report.[60]

Progressive support for surrogacy

By coming together and working with others, the UK surrogacy community has fought (and continues to fight) for change and improvement in the conditions for surrogates, IPs, and people born through surrogacy. The 2023 Law Commissions' report demonstrates how much societal attitudes towards surrogacy have evolved in the 40 years since the Warnock Report, and the potential of well-organised grassroots campaigns to influence progress in policy and law.

The Law Commissions' review, and the DHSC guidance on surrogacy, demonstrate the state's journey from wilful neglect of surrogacy to progressive support for it. In Natalie Smith's view:

> I think supportive is the way to describe it, but I think it's more than that. It's also about the *process* of the Law Commissions' review itself, as well as the outcome. My biggest concern – because it was the Law Commissions doing this review – was that the words of lawyers would have more prominence than the words of people who have lived experience of surrogacy, but I don't think that's happened. I think they've done a really good job of listening to people talk about their

[60] Horsey (2018), n21.

> real experiences, and of those working in this area of law. The *process* of reforming the law, I think, sends very strong signals about how the government feels about surrogacy.

SurrogacyUK does not speak for all surrogacy organisations, but we are very supportive of the Law Commissions' proposals and, learning lessons from the past, began preparing for prospective changes in early 2023. While the full implications of the changes will not be clear until the law is passed (if, indeed, it is) and associated guidance is published by the HFEA, we are preparing for future regulatory oversight, reviewing our approach to expenses and considering implications for our future staffing and sustainability.

There are cost implications for us, which will require an increase in our membership fees, but also potential opportunities to grow our membership. For example, the proposals will allow RSOs to advertise their services.[61] We have some reservations about this and are concerned that it could encourage predatory practices that would go against our values and, we believe, the spirit of ethical surrogacy in the UK (for example, advertising for surrogates on university campuses), so we still believe there should be limits on advertising. However, advertising should allow us to enhance our mission to make surrogacy more accessible and better understood.

The reforms may increase interest in domestic surrogacy from both IPs and prospective surrogates, encouraged by a new pathway that allows IPs to hold legal parenthood from birth and provides surrogates with recourse to the courts for unpaid expenses. There is some concern that the proposals may have unintended consequences, reducing incentives for surrogacy teams to maintain contact after birth, with negative implications for people born through surrogacy, and ammunition for those who are morally opposed to it. Sarah Jones sees this as an opportunity to further develop and embed the organisation's expectation of enduring, lifelong relationships:

> What we'll do instead is build [that expectation] into the new pathway through implications counselling and the welfare of the child assessment and make it much more child-centred. I think that, as an organisation, we have wavered between being very IP-focussed or very surrogate-focussed and moving forward we need to make surrogacy journeys child- and child-welfare led. If we do that, I don't think we can go wrong.

SurrogacyUK believes that, if passed, the reforms *will* improve domestic surrogacy journeys, both on the new pathway and through reforms to the

[61] Law Commissions, n19, paras 14.120–14.121.

existing pathway (for example, by removal of the requirement for surrogate partners' consent to parental orders). The proposed surrogacy register will give people born through surrogacy comparable rights to those born through adoption and donor conception to discover their origins.

We will advocate for beneficial amendments to be made as the law passes through parliament and will continue to campaign – with our partners – on areas that the Law Commissions' review declined to change (such as double-gamete donation), or which were not within the scope of their review. For example, access to NHS-funded IVF treatment is exceptionally difficult to obtain where a surrogate is required to carry a resulting pregnancy, and remains a significant inequality in terms of access to fertility treatment for people wishing to pursue parenthood through surrogacy.

Surrogacy is about creating and growing families. Despite 1980s legislation that hoped that surrogacy would 'wither on the vine', the UK's surrogacy community has developed, and self-regulated, a distinctive, altruistic approach to the practice of surrogacy. We are delighted that the proposed reforms maintain the altruistic foundations of the UK's approach to surrogacy and believe that international jurisdictions will continue to look to the UK for inspiration and guidance as they also regulate surrogacy or review existing regulations.

The Law Commissions' review and resulting recommendations represent a once-in-a-generation opportunity to reform surrogacy law. For those who were involved in campaigning for change, like Natalie Smith:

> For me personally it's a no brainer. The Department [of Health and Social Care] have made an investment, they've followed an exemplary process, the Law Commissions have managed the process incredibly and they've got a fantastic set of recommendations and a draft law. The work's been done, they just need to action it.

3

How UK Surrogates Navigate Arrangements, Processes and the Law

Kirsty Horsey

Introduction

In autumn 2021, I conducted two online surveys – one with women who had been/were acting as surrogates, and another with parents/those seeking to become parents through surrogacy (in this chapter I refer to both under the umbrella term 'intended parents' (IPs)).[1] All the surrogacy arrangements involved IVF treatment at one licensed group,[2] with embryo transfer occurring between March 2014 and October 2021.

Some survey respondents consented to follow-up interviews. Twenty-five surrogates were subsequently interviewed between December 2021 and March 2022.[3] Interviewees were informed that their responses could be used in outputs feeding into wider academic and political debates on

---

1 Ethical approval for the entire study was granted by Kent Law School's Research Ethics Advisory Group, University of Kent (21 October 2021). Papers analysing the survey responses have been published: Horsey et al, 'UK Surrogates' Characteristics, Experiences, and Views on Surrogacy Law Reform' (2022) 36(1) *International Journal of Law, Policy and the Family* 1–29; Horsey et al, 'UK Intended Parents' Characteristics, Experiences, and Views on Surrogacy Law Reform' (2023) 37(1) *International Journal of Law, Policy and the Family* 1–28.

2 London Women's Clinic, with embryo transfer taking place in either London or Cardiff, and additional consultations occurring in some satellite centres around England and Wales. The sample of surrogates thus included no 'traditional' surrogates.

3 All interviews (semi-structured, lasting 45–120 minutes) took place via the Zoom online platform, the most appropriate means of interviewing when some COVID-19 restrictions remained. All but one interview was recorded (one surrogate did not give permission to

surrogacy, in the context of potential law reform. Surrogates were asked about various aspects of their experiences, including how they came to surrogacy and (where relevant) how the pregnancy proceeded, whether they experienced issues with their care; the financial part of the arrangement; ongoing relationships; and opinions on the legal position and potential reforms, especially with regards to the Law Commissions' initial consultation recommendations.[4] Interviewees had the opportunity to voice any reflections on their overall experience. Qualitative analysis was undertaken using an inductive coding method to identify key themes, which involved an iterative process, before assigning primary codes, then grouping these into final thematic strands. More than one code could be assigned within an interview response and thus some responses overlap across themes.

This chapter uses interview material to highlight how surrogates navigate the journey and view the law on surrogacy. To avoid identification of the interview participants, comments are anonymised and neutral identifiers used (for example, S1 refers to the first surrogate interviewed, chronologically). Potentially identifying information (such as location, names of partners or IPs) has also been removed/anonymised. Considering insights derived from the interviews, the chapter concludes on whether and how the recommendations made by the Law Commissions in their final report published in March 2023 might better match the interests and expectations of participants in domestic IVF surrogacy arrangements.[5]

Interviews with surrogates

Ten surrogates had been a surrogate (in their most recent journey) for a male same-sex couple, 14 for a heterosexual couple and one for a solo (female) IP. Six surrogacies were undertaken for the surrogate's brother (whether in a same-sex or heterosexual couple), two for the surrogate's sister and one for the surrogate's own adult daughter. Seven surrogates had been a surrogate before (some for different previous IPs, some were undertaking a 'sibling journey' for the same IPs). Eight surrogacies discussed had been facilitated by one of the UK's non-profit surrogacy organisations. All the surrogates had their own children. Two surrogates' journeys were ultimately unsuccessful, while one was pregnant at the time of interview.

record) and transcribed verbatim. Notes were taken for the unrecorded interview and a transcript constructed from those notes as best as possible.

4 Law Commission and Scottish Law Commission: Joint Consultation Paper, *Building Families Through Surrogacy: a New Law* (Law Com Consultation Paper No 244, Scot Law Com Discussion Paper No 167, 6 June 2019).

5 Law Commission and Scottish Law Commission, *Building Families Through Surrogacy: a New Law: Volume II: Full Report* (Law Com No 411, Scot Law Com No 262, 2023).

What led to the decision to become a surrogate?

Several surrogates had experienced fertility issues themselves,[6] or had discussions with friends, family members or others about infertility and empathised with those who needed help to have a child. For example, S10 said: 'I understand the whole "not being able to have kids" thing'. S4 'had undergone IVF several times to have my own children' and was 50 when she became a surrogate. Similarly, S13 explained: 'I had IVF for our own kids (age 7 and 5) so had experienced infertility and wanted to help. I knew what IVF was like. Bumped into a past client who had had children through surrogacy and that "sowed the seed"'. S20 had experienced miscarriage and took a long time to recover and to conceive again. She explained that 'in my head I felt "I'm never going to be a mum"'. She eventually had two children and following counselling 'said to my husband that "now I know how it feels, if I wanted to be a surrogate, how would you feel?" and he was very supportive about it'. Some had been a surrogate before and wanted to do it again.[7] S5 had done so twice and reflected that 'when I was pregnant with my first baby, I found it just incredible that some people couldn't have them very easily'. S22 said: 'There was a gay couple [at work] who I knew had been looking at adoption. I wanted to do surrogacy again – so I offered'. Others said they enjoyed their own pregnancies and/or found them easy. Others were inspired by reading about surrogacy or seeing surrogates speak, on TV or in person. S11 said: 'I saw a surrogate on a morning TV programme when I was a student – it stayed with me and I thought about it often … I had my own son easily, surrogacy was still in the back of my mind'. Similarly, S18 said she

> was about 17/18 and watching *This Morning* and there was a surrogate on there. I had never heard of it before but gut feeling was 'I would love to do that'. Didn't have my own kids at the time – had first one aged 20 and by 33 I had 4 – the idea came back – I like being pregnant and had easy pregnancies.

Some surrogates had a gay sibling they wanted to help. S2, who underwent IVF herself 'empathised with [her] brother's situation because of my own fertility issues'. S6, a surrogate for her brother/his husband, explained 'they had decided early on that they wanted kids and I offered to help'. S24 also had a child for her brother and his husband:

---

6 Miscarriage was mentioned by two surrogates, IVF by three PCOS (polycystic ovary syndrome) by two and unexplained infertility by one.

7 S3 also intended to be a surrogate again for the same IPs, who still had embryos in storage (that is, a sibling journey) – but 'only for them'.

> I'm a single mum via donor sperm – I had two kids before surrogacy and another one since. My brother got married and started looking at surrogacy – my youngest was one and a half – we were chatting about it and he was worried about the cost and the legal implications and everything. So I said 'why don't I do it?'. He didn't think I was serious, but we talked more. My pregnancies were easy and we'd always have a tie and it would save them thousands on top of clinic costs.

Others offered to help a sibling or other family member who was ill or struggled with infertility. S9's younger sister had gynaecological/fertility issues and she 'always wanted to do this', having had her own children quite young. S14 explained that her brother and sister-in-law

> had trouble conceiving for many years and I'd always considered it. They went through several rounds of IVF by then but fibroids meant she just couldn't carry. My brother asked me if I was still OK to consider it. I was totally fine … my husband was supportive as knew I wanted to do it.

S12 (32 weeks pregnant at interview) was carrying for her sister who already had one child via IVF and had frozen embryos in storage – but had since been ill and could not carry another baby. Similarly, S16 was a surrogate for her brother and sister-in-law's second child. They also had a child via IVF and embryos in storage, but subsequently the intended mother was diagnosed with cervical cancer. S19's half-sister had an illness that made it impossible for her to carry a child and had tried surrogacy before, unsuccessfully: 'we offered to help – it was a team effort, very much'. S15's daughter preserved her eggs prior to fertility-ending cancer treatment. She explained:

> A nurse told [her] that her journey to motherhood wasn't necessarily over and she could look into surrogacy – that started me thinking about it and while she was having treatment I got fit, had health checks etc – once we got over the cancer we spoke about it – then had to speak to consultant to "put the case" for it to be me.

Other surrogates did it for a friend. S20's long-term friend had experienced long-term infertility, IVF attempts and recurrent miscarriage:

> We'd had our second baby – I hadn't seen [the intended mother] much during this time and found out she was finding it difficult to be round people with young kids or who were pregnant. I … emailed her, asked her if she'd ever considered surrogacy and if it was something we could

> help with. Got email back a bit later in return through tears – from that day we talked a lot more about it.

S25 explained that a long-term family friend had MRKH:[8] 'the couple started surrogacy but it hadn't worked out. I'd just had the second of my children and thought I could help – so I offered'.

Some helped IPs who were initially strangers. S18 applied to SurrogacyUK (SUK) to join as a surrogate, explaining:

> The [support worker] contacted me and the email was so lovely – I felt welcomed into a supportive group. I met [the IPs] at a SUK social. I was the only surrogate there who hadn't done it before. There was just something about the IPs – you connect – they didn't look like the normal couples there, they seemed shy – well, he was shy but chatty, she was strong but shy. I knew from day one it was them.

How the surrogacy journeys began

Many surrogates undertook internet research, often discovering web-based (independent) surrogacy groups or one or more of the UK's non-profit surrogacy organisations.[9] S1, for example, said that she 'joined a few groups to be nosy' and seeing 'lots of sad stories made my desire to help stronger. I did some research on Facebook groups, Google and YouTube, then I discovered the government document – within a week I knew all the laws'. S18 said she had no idea where to find information initially: 'I googled on a night shift and SUK came up – I liked the look of it. Followed my gut'. S3 initially offered to help her sister who struggled with infertility, but she wasn't ready to proceed. She joined Facebook groups to find out more and 'went from there'. While pregnant on her first journey she started talking to the IPs on her latest journey (baby born four weeks pre-interview). S9 separated from her husband and investigated surrogacy: 'I looked in Facebook groups and saw loads of people's stories and decided I could give someone else the gift of that love you get with a baby'. S13 also viewed Facebook groups, explaining she 'lurked in the background for a while, reading lots, building relationships, finding information'.

---

8 Mayer-Rokitansky-Küster-Hauser syndrome, a congenital condition characterised by a shortened vagina, absent cervix and absent or undeveloped uterus.

9 Four are mentioned in the Department of Health and Social Care's guidance on surrogacy: COTS, SurrogacyUK, Brilliant Beginnings and My Surrogacy Journey ('The Surrogacy Pathway: Surrogacy and the Legal Process for Intended Parents and Surrogates in England and Wales' (2018, last updated April 2024), available at www.gov.uk/government/publications/having-a-child-through-surrogacy (last accessed 29 June 2024).

S4 'found out about surrogacy on the internet and lighted on SUK quite quickly' thinking they had a good approach. S10 also contacted SUK as she saw 'they had a big network, were very well known and respected'. S11 also researched and 'ended up at SUK – started going to socials and meeting loads of people' adding 'all have compelling stories, though you bond with some more than others'. S7, who had been a surrogate twice (sibling journeys supported by SUK) reached out to Brilliant Beginnings, as they 'supported the way I wanted to do it this time. Personally, I prefer the "matching" approach. It takes a bit of the decision away, which is a lot on one person's shoulders'. S8's brother and sister-in-law had struggled for years and had joined SUK – S8 surprised them by going to a 'social' and then offered to be their surrogate. S25 and her friend 'joined SUK as a team, went to their annual conference and that was really enlightening – we heard [a surrogate] talk about how to talk to your own children about it'. S19 said that her IPs had attended SUK socials, adding:

> I got info from them and also did my own research – [my sister] really wanted to make sure I was 100% ready to do it. Looked into side effects, possible medical issues etc, especially as I was a bit older [mid 40s] – I wanted my son [17] involved too, made sure he was happy.

S11 asked SUK to set up a call with [the IPs] to establish 'where the lines are. The hardest question was "what if it doesn't work the first time?" I think where I was willing to try the IPs were a bit more nervous about maybe doing it again – maybe because they only had a finite number of embryos'. S13 explained: 'Once I posted, there were lots of responses; I slowly sifted through and came to [the IPs] – conversation with them flowed easily, unlike with some others – it didn't feel forced … They already had one child through surrogacy so maybe their experience helped'. S23 wrote an introductory post, describing this as 'like dating! People commented on it and I just liked [intended mother's] response – she was a single woman and I'm not a feminist but I did think I wanted to help her … I liked the fact [she] was about the same age – we could chat about stuff'. S17's journey was a sibling journey. The IPs' first child was born through traditional surrogacy, and they tried for a sibling the same way for nearly two years with no luck. Instead, they tried IVF surrogacy (using S17's egg in a fresh cycle): 'it was important for [the IPs], they wanted the children to be genetically related to each other but had used different partner's sperm each time – the eggs were a constant'.

Many surrogates described conversations they had with the IPs before entering arrangements, setting parameters and ensuring all parties agreed on specific, often difficult, matters. For example, S3 said she 'spent a lot of time getting to know [the IPs] before making the agreement. We discussed everything – no-one was shy!' S8 had no written agreement – 'I left everything to them'. The IPs had decided they would want to terminate if the baby had Down's and 'I agreed with that, saying "because it's your baby"'. S9 explained that they 'had good chats early on with all the awkward questions – the "what would you do if..." questions. It was their baby and my body so all questions re the baby were down to them and anything about labour/birth etc down to me'. S10 said there were 'lots of things to think about, like "who should be on the birth certificate?" "What if the baby dies?" It makes you have those really serious conversations – it's good, so you know exactly where the others stand, e.g. with questions about termination'. S17 said that 'everything was spoken about before we approached the clinic, worst-case scenarios, how many transfers to try – all the "what ifs" through the pregnancy including when and if termination was appropriate, birth plan, who's there, what happens if anyone dies etc'.

Others discussed similar issues in counselling. In S16's journey, both couples had counselling together, 'delving into things that are really personal'. She added 'my biggest concern was what if I lost the child – how would they react? This was covered, [the IPs] agreed it would be down to nature if it happened'. S21 had clinic-based counselling, together with the IPs and separately: 'it just covers everybody'. Some surrogates questioned the value of counselling. S19 said it felt 'like ticking a box', adding that she could 'see the value if people were strangers maybe, but maybe needs tailoring for family relationships?' S22 said: 'The whole focus ... was on whether I'd be able to give up the baby or not – I found it kind of tick box rather than therapeutic'.

Some had written agreements, often using templates from an organisation. S5 had been a surrogate with COTS (Childlessness Overcome Through Surrogacy), but this journey was without organisation support. She used a template from her previous journeys. S21 also used COTS' template, explaining 'all the difficult questions were covered'. S23 said: '[The intended mother] made the agreement from a template I'd seen on the groups and asked if I was happy with it – I made one change'. S18 used SUK's template: 'it helped us put everything in order and helped me plan – for example to let [the intended mother] be in the room for the birth. It felt like a bunch of friends doing something together'. S20 said: '[The intended mother] had found a template. A lot of it was about wishes about our birth plan and what could/should happen and ... any medical decisions that would have to be made'. Some surrogates' anxieties were allayed by early conversations or agreements. S1 explained she was 'obviously anxious about "what if they didn't want the baby?"'. Likewise, S4 was anxious the IPs would change their mind but said that, once she got to know them, she knew they were 'totally on the same page'.

Others relied on legal advice, whether or not they had a written agreement. S12 and her sister had 'no formal agreement, just a loose discussion really, and ongoing conversations. The clinic insisted [both couples] had legal advice'. S23 said the intended mother obtained legal advice, on the clinic's insistence, perhaps especially apposite because both women were single. S14 explained that she and her brother had no written agreement, though he consulted a solicitor to 'get the lay of the land'. S22 had no written agreement, saying it was 'just done on trust'. However, she 'did get legal advice and was told to keep records of everything. I didn't realise that needed to update wills and life insurance cover – I hadn't really thought about what if I died?'.

Others found legal advice unnecessary, sometimes because they were in sibling/family relationships, or because they had organisational support. For example, S20 said: 'The clinic made us get independent legal advice – they just checked our understanding etc', adding 'it seemed a bit of a waste of time because of our circumstances but can see it might be valuable for others'. S17 explained she 'didn't have legal advice with these IPs as I felt completely supported by SUK – I was pretty confident I had good understanding – I'd been to legal sessions at [SUK] conferences'.

How the journey was experienced

S1 compared being a surrogate to running a charity marathon. Having initially thought she would 'help a mum', she 'happened to meet "the boys" ... the best people I've ever met'. The journey went well: 'The best thing I've ever done. It's massive – trusting a stranger with the biggest thing in your life'. S10 found out about the 'practical side of things from SUK, boards and support worker – "like how does it happen, what do we do? etc"'. She explained she already cared for children (in work), adding: 'I just see it as an extension of that – looking after someone else's baby'.

Some surrogates mentioned reactions of/comments from others. S14 said:

> The reactions of people are the funniest thing – at the time I worked in a shop – all colleagues and regulars knew about it and were supportive, but when other people asked questions I felt I had to explain "it's not my baby" and then they were amazed, like, "I've never met a real surrogate before!" A lot of people asked how it all worked biologically, what with it being my brother's baby.

S18 said:

> Everyone's question to me was 'will you be able to give the baby up?' and I said 'it's not my baby'. I knew that if I used my egg it might be

different – there might be similarities with my own kids. I saw this as looking after a child for its parents.

S24 said: 'Friends questioned why I was doing it. Some thought it was amazing and some said "I can't understand how you can do it". I'm a very headstrong person, and if I say "she isn't mine" then she isn't mine. I love her because she is family'.

One surrogate (S23) described difficult situations with work and family members:

> My boss was very anti – so I felt awful about having to ask for any time off. My wider family weren't very supportive either… First time I told them mum gave me a funny look. Second conversation she just asked me where [the intended mother] lived and whether my kids knew! My sister was pretty supportive though.

Healthcare experiences

Some surrogates commented on the fertility clinic or maternity service settings.[10] Clinical issues sometimes related to privacy. For example, S2 described her experience as 'a bit strange as on embryo transfer day I was there with my brother-in-law as my brother couldn't attend – he had to avert his eyes!' S17 explained that the processes at the fertility clinic were

> very complicated as I was using my own egg – there were no specific forms for doing GS with your own eggs, so I had to complete donor forms so the eggs didn't belong to me – but then I was signing surro [sic] forms for the embryos to be put back in!

S19 said that the clinic's treatment of her 'felt a bit blasé, like they do that all the time – they need to appreciate that for us it was all new and daunting'.

Several surrogates had undertaken their journey during the COVID-19 pandemic, experiencing issues relating to the legal restrictions in place. For example, S23's embryo transfer was towards the end of 2019, 'so everything happened during lockdowns. [The intended mother] wasn't allowed to lots of appointments etc but she had been there for embryo transfer'. She had an elective Caesarean section and explained that 'because of Covid I was in theatre by myself … [The intended mother] waited in the car while I was in [theatre] – she was a blubbering wreck. The doctor was asking what

---

[10] For wider discussion of healthcare experiences of surrogates, see Zaina Mahmoud, Chapter 8, this volume.

I wanted and how I wanted to find out the gender – I said they should be asking [her]'. S25's pregnancy occurred at a similar time: '[The intended parents] came down despite lockdown … they managed to come to the early scan and just got to the 12-week scan. It was a Covid birth – [the intended father] couldn't come in but [the intended mother] could – they were given a separate room after'. Much of S7's pregnancy was also during lockdown: 'We never quite achieved what we wanted to as couldn't see each other so much. [The IPs] still drove to hospitals for appointments to debrief in the car park. It was just what we had to do at that time'. S12 (32 weeks pregnant at time of interview) was worried further restrictions would be put in place. 'I'm planning for my sister to be at the birth. We have a specialist midwife who has dealt with surrogacy before, so depending on Covid restrictions that will happen'. She added: 'I don't want to be in a hospital looking after the baby and not her – that would be detrimental to the baby, my sister, me and everything'.

Some interviewees described their care in hospital. S14 said that 'the hospital was really good – they'd had experience of surrogacy before. There was a separate room for the IPs and the baby and I told the midwives that [the IPs] could make all the decisions for the baby'. S20 who was overdue, faced concern about pre-eclampsia, was hospitalised pre-birth and subsequently induced. She said: 'My husband was straight in with me and [the intended mother] in a private room – she was allowed in for the delivery though – the midwives were brilliant. They said "this doesn't happen every day so we'll do it however you want"'. S11 said:

> Labour was fine – no worse than for [son] – but later there was a massive bleed, needed to go to operating theatre, had a transfusion and later a bad infection – had to stay in to recover for ages. But the hospital put me and my partner in a private room and [the IPs] and baby in another private room – they were really good at facilitating what we needed – me expressing milk etc. On discharge the lady was very respectful of the surrogacy – the hospital didn't have a policy at the time, but they *were* informed and understood the legality.

Other surrogates mentioned lack of knowledge. S6 said the 'hospital hadn't really come across surrogacy before, so we had to write a detailed birth plan, but they were very accommodating. My brother had the first skin-on-skin and the first feed and nappy'. S24 said her IPs were there for the delivery:

> But they wouldn't have been able to take [her] home – the hospital said. So if I'd had to stay in for a couple of days they wouldn't have been able to take her. They tried to do all the tests without [the intended

> parents] – the midwives hadn't really seen surrogacy before. The boys should have been more involved.

S3 said the care she received during birth was good, but the 'rest of the stay in hospital didn't go as planned' because all parties were separated. In addition, 'one midwife said "why are you breastfeeding? It'll confuse the baby!". I couldn't see [the IPs] and share the experience with them. [The hospital] wasn't consistent – one minute it's "because of Covid" and the next it's that "we can't have men wandering around among all the women"'. Others received good medical care, but experienced other issues related to being a surrogate. For example, S2 said: 'Though the birth didn't go as planned, the care was good. I was the first surrogate they'd ever had at the hospital. It was good as they allowed [the IPs] to care for the baby immediately. The only thing was that all the way through I was addressed as "mother"'.[11] S4 explained 'some nurses didn't get it but were OK after the situation was explained. But it drove me mad that they constantly called me "mum"'. At the more extreme end was S18 who explained:

> When I went to hospital for the booking in appointment they called social services! But luckily social services were OK with it when I explained it was surrogacy. The NHS seemed not to know anything about surrogacy at all – but the hospital drew up a policy and asked me and IPs to comment on it. By the end, we had two private rooms – all good BUT they didn't want to let me leave before the baby was discharged – they had to draw up a document and get me to sign it.

Expenses and payments

There was a wide variety in the way expenses were calculated and the sums that were reimbursed. S1 used templates found in surrogacy groups and on YouTube and calculated expenses based on her own most recent pregnancy. She explained: 'I worked out at the beginning it would be about £12,500 – as we went through this varied as some things cost more and others cost less than expected'.[12] S7 was advised by an organisation. She said: 'There was a thorough process and conversation around expenses, it was all broken down – childcare, lost wages etc – it came to £17.5K. I think expenses are individual to everyone's situation'. S9 said she had 'had heard lots of stuff about expenses on group chats – including guidance from organisations on

[11] See Mahmoud, ibid, who details similar comments from surrogates about unwanted terminology used in healthcare settings.

[12] COVID-19 lockdowns were one of the reasons for some of the variations.

what should be included', explaining that she was initially guided by this. She added: 'Obviously the IPs paid for transport to/from London – they just booked it all and sent tickets. For medications I just paid upfront and sent them receipts … I think it came to about £15,000 all told'. S10 explained that expenses were calculated in advance for the entire journey then that sum was 'broken down to 10 payments – the first on positive test result, then monthly. Mine was mainly about travel, which we did on a pre-paid credit card, meds, childcare, time off work to go in'. She added 'SUK said the average is usually about £12–15,000 – we came in under that'.

Those amounts were fairly typical. S21, who was in the early stages of a journey and not yet pregnant, said that she discussed in advance with the IPs what her expenses might be: 'I came up with range £13–15K based on various things that might happen but they said they were happy to go with £15,000 and I accepted'. S23 said: 'I hadn't really thought about it as when you have your own kids you obviously just absorb all those costs', adding: '[The intended mother] proposed a cost and I had roughly calculated mine and it worked out about the same – we covered food, maternity clothes, childcare for appointments, travel, time off work, a cleaner near the end. It was about £13Kish, paid weekly'. S5 had been a surrogate twice before but explained 'on this [journey] I reduced expenses a bit as I didn't need childcare'. Similarly, S17 'took the expenses for my previous journey and amended according to circumstances for this one – actually they had reduced.[13] It was approximately £14K'. S3 also based expenses on a previous journey, explaining it formed part of the initial agreement: 'I said "this is my expenses [sic] and if you can't afford that then we can't go on". But I knew they were bang-on average according to groups and chats'. S13 took advice from people who had been surrogates before. She said:

> Some surrogates say there's an average sum and just to go with that, but I broke it down – it was £21K. I explained to the IPs that it was higher than average – because I was self-employed – and we had a long conversation about it and [the IPs] were totally OK with the breakdown. We did 5% of that per month and the remainder at birth.

Others operated expenses differently. S2 explained that the IPs 'paid all the medical side of things so I never saw how much that all costed'. They also paid for her travel, maternity clothes, medication, healthy snacks: 'I just noted any bits down in a Notes document. The total was under £1,000'. S12 said: 'My sister buys all the bits like hospital stuff and maternity clothes – she

[13] When asked why she explained 'because own oldest child not living at home, I separated from my husband, it was different circumstances'.

just makes sure I'm not out of pocket like taxis to hospital'. S24 explained that the IPs bought maternity clothes, medicines and travel, adding:

> As long as I wasn't out of pocket we were ok. My brother paid for me and [own children] to go to Spain for a week before it all started. And he bought me a Pandora bracelet and I get a charm every year. When we were looking into it we found people who said they 'charged X amount plus expenses'. The way I look at it you're doing this as a gift for someone who can't do it for themselves.

S7 said that the IPs did food shopping for her to save her going to the supermarket during the COVID-19 pandemic: 'Literally every Friday they would rock up with a food shop and have a 10-minute chat on the doorstep'. S8 said she refused to take money but said that the 'IPs put £100pcm in an account to cover my transport to hospital – there was a lot of travel – they believed they *needed* to show that expenses were covered which is why I agreed'. S14 said expenses were first mentioned during counselling, adding: 'After that they just got a credit card in my name and I bought everything pregnancy-related with that so didn't have to go back and forth all the time – maternity bras, vitamins, travel to clinics, stuff like that'.

Some mentioned discomfort around expenses. S11 said: 'I found it awkward – I didn't know expenses were even recoverable until [SUK support worker] said so. I kind of wish it wasn't… It kind of made the relationship not as good as it could have been'. S13 said it was 'difficult' telling the IPs what her expenses would be. S22 described it 'the most awful part – I didn't want to spend their money'. S18 said:

> I felt a bit uncomfortable – we did it as monthly payments but I didn't touch it for months. I was using my own money – struggling to process that I could use the money. Never any bad feeling but felt funny about it and asking for things. I didn't want to use their money but they were like 'it's fine, if you need something because you're pregnant'. It ended up being just under £10,000.

Similarly, S25 said: 'I hate doing it … I find it quite frankly embarrassing – it's always awkward to talk about money. We covered travel, childcare, after school clubs, cleaner, dog walking, some takeaways and convenience foods etc – healthy foods - and a mini-break for the family. It came to just under £9K'.[14] S20 also described some awkwardness, saying that 'it's weird asking your mate for money to buy clothes'. She added '[the IPs] covered anything

14 At time of interview S25 was preparing for a sibling journey where expenses were £9,700.

I needed in that respect – worked out what to give me per month – we never really thought too hard about it'. S16 explained she 'was out of pocket. I had unpaid leave for the two days I had to take off work. I paid for trips to clinic myself – my brother offered and I said "no". So he left a cheque out for me one day and I tore it up'. Explaining why, she said: 'I did it for love – had it been a stranger then I could see why you might claim. If starting as strangers, then maybe the law should step in to protect surrogates being out of pocket'. Only one surrogate believed that surrogates should be able to receive more than expenses. S4 said that she had 'strong views on payments' and that 'surrogates should be reimbursed for all their expenses and receive a modest sum on top'.

Ongoing relationships

Most surrogates maintained ongoing contact with the families they helped to create, though the extent varied.[15] Several commented on the relationship their own children had with the family. S1 explained that there was regular contact between both families – explaining 'my kids were aware of what was happening from the start'. S4 said that her own teenage children have a 'positive relationship' with the surrogacy-born child, adding that they were 'OK with everything' because it was explained to them and 'our normal is their normal'. She gave a recent example of a trip to a park where her eldest pushed the child on a swing. She said: 'They [the surrogacy-born child, then aged four] were quite shy initially but I think things will develop over time as [child] gets more used to us'. S20's children were seven and five years old. She explained:

> They have a really good bond with the baby. We go round and play. They met her at the hospital straight after the birth. My [daughter] says '[baby] is a bit like a cousin, isn't she?' While I was pregnant, we talked to the kids about it – used a story book to introduce the fact I was being a surrogate.

S6 said: 'Since birth we share family albums, WhatsApp groups etc – we're in pretty much daily contact'. S3 detailed a good relationship with the IPs, adding 'they're coming round with the baby for New Year's'. S18 said that when she started the process, she spoke to all her own children (her youngest was six at the time): 'They were OK with it and asked questions whenever

15 Where surrogates had children for family members the contact was generally high and physical visits only limited by geography, as might be expected between aunts/cousins generally.

they wanted. We have ongoing contact – I was expressing to start with. [The IPs] sent a pic of the baby at Christmas which was lovely. They called on [baby's] 1st birthday [during lockdown]'. Many surrogates were extremely positive about the relationships they had built and viewed ongoing contact as important. S9 explained: 'It was always more about our connection than their background and their story – everyone deserves a baby. For me it was about how my kids would get on with them – which turned out to be really well!'[16] S10 was also positive about ongoing relationships:

> When we joined SUK [the IPs] were one of the first to welcome us– we kept coming back to them and their profile and it was like we'd always known them – my husband was the same – he'd talk to them independently of me! We were friends from the offset and still now, four years on – our kids have met their kids – there's no negativity.

S13, who had recently given birth, explained that she:

> Still express[es] milk for the baby and am going to try to keep that up for at least six months, so we have lots of contact – they're only 20–30 minutes away. With our own kids – that was my husband and I's only concern – about how they would handle it, so we were open about it all from the start. They completely got it! They met [the IPs] and we all kept explaining how it all worked. They were really good. I heard one of them explaining to a friend that 'mummy had a baby for someone else'. It helps seeing [the baby] post birth and in her own family unit – the kids can see it's all completely normal.

S17 also had lots of ongoing contact and believed this was important to consider when undertaking surrogacy. She said: 'My children have been raised with complete openness about the surrogacies I have done. The child should have the opportunity to have ongoing contact with the surrogate and her family – especially these days with home DNA kits – everything's out there anyway'. In intra-family relationships there were generally high levels of contact, and ongoing relationships forged through being aunts/ cousins etc, as well as with grandparents. S2 said that 'the twins understand that they grew in [auntie's] tummy', adding 'my son knew all about it at age-appropriate levels. He describes his cousins as "womb mates"'. S14 explained that her niece 'knows she grew in my tummy – it's talked about

[16] This comment relates to S9's first journey with these IPs – at time of interview she was pregnant on a sibling journey for them.

often', adding that 'mum/grandma was day to day support and has been very involved on both sides'.

S8 said: 'My son was a bit disappointed [that she wasn't going to be a sibling for him] when we told him at 13 weeks. He was 12 – but he got his head around it. He has a great relationship with her as a cousin'. S12, who was a surrogate for her sister, said:

> Obviously we'll be in touch all the time as we're sisters and live near each other! The kids know about it all – actually telling them was easier and we got a better reaction than some adults! And we've documented the journey and made a book for the baby, so he'll know all about it when the time comes.

S24 said that 'we see them all about twice a month but that's because we're family – I always did see him [brother] about that often'. She added:

> [The IPs] have spoken to [her] from day one about how she was conceived – no-one's ashamed of it – we're all open about it and all the children in the family know the truth. We all have healthy happy children who were very much wanted and that's all that matters. I wanted my children and planned them – my brother wanted his daughter just as much.

Some surrogates, although in contact, did not want/expect this to occur so frequently. S5 explained that she stays in touch 'to the extent I wanted', adding 'I don't want to go to birthday parties all the time, just a few updates'.

Legal understandings

Most interviewees had some legal understanding, particularly the fact that they would be/had been the child's legal mother at birth. Many commented on this, and/or their husband being the legal father. S1 said that she understands 'why it is as it is' but added that it is 'black and white I am not the baby's mother. I should not be that baby's legal mother and nor should my husband [sic]'. S5 said:

> I kind of see why the surrogate is the legal mother, to protect the kids, but it bothered me more that the IPs had no legal rights. I'd be happy to lose any legal rights the second the baby is born. And it's weird that my husband was the legal father when he had nothing to do with it – he went to one counselling appointment but here he is, the legal father!

S18 said she initially had 'no awareness of the legalities about it', adding: 'I had no idea that if I was married the person I'm married to goes on the birth cert [sic]. The law to me just didn't make sense … Didn't know the surrogacy agreement, all that we agreed, none of it was legally binding'. S17 was undertaking a sibling journey. She thought it 'weird that legal fatherhood rested with my ex-husband unless he said he didn't consent to my treatment. We had an amicable relationship, so he just did that, so the form is being *used* as "do not consent to being legal father" when this isn't its true purpose'. S13 said: 'I had done a fair amount of research … and understood I would be legal mother. I didn't agree with that and [husband] being on the birth certificate. It's not our baby'. S7 thought the law was 'very dated', adding 'I think I should be able to say that I don't want to be on the birth certificate. All start this process knowing who the parents are intended to be'. S8 thought the IPs should be legal parents: 'It would make it easier – it was quite an emotional journey, especially for my sister-in-law – all clinicians had to talk to her about everything. The day after I had the baby the midwife referred to her as "mum" and she sobbed'. Similarly, S12 explained:

> It will be hard for my sister and her partner to know they're not the legal parents, especially when the embryo was from the same batch they used for [their existing child]. It's another kick in the teeth for them – they have the small privilege of being named the legal parent taken away from them – so there's a cloud over it. It makes me really sad.

S22 said that she found it 'insane that those children could have come back to me even though they're not mine', adding 'I'd much rather the IPs were parents at birth'. S19 said:

> When I first looked into it I was a bit concerned [because of sister's health] – I didn't want to be left with a baby … It was none of my doing, it was all theirs and they were just borrowing a bit of my body … I was only on the journey for my sister and her partner; the embryo was made from their sperm and egg and the journey was funded by them. Therefore, I shouldn't be the legal mother.

S15, who intended to be a surrogate for her daughter, said: 'I feel like I'd just be a host, helping by using my womb… The fact the baby would be registered by and to me feels really weird. We looked into whether [my daughter] could be on the birth certificate e.g. as a second parent'.

Two interviewees were solicitors and had good legal understanding. S12 said she found it 'mind-boggling and archaic', adding: 'Times and treatments have changed so much. Law, like in other areas, just doesn't match up with modern society. Maybe if there's a biological connection, I can appreciate you might want a safeguard but in our kind of situation it's no good for anyone'. In S11's case, one IP was also a solicitor. S11 said she was 'not put off knowing I would be the legal mother', but added: 'it is a risk though, isn't it? Your brain takes it into account I guess, you have to work out who you can trust'. S4 understood that she would be the legal mother but did not think she should be, explaining: 'I had absolutely no emotional attachment at all – it wasn't my baby. If [the IPs] had done a runner I still wouldn't have kept the baby'. S5 also mentioned that 'it must be really worrying for the parents that I will run away with their baby'.

For some, the fact they would be the legal mother was less concerning. S3 said: 'I found out I would be the legal mother but it never bothered me – we drew up a big agreement between me and my husband and [the IPs] and sorted wills'. S25 said: 'I knew I would be the legal mother. It doesn't really bother me as knew it wasn't going to be my baby – it was just a bit of paper. I can understand why the IPs would want it though, obviously'.

S20 said that '[the intended mother] started doing all the research once we'd made the offer. I knew that I would be legal mum and [my husband] the legal father. [I] was not worried about being left with the baby (some people did ask!) – we'd been friends for a long time, since college'. Similarly, S10 said:

> SUK made me aware I'd be the legal mother very early on – didn't bother me. I think because we did GS I knew the baby didn't have a biological link to me. It was just a process. More important for the actual parents. I don't know how I would have felt if it had been my own egg.

S14 said she had 'no worries' about being the legal mother but 'thought it was weird as the baby's not mine'. She said she would not have done surrogacy using her own eggs: 'I couldn't anyway as he [one of the IPs] was my brother, but not at all – it would be so different as when you give birth it might look like you a bit or feel a bit like yours'. Others also mentioned they may feel differently about being the legal mother if they were genetically related. S21 said: 'I'm not entirely sure that I agree I should be the legal mother. It might be more appropriate if a surrogate uses her own egg'.

The Law Commissions' proposals

At the time of the interviews, the Law Commissions' consultation containing initial proposals for potential reform of the law on surrogacy had been concluded.[17] The interviews focused on three key areas of the proposals: legal

[17] Law Commissions, n4. The Commissions' full report and recommendations were published later, in March 2023 (n5), alongside a new Surrogacy Bill.

parenthood (specifically the new 'Pathway to Parenthood' for IPs), advertising and expenses/payments.

'Pathway to Parenthood' and related reforms

The proposed new 'Pathway', if followed by IPs undertaking domestic surrogacy, would enable them to acquire legal parenthood at birth. The pathway contains several pre-conception steps (including, inter alia, criminal and medical checks, independent legal advice and counselling for all parties) leading to a 'regulated surrogacy agreement' supported by a 'regulated surrogacy organisation (RSO). Non-profit surrogacy organisations would apply to become RSOs and be regulated by the fertility sector regulator, the Human Fertilisation and Embryology Authority (HFEA). IPs who did not or could not follow the new pathway would still be able to apply for a parental order, with post-birth checks as occur at present.

Most surrogates supported the pathway proposal. S11 said it 'seem[s] to follow what you go in with the intention of anyway', adding that it would 'give clarity and recognise the point of the journey'. S23 said: 'It seems sensible – these are things you should do anyway'. S3 said: 'apart from it being my body, the IPs should be parents from birth and recognised sooner'.[18] S10 said: 'The surrogate should not be the mother. At no time does that surrogate consider the child to be theirs'. S9 said that 'if the law changed and both IPs went on the birth certificate that would be better'. S18 thought the pathway was 'brilliant', adding: 'That was the hardest bit, one of the nurses knocked and said "mum" – I said the mum was next door and the nurse said legally I was – I know I gave birth and everything but I'm not the mother'. S20 agreed with the pathway 'because of the surrogate's freedom and the role of medical decision making', adding: 'If you're left responsible for a child that isn't yours it doesn't make sense. The thing I was looking forward to most was handing her over and her not being my responsibility'. S1 thought the pathway was 'really important', adding: 'people need to feel safe that the surrogate won't take the baby, and the surrogate needs to be protected as well. The baby should be protected as well'. Similarly S25 asked:

> If the IPs are the mum and dad – as they should be, rightly, what about the surrogate? She shouldn't be forgotten about. I don't want to be seen as the mum but there does need to be some protection. It would have been great if [the pathway] had been there for this journey!

18 S3 also thought the surrogate should have PR at birth (jointly with IPs) so that if 'something happened medical [sic] and the IPs can't be there on time the baby would be OK'.

Some surrogates made direct reference to whether the surrogate was genetically related to the baby. S13 said: 'I agree with the pathway – maybe a bit more tricky for me personally if the surrogate used her own eggs. But the law should not treat it differently – it's a matter of personal choice for surrogates'. S17 – the only surrogate in the sample who used her own egg – said: 'I would rather not be the legal mother – I think at birth the IPs should be recognised as the parents as I don't want to be legally or financially responsible. Even though my egg was used I think I should be classed as an egg donor, *and* a surrogate'. S20 said she thought legal parenthood should follow whoever the egg belongs to: 'So if a donor egg it's more like an adoption – donated to the IPs and follow the same pattern'. S22 supported the pathway because 'counselling needs to come much earlier than it does now – i.e. before you even get to the clinic (and especially with your own eggs)'.

S4 described the pathway as 'pretty strict' adding that IPs becoming parents at birth might help 'take away a fear on both sides'. S6 thought 'agreements should be in place from the start. The parties shouldn't be able to change mind once the baby is viable'. S12 said: 'It's ludicrous that the biological parents are not immediately named as legal parents'. S16 also said she thought it was wrong that she would be the legal mother:

> We're enough in the 21st century that this seems odd – you can have surrogacy for gay couples and so this seems outdated. For me, what was being implanted was nothing to do with me – it was 100% their genes. It was theirs, so they should be the parents, legally *or* if I am legal mother then they should be too [sic] and I can 'drop off' after a certain time. The idea of the surrogate being the legal mother messes with my mind – to know you could go through all that and then have to deal with the legal stuff.[19]

Several surrogates were alert to the fact that their own journey would not have met the pathway's requirements. Often this was because of the need to have organisational support (that is, an RSO). S2 said that the proposal did not encompass the surrogacy she undertook for her brother, questioning why her brother should not be able to achieve parenthood at birth, saying: 'I only did it because of my brother so we didn't need an organisation involved'. Likewise, S14 was concerned the pathway would not have applied to her

[19] S16 was the only surrogate who spoke about the proposed new surrogacy register, saying 'I think it's important that children know how they were born – also maybe they need to know for their own medical histories'. For more discussion of the register, see Wade, this volume, Chapter 7.

situation, 'doing it for brother and outside an organisation, even though we had legal advice and counselling'. S15 said: 'It seems weird that we might not fit within their proposals. Inter-family relations are different – they should be somehow included even if there's no surrogacy organisation involved'. S19 liked the pathway proposal but asked: 'Would our agreement have fit? Needs rethinking a bit for family arrangements?'

On RSOs specifically, S1 said that she could see their potential value but that 'it depends how many cases go wrong'. She thought that '"indy" groups should be kept, but they should be smart – and do the DBS checks and medical checks etc'.

Advertising

The question of who should be able to advertise in surrogacy generated less discussion, but the variety of responses is interesting. S10 disagreed with any advertising being allowed. S20 disagreed there should be any advertising 'except maybe IPs advertising they're looking for help'. S12 said she was 'not sure about advertising', adding 'maybe only surrogates'. S4 thought advertising 'should only be for the non-profits'. S17 thought it 'too risky' to allow surrogates or IPs to advertise, adding 'clinics and not-for-profits should probably be able to in line with how it's done for egg donors'.

Expenses/payments

The Law Commissions made no concrete proposals regarding expenses/ payments in the consultation, merely outlining the kinds of costs that could potentially be covered and asking for respondents' thoughts. S7 described this approach as 'too wishy washy', adding that 'people need more direction. The surrogate needs to be protected but IPs need to be protected too – it's about transparency. People's perceptions are influenced by the law and what it says or what they think it says'. S15 said: 'Expenses are difficult and it has to be taken into account that there could be unforeseen costs that could be incurred and hadn't been planned for – but outlining skeleton expenses would be good – can personalise to each surrogacy then'. Similarly, S17 said:

> What's reasonable is different for different people. My head says the Law Commissions should provide guidance on what should be included but my surrogate head says that won't work! Categories like 'essential' don't work. It might be better to say what's not included. I think it's OK to include e.g. recoup holiday because good for physical recouperation and reconnecting with own family. But it should be capped – fits with ethos of what expenses are about and shouldn't be a new thing.

S22 said: 'I don't want to see the whole process being abused … it's good to detach money from parenthood but people could take the mickey and spend IPs' money willy-nilly like if a surrogate "craved" Chinese four times a week'. S5 said the law 'definitely needs to change. It needs to recognise that everyone is a different type of surrogate and every journey is different'.

Linked to some comments about parenthood, some interviewees who were surrogates for family members thought that expenses/payments needed more clarity. S12 said:

> Even for us we didn't know if any money should be changing hands. Then we figured out that as long as no gratuitous payments but just covering what we needed for the pregnancy it would be OK. So it needs to be made clear for everyone what needs to be recorded, so the issue isn't hanging over people, even sisters.

Some mentioned going 'beyond' expenses or allowing 'payments'. S11 thought a modest payment above expenses should be allowed. S15, however, commented that 'even a modest one on top is more difficult – might price some IPs out of the market, especially some who have had long, expensive IVF journeys already'. Most others who commented disagreed with payments beyond expenses, often because the 'wrong people' might become surrogates. S13 thought 'you shouldn't be able to do it "as a job" but also you shouldn't be out of pocket', adding 'ethically I don't think it's OK to be "paid"'. S14 said: 'Payment doesn't feel right especially if you say you can advertise. There shouldn't be a commercial side of this as the wrong people might come forward'. Similarly, S19 said:

> I just feel that if you put payments in there for extra things you might attract the wrong kind of people. Within a family it's a bit different as you're definitely doing it because you care. I don't like the USA where you can do it as a job – fixed pricing doesn't seem right. It would be payment enough to see my sister happy with a family.

S24 said: 'I don't think people should profit from it, but they should never be out of pocket. It might make people do it for the wrong reasons'. S22 agreed: 'If someone goes into it even for a £2,000 flat fee they may be doing it for the wrong reasons'.

Some surrogates, however, thought a 'bonus payment' might be acceptable. S23 acknowledged 'it's already a very expensive process – but if [the intended mother] had said at the end "thank you and here's a bonus", I think that should be OK'. S25 spoke of 'an "inconvenience payment" or modest sum on top of expenses – a "thank you payment on top". Why not? Most surrogates want to thank their own family and do something with/for them – to have that, guilt free, say "go and treat your family" etc would be OK'. But, she thought such a payment should be capped adding 'but don't ask me how much – I guess you could compare it to CICA – I know it's not the same – or PSLA'.[20]

Advice and reflections

Lastly, the interviewees were asked what advice they would give to others or for final reflections they had on their experience. Several said it was important not to rush into decisions and advocated the value of undertaking comprehensive research. S9 said: 'No two journeys are the same – there's a wealth of knowledge on the groups so use it!' S3 said: 'Take your time – if you're in a rush, don't do it', adding: 'Do your research, talk to everyone, take advice seriously and listen'. S23 agreed: 'Do your research beforehand and don't be pushed into anything'. S8 said: 'Don't go into it lightly'. S9 said: 'If anything doesn't sit right, don't ignore it'. S14 said: 'Make sure you have support around you, through all the pregnancy and afterwards, think about the logistics'. S13 advised: 'Do it! But definitely make sure your head's in the right space – you don't know how you're going to deal with this until it happens – don't rush it – so make sure counselling and other things are in place for your own support'. S1 cautioned against rushing, advising that 'even if you don't go with an agency, do what they'd do'. S17 said: 'Take your time. Research. Don't rush into anything. Take 3–6 months to find out. Maybe get counselling before even going near an organisation or clinic. Self-reflection is important. Make sure you have support. Retain your own voice in the agreement and throughout the arrangement'. S23 said potential surrogates should 'be headstrong and know you're going into this yourself. You're giving up nine months and have to take medications etc – you need to be in a mental state to deal with all the hormones while also dealing with your own life'.

Others stressed the value of support from surrogacy organisations. S7 explained: 'You need to be in the right place, ready for the commitment etc. I think it's crucial to have support from organisations, I worry about people who go independent as then they don't have the same support'. S4 said that you should 'go through an agency' explaining that the reason for this was situations she'd 'read about where things have gone wrong tend to be private arrangements – even made via Facebook and people have agreed before they've even met!'. S11 said it was important to 'go into it informed. It is an amazing thing to do but you have to hear different experiences and

[20] CICA = criminal injuries compensation; PSLA = a component of damages payments in tort personal injury claims for 'pain, suffering and lost amenity'.

have the confidence to ask the questions you want. There's plenty of support from SUK (and presumably the other organisations) – that's why networks, groups etc are so good'. S21 also advised 'always do it through an agency – some people offer more to surrogates to do it outside an agency but you shouldn't be swayed, they really look after your own wellbeing – and it can be emotionally difficult'.

Some discussed the importance of trust and good relationships. S10 said that 'everyone comes to it for different reasons, but my advice would be to find someone you can be yourselves with and 100% can be honest with. If you're drawn to it, do it!' S13 said: 'There's a lot of trust in this. It goes both ways, there's a big assumption that the risk is undertaken by the IPs only but e.g. what if the IPs died in a car accident?' S22 said that surrogates 'must have a really strong relationship with the IPs first', adding 'without that there's risk. It's about trust and friendship at the end of the day'. S23 said: 'Make sure you're comfortable with the person/people – you'll spend loads of time with them and talk about all kinds of personal things – and sometimes be half dressed!' S25 said surrogates should 'be sure in your gut that you want to do this before you start. Be clear with your expectations about the birth. Make sure you can be friends – I can't imagine not wanting to hang out with them now'. Others explained their worries about other people's opinions. S6 said: 'No-one ever said anything negative other than a few people questioned beforehand "are you sure?"' S13 said potential surrogates must 'be prepared for difficult conversations – people asked about it when I was showing – they'd say "how will you give your baby away?" and if I said "it's not my baby" people struggled to understand that'. Similarly, S14 said that 'people ask a lot of questions all the time, but it's mostly none of their business – you just have to be polite!' S20 explained she had been 'very scared of coming across "anti" views, but in fact came across a lot of positives [sic]'. She added: 'I was even worried about telling my dad – but in fact it was all OK and he was very supportive and more sad that I'd found it hard to tell him'. S18 said:

> Don't worry about what people's opinions are. I chose it – it's not the fact someone has asked me. I had friends who thought it was wrong – but you've got to be strong. Almost fell out with one friend who said they thought it was dangerous – but when it all went right she changed tune and said I'd done something good … I was scared of my mum's opinion – didn't tell her until I was six months pregnant – but she was really good about it and still asks about the baby! I never thought beyond the IPs but got a card from [the intended father]'s mum and dad saying that I had done something really special by making them grandparents – I'd forgotten the infertility of [the intended mother] would extend further.

As before, some indicated different feelings about traditional and gestational surrogacy. S4, for example, said she would not consider traditional surrogacy because 'then it might have felt like giving my baby away, probably because of my own children and it being a true half sibling'. S5 said: 'I was always very clear that I wouldn't donate eggs or be a traditional surrogate because then it would feel like "my child". I just wanted to donate by growing people's babies. People do different things to help like shave their heads or climb mountains, but that's not me'.

Various interviewees wanted to share positive thoughts about surrogacy. S8 said that 'it was a very rewarding experience – the feeling of helping someone is a good feeling'. S25 said that 'strong surrogates do it for a particular reason', adding: 'Lifting up what surrogates do is what's important'. S24 said: 'I think there's a stigma about it and there shouldn't be. It's different when your own kids go away and you always want them back'. Similarly, S16 observed that 'we should be open about surrogacy a little bit more – like abortion used to be more "taboo", times have changed, and I think surrogacy will gradually get even more acceptable'. S18 said she had 'no regrets', adding that 'it was the best thing I've ever done'. S2 wanted to highlight how her IPs (her brother and his partner) had faced no discrimination where they lived (a London borough) and had made links with several other (gay) families created via surrogacy, adding 'there's a bit of a community'.

Conclusion

Motivations to become a surrogate were often based on empathy and/or altruism. Many surrogates had experienced fertility issues themselves, known someone who had, or had family members/friends who had experienced infertility and/or illness. While eight surrogates had support from a non-profit surrogacy organisation, others had previously had organisational support but were now 'independent'. Some were surrogates for family members (of those, some said this was the only reason they considered it). Whether or not they ended up working with an organisation, many conducted internet research to find out about surrogacy and/or to find template agreements or guidance on expenses.

Surrogates placed different value on counselling and legal advice. Some felt that either or both were unnecessary, sometimes because they had been a surrogate before, or because they felt fully supported by an organisation. These things were particularly questioned when arrangements were between friends or family members. This has potential implications for the Law Commissions' final proposed 'Pathway to Parenthood' under which IPs can achieve legal parenthood at birth, providing they have support from an RSO and take several required steps pre-conception, including the receipt of counselling and independent legal advice for all parties.

Expenses to surrogates varied (the range from those who mentioned a total amount was £1,000–£21,000), though seemed to fall within normal parameters. Several surrogates mentioned that expenses were dependent on individual circumstances and two who had been surrogates before mentioned that their expenses had *decreased* due to changes in their own lives between journeys. When asked about reform to expenses/payments, most favoured retaining an expenses-only approach, though some agreed that a modest gift or recuperative holiday could be allowed. A few expressed support for a small token payment on top of expenses, but those who did thought this should be modest or capped. Concern was expressed by some that going beyond this might make the 'wrong people' become surrogates, or women would do it for the 'wrong reasons'. This is generally reflected in the Law Commissions' final recommendations, where an expenses-based/altruistic approach is recommended. Some surrogates expressed a desire for 'clarity' about what might be 'allowed' in expenses and the Law Commissions have gone some way towards this. However, from the way expenses worked in practice, it may be that the Law Commissions' rigidity about *how and when* expenses are reimbursed needs rethinking.

Most interviewees maintained ongoing contact with the families they helped create, including those who were not surrogates for friends/family members. Though the extent of contact varied, all viewed it as important. Also thought important was openness with surrogates' own children and wider family. Only one surrogate mentioned the proposed surrogacy register (expressing support), but given the feelings about contact and openness it seems that this would be widely supported. Most said they (and their husbands/partners where appropriate) should not be viewed as legal parents of surrogate-born children. Sometimes this was because there was no genetic relationship (so answers may have differed in relation to traditional surrogacy) and sometimes because of a wish to reflect parties' intentions. The one surrogate who used her own egg, however, did not view herself as the mother of the child(ren) she carried for the IPs, seeing herself as both an egg donor *and* a surrogate. Others were ambivalent about legal motherhood (often explained by the relationship of trust they had with IPs), but none said they thought the current position was absolutely correct. When discussing the proposed 'Pathway to Parenthood', there was – understandably – substantial support. Some whose arrangements would not have met the conditions for the new pathway (especially in intra-family arrangements and/or because of the need for RSO support) thought that the parameters should be extended to include them.

It seems, therefore, that much of what is proposed in the Law Commissions' final recommendations and draft Surrogacy Bill would find support among surrogates. However, consideration may need to be given to amendments to incorporate existing good/common practice (such as in relation to how expenses are reimbursed, for example by monthly instalments); or different types of relationship that may not require the level of support and scrutiny required under the proposed new pathway, for example where surrogates and IPs are undertaking sibling journeys, or in intra-family relationships where surrogates would not have undertaken the journey but for their sibling or other relationship. While support from RSOs, counselling and legal advice may still be desirable, it may be that a lighter touch could be possible.

4

Why UK Parents Go Overseas: The Challenges, and What it Means for UK Law Reform

Natalie Gamble

Introduction

I write this chapter as a practising lawyer who works with intended parents (IPs) and manages legal issues associated with UK and international surrogacy on the ground. In 2007 I represented a British couple who had twins through surrogacy in Ukraine following a long history of failed infertility. This became *Re X and Y*,[1] the UK's first reported international surrogacy case, in which the High Court addressed the conflict between children's welfare and public policy, issues that countries around the world still struggle to deal with effectively.

Over the past 15 years international surrogacy has grown, not just for IPs from the UK but from many other countries. In a world in which online information about surrogacy services is readily available and parents can connect on social media to share their experiences, it has become a global phenomenon.[2] The United Nations,[3] the International Social Service (ISS),[4] the Hague Conference on Private International Law (HCCH),[5] and the

---

1 *Re X & Y (Foreign Surrogacy)* [2008] EWHC 3030 (Fam).

2 The Economist Films, 'What's Driving the Baby-Business Boom?' (21 September 2023), available at www.economist.com/films/2023/09/21/whats-driving-the-baby-business-boom (last accessed 2 July 2024).

3 United Nations, 'Surrogacy', available at www.ohchr.org/en/special-procedures/sr-sale-of-children/surrogacy (last accessed 2 July 2024).

4 ISS, 'Surrogacy', available at https://iss-ssi.org/surrogacy/ (last accessed 2 July 2024).

5 HCCH, 'The Parentage/Surrogacy Project', available at www.hcch.net/en/projects/legislative-projects/parentage-surrogacy (last accessed 2 July 2024).

European Court of Human Rights (ECtHR)[6] have all grappled with its consequences. The second International Surrogacy Forum in Copenhagen in June 2023 was attended by hundreds of lawyers, academics and judges from around the world, there to discuss experiences and challenges arising from IPs crossing borders to build families through surrogacy. Such was its success, a third International Surrogacy Forum is taking place in Cape Town in March 2025. International surrogacy is well established and here to stay.

Seventeen years on from *Re X and Y*, international surrogacy for UK parents has grown from being a single case to the point where there are now specialist surrogacy judges in the English High Court making parental orders for approximately 200 families created through international surrogacy each year,[7] and there is even official government guidance for prospective IPs published by the Foreign Commonwealth and Development Office (FCDO).[8]

Why are intended parents engaging in international surrogacy?

Globally, most IPs seeking surrogacy abroad unsurprisingly come from countries (including in Europe, the Middle East, China and Australia) that take a cautious or prohibitive approach to surrogacy domestically. IPs who engage in surrogacy typically have no option to conceive a child other than with the help of a surrogate (whether for medical reasons or due to their relationship status) and, if they cannot access surrogacy at home, they instead seek surrogacy services abroad.

UK IPs do not face the same predicament as parents from other European countries such as France or Germany, where surrogacy is banned and for whom international surrogacy is the only choice. In Italy, surrogacy is not just prohibited domestically, but the current government has recently criminalised those engaging in surrogacy overseas, such is their concern about international surrogacy. By comparison, the domestic policies of the UK fall at the more moderate end of the range of 'exporting' countries, since the UK permits surrogacy (within certain parameters) rather than prohibiting it.

---

6 ECtHR Factsheet, 'Gestational Surrogacy', available at www.echr.coe.int/documents/d/echr/fs_surrogacy_eng (last accessed 2 July 2024).

7 Child and Family Court Advisory and Support Service (CAFCASS) response dated 6 May 2021 to freedom of information request made by Brilliant Beginnings: CAFCASS records show that the numbers of parental order applications made showing the place of birth of the child being other than England and Wales or Scotland was 172 in 2018–2019, 235 in 2019–2020 and 190 in 2020–2021 (average 199 pa).

8 FCDO, 'Surrogacy overseas', available at www.gov.uk/government/publications/surrogacy-overseas/surrogacy-overseas (last accessed 2 July 2024).

However, the limitations of the current UK legal framework are what drive many UK parents to undertake international surrogacy instead of pursuing domestic surrogacy arrangements.[9]

Current UK law has its genesis in the 1980s when surrogacy was in its infancy and the primary policy objective was to discourage it, the authors of the Warnock Report expressing a hope that their recommendations would make surrogacy 'wither on the vine'.[10] The Surrogacy Arrangements Act 1985 and the Human Fertilisation and Embryology Act (originally passed in 1990 and updated in 2008) made UK surrogacy arrangements unenforceable, prohibited professionals from negotiating surrogacy agreements, barred surrogates and IPs from advertising, restricted third party matching services in the UK, sought to limit payments to surrogates and treated the surrogate as the legal mother. Without prohibiting surrogacy, UK law therefore deliberately makes it difficult for IPs and surrogates to connect and denies legal security to those entering surrogacy arrangements. To the extent that there is a legal framework underpinning the practice of surrogacy in the UK, it only regulates what happens after the child is born, providing a judicial mechanism – the parental order – to reassign legal parenthood to IP(s) in retrospect.[11]

Surrogacy has grown in the UK notwithstanding the limitations of the legal framework. We know from statistics collected by CAFCASS, which is involved in every parental order application in England and Wales, that the number of parental order applications made each year has risen steadily, with 67 applications made in 2008 in respect of UK surrogacy cases, rising to at least 259 in 2022–2023.[12] With limited professional services available, parents must find their own surrogate and many find the process of doing so (notwithstanding the existence of supportive non-profit organisations and social media groups) not just lengthy but uncertain, dependent on luck or how well they are able to promote themselves to potential surrogates, of whom there are not enough. Even if IPs are lucky enough to find a surrogate willing to help them, the surrogacy arrangement they enter is based entirely

[9] Vasanti Jadva, Helen Prosser and Natalie Gamble, 'Cross-border and Domestic Surrogacy in the UK Context: an Exploration of Practical and Legal Decision-making' (2018) 24(2) *Human Fertility* 93–104. See also Claire Fenton-Glynn, *International Surrogacy Arrangements: a Survey* (Cambridge Family Law 2022).

[10] Margaret Brazier, Alastair Campbell and Susan Golombok, *Surrogacy: Review for Health Ministers of Current Arrangements for Payments and Regulation - Report of the Review Team* (HMSO 1998) (the 'Brazier Report'), summarising the Warnock Committee's 25 conclusions, para 2.23. The history of the regulation of surrogacy is outlined in Chapter 1 of this volume.

[11] Human Fertilisation and Embryology (HFE) Act 2008, ss54 and 54A.

[12] Freedom of information request, n7.

on trust with no legal certainty. Although IPs understand that disputes over surrogacy arrangements are incredibly rare in practice, I have heard many who choose international surrogacy options say that they are not willing to take even a tiny risk of a surrogate changing her mind when it comes to something as important as the conception and birth of their child.

Research has confirmed our experience on the ground that the main drivers for UK parents seeking surrogacy overseas (and rejecting domestic surrogacy options) are the lack of legal certainty in the UK, and the challenges finding a UK surrogate.[13] That is the context in which more UK parents now conceive through international rather than through domestic surrogacy arrangements each year.[14]

Where are intended parents going for surrogacy?

The US is the main global destination for international surrogacy. From a UK perspective it represents just under half of all parental order applications made following surrogacy births overseas.[15] Surrogacy in the US is socially accepted and legally recognised in many states, with established professional agencies, lawyers and clinicians who work together to match IPs and surrogates (following screening and safeguarding checks), provide high quality fertility treatment and support everyone through the process, with a clear track record of success. The specifics of the legal process vary depending on the state, but typically there is a legal framework that honours the parties' intentions (as reflected in legal agreements and often with judicial oversight during the pregnancy or immediately after the birth) so IPs are recorded on their child's US birth certificate as the legal parents. However, US surrogacy is expensive, now costing upwards of £250,000 per surrogacy journey. While much of that cost reflects professional services that play a valuable safeguarding role (as well as the expenses and compensation paid to surrogates and donors), some relates to the unique context of the US, including the limited access and narrow state-funded healthcare system, resulting in expensive hospital and insurance fees.[16]

---

[13] Jadva et al, n9. See also Fenton-Glynn, n9.

[14] CAFCASS response, n7: CAFCASS records show that, of the total parental orders made by the English Family Court, applications relating to children born in England and Wales or Scotland accounted for 126 out of 298 applications in 2018–2019 (42%), 154 out of 389 applications in 2019–2020 (40%), and 145 out of 335 applications in 2020–2021 (43%).

[15] CAFCASS response, ibid: CAFCASS records show that the number of parental order applications in respect of children born in the US were 83 in 2018–2019, 110 in 2019–2020 and 76 in 2020–2021 (average 90).

[16] In the US it is typical to pay: (1) some identified/quantified out-of-pocket expenses (for example, insurance co-pays, lost wages); (2) some allowances for expenses without being

For many IPs, the US option is out of financial reach. Historically, India was a significant alternative surrogacy destination until changes to Indian immigration rules restricted it, first for single, same-sex and unmarried parents and then, from 2015, for all foreign IPs. More recently, Ukraine has been the second most popular global surrogacy destination for UK parents[17] (albeit only available to different-sex married couples with proven medical need), with a large number of clinics offering both fertility treatment services and surrogacy matching/support at a fraction of the cost of the US. The Ukraine Civil Code explicitly provides that different-sex married parents are the legal parents of a child born through surrogacy.[18] This means that IPs have legal certainty and are recorded on their child's (Ukrainian) birth certificate, albeit that (as was the case in *Re X and Y*) that position will not be recognised in the UK. However, the surrogacy process works differently from surrogacy in the US in practice, typically managed by a single clinical organisation rather than a collaborating group of independent professionals, and with usually (although not always) a more limited direct relationship between the IPs and the surrogate.

International travel restrictions introduced during the COVID-19 pandemic in early 2020 disrupted cross-border surrogacy services. The biggest challenge of the early pandemic was managing the births of children born abroad whose parents were unable to reach them.[19] The UK and many other governments instituted travel exemptions for parents and expedited issue of travel documents for babies to ensure that parents could bring their babies home swiftly. Those seeking to engage in international surrogacy were for a period of time unable to travel overseas to engage in the necessary fertility treatment processes, although export of gametes and embryos became more common, leading to a change in HFEA (Human Fertilisation and Embryology Authority) guidance.[20] Some parents were

quantified, for example, a maternity clothing allowance, a monthly 'expenses' fee of around $200; (3) various compensation amounts that are not really referable to expenses, and are given varying terminology (base compensation, pregnancy reimbursement, expenses for inconvenience, pain and suffering and so on). There is typically a base amount, but also other compensatory figures may be included, such as payments made for embryo transfer, additional amounts for multiple pregnancies and so on. See also Mahmoud, Chapter 8, this volume.

17 CAFCASS response, n7: CAFCASS records show that the number of parental order applications in respect of children born in Ukraine were 31 in 2018–2019, 44 in 2019–2020 and 44 in 2020–2021 (average 40), second only to the US (average 90).

18 *Re X & Y (Foreign Surrogacy)* [2008] EWHC 3030 (Fam) at [8].

19 Daniela Prugger and Oksana Parafeniuk, 'Surrogacy is Complicated – Then Add a Global Pandemic' *Marie Claire* 17 May 2020.

20 Human Fertilisation and Embryology Authority, 'Exporting Gametes or Embryos for Patients Seeking Surrogacy Abroad', available at https://portal.hfea.gov.uk/knowledge-base/news-for-clinics/2020-clinic-news/exporting-gametes-or-embryos-for-patients-seeking-surrogacy-abroad/ (last accessed 2 July 2024).

also able to conceive using embryos that had been stored overseas prior to the pandemic (including parents conceiving second or subsequent children following prior international surrogacy journeys).

Since 2022 the war in Ukraine has caused more significant disruption, effectively removing Ukraine surrogacy as an option for all but the most risk-hardened IPs (surrogacy agencies are still offering services there).[21] A resulting influx of IPs seeking surrogacy services in neighbouring Georgia (which has a similar framework to Ukraine but with only a handful of operating clinics) prompted the Georgian prime minister to announce in July 2023 that surrogacy would be prohibited for foreign IPs in Georgia. He cited concern that too many foreign IPs were 'turning it into a business' and said it was 'disturbing to leave this issue unregulated'.[22] Implementation of the proposed ban would leave various Canadian provinces and Greece as the only significant remaining jurisdictions that offer legally recognised surrogacy to foreign IPs outside the US. Both countries permit surrogacy but with limitations on the amounts that can be paid to surrogates (seeking to limit this to expenses). My experience is that these are not common surrogacy destination choices for UK IPs given the long and uncertain timeframes for being matched with a suitable surrogate and the poor quality of surrogate screening. This is reflected in the relatively low numbers of parental order applications that have been made in respect of children born in Greece (11 since 2014) and Canada (87 since 2014).[23]

Surrogacy practice has also emerged in a broad range of other countries where there is no legal framework. Those in which surrogacy is currently being offered to international IPs include Cyprus, Mexico, Colombia and newly emerging options in Africa, South America and Central Asia. The absence of law and regulation that enables such services to develop means that there is little structure to ensure the quality, ethics and safety of services being provided. There has also been a historic pattern in unregulated destinations that surrogacy services emerge before the practice is (often abruptly) shut down by governments that do not support it or are concerned about a significant influx of demand. India and Thailand, for example, were both popular unregulated international destinations for surrogacy until the practice

[21] Anika König, 'Reproductive Entanglements in Times of War: Transnational Gestational Surrogacy in Ukraine and Beyond' (2023) 42(5) *Medical Anthropology* 479; Alison Motluk, 'Ukraine's Surrogacy Industry Has Put Women in Impossible Positions' *The Atlantic* 1 March 2022.

[22] Anon., 'Surrogacy in Georgia to be Allowed Only for Citizens, Says PM' (agenda.GE 12 June 2023).

[23] CAFCASS response, n7.

was outlawed (very suddenly) for foreign IPs in 2015.[24] There is obvious risk for those in the midst of a surrogacy arrangement of experiencing a change to the law mid-process, which includes surrogates and IPs suddenly not knowing whether they will be liable to criminal prosecution, children's identity and parentage being jeopardised and, if intermediaries are closed without warning, withdrawal of professional support leading to loss of identity information for the child and even loss of contact between IPs and surrogates.

Legal parentage of children born through surrogacy

Prime destination countries for IPs are typically ones in which they will be recorded on their child's birth certificate as the parents. However, difficulties associated with recognition of parentage at home are common: when parents travel from countries that do not recognise surrogacy to countries that do, a conflict of law almost always arises in which one or both parents are not recognised as their child's legal parent in the country in which they live.

Under UK law, for example, the surrogate and her spouse, if she has one, are the legal parents of any child born through surrogacy irrespective of what the overseas birth certificate records, by virtue of the HFE Act 2008.[25] In such cases neither IP is recognised as a legal parent for any purpose in the UK and cannot pass on their British nationality. If the surrogate is not married, the intended father will (if he is the child's biological father) be recognised as a legal parent in the UK for some purposes, including British nationality. However, the other IP will not be recognised as a legal parent, and will not be able to pass on their British nationality when their child is born. Even where the biological father is the legal father, the surrogate will remain the legal mother and the only person who, for the purposes of UK law, can exercise parental responsibility for the child.

From the child's perspective this conflict of law means that some children are effectively born in a legal black hole in which neither the country of their birth nor the country of their parents recognises the adults within its own jurisdiction as their parents. Hedley J famously described the twins born to UK parents in Ukraine in *Re X and Y* as having been 'marooned stateless and parentless'[26] because they had no nationality and no adults

[24] Anon., 'India Bans Foreigners from Hiring Surrogate Mothers' *The Guardian* 28 October 2015; Anon., 'Thailand Bans Commercial Surrogacy for Foreigners' *BBC News* 20 February 2015.

[25] ss33, 35 and 42

[26] *Re X & Y (Foreign Surrogacy)* [2008] EWHC 3030 (Fam) at [10].

who were legally responsible for them in the country where those adults lived. In other cases, the consequences are less stark but no less significant. Children born in the US and Canada, for example, obtain citizenship in their country of birth so are not born stateless. However, if the surrogate is married, they are still born without a legal connection with either of their IPs or a right to live permanently in the UK with them. In international surrogacy cases where the surrogate is not married, children may be born British via their biological father, but will have no legal connection with their other IP, and neither of their UK parents will automatically have parental responsibility for them to make important decisions to safeguard their welfare.

For UK parents, the legal difficulties children face are usually temporary since most parents can apply to the Family Court for a parental order that, when granted, makes them their child's parents for all legal purposes and confers British nationality on the child if either parent is British. However, some parents are excluded from this option – for example, those conceiving with donated eggs and sperm and those who are not domiciled in the UK. Single parents were also excluded until 2019.[27] Even for those who are eligible, the parental order process takes 5–12 months and requires the family's presence in the UK, which means that parents must first grapple with complex immigration issues to bring home children who are not yet legally theirs. Parents travelling home with newborn children from the US or Canada can in the short term use their child's US/Canadian passport, but parents and their newborns travelling from most other jurisdictions face a long and stressful wait for UK travel documents, which can take many months, even if the children are born British. Special processes were established during COVID-19 and in response to the outbreak of the Ukraine war to speed up access to safe passage home, but these emergency measures are not routinely available and in my extensive professional experience it is routine for surrogate-born children and their British parents to be stranded in the country of birth for 4–6 months or more, separated from wider family support and any NHS medical care they need.[28]

Conflicts of law in respect of parentage recognition mean that children born through surrogacy lack the basic right to a secure legal identity that almost all other children enjoy without question. Whatever the wider concerns about surrogacy, this is a children's rights issue.

---

27 Human Fertilisation and Embryology Act 2008 (Remedial) Order 2018.

28 See, for example, *Re Z (Foreign Surrogacy: Allocation of Work: Guidance on Parental Order Reports)* [2015] EWFC 90

Can this be resolved at an international level?

The consequences of international surrogacy for children's rights is not just a UK problem. Marianna Iliadou has written in this book about the approach of the ECtHR, which has grappled with the need to safeguard children's parentage and nationality within Europe.[29] The HCCH has also, since 2010, been considering whether a private law instrument – a voluntary treaty entered into between nations similar to the ones regulating child abduction and inter-country adoption – could help resolve cases of what it calls 'limping legal parentage'. The appointed Experts' Group on Parentage and International Surrogacy Arrangements recently produced its final report, concluding that an international treaty may be feasible and describing its aim as being to create 'greater predictability, certainty and continuity of legal parentage in international situations, with the child's best interests the primary consideration'.[30] However, the report acknowledges the challenges of designing a treaty that will attract as signatories both those countries that support legally enforceable compensated surrogacy arranged commercially (permissive countries in which children are being born through surrogacy), and those countries in which surrogacy and the creation of non-traditional families are regarded as morally or ethically unacceptable (conservative countries from which IPs mainly travel).

The Experts' Group proposes several possible solutions. One is that international surrogacy arrangements could be dealt with in a separate 'optional protocol' to a main treaty on cross-border recognition of parentage, so that those countries that fundamentally oppose surrogacy could opt out.[31] Such an approach seems unlikely to protect children adequately, given that the countries that do not want to recognise parentage in surrogacy cases will simply choose not to do so and we will be no further forward than we are now.

Another suggestion is to set internationally agreed minimum standards for surrogacy on which recognition of parentage could be contingent.[32] That sounds sensible – in exchange for agreeing to recognise the parentage of children born in permissive countries, conservative countries would get some assurances that the surrogacy has been conducted responsibly. However, there is enormous difficulty lurking beneath this benign-sounding proposal. What safeguards should look like is not just detail to be worked

29 Chapter 9.

30 HCCH Parentage/Surrogacy Experts' Group: Final Report, 'The Feasibility of One or More Private International Law Instruments on Legal Parentage' (November 2022), introduction, para 5.

31 ibid, chapter 4.

32 ibid, chapter 4.3.4

out, but something that goes to the very heart of whether surrogacy is considered acceptable as a concept. For example, the Experts' Group says that 'financial considerations' are one area in which safeguards could be agreed, something that puts a gloss of ease on the chasm between the views of permissive and conservative countries over the acceptability of commercial surrogacy (including surrogate compensation, arrangement by profit-making intermediaries and legally recognised surrogacy agreements). Another example is 'requiring the consent of the surrogate'. Whether this should mean that women acting as surrogates must give informed consent before they enter a binding surrogacy arrangement or must consent to the transfer of parentage after the birth with a right to change their minds goes to the essential validity of surrogacy itself. With such different perspectives on basic issues, it seems unlikely that it will be possible to find common ground on agreed safeguards any time soon. A private law international treaty dealing with parentage recognition should therefore remain a global aspiration, but it seems unlikely that it will offer a practical solution for resolving parentage issues in international surrogacy cases in the foreseeable future.

The Law Commissions' approach to parentage following international surrogacy

For UK parents, that leaves issues of parentage recognition to be resolved via domestic legislation, making the Law Commissions' recommendations of key significance. The Law Commissions' final report accepts that, in principle, children born through surrogacy can and should be recognised as the legal children of their parents. Within its proposed new regulated framework for UK surrogacy, IPs would – for the first time in UK law – be recognised as their child's legal parents from birth without the need for a post-birth court process and the period of legal limbo it creates.[33] Fundamentally, this recognises the validity of the shared intention at the heart of any surrogacy arrangement. However, it is only proposed that children born through UK surrogacy whose parents have followed the requirements of the proposed new 'pathway' should have at-birth legal parentage; it is not proposed that children born through international surrogacy should be afforded the same protection.

In their provisional proposals published in 2019, the Law Commissions suggested that the UK government should have the power to create a designated list of countries from which overseas court orders or birth

[33] Law Commission and Scottish Law Commission, *Building Families Through Surrogacy: a New Law: Volume II: Full Report* (Law Com No 411, Scot Law Com No 262, 29 March 2023), chapter 2.

certificates conferring parentage in international surrogacy cases would be automatically recognised in the UK (similar to law that applies to overseas adoptions).[34] That would have meant that some children born through international surrogacy – although not all – would have been automatically recognised as the children of their UK parents from birth. This proposal needed further consideration, including deciding who would decide which countries would be approved and which would not (and on what basis), how the list would be maintained to respond to an international surrogacy landscape that is constantly changing, and whether children would have automatic British nationality (which children subject to recognised overseas adoptions do not). However, in their final proposals the Law Commissions stepped away from this recommendation altogether. The report states:

> We have also decided not to recommend that it be possible for legal parenthood obtained in a foreign jurisdiction following a surrogacy arrangement there to be automatically recognised in the UK, without it being necessary for the intended parents to apply for a parental order. Having considered the consultee responses, we retain concerns about the risks of exploitation and do not consider that the proposed reform is compatible with the rest of our recommendations.[35]

The Law Commissions' final recommendation is therefore that the existing parental order system should be retained for families created through international surrogacy, with no significant changes to the current court process or criteria, and with 'clearer guidance' only on existing immigration rules.[36] This is a missed opportunity to help safeguard the welfare of children born through international surrogacy and avoid them being born into a legal vacuum. The Law Commissions could, for example, have recommended that the parental order process could be started before the child is born. Doing so would have reduced (or, if pre-birth orders were permitted, eliminated entirely) the period of legal limbo currently experienced by children born through surrogacy.

The Law Commissions could also have reviewed the criteria the court must consider when a parental order application is made and rationalised them to reflect changes already made through case law. The criteria in s54

[34] Law Commission and Scottish Law Commission: Joint Consultation Paper, *Building Families Through Surrogacy: a New Law* (Law Com Consultation Paper No 244, Scot Law Com Discussion Paper No 167, 6 June 2019), p391, consultation question 99. The recommendation for a designated list mirrors the designated list for overseas adoptions in the Adoption (Recognition of Overseas Adoptions) Order 2013.

[35] Law Commissions, n33, para 16.33.

[36] ibid, para 16.211 (recommendation 83).

HFE Act 2008, written as a last-minute amendment to the law in 1990 and without a proper policy review, comprise a long list of requirements that the court must consider in every parental order application, something that contributes to how long and complex these court applications can be. However, in reality, the court's commitment to safeguarding the welfare of children has led to the dilution of the statutory criteria, leaving a significant mismatch between what s54 appears to require and how it is applied in practice.

The starkest example is s54(3), which states that parents 'must apply for the order during the period of six months beginning with the day on which the child is born'. In fact, there is no longer any time limit for making a parental order application. In *Re X*, former President of the Family Division Sir James Munby was faced with an out-of-time application and a child born through surrogacy in India who needed legal security. He ruled that Parliament could not actually have intended to create an inflexible deadline and that enforcing the six-month statutory deadline would be 'nonsensical'.[37] His decision has been followed in many subsequent cases. In one recent case the court made a parental order in respect of an adult, 22 years after their birth.[38]

Similarly, the requirement for joint applicants to be married, civil partners or 'living as partners in an enduring family relationship',[39] and for the child to have their home 'with' the IPs,[40] have both been interpreted broadly, enabling parental orders to be made in favour of parents who have separated, died or never been in a relationship with each other at all.[41] Relationship status is no longer a meaningful criteria and yet it must be addressed in every application. In addition, the retrospective authorisation of payments of more than reasonable expenses in s54(8) is now routine in parental order applications, particularly those involving international surrogacy arrangements. Authorisation of substantial compensation payments to surrogates over and above their expenses was described by a High Court judge as a 'non-controversial matter'.[42]

On the ground, the only three criteria that really remain significant are the parents' domicile, the need for at least one IP to have a genetic connection to the child and a rigorous requirement for the surrogate's consent, yet parents have to provide detailed evidence addressing each of the remaining criteria

---

37 *Re X (A Child) (Surrogacy: Time Limit)* [2014] EWHC 3135 (Fam).

38 *X v Z (Parental Order: Adult)* [2022] EWFC 26.

39 HFE Act 2008, s54(2).

40 ibid, s54(4).

41 See for example *Re N (Surrogacy: Enduring Family Relationship; Child's Home)* [2019] EWFC 21, *Re DM and LK* [2016] EWHC 270 (Fam) and *Re X* [2020] EWFC 39.

42 *Re AB (Surrogacy; Domicile)* [2016] EWFC 63, at [11].

to show how either they meet them or, if they do not, where the case law varies the prima facie statutory rules to accommodate their application. To be modern and effective, any new law should reflect how it actually works in practice.

There was also the opportunity to do more to address the concerns the Law Commissions expressed about the risk of exploitation in international surrogacy. Parental orders (or indeed any UK law) cannot, of course, directly regulate what happens overseas, but that does not mean that UK law does not influence how things work. If demands are placed on IPs by the family court to produce evidence that a surrogacy arrangement overseas has been entered into ethically and without exploitation, IPs will be incentivised to choose service providers overseas that can demonstrate they can meet those requirements. Such a requirement could have helped shape overseas practice positively, as service providers seek to meet the needs of IPs from the UK.

To give an example of how this works on the ground, current UK law incentivises parents to choose foreign surrogates who are not married (because British nationality law then enables a British father to be recognised as the legal father and for the child to be born British, which allows the child to be issued with a UK passport or emergency travel document enabling them to travel to the UK). A requirement for surrogates to be unmarried was not a deliberate policy decision and it does little to safeguard surrogates' welfare. But as a direct result of the demands of the UK legal system, agencies in places like Ukraine and Georgia have learned that UK parents would like them to find an unmarried surrogate, and their surrogate recruitment policies have adapted to provide that.

Just imagine, therefore, that the parental order criteria, instead of incentivising a choice of unmarried surrogates, actively sought to incentivise ethical surrogacy practice. IPs could be explicitly asked to demonstrate to the court that they have complied with legal requirements in the country of birth, or that their surrogate has had independent legal advice, or that safeguarding checks were done to ensure that their surrogate was not being exploited, or that information about their children's genetic heritage was available for them to share with them, for example. Such requirements would be relatively easy to satisfy for surrogacy arrangements in jurisdictions that already have such safeguards, such as the US, incentivising parents to choose such jurisdictions. However, they would also drive IPs engaging in surrogacy in other countries (particularly countries in which surrogacy is entirely unregulated) to ask agencies to apply such safeguards to ease the parents' court application, thereby creating a demand for more ethical surrogacy practice. Ultimately, the welfare of the child must be the court's paramount consideration, and this means that these criteria would have to be flexible to some degree, as the existing criteria are. However, focusing explicitly on issues that affect the ethics of the surrogacy arrangement would be far more meaningful than the existing criteria, and anticipating that the court will demand evidence of good practice could help steer IPs toward providers and destinations which can offer it.

Why did the Law Commissions step away from reform for international surrogacy?

The Law Commissions' final report expresses concern about the great risk of exploitation in international surrogacy, while acknowledging that the landscape is complex.[43] Concern about the risk of exploitation seems to be the basis for the Law Commissions' recommendation not to reform the law in relation to international surrogacy. The report states:

> We acknowledged in the Consultation Paper that the extent to which international surrogacy arrangements give rise to cause for concern is dependent, to an extent, on the level of regulation provided in each country, as well as the general legal and socioeconomic context. The risks of exploitation will depend, for example, on the effectiveness of regulation provided by national laws in different countries, and the impact that the payment available to women to be a surrogate can have on the lives of the surrogate and her family. Concerns may be greatest where regulation is inadequate, the sums of money payable to women who act as surrogates are lifechanging, and where women do not have equal access to employment, education or other opportunities. While we do not consider that all international arrangements will necessarily be exploitative, we consider that the risk of exploitation is considerably higher than in domestic agreements and that those risks cannot be controlled by the domestic laws of England and Wales, or Scotland.[44]

It is absolutely right that the Law Commissions should highlight concerning practice overseas, particularly in unregulated surrogacy destinations with few controls. The risk of exploitation is, in my experience, greatest where there is an imbalance of wealth and power between the surrogate and IPs that is not carefully managed, and/or where an intermediary controls the surrogacy process without the checks and balances of a collaborative professional approach or judicial/regulatory oversight. Having said that, care should be taken not to presume that women living anywhere other than the UK and

43 Law Commissions, n33, paras 16.9–16.21.

44 ibid, para 16.10.

the US are incapable of giving informed consent to acting as a surrogate. Furthermore, the UK can learn some valuable practices from some surrogacy destinations, particularly in relation to compensated surrogacy in the US. A professionally-supported surrogacy arrangement in which a surrogate has been through a screening process (including financial, medical, social and psychological screening), is represented by her own independent attorney, has excellent practical, medical and mental health support, is being fairly compensated (if she wishes) for her risk and inconvenience as well as being reimbursed for her out-of-pocket expenses, and benefits from a legally recognised arrangement that is scrutinised and endorsed by the court contains far more safeguards than current UK surrogacy practice. Such arrangements in my experience reflect a strong, balanced and enduring relationship between all those involved.

What makes surrogacy ethical or unethical is, therefore, about how, and not just where, it takes place.[45] As with surrogacy in the UK, the important questions are:

- Have all those involved given informed consent? What safeguards are in place to ensure that?
- What is the nature of the relationship between the IPs and the surrogate? Is there direct contact between them, and are they able to develop a personal relationship? Is there a fair balance of power between them? What safeguards are in place to ensure that?
- What is the role of any third-party intermediaries? Are they controlling the process in a problematic way or providing support and safeguards to protect all involved? Are they regulated, subject to judicial oversight or required to comply with a legal process?
- Is there a clear legal framework? Is it being followed?
- Is there a culture of support for surrogates, IPs and those surrounding them to ensure that everyone's medical and mental welfare is considered?
- How is the welfare of the child being planned for, including in relation to retention and disclosure of information about their genetic and gestational origins and birth story?

We need to understand the answers to these questions to assess the risk of exploitation (and ideally to minimise it).

[45] Lavanya Fischer, Natalie Gamble, Kirsty Horsey, Emily Jackson, Denise Seidelman and Richard Vaughn, 'Surrogacy Needs to be Regulated, not Prohibited' (2024) *British Medical Journal* 386:e079542.

So, what should we do? How should law reform approach international surrogacy?

UK law reform needs to be pragmatic and to accept that the ethical and welfare implications of international surrogacy should be managed rather than ignored. The law for UK surrogacy appears (quite rightly) to be moving away from restriction toward regulation, reflecting the previous government's now longstanding policy to 'support surrogacy as part of the range of assisted conception options'.[46] Hopefully, the current government maintains this policy and drives forward much-needed changes to existing law. Regulating surrogacy arrangements is very clearly the best way to safeguard all involved and protect the welfare of children. The same approach needs to be taken with international surrogacy as with domestic arrangements.

UK law reform could therefore comprise three separate policy strands in relation to international surrogacy:

Recognising parentage from birth for all children born through surrogacy

The Law Commissions' proposals for parentage from birth for some children born through UK surrogacy are positive, and equivalent at-birth status needs to be given to all children born through surrogacy, including those born overseas. While it may be justifiable to retain judicial oversight in respect of international surrogacy arrangements, the current parental order process (which only starts after the birth) is outdated and complex, and leaves children unnecessarily vulnerable for too long. The current s54 criteria should be reviewed to remove obviously redundant hurdles (such as the six-month deadline and the stipulations as to relationship status that have effectively already been removed through case law) as well as the criteria that deny certain categories of children born through surrogacy resolved parentage (including children conceived with both donated eggs and sperm, and children born to UK resident or British parents who cannot satisfy the domicile requirement). The child's welfare and the free consent of the surrogate are the core issues the court should focus on, together with whatever other considerations would help encourage parents to choose the most ethical surrogacy practice overseas. In addition, the whole process should be shifted forward so that orders can be made pre-birth.

---

[46] Department of Health and Social Care, *The Surrogacy Pathway: Surrogacy and the Legal Process for Intended Parents and Surrogates in England and Wales* (first published 2018), available at www.gov.uk/government/publications/having-a-child-through-surrogacy/the-surrogacy-pathway-surrogacy-and-the-legal-process-for-intended-parents-and-surrogates-in-england-and-wales. Restated in the introduction to the Law Commissions' final report, March 2023.

Making regulated UK surrogacy as accessible as possible

The Law Commissions' recommendations seek to create an assured standard for ethical surrogacy practice in the UK, with HFEA-regulated agencies, a requirement for legal advice and counselling, written agreements and other safeguards applied before conception. This is all sensible, but it is critical to ensure that this new form of UK surrogacy thrives if, as the Law Commissions wish, domestic surrogacy is to be encouraged over international surrogacy.[47]

First, surrogacy in the UK needs to attract women who can and wish to act as surrogates safely, to address the current shortage of UK surrogates. The Law Commissions' proposal to tighten up the rules on payments to UK surrogates so they receive no financial benefit is counterproductive in this regard. The current rules on expenses, despite popular misconception, are flexible enough to enable UK surrogates to receive some financial acknowledgment beyond their out-of-pocket expenses, and it is not (and never has been) illegal to pay or receive a compensatory amount. In practice most UK surrogacy teams currently agree an upfront figure that is then paid over the course of the pregnancy. Some surrogacy teams do try to cost this against anticipated expenses, but many take a much looser approach to agreeing what they feel is fair or reasonable (or simply pay what they can afford). Costed expenses also commonly include items like family holidays (which might be considered a 'nice to have' or a 'thank you' rather than an out-of-pocket expense), and fixed amounts for embryo transfers, multiple pregnancies and caesarean births (which reflect compensation rather than reimbursement).[48]

While the system is not as open or transparent as it could be, many UK surrogates do receive some financial benefit as compensation beyond out-of-pocket expenses, and yet there has never been a case in which the court has refused a parental order due to the level of payments made. However, the Law Commissions have recommended the law is tightened up to ensure that UK surrogates are paid no more than their actual expenses, with narrower categorisation of permitted payments and a new requirement for surrogates to account for their costs as they go along.[49] This is a step backwards, which risks being both impractical and demeaning if surrogates, rather than being trusted and respected, are expected to justify everything they spend and produce receipts for even such items as vitamins and sanitary towels. It also buys into the false narrative that surrogates are either motivated by altruism *or* money, when in reality the fact that a surrogate and her family can receive some financial acknowledgement does not detract from their motivation to

[47] Law Commissions, n33, para 16.9.

[48] ibid, paras 12.96–12.102.

[49] ibid, para 12.119.

help someone else have a family. Within a regulated framework in which safeguards ensure that women are not being exploited, the law should permit those surrogates who want to be compensated through a financial acknowledgement that goes beyond a reimbursement of her out-of-pocket expenses to receive a sensible level of compensation for the enormous effort and commitment surrogacy entails for them and their families.

Secondly, more needs to be done to resolve the perception of UK surrogacy as risky. While disputes are rare in practice, it is the perception of legal insecurity that drives so many IPs overseas.[50] The law should seek to ensure that surrogates give informed consent at the outset and maintain bodily autonomy throughout the surrogacy process, but they should not (as the Law Commissions propose) retain the right to change their minds and become the legal parent up to six weeks after the birth.[51] If UK law reform does not change the current dynamic in which there are too few UK surrogates and IPs perceive UK surrogacy as risky and uncertain, the new safe regulated form of UK surrogacy will be accessed only by a tiny handful of people. Law reform in its current guise will then achieve very little in practice, and the UK will continue to export rather than resolve the risk of exploitation.[52]

Doing everything we can to encourage ethical practice abroad

While UK law cannot directly regulate surrogacy practice overseas, that does not mean that it cannot have any impact on how surrogacy is practised abroad. The parental order criteria could be reformed in such a way that they incentivise UK parents to demand ethical surrogacy practice overseas, and thereby help shape surrogacy outside our borders.

The UK should also continue to encourage international efforts to achieve cross-border consensus on parentage and ethical global standards. As already highlighted, the HCCH is exploring the creation of a treaty on cross-border recognition of parentage. Other bodies have begun to consider proposed international standards for surrogacy (including the Verona Principles published by the ISS (the International Social Service) in 2021).[53] There remains very little global consensus about even the basic question of whether surrogacy as a concept is acceptable, but the UK has been on a journey in

50 Jadva et al, n9.

51 Law Commissions, n33, paras 4.124–4.127 (recommendation 3).

52 Claire Fenton-Glynn, 'Outsourcing Ethical Dilemmas: Regulating International Surrogacy Arrangements' (2016) 24 *Medical Law Review* 59.

53 ISS, 'Principles for the Protection of the Rights of the Child Born Through Surrogacy', available at https://bettercarenetwork.org/sites/default/files/2021-03/VeronaPrinciples_25February2021.pdf (last accessed 2 July 2024).

which policy has shifted from discouragement of surrogacy to acceptance and regulation,[54] and we should share our experience and understanding as part of such global discussions. International bodies need to understand the positives of surrogacy as well as the concerns, and the world needs to work together to achieve a pragmatic approach that will be far more effective in safeguarding vulnerable parties overall than a prohibitive one. This is a very long-term project.

Conclusion

Surrogacy is a family-building practice that is here to stay. With international efforts to regulate it stalled by the disparity of views around the world, the UK has a domestic responsibility to grapple with international surrogacy properly, as well as surrogacy that takes place at home. Current efforts towards law reform must not become another missed opportunity. The most important priority must be to safeguard the welfare of children born through surrogacy, who are often currently left vulnerable and exposed. Children born overseas are no less deserving of protection than children born through UK surrogacy, and urgent reform is needed to ensure they are no longer born in a legal black hole.

We must also do everything possible to promote ethical surrogacy practice, wherever surrogacy takes place. Proper regulation in the UK is a positive step, but we need to make safe regulated UK surrogacy available and attractive to as many families as possible, so that fewer are driven to pursue surrogacy outside those safeguards. We also need to do what we can to manage the ethics of international surrogacy. International surrogacy is not inherently exploitative[55] and the UK can encourage good practice both by engaging in collaborative international law work and through its own domestic legislation.

Surrogacy law reform in the UK represents a once-in-a-generation opportunity to get the law right. It must be pragmatic and seek to both safeguard the welfare of children and promote an ethical approach to surrogacy, whether the surrogacy takes place in the UK or abroad.

[54] See Pott and White, Chapter 2, this volume.

[55] Fischer et al, n45.

PART II

Specific Issues in the Law Commissions' Recommendations

5

The Genetic Link Requirement: Reconsidering the Arguments for Double Donation

Lottie Park-Morton

Introduction

For the intended parents (IPs) of a surrogate-born child to be recognised as the legal parent(s), a parental order must be granted under s54 or s54A Human Fertilisation and Embryology (HFE) Act 2008. The effect of this is to remove the surrogate's (and, if applicable, her partner's) legal parenthood, reissuing the birth certificate to list the IPs as the child's legal parents.[1] Numerous requirements must be satisfied before the court can grant the parental order. Some requirements, such as for the application to be made within six months of the child's birth[2] and for the IPs to be in a formalised or enduring family relationship,[3] have been liberally interpreted by the court to allow parental orders to be granted in circumstances where a strict reading of the legislation would not permit this.[4] The lifelong welfare of

1 There are procedural differences to the court processes in England & Wales and Scotland. For more information on the court procedure, see Law Commission and Scottish Law Commission: Joint Consultation Paper, *Building Families Through Surrogacy: a New Law* (Law Com Consultation Paper No 244, Scot Law Com Discussion Paper No 167, 6 June 2019), chapter 6.

2 HFE Act 2008, s54(3).

3 ibid, s54(2).

4 For example, *Re X (A Child) (Parental Order: Time Limit)* [2014] EWHC 3135 (Fam); [2015] Fam 186 with numerous cases since adopting the same liberal approach to the statutory requirements.

the child is the basis upon which the courts have taken this approach, an obligation since 2010 when the paramountcy standard from adoption[5] was inserted into the legislation.[6]

Despite the liberal approach taken to some of the s54 requirements, others remain absolute. One such requirement is s54(1)(b): that 'the gametes of at least one of the applicants were used to bring about the creation of the embryo', meaning that at least one IP must have a genetic link to the child. Single IPs have been eligible for parental orders since 2019,[7] and in such cases that IP must be the genetic parent of the child under s54A(1)(b). This means that in traditional surrogacy arrangements – where the surrogate's egg is used – IPs cannot establish legal parenthood by way of a parental order if they used donor sperm. In gestational surrogacy arrangements – where the surrogate has no genetic link to the child – 'double donation' (that is, donor egg and sperm or donated embryos) also prevents an order from being granted.

This requirement can be contrasted with the approach taken to establish legal parenthood following other assisted reproductive techniques (ART) where double donation *is* permitted. The distinction between the use of double donation in surrogacy and other ART therefore exposes inconsistency in how the law attributes and values genetics and gestation in the determination of parenthood. The Law Commission of England and Wales and the Scottish Law Commission (the Law Commissions) made provisional proposals in their consultation paper[8] to move away from the absolute nature of the genetic requirement in circumstances where double donation was a medical necessity. However, in their final report they departed from this, recommending that the genetic link requirement be retained in all but very limited circumstances.[9]

In this chapter, a brief context to the current legislative framework is provided, before reflecting on the approach taken in the Law Commissions' provisional proposals and final recommendations. The chapter then thematically analyses the conceptual and practical arguments for retaining or removing the genetic link requirement that were explored in the consultation project. It argues that, despite some legitimate concerns, the removal of the requirement better reflects the intention of all parties to the surrogacy arrangement, represents modern family formation, and satisfies the interests of the parties involved. Therefore, it argues that legal parenthood following

5 Adoption and Children Act 2002, s1.

6 Human Fertilisation and Embryology (Parental Orders) Regulations 2010.

7 Human Fertilisation and Embryology Act 2008 (Remedial Order) 2018.

8 Law Commissions, n1.

9 Law Commission and Scottish Law Commission, *Building Families Through Surrogacy: a New Law: Volume II: Full Report* (Law Com No 411, Scot Law Com No 262, 29 March 2023).

double donation in surrogacy should be permitted in wider circumstances than currently recommended.

Tracing the genetic link requirement

When the Human Fertilisation and Embryology Bill (the Bill), later the Human Fertilisation and Embryology Act (HFE Act) 1990, was debated, there was very little discussion relating to surrogacy. The Bill covered a wide range of other ethically sensitive issues, such as embryo research, which dominated parliamentary debate. References in Parliament to surrogacy were few and demonstrated the cautious approach to the practice, such as the Lord Chancellor of the time stating that the government would be 'appalled' to see an upward trend in the use of surrogacy.[10] To treat the woman who carried the child as anything other than the child's mother, was seen as ignoring the 'practical, physical and emotional relations' between the surrogate and the child, during and after birth, and would remove the certainty provided by the law.[11]

Despite this clear messaging on the government's view on parenthood following surrogacy, during its passage through the House of Commons the Bill was amended to make specific provisions for IPs' recognition as the child's legal parents. Michael Jopling MP spoke of a couple in his constituency who had to adopt their children born through surrogacy. Jopling moved an amendment to allow IPs to be given parental responsibility where there was a genetic link to the IPs and the surrogate did not object. Given the declaration by the Lord Chancellor of the government's policy in relation to surrogacy, Jopling stated 'I cannot believe that an amendment of the sort… would in itself encourage surrogacy… it would add common sense to an unusual, unsatisfactory and unfair situation'.[12]

Following the Commons Committee Stage, clause 9 was introduced, which became s30 HFE Act 1990 (subsequently s54 HFE Act 2008). The clause, laying out the parental order requirements, went further than Jopling's proposal, allowing legal parenthood, rather than just parental responsibility, to be transferred to the IPs. There was no parliamentary discussion of this clause, and it appears to have been introduced solely in response to Jopling's proposed amendment based on the plight of one couple. As Norrie identifies, '[t]he policy behind the introduction and re-enactment of parental orders remains, therefore, obscure' although it seems that 'Parliament intended

10 *Hansard* HL Deb, vol 517, col 207, 20 March 1990.

11 ibid.

12 *Hansard* HC Deb, vol 170, col 945, 2 April 1990.

a mechanism to avoid the need for adoption when at least one of the commissioning couple is the genetic parent'.[13]

The parental order requirements have changed only subtly since their introduction in 1990, with minor amendments in 2008, and eligibility extended to single IPs passed into law in 2018. S54(1)(b) remains unaltered and is one of only a few of the requirements to remain a hard line of the legislation. However, it is not possible to ascertain parliamentary intent in the inclusion of the requirement. If clause 9, now s54, was introduced solely based on Jopling's proposal, the inclusion of the genetic link requirement may be due only to the fact that his constituents were the genetic parents of the surrogate-born children.

In the Law Commissions' consultation, a new 'Pathway to Parenthood' was first proposed. This proposal was maintained in their final report,[14] under which IPs would be recognised as legal parents from birth, provided certain pre-conception processes are completed and the surrogate does not withdraw her consent. For IPs who are ineligible for the new pathway, due to failing to comply with pre-conception processes or in circumstances where the surrogate withdraws her consent, or those who engage in international surrogacy arrangements, it is proposed that the parental order pathway be retained, with amendments.

In the consultation, in the context of the proposed new pathway and amended parental order pathway, two provisional proposals relating to the genetic link requirement were made. First, that double donation be permitted on the new pathway in cases of 'medical necessity' (where no IP can provide gametes); and, secondly, retaining the requirement for a genetic link for IPs requiring a parental order following international surrogacy arrangements. A further question was posed, without a corresponding proposal, regarding whether double donation should be permitted outside the new pathway where IPs need to obtain a parental order following a domestic surrogacy arrangement.[15]

The final report saw a change in approach. The provisional proposal to allow double donation based on medical necessity was removed, thus recommending retention of the genetic link requirement to establish legal parenthood following surrogacy.[16] This also closed the distinction between the genetic link requirement in domestic and international arrangements. Under the recommendations, there remains one very limited exception

13 Kenneth Norrie, 'English and Scottish Adoption Orders and British Parental Orders after Surrogacy: Welfare, Competence and Judicial Legislation' (2017) 29 *Child and Family Law Quarterly* 93, 96.

14 Law Commissions, n9, chapter 2.

15 Law Commissions, n1, paras 19.72–19.74.

16 Law Commissions, n9, 163.

when a parental order could be granted without an IP having a genetic link – in circumstances where there has been a relationship breakdown, and the genetic IP is no longer involved in the arrangement.[17]

To understand why a different approach was suggested in relation to the new pathway and parental order process, and why the stance of the Law Commissions changed during their project, it is necessary to reflect on the initial findings and consultation responses and the final report.

Domestic arrangements: a departure from, and retreat to, prioritising genetic relatedness

The provisional proposals

In the discussion relating to the genetic link requirement, stakeholder views were finely balanced. The requirement was viewed as a clear distinguishing factor from adoption and a way to protect against child trafficking and 'designer babies'.[18] Equally, however, it was stated that a genetic link (or lack thereof) does not affect quality of parenting, and the different treatment of surrogacy compared with other ARTs, which do not require a genetic link, was highlighted as potentially discriminatory.[19]

Balancing these opposing views, it was provisionally proposed that for cases on the new pathway, the requirement for a genetic link should be removed in cases of medical necessity. The Law Commissions argued this would ensure double donation be used only when 'necessary', thus safeguarding against concerns raised about the general removal of the genetic link requirement. Medical necessity was defined as where 'either the single intended parent is not, or neither of the intended parents in a couple are, capable of contributing gametes for conception due to medical infertility'.[20]

The final recommendations

Many consultation responses related to double donation focused on the exception being framed around 'medical necessity'. However, comments varied as to why that framing would not be appropriate. Some respondents argued for no restriction on double donation, while others thought 'medical necessity' would be too difficult to define and apply. For example, Brilliant Beginnings, a surrogacy organisation that supports surrogates and IPs,[21]

17 ibid, 267.

18 Law Commissions, n1, 279–281.

19 ibid, 278–279.

20 ibid, 283.

21 Brilliant Beginnings is recognised by the Department of Health and Social Care as one of the national non-profit surrogacy organisations: DHSC, 'Care in Surrogacy: Guidance

and their sibling organisation, NGA Law, a law firm specialising in fertility and surrogacy law, were concerned that the exception could marginalise those who may have a valid reason, outside medical necessity, for using donors, such as women suffering from tokophobia, the fear of pregnancy or childbirth.[22] The Family Law Bar Association highlighted another example of where the IPs are not infertile, and are able to contribute gametes, but use donor gametes to avoid the risk of a genetic disorder being transmitted to the putative child.[23] This would reasonably be defined as a valid reason for using donor gametes, but under the Law Commissions' framing of 'medical necessity', would not have fallen within the exception.

In recommending the retention of the genetic link requirement, the Law Commissions stated they were 'heavily influenced by the difficulties and disadvantages in seeking to tie double donation to the need for medical necessity'.[24] If the definition of medical necessity was too prescriptive, it could inadvertently prevent individuals from being included,[25] whereas a wider and less prescriptive framing could introduce ambiguity as to whether it would be acceptable.[26] Resultantly, the provisional proposal to allow double donation in cases of medical necessity was deemed unworkable.

Given the Law Commissions only consulted on allowing double donation in cases of medical necessity, they were compelled to make their recommendations in accordance with the consultation questions posed, and views received. As such, they were not in a position to make any other final recommendations on double donation generally, as consultees' views would not have informed them.[27]

Nonetheless, despite the lack of recommendation in this regard, the Law Commissions commented that the government 'may wish to consider whether a policy permitting double donation in surrogacy agreements could be introduced'.[28] This suggests they see potential merit in removing the genetic link requirement but were constrained to only make recommendations aligned with the consultation questions and comments. It is notable that this is the only aspect of the final report where the Law Commissions suggest the government review the law other than in accordance with their

for the Care of Surrogates and Intended Parents in Surrogate Births in England and Wales' (2018, updated 25 April 2024).

22 Law Commissions, n9, 161.

23 ibid.

24 ibid, 162.

25 The Law Commissions used the example of individuals who, due their age or health, would have a very small chance of their gametes producing an embryo: ibid.

26 ibid.

27 ibid.

28 ibid, 163.

recommendations.[29] It may therefore be reasonably assumed that the Law Commissions would be open to a departure from their recommendations if the policy decision were to be to permit double donation.

International arrangements: genetic link as a safeguard

The provisional proposals

While the provisional proposals moved away from the absolute necessity for a genetic link in domestic cases on the new pathway, a different approach was advocated for international surrogacy. For international arrangements, it was provisionally proposed that the genetic link requirement be retained when applying for a parental order. There were three bases upon which the Law Commissions justified this approach.

First, given that many jurisdictions where IPs access surrogacy permit the use of anonymous gametes, allowing double donation could result in a situation where the child had no possibility of access to information about their donors, contrary to the Law Commissions' stance that a child has the right to know information relating to their genetic origins.[30] Requiring a genetic link with an IP increases at least the possibility that information about one genetic parent would be available to the surrogate-born child. Secondly, there were concerns that, at present, the court and parental order reporter can have difficulties contacting the surrogate. Without that contact with the surrogate to confirm the nature of the surrogacy arrangement, absent a genetic link, it would be difficult to prove that the child was born as a result of a surrogacy arrangement.[31] Thirdly, the approach was justified based on there being less pre-conception oversight of the arrangement than in cases on the new pathway, with the genetic link requirement seen as a safeguard against concerns of child trafficking.[32] These concerns are addressed later in the chapter, to analyse whether they provide an adequate basis for retaining the genetic link requirement. What is clear is that the proposed retention of the requirement in international arrangements stemmed from the Law Commissions' concern of there being less oversight or safeguards in place

[29] The final report does comment that the government may wish to consider wider policy and law reform that would indirectly affect surrogacy, such as recognition of co-parenting, enforcement powers of the Human Fertilisation and Embryology Authority (HFEA) and the scope of the HFEA register for donor conceived individuals. It also made clear that it is a governmental decision as to whether to enforce a civil penalty scheme relating to prohibited payments. None of these, however, directly suggest that the government look to adopt a different stance than that recommended.

[30] Law Commissions, n1, 283.

[31] ibid, 283–284.

[32] ibid, 284.

in overseas arrangements, with a genetic link providing a level of assurance as to the nature of the arrangement.

The final recommendations

The final report's recommended retention of the genetic link requirement in all cases removes the distinction drawn in the provisional proposals between domestic and international surrogacy arrangements. However, given the seeming encouragement by the Law Commissions for the government to review the position of the law on double donation in surrogacy, it is important that the justifications in the provisional proposals for retaining the genetic link requirement in international arrangements are properly analysed. Any legal distinction based on where the surrogacy arrangement took place will be subject to scrutiny. As I have argued elsewhere, it is important from a children's rights perspective that there is parity, to ensure a child is not disadvantaged by not permitting IPs to be recognised as the legal parents based on where they were born.[33]

The exceptional case

The provisional proposals

The Law Commissions stated that requiring a genetic link on the parental order pathway for domestic arrangements that fall off the new pathway was 'finely balanced'[34] – evidenced by the fact that they sought consultees' views, rather than making any provisional proposals. However, the Law Commissions made provisional proposals in relation to two specific problematic situations in terms of the genetic link requirement.

First, reference was made to the situation where IPs began the surrogacy arrangement on the new pathway, only to revert to a parental order application (for example, as a result of the surrogate withdrawing her consent).[35] In such situations, if double donation were permitted on the new pathway, but not within parental order applications, the IPs would not be able to establish legal parenthood through a parental order, despite complying with the legal framework at the time of entering into the arrangement. A provisional proposal was put forward to allow a parental order to be granted, absent a genetic link, in such circumstances 'to avoid

[33] Lottie Park-Morton, 'The Role of Non-Genetic Parents in a Surrogate-Born Child's Identity: an Argument for Removal of the Genetic Link Requirement' (2024) 32(1) *Medical Law Review* 61.

[34] Law Commissions, n1, 283.

[35] ibid, 284.

putting intended parents into a trap where they could unintentionally be placed in a situation in which they could not become the legal parents of the child despite their initial expectations'.[36] The terminology used by the Law Commissions in the framing of the provisional proposal was that of 'good faith', in relation to the IPs' belief that they had met all of the requirements at the time of entering the new pathway.[37]

Secondly, the situation was envisaged where a non-genetic IP may be applying for a parental order as a single IP because of a relationship breakdown where the other IP, with the genetic link, no longer has any involvement in the arrangement. Again, the Law Commissions provisionally proposed that in such cases the non-genetic IP should still be able to obtain an order despite the lack of a genetic link,[38] although no reasoning was given as to why this should be permissible beyond the fact that the IP raising the child would not be able to secure a parental order.

The final recommendations

Given the Law Commissions' decision to retain the requirement for a genetic link in all cases, regardless of whether the arrangement was on the new pathway or not, the first proposed exception – where the IPs started on the new pathway in good faith but had to revert to the parental order pathway – was stated to 'fall away'.[39] The second proposed exception – where IPs separate, leaving the non-genetic IP to pursue a parental order as a single applicant – did, however, continue to be recommended in the final report.

The consultation responses received in relation to this proposal were divided, with many arguing that the genetic IP should continue to be recognised as the child's legal parent irrespective of relationship breakdown.[40] However, the Law Commissions took the view that such an approach could be contrary to the best interests of the child in forcing a genetic parent to be a legal parent against their will.[41] Therefore, they recommended allowing a single non-genetic IP to apply for a parental order provided that, at the time the surrogacy arrangement was entered into, there was another IP who had a genetic link to the child.[42] To recommend otherwise would be to allow

36 ibid, 285.
37 ibid.
38 ibid, 286.
39 Law Commissions, n9, 159.
40 ibid, 261.
41 ibid, 264.
42 ibid, 263.

the genetic IP to prevent an order being granted where it would best meet the child's welfare.[43]

There are associated recommendations made that mitigate some of the concerns raised by consultees relating to the ability of the genetic parent to renege from the arrangement. These include joining the genetic IP to the parental order application,[44] and for that IP's details to be recorded on a surrogacy register.[45]

Reflections on the project

As the above discussion demonstrates, there was a marked shift in the Law Commissions' approach to the genetic link requirement between their consultation paper and final report. The provisional proposal for removing the genetic link requirement in domestic cases framed around medical necessity was unfortunate. The narrow framing of the exception, generally agreed to be unworkable, meant that broader consultation and discussions around the genetic link requirement in general were hampered. However, there was recognition in the consultation responses that the genetic link requirement can be simultaneously justified and challenged based on how the law values genetics and intention in parenthood. As such, the final report's suggestion that the government should reconsider the requirement demonstrates that the Law Commissions see the value in a more broadly encompassing debate as to the retention of the necessity for a genetic link.

Given the decision to retain the genetic link requirement in all but very limited circumstances, the distinction between international and domestic arrangements, as well as arrangements on the new pathway and parental order pathway, is removed. Nonetheless, if the government were to review the genetic link requirement, it is important that any differing approaches be properly scrutinised and justified to ensure surrogate-born individuals are not treated differently based on where they were born or the circumstances around their conception and birth.

The one proposal remaining in the final report relates to ensuring a non-genetic IP can be recognised as the child's legal parent following a relationship breakdown with the genetic parent. The acknowledgement that the non-genetic IP should not be prevented from establishing legal parenthood based on the actions of the other IP would ensure that the best interests of the child can be met. However, this is a very narrow exception and there are

43 ibid.

44 ibid, 266.

45 ibid, 387. For discussion of the proposed surrogacy register, see Wade, Chapter 7, this volume.

other potential circumstances where a genetic link may be lacking between the child and IP(s) which would also justify a more radical departure from the necessity for a genetic link.

To assess the coherence of the recommendation to retain the genetic link requirement, it is necessary to consider the thematic arguments that arose in relation to the requirement within the consultation project. Four themes emerged from the consultation paper and final report: the role that the requirement has in distinguishing surrogacy from adoption; inconsistency and potential discrimination that the requirement may create when compared with other ARTs; arguments framed around harm to surrogate-born children; and issues relating to the child's identity. These will be considered in turn. The following section demonstrates that, notwithstanding seemingly legitimate reasons for retaining the genetic link requirement based on some of these themes, there are more compelling arguments that demonstrate that prioritising genetics in surrogacy arrangements cannot be conceptually or practically justified.

Emerging themes from the consultation project

Distinguishing between surrogacy and adoption

One key argument for retaining the genetic link requirement is to retain a clear distinction between surrogacy and adoption. An adoption order and parental order have the same effect of transferring legal parenthood from the birth mother to those who will undertake the social function of parenting, with parental orders having been termed 'a form of fast-track adoption'.[46] However, while parental orders are typically an entirely private law matter, adoption requires state involvement and public law proceedings. There is therefore less regulatory oversight of surrogacy arrangements leading to parental orders compared with arrangements leading to an adoption order. This is reflective of the different factual circumstances arising in surrogacy and adoption. These different factual considerations are, under existing law, two-fold. First, surrogacy is premised on a private agreement between parties, whereas adoption often arises in the context of state involvement and with a pool of potential parents that have not been pre-selected. Secondly, under the current law, although contested within this section of the chapter, parental orders can be seen as having the additional purpose of aligning genetic and legal parenthood with at least one IP.

The idea that the genetic link between an IP and child is the distinguishing factor between an adoption order and parental order is one supported by

46 Kirsty Horsey, 'Challenging Presumptions: Legal Parenthood and Surrogacy Arrangements' (2010) 22 *Child and Family Law Quarterly* 449, 453.

case law, with various cases taking the view that a parental order is the preferable legal mechanism following surrogacy.[47] For example, in *Re X (A Child) (Parental Order: Time Limit)*,[48] it was stated that adoption would 'not be an attractive solution' for recognising the relationship between the child and IPs on the basis that a parental order would confirm '[t]he important legal, practical and psychological reality of X's identity: the commissioning father is his biological father and all parties intended from the outset that the commissioning parents should be his legal parents'.[49] There was therefore judicial affirmation that a distinguishing factor between surrogacy and adoption is the genetic link with one IP, in this case the intended father. However, in the same sentence, Sir James Munby P also emphasised a further distinguishing factor: intention. By stating that 'all parties' intended for the IPs to be the legal parents of the child from the outset, recognition was given to how such intention was a determining feature of the surrogacy arrangement, and an important aspect of the child's identity.

AB v CT further supports the distinction between adoption and surrogacy based on the genetic link.[50] There, Theis J asserted that the effect of an adoption order was to treat the child 'as if' the child was a child of the adopters whereas, in surrogacy arrangements, this does not reflect the reality that the child is genetically related to one of the IPs.[51] Instead, it was stated that a parental order is a 'more honest order which reflects the reality of what was intended, the lineage connection that already exists and more accurately reflects the child's identity'.[52] Again, in stating that a parental order better reflects the situation than an adoption order, there was emphasis on the genetic link, but also an explicit reference to intention, with the parental order better reflecting the reality of what was intended.

In *D v ED (Parental Order: Time Limit)*, Russell J stated that a parental order was required, 'rather than giving [the children] the wholly artificial and, in their case, inappropriate' status of adopted children.[53] As to why adoption would be inappropriate, there was again focus not only on the genetic link but also the role of intention:

---

47 The court has, however, granted an adoption order instead of a parental order at the request of IPs, demonstrating that an adoption order is not necessarily an inappropriate way to transfer parenthood following surrogacy in some circumstances: *Re H (Surrogacy: step-parent adoption)* [2023] EWFC 214.

48 *Re X* (n4).

49 ibid, at [7].

50 *AB & CD v CT (Parental Order: Consent of Surrogate Mother)* [2015] EWFC 12.

51 ibid, at [71].

52 ibid.

53 *D v ED (Parental Order: Time Limit)* [2015] EWHC 911 (Fam) [61].

> It is undeniably a basic and fundamental part of these children's identity as human beings that the Applicant/father is their biological father, and that the Applicant/mother played a full part in the process of their conception having selected an egg donor, as she has herself explained to them and as they have grown up believing. The Applicants were their planned and intended parents from before conception and since the day on which they were born. All of these facts, fundamental to these children's very existence and identity are far from those present in adoption.[54]

Therefore, the judiciary clearly perceives a genetic link as a key distinguishing factor between surrogacy and adoption. However, to conclude on this basis alone would be an incomplete analysis of the case law. As each of the passages from the judgments above demonstrate, along with the genetic link requirement, there is also an emphasis on how intention distinguishes surrogacy from adoption. The Law Commissions' consultation also framed the significance of the genetic link in terms of intention by stating:

> [A] genetic link does offer proof that the intended parents were involved in bringing about the conception of the child. It appears to us that the distinction between surrogacy and adoption (and the protections of adoption) could be preserved so long as the intended parents are involved in the child's conception. Safeguards may be needed to ensure that, absent a genetic link, there is evidence of their involvement in conception.[55]

This suggests that the importance of the genetic link is not the genetic relatedness in and of itself, but rather what the genetic link evidences: the intention to bring about the conception of the child and to become the child's social parents.

In surrogacy, the IPs are the planned parents from birth – and before. From before conception, there is an understanding between the parties that the IPs will act as the social, and legal, parents of the child. This is a key distinction from adoption, whereby the child must have been born before intended adoptive parents can be matched with her/him. It can therefore be argued that there need not be reliance on the genetic link to distinguish surrogacy from adoption: the distinction could reasonably be drawn based on intention. This was acknowledged by the Law Commissions where they stated that '[s]urrogacy can still robustly be differentiated from adoption even

[54] ibid, at [62].

[55] Law Commissions, n1, 281.

without maintaining a genetic link between parent and child, because of the clearly evidenced preconception intention of the parties'.[56] Nonetheless, given the reduced oversight of surrogacy compared with adoption, the Law Commissions commented that removal of the genetic link requirement could heighten the risk of individuals using surrogacy to circumvent adoption law protections.[57] However, this risk could be mitigated through means other than continuing to require a genetic link. For example, drawing on the recommendations from the Law Commissions, the regulated surrogacy statement (RSS), a document agreed between the IPs and surrogate prior to the arrangement proceeding on the new pathway, would evidence the IPs' role in the conception of the pregnancy, even in circumstances where there is no genetic link. The pre-conception stage would include a welfare of the child assessment and criminal record check, mitigating concerns that surrogacy could be used to evade safeguards in the adoption process. In acknowledging that not all cases would proceed on the new pathway, such as international arrangements, it could be harder to evidence pre-conception intention to distinguish surrogacy from adoption. Nevertheless, there could be other means of evidencing intention in the parental order proceedings, such as written surrogacy agreements and related documents. Further, the court needs to be satisfied that the lifelong welfare of the child would be satisfied by the granting of the order – if there were concerns in relation to the quality of parenting of the IPs, the court could refuse to grant a parental order, in a similar protective way as adoption proceedings would.

Therefore, the genetic link requirement does not need to be retained to preserve the distinction between surrogacy and adoption: as the Law Commissions have commented, and as case law has acknowledged, intention can equally act as a differentiator. Concern that individuals would resort to surrogacy to avoid adoption law protections does not justify retaining the genetic link requirement given that there are other mechanisms, both procedural and judicial, within the recommendations that would ensure the legitimacy of the arrangement and protect the welfare of the child.

Inconsistency in parenthood attribution following assisted reproductive techniques

One argument advanced in support of removing the genetic link requirement relates to how the provision is inconsistent with other ways of starting a family. As stated earlier, the requirement for a genetic link as a precursor to legal parenthood is not one that is present for other ARTs. When a woman

56 Law Commissions, n9, 162.

57 Law Commissions, n1, 279–280.

has a child through IVF or donor conception, the law is clear that she will be the child's mother[58] and her partner (if applicable) can be recognised as the child's father or second parent.[59] This is the case irrespective of whether she or her partner have used their gametes in the treatment, meaning donated egg and/or sperm, as well as donated embryos, can be used.[60]

A comparison of how parenthood is determined following surrogacy and other ARTs exposes inconsistencies in how parenthood is attributed, and gestation or genetics prioritised. These inconsistencies were also identified in the Law Commissions' project, with a view that it could be perceived as discriminatory on the basis of infertility and single-person status.[61] Brown and Wade have analysed whether, in such circumstances, the requirement for a genetic link could be challenged as an interference with a single applicant's right to family and private life under Article 8 and prohibition of discrimination under Article 14 ECHR.[62] Given the wide margin of appreciation afforded to states in relation to surrogacy, it is likely that the requirement, and interference, would be justified. Nonetheless, when considered in combination with the child's right to identity, discussed further below, the interference becomes harder to justify.

It was acknowledged by the Law Commissions that the requirement could be felt particularly acutely by single women who are both infertile and unable to carry a pregnancy to term.[63] In such circumstances, where a surrogate and donated gametes would be required, the intended mother would not be able to satisfy the genetic link requirement and could therefore not become the legal parent. In contrast, if she was infertile but able to carry and maintain a pregnancy, she would be able to become a legal mother through operation of s33 HFE Act using donated gametes and IVF.

The defining distinction in this situation, therefore, is the woman's ability to gestate, with gestation and giving birth being the determinants of legal motherhood in UK law under the maxim of *mater semper certa est* (the mother is always certain).[64] Despite the law relating to parenthood following surrogacy seeming to prioritise a genetic link, true priority is given to gestation. A genetic link, however, is an alternative basis for

58 HFE Act 2008, s33.

59 ibid, ss35–37 and 42–44.

60 HFE Act 2008, ss3(2) and 3ZA.

61 Law Commissions, n1 above, 278–279; Law Commissions, n9, 160.

62 Alan Brown and Katherine Wade, 'Parental Orders for Deceased Intended Parents: *Re X (Foreign Surrogacy: Death of Intended Parent)* [2022] EWFC 34' (2022) *Medical Law Review* 744, 6.

63 Law Commissions, n1, 278–279; Law Commissions, n9, 160.

64 For critical analysis of the allocation of motherhood to the woman who gives birth, see Zaina Mahmoud and Elizabeth Chloe Romanis, 'On Gestation and Motherhood' (2023) 31(1) *Medical Law Review* 109.

establishing parenthood, providing the ability to displace the gestational basis for motherhood.

Neither gestation nor genetics, however, necessarily reflects who intends to act as a parent. This is recognised in the parenthood provisions for other ARTs, such as non-genetic partners of the mother. Under these provisions, where donated gametes are used, the claim to paternity or second parenthood is based on consent or intention, as opposed to any biological connection to the child. The non-genetic partner of the mother consents to the woman receiving treatment,[65] or consents to being treated as the parent[66] and, on that basis alone, the legislation provides for them to be a legal parent. The is one example of the law already having provision in certain circumstances for intention-based parenthood.

Arguments for intention-based parenthood following surrogacy are well-established, evidenced in the consultation paper, where it is acknowledged:

> [I]n surrogacy, social or psychological parenthood is seen by the parties as at least as, if not more, important than genetic or gestational parenthood. The need for a genetic link does not reflect this emphasis on social parenthood in the context of surrogacy, and may even be seen to undermine the parental role of intended parents who do not have a genetic link to the child.[67]

There are two points to note from this statement. First, the recognition that the genetic link requirement could operate to undermine a non-genetic parent, viewing them as 'inferior' to the IP with a genetic connection to the child.[68] This is not something that the law should look to reinforce, particularly given that genetics is not a determinant in allocation of parenthood following other ARTs. Secondly, in surrogacy, social parenthood – which stems from the intention to parent – is seen as paramount. If parties to surrogacy arrangements see intention as the most important factor in the attribution of legal parenthood, to continue necessitating and prioritising a genetic link undermines the role of non-genetic parents in their social parenting role. This would be felt most acutely by single applicants who would be unable to obtain a parental order without a genetic link to a child. However, even where a parental order is sought by two applicants, the genetic link requirement could still be perceived as undermining the role of the non-genetic IP in the

65 Where the woman is married or in a civil partnership: HFE Act 2008, ss35 and 42.

66 Where the agreed fatherhood or agreed female parenthood provisions apply: ibid, 36–37 and 43–44.

67 Law Commissions, n1, 281.

68 Lydia Bracken, 'Surrogacy and the Genetic Link' (2020) 32 *Child and Family Law Quarterly* 303, 309.

messaging of the legislation in prioritising the genetic relationship between an IP and child as a 'gateway' to obtaining a parental order.

The law should better align with parenthood following other ARTs and move away from the absolute requirement for a genetic link. To do so would move the law towards an intention-based model, requiring, as Horsey advocates 'an acknowledgement that parenthood following assisted conception does not depend upon anything inherently biological, but rather upon a pre-conception intention to have a child, and to initiate the process with which that child is to be brought into the world'.[69]

Harm to children

A further theme explored in the arguments regarding the genetic link requirement relates to the broad issue of the harm potentially caused to children. In the consultation paper and final report, two main concerns fell within this definition: child trafficking and commercialisation, and an undesirable move towards 'designer babies'.

Some stakeholders, including CAFCASS, were concerned that removing the genetic link requirement increases the risk of child trafficking and commercialisation of children.[70] Particularly in relation to international arrangements, when it can be harder to make post-birth contact with the surrogate to confirm the nature of the arrangement, safeguards may be harder to impose and enforce.[71] Requiring a genetic link is one way to demonstrate that the child was actually born as a result of surrogacy, thus reducing the risk of child trafficking.[72] However, the Law Commissions' consultation acknowledged that there are ways other than maintaining the genetic link requirement to combat concerns relating to child trafficking, such as criminal law provisions, and the enhanced criminal record checks that would take place on the new pathway.[73] It must be acknowledged that international surrogacy arrangements, where concerns of child trafficking would be most prevalent, are ineligible for the new pathway, meaning those checks would not necessarily take place. Therefore, the stance of the Law Commissions, in resorting to criminal law provisions in the event of child trafficking, would only be able to punish the offence after it has been committed. This would not prevent the practice in the same way that retaining the genetic link requirement may be seen to do.

---

69 Horsey, n46, 472.
70 Law Commissions, n1, 280.
71 ibid, 284.
72 ibid.
73 Law Commissions, n1, 282.

However, the final report stated that nearly all consultation responses raising arguments relating to trafficking and commercialisation of children as a reason for retaining the genetic link requirement were from those opposed to surrogacy in general.[74] This may indicate that the arguments were advanced due to concerns around the practice of surrogacy *per se*, as opposed to the precise issue of the genetic link requirement. It appears that the Law Commissions were not persuaded by arguments relating to commercialisation and trafficking alone as reasons for maintaining the genetic link requirement. In the final report, there is only brief acknowledgement of the arguments received during the consultation, and they did not feature in the substantive analysis as to the recommendations.

Linked closely with concerns of commercialisation, the second argument advanced for keeping the genetic link requirement was that removing it could be a step towards allowing 'designer babies', with people choosing gamete donors with 'desirable' traits.[75] If there was no requirement for a genetic link, IPs could choose gamete donors on the basis of physical attributes, which was cited as risking a move towards eugenics within assisted reproduction.[76] It was acknowledged that preventing this could be harder to achieve if the genetic link requirement were removed and it is seemingly on this basis that the provisionally proposed exception to the genetic link requirement was based:[77] in only permitting double donation where it is a medical necessity, it would limit the potential for people to use double donation on the basis of genetic preference.

The subsequent decision to retain the genetic link requirement, due to concerns over the application of 'medical necessity', would therefore allay the concerns over double donation leading to a practice of designer babies. However, this is a hypothetical concern: no evidence was advanced to suggest that allowing double donation would result in such practices, and it would seem an overly restrictive approach to maintain the genetic link requirement based on such a theoretical concern where there are other valid reasons for moving away from it.

Equally, arguments can be made from the child's perspective that the retention of the genetic link requirement could operate in a manner that is detrimental to their welfare. Given the absolute nature of the genetic link requirement under the current legal framework, a parental order cannot be granted even if a welfare of the child assessment indicates that this would be best for the child. As Jackson has highlighted, permitting double donation

[74] Law Commissions, n9, 160.

[75] Law Commissions, n1, 280–281; Law Commissions, n9,161.

[76] Law Commissions, n1, 281.

[77] ibid, 282.

would therefore actually support the welfare of the child by allowing a parental order to be granted in circumstances where it currently would not be possible, so long as the child's welfare demanded it.[78] Bracken similarly emphasises that a blanket ban on the transfer of parenthood on the basis of a lack of genetic link prevents an individualised best interests assessment.[79]

However, these criticisms could only be overcome if double donation were permitted more broadly than originally envisaged in the consultation. The provisional proposal to allow it only in cases of medical necessity would have, arguably, been subject to the same criticism as the existing law in that transfer of legal parenthood could not take place if double donation were used but the circumstances fell outside the definition of 'medical necessity'. Resultantly, from a child welfare perspective, a more radical move away from the genetic link requirement can be justified, ensuring that the court can grant a parental order in accordance with an individualised assessment of the welfare of the child.[80]

Identity of the child

In the Law Commissions' consultation and final report, a final justification for retaining the genetic link requirement centred on the identity rights of the surrogate-born child. The child's right to identity, as an emerging right, can be articulated based on the United Nations Convention on the Rights of the Child (UNCRC) and European Convention on Human Rights (ECHR). Article 7 UNCRC states that a child has the right to know their parents, which has been interpreted to mean social, genetic, and gestational parents,[81] while Article 8 provides that a child has the right to preservation of identity, including family relations. This concept of identity has been applied in relation to Article 8 ECHR, the right to family and private life, with the right to know biological origins and circumstances relating to the nature of an individuals' birth being understood as a component of identity, falling within private life.[82]

In the Law Commissions' consultation, it was stated that permitting double donation, particularly in international arrangements where anonymous gamete donation is permitted, could prevent a child from being able to access information about their origins. Therefore, retaining the current genetic link

78 Law Commissions, n9, 160.

79 Bracken, n68, 312.

80 The Law Commissions consultation project did not engage with the broader welfare question of whether it is better for children to be brought up with one genetic parent.

81 Rachel Hodgkin and Peter Newell, *Implementation Handbook for the United Nations Convention on the Rights of the Child* (3rd edn, Unicef 2007) 105–106.

82 *Odievre v France* (2004) 38 EHRR 43.

requirement was stated to ensure preservation of information about at least one genetic parent.[83] If respecting a child's right to identity is understood to include an ability to access information relating to genetic parents, the retention of the requirement can be justified on this basis.

However, as Bracken recognises, the requirement for a genetic link only 'half vindicates the child's right to identity' given that a genetic link to both IPs is not required.[84] At best, the genetic link requirement can only partially ensure this right is realised, as the child would be able to access information relating to the heritage of the genetic IP but may not have origin information relating to an anonymous overseas donor. Notwithstanding, the retention of the requirement, particularly in international surrogacy arrangements, ensures *some* origin information is available for the surrogate-born child. The Law Commissions' recommended introduction of a surrogacy register (which would record information relating to the surrogate and genetic parents) exemplifies the importance of surrogate-born children having access to origin information.[85] However, a surrogacy register would be of limited utility when IPs engage with surrogacy overseas using anonymous gametes. Under the recommendations, the parental order requirement to provide information for inclusion on the surrogacy register can be dispensed with where the surrogate or gamete donor cannot be identified, provided this fact is recorded on the register.[86] With the court's ability to dispense with the requirement to provide origin information, retaining the genetic link requirement becomes significant in relation to the child's right to identity: it will ensure at least one genetic parent's information can be stored and made accessible to the child.

References in the Law Commissions' consultation paper and final report refer to the child's right to identity exclusively in relation to their ability to access information relating to their genetic and gestational origins. However, there is a further component of the child's identity that is relevant to the genetic link requirement: their lived reality and relationship with the IPs. Case law of the ECtHR has been significant in developing the concept of identity as an aspect of private life. While there is still evidence of priority being given to genetic relatedness in the decisions,[87] there is also growing

83 Law Commissions, n1, 280.

84 Bracken, n68, 318.

85 For a detailed analysis of the recommendations for the introduction of a surrogacy register, see Wade, Chapter 7, this volume.

86 Law Commissions, n9, 282.

87 For example, the ECtHR has held that there is no requirement for a state to recognise the relationship between IPs and child where both IPs lack a genetic link: *Paradiso & Campanelli v Italy* App no 25358/12 (24 January 2017); *Valdis Fjölnisdóttir and others v Iceland* App no 71552/17 (18 May 2021).

recognition of how non-genetic IPs are formative in a surrogate-born child's identity. For example, in the ECtHR's 2019 advisory opinion,[88] it held that there must be a legal mechanism by which a non-genetic IP can have their relationship with the child legally recognised to align with the child's identity, a decision subsequently supported by, and applied in, more recent case law.[89]

There is also growing recognition of how non-genetic IPs are formative in children's identity within domestic case law.[90] In *D v ED*, Russell J stated that the non-genetic parent was fundamental to the children's identities having 'played a full part in the process of their conception', with the IPs being 'planned and intended parents from before conception and since the day on which they were born'.[91] Therefore, the case law of the ECtHR and domestic courts increasingly refer to children's identity rights as a basis for requiring recognition of the relationship between the non-genetic IP and child, appreciating the formative role that a non-genetic IP plays in the conception of the surrogate pregnancy and their intention to act as a social parent. On this basis, it can be asserted that – even absent a genetic link with at least one IP – non-genetic IPs should have the ability to have their parenthood recognised, in accordance with their actions and planned intention since before conception.

Resultantly, the child's right to identity can be used both to support and contest the retention of the genetic link requirement. Retaining the requirement will ensure surrogate-born children have access to information about one genetic parent when IPs engage with international surrogacy and utilise anonymous gametes. However, it can also be argued that the genetic link requirement fails to respect the role of non-genetic IPs in the child's identity.

Conclusion

The themes emerging from the consultation project would appear to justify a departure from the genetic link requirement. Allowing parenthood

88 European Court of Human Rights Grand Chamber, 'Advisory Opinion Concerning the Recognition in Domestic Law of a Legal Parent-Child Relationship between a Child Born through a Gestational Surrogacy Arrangement Abroad and the Intended Mother' (Request no P16-2018-001, 10 April 2019).

89 *KK and Others v Denmark* App no 25212/21 (ECtHR, 6 December 2022); *DB and Others v Switzerland* App nos 58817/15 and 58252/15 (ECtHR, 22 November 2022) (French judgment machine translated 6 March 2023). For further discussion of recent ECtHR case law, see Iliadou, Chapter 9, this volume.

90 A systematic review of reported s54 decisions and the use of the concept of identity within the judgments is undertaken in Lottie Park-Morton, n33.

91 *D v ED (Parental Order: Time Limit)* [2015] EWHC 911 (Fam) [62].

following surrogacy to be recognised absent a genetic link ensures consistency with other forms of ART, better reflects the intention of all parties, and can support the child's welfare and identity interests. Concerns over the commodification and commercialisation of children, and a blurring of the divide between surrogacy and adoption, can be combatted through means other than continuing to prioritise genetic relatedness in the attribution of legal parenthood.

The recommendation for a non-genetic single applicant to be able to be recognised as a legal parent following a relationship breakdown is a very narrow exception that recognises the importance of the non-genetic IP's role in the child's conception and their intention to become the social parent of the child. The justifications for this exception to the genetic link requirement, however, can – and should – be applied more broadly.

There are circumstances where a genetic link between the IP(s) and child may be lacking, thus preventing parenthood from being established, despite the legitimate intentions of the IPs to become the parents of the child. To take one example, although the risk may be low, there is the potential that incorrect embryos or gametes are used during fertility treatment, resulting in the child not being genetically related to the IPs despite the actions and intentions of the IPs to use their own gamete(s). In such circumstances, the IPs would have acted in good faith, and with a legitimate expectation of parenthood, but through no fault of their own would not be able to be recognised as the child's legal parents either on the new pathway or through a parental order. This risk is not just hypothetical – there have been reported cases of clinical error resulting in incorrect gametes being used. In *Paradiso & Campanelli v Italy*,[92] a DNA test found no genetic link between the intended father and child, despite the intended father having provided his sperm for treatment. It was unknown how the error at the clinic arose.[93] Although not a surrogacy case, *Leeds Teaching Hospitals NHS Trust v A* also exemplifies the possibility of clinical error resulting in incorrect gametes being used.[94] There, it was held that the intended father could not be said to have consented to the incorrect sperm being used in treatment, resulting in him being unable to obtain legal parenthood.

Therefore, the exception to the genetic link requirement following relationship breakdown is welcome: it is an important exception that recognises the intention of the non-genetic IP and would best meet the interests of all parties. However, it does not go far enough. If the Law Commissions acknowledge that, in such circumstances, genetic relatedness

92 *Paradiso & Campanelli v Italy*, n6.

93 ibid, at [31].

94 *Leeds Teaching Hospitals NHS Trust v A* [2003] 1 FLR 412.

should not determine legal parenthood, this should be recognised and applied in a broader range of circumstances. This could be done in two ways. First, the requirement for a genetic link could be removed in its entirety, adopting an intention-based model for parenthood. However, it must be acknowledged that such an approach could result in a surrogate-born child not having access to any origin information following international surrogacy arrangements, contrary to their right to identity. Alternatively, the genetic link requirement could be retained, but with the exception being framed more broadly to ensure the law caters for the exceptional cases – such as clinical error – and does not operate to prevent legal parenthood being established contrary to the legitimate expectations of the IPs and what would best secure the interests and rights of all parties.

6

Reconsidering Payments to the Surrogate: Can the 'Ambiguities' be Resolved?

Alan Brown

Introduction

In March 2023, the Law Commissions of England and Wales and the Scottish Law Commission published their final report and recommendations for changes to surrogacy law,[1] alongside a draft Surrogacy Bill.[2] The 587-page report[3] represented the culmination of a lengthy law reform project.[4] The project was situated against the background of calls for reform of the existing legal regime regulating surrogacy arrangements in the UK.[5] The Law Commissions concluded that 'the current law governing surrogacy does not work in the best interests of any of the people involved: children born though surrogacy, women who become surrogates, or intended parents',[6]

1 Law Commission and Scottish Law Commission, *Building Families Through Surrogacy: a New Law: Volume II: Full Report* (Law Com No 411, Scot Law Com No 262, 29 March 2023).

2 Surrogacy Bill, available at https://s3-eu-west-2.amazonaws.com/lawcom-prod-storage-11jsxou24uy7q/uploads/2023/03/3.-Surrogacy-draft-bill.pdf (last accessed 3 July 2024). Part 3, clauses 39–50, provides the proposed new statutory regime relating to payments.

3 The draft Bill is similarly lengthy: 129 clauses and seven schedules.

4 Law Commission and Scottish Law Commission: Joint Consultation Paper, Building Families Through Surrogacy: a New Law (Law Com Consultation Paper No 244, Scot Law Com Discussion Paper No 167, 6 June 2019).

5 See, for example, Kirsty Horsey and Sally Sheldon, 'Still Hazy After All These Years: the Law Regulating Surrogacy' (2012) 20 *Medical Law Review* 67 and Amel Alghrani and Danielle Griffiths, 'The Regulation of Surrogacy in the United Kingdom: the Case for Reform' (2017) 29 *Child and Family Law Quarterly* 165.

6 Law Commissions, n1, para 1.8.

and that '[i]t is clear from the engagement we have had with consultees throughout this project, and in particular from those personally affected by the impact of the current law, that the law must be reformed'.[7] These are statements with which almost all familiar with the legal regime would agree. However, determining *how* that regime should be reformed to address those issues represents a less straightforward task, as the law reform project illustrated.[8] The previous UK government issued an 'interim response' to the report in November 2023, which stated 'parliamentary time does not allow for these changes to be taken forward at the moment'.[9] Given there is now a new government in place, it is to be hoped that these proposals will one day be brought before Parliament.

The focus of this chapter is on only one aspect of the proposals – payments (generally payments from intended parents (IPs) to the surrogate) within surrogacy arrangements. The current approach has been the subject of much academic criticism.[10] This criticism provides my foundation, as I consider the proposed law reform within this context, before adopting a wider perspective and, through this, offer some potential solutions that may better address the issues with the current law. Thus, I first set out the current approach to payments, and the criticisms of that regime. Thereafter, I consider the Law Commissions' proposals, and whether they are likely to successfully address the criticisms of the existing regime. I argue that the proposals have been designed to address some of the criticisms of the existing law without fundamentally altering (or properly reconsidering) the policy underpinning the existing legal framework. Given this, I set out some different policy rationales that could underpin a reformed regulatory regime governing payments within surrogacy arrangements. Finally, I explore whether the 'ambiguity' regarding the position of payments within surrogacy arrangements that is apparent in both the existing regime and the Law Commissions' proposals, is inherent to *any* attempt to regulate such payments, or whether the ambiguity results

7 ibid, para 1.9.

8 ibid, paras 1.44–1.69, detail the significant opposition to the proposed reforms from organisations (for example, Nordic Model Now!) that advocate for the complete prohibition of surrogacy. However, the terms of reference of the reform project were premised upon 'a context in which Government supports [surrogacy's] use' (para 1.7). As such there was no consideration of prohibiting surrogacy in the report.

9 Letter from Maria Caulfield MP, 8 November 2023, available at https://cloud-platform-e218f50a4812967ba1215eaecede923f.s3.amazonaws.com/uploads/sites/30/2023/03/Law-Commission-Letter.pdf (last accessed 3 July 2024).

10 Claire Fenton-Glynn, 'Outsourcing Ethical Dilemmas: Regulating International Surrogacy Arrangements' (2016) 24 *Medical Law Review* 59; Emily Jackson, Jenni Millbank, Isabel Karpin and Anita Stuhmcke, 'Learning from Cross Border Reproduction' (2017) 25 *Medical Law Review* 23; Alan Brown, 'Surrogacy Law Reform in the UK: the Ambiguous Position of Payments to the Surrogate' (2021) 33 *Child and Family Law Quarterly* 95.

from the lack of a clearly explained and asserted regulatory rationale for either the current law or its proposed replacement.

The current law concerning payments

Before considering the proposals, it is necessary to set out the current legal regime and summarise the criticisms of that regime. The current law, and these criticisms, provides the starting point from which the Law Commissions proceed, and addressing the criticisms represented a core part of the law reform project.[11]

Previously, I have described payments within surrogacy arrangements as being 'situated in an ambiguous regulatory position'.[12] This ambiguity arises because of the interaction of different legislative provisions passed at different times for different purposes, and the 'creative' approach to statutory interpretation subsequently adopted by the judiciary when determining legal parenthood.[13] Section 2 of the Surrogacy Arrangements Act (SAA) 1985 Act prohibits various activities relating to surrogacy arrangements if they take place 'on a commercial basis'.[14] However, those prohibitions do not apply to the surrogate[15] or to IPs.[16] Therefore, the SAA 1985 only prohibits third-party commercial involvement in surrogacy arrangements.[17] This was a deliberate policy choice reflecting the views expressed by the Warnock Committee.[18] The SAA 1985 began the ambiguous treatment of payments through this approach of partially prohibiting commercial surrogacy, but not prohibiting the making of *any* payments between the parties. There is some apparent regulation of payments[19] through the process for granting a parental order – a post-birth order transferring legal parenthood from the surrogate[20] to the IPs. The 'conditions' for parental orders are provided by

[11] Law Commissions, n1 (see, for example, paras 12.16 and 12.41).

[12] Brown, n10, 96.

[13] See Mary Welstead, 'Surrogacy: One More Nail in the Coffin' (2014) *Family Law Journal* 1637.

[14] SAA 1985, s2(1).

[15] ibid, s2(2)(a).

[16] ibid, s2(2)(b).

[17] ibid, s2(5)–(8) prohibit the involvement of profit-making bodies in surrogacy arrangements, preventing the operation of a commercial marketplace for surrogacy arrangements.

[18] Committee of Inquiry into Human Fertilisation and Embryology, Report Cmnd 9314 (HMSO 1984) ('Warnock Report'), para 8.19.

[19] Horsey and Sheldon describe this regulation as 'visibly ineffective' (n5, 87).

[20] And potentially her husband (or male civil partner), if he is a legal parent by virtue of Human Fertilisation and Embryology (HFE) Act 2008, s35, or wife (or female civil partner) if she is a legal parent by virtue of s42.

s54 HFE Act 2008. However, the judicial interpretation of these conditions has been extensively criticised.[21] Section 54(8) provides:

> The court must be satisfied that no money or other benefit (other than for expenses reasonably incurred) has been given or received by either of the applicants for or in consideration of – (a) the making of the order, (b) any agreement required by subsection (6), (c) the handing over of the child to the applicants, or (d) the making of arrangements with a view to the making of the order, unless authorised by the court.

The approach of the parental order regime on payments is based on three principles: (1) reimbursement of 'expenses reasonably incurred' is permitted; (2) other payments can be 'authorised by the court'; and (3) beyond those two circumstances 'no money or other benefit' can be paid if the order is to be granted. The HFE Act 2008 appears to provide the bases ('expenses reasonably incurred' and judicial authorisation) on which payments are subsequently sanctioned through the transfer of legal parenthood to IPs. The difference between the approaches of the SAA 1985 and the HFE Act 2008 – which results from their different purposes – furthers the ambiguity regarding payments within the current legal regime.

However, the statutory language is not the end of the story. First, there is no statutory definition of 'expenses reasonably incurred', and this has been described judicially as 'a somewhat opaque concept'.[22] This has led to an absence of judicial clarity about what payments are permitted as 'expenses reasonably incurred'. The courts have not always engaged in detailed assessments in individual cases (particularly in domestic surrogacy arrangements) of what is included within such expenses, preferring to accept the information provided by IPs when considering parental order applications.[23] Second, due to the importation of the 'welfare principle' into

[21] See Claire Fenton-Glynn, 'The Regulation and Recognition of Surrogacy under English Law: an Overview of the Case-Law' (2015) 27 *Child and Family Law Quarterly* 83, Kirsty Horsey, 'Fraying at the Edges: UK Surrogacy Law in 2015' (2016) 24 *Medical Law Review* 608, Kenneth Norrie, 'English and Scottish Adoption Orders and British Parental Orders After Surrogacy: Welfare, Competence and Judicial Legislation' (2017) 29 *Child and Family Law Quarterly* 93 and Alan Brown, 'Two Means Two, but Must Does Not Mean Must: an Analysis of Recent Decisions on the Conditions for Parental Orders in Surrogacy' (2018) 30 *Child and Family Law Quarterly* 23.

[22] Hedley J in *Re L (A Child) (Parental Order: Foreign Surrogacy)* [2010] EWHC 3146 (Fam) at [7].

[23] See *Re Human Fertilisation and Embryology Act 2008; Re A, B and C (Infants)* [2016] EWFC 33.

s54 HFE Act 2008,[24] the judicial authorisation envisaged by the legislation has effectively become a rubber-stamping exercise. As Hedley J put it, 'it will only be in the clearest case of the abuse of public policy that the court will be able to withhold an order if otherwise welfare considerations support its making'.[25] This position has occurred because, as Fenton-Glynn has commented, 'it will rarely be in the child's best interests to refuse to recognise the parenthood of the persons who are acting as such'.[26] Thus, the courts have consistently granted legal parenthood to IPs in cases where they have paid significant sums of money to surrogates,[27] and third-party agencies.[28] The Law Commissions noted that they were 'not aware of a case where a parental order has been refused on the basis of payments exceeding what is reasonable, under section 54(8) of the HFEA 2008'.[29] The role of judicial authorisation of payments has been described by academic commentators as 'a fait accompli'[30] and as 'undermin[ing] the rule of law'.[31] Despite what seems implied by s54, the parental order process does not, in practice, operate as an effective regime for regulating payments, because orders appear to be *always* granted regardless of the scale of payments made. Thus, as Jackson et al argue, '[t]he legislation therefore fails to stop payments, while failing to provide legal certainty about what is and is not allowed, and also potentially deterring the acquisition of legal parenthood'.[32]

There is a contrast between policy and practice when it comes to payments within surrogacy arrangements. The policy envisages a restrictive approach to

---

24 Human Fertilisation and Embryology (Parental Order) Regulations 2010, Schedule 1. This imported the Adoption and Children Act 2002, s1(2), which provides: 'The paramount consideration of the court or adoption agency must be the child's welfare, throughout his life'.

25 *Re L*, n22, at [10]. See further *J v G (Parental Orders)* [2013] EWHC 1432 (Fam) and *Re WT (Foreign Surrogacy)* [2014] EWHC 1303 (Fam).

26 Fenton-Glynn, n10, 62.

27 For example, payments of $47,715 to the surrogate (plus 'reasonable expenses') in *Re W* [2013] EWHC 3570 (Fam), and $56,750 in *J v G (Parental Orders)* [2013] EWHC 1432 (Fam).

28 For example, payments of $65,700 ($48,000 paid to a surrogacy agency) in *P-M (Parental Order: Payments to Surrogacy Agency)* [2013] EWHC 2328 (Fam) and of around $48,000 (the vast majority not to the surrogate) in *Re X (Foreign Surrogacy: Child's Name)* [2016] EWHC 1068 (Fam).

29 Law Commissions, n1, para 12.40.

30 Jackson et al, n10, 35.

31 Claire Fenton-Glynn and Jens Scherpe (on behalf of Cambridge Family Law), *Surrogacy: Is The Law Governing Surrogacy Keeping Pace With Social Change?* (2017), Response to the Law Commission of England and Wales Consultation on its 13th Programme of Law Reform, 4, available at www.law.cam.ac.uk/sites/www.law.cam.ac.uk/files/images/www.family.law.cam.ac.uk/documents/cambridge_family_law_submission.pdf.

32 Jackson et al, n10, 35.

payments. However, in practice, the exclusion of the parties to the surrogacy from the prohibition on 'commercial activities' under the SAA 1985, and the 'creative' judicial interpretation of s54(8) HFE Act 2008, particularly in cases involving international commercial surrogacy arrangements,[33] means that there is (at best) limited enforcement of this restrictive framework. Ultimately, this contrast led to my previous description of payments as having an 'ambiguous position' within the regulatory framework. Therefore, it has become difficult to describe (or locate) the policy rationale that underpins the approach to payments within the current legal regime. Unsurprisingly, these issues did not escape the Law Commissions[34] and, in the next section, I consider the extent to which the proposed reforms effectively address the ambiguities of the current approach.

The Law Commissions' proposed reforms

The Law Commissions propose a new regime for regulating payments within surrogacy arrangements.[35] Chapter 12 makes clear that 'asking whether surrogacy in the UK should be able to operate commercially, or altruistically, does not answer the question of what payments the IPs should be permitted to make to the surrogate'.[36] The approach of chapter 12[37] is to deliberately not engage with the underlying policy question of whether surrogacy should be available commercially in the UK.[38] Neither does it start from the related question of whether surrogates should be paid for being surrogates,[39] even while continuing to prohibit an overarching commercial regime.[40] I accept there is not necessarily a clear and simple distinction, either conceptually or in practice, between 'altruistic' and 'commercial' models of surrogacy.[41]

33 Law Commissions, n1, para 16.3 notes: 'It appears to be the case that international surrogacy arrangements may now account for up to half of parental order applications'.

34 ibid, para 12.41.

35 ibid, chapter 12.

36 ibid, para 12.5.

37 This reflects the approach taken in the joint consultation paper (n3), paras 2.12–2.18 and 14.3.

38 See Kirsty Horsey, 'Surrogacy in the UK: Further Evidence for Reform', Second Report of the Surrogacy UK Working Group on Surrogacy Law Reform, (December 2018), 15–19, which suggests that the classification of regulatory approaches to surrogacy arrangements requires greater nuance than simply distinguishing between 'altruistic' and 'commercial'.

39 I thank Kirsty Horsey for raising this point.

40 The existence of a 'commercial surrogacy' regime is determined by the legal regulation around the surrogacy arrangement itself – the extent to which third party commercial involvement in various activities is permitted or prohibited.

41 See Sharon Roach Anleu, 'Surrogacy: For Love but Not for Money?' (1992) 6 *Gender and Society* 30 and Anita Stuhmcke, 'The Regulation of Commercial Surrogacy: the Wrong Answers to the Wrong Questions' (2015) 23 *Journal of Law and Medicine* 333, 334, who

However, I argue the question of the permissibility of commercial surrogacy, or of the possibility of payment being permitted for being a surrogate,[42] should have been a more fundamental question than it is in the law reform project. Instead, the Law Commissions state that: '[o]ur overall approach has been to seek to provide greater detail on what payments it should be permissible to make to the surrogate rather than relying on the formula of "expenses reasonably incurred", found in section 54 of the HFEA 2008'.[43] The report proposes an alternative framework for payments, not based upon an 'expenses' model.[44] Chapter 12 acknowledges this, explaining that 'we are not simply trying to capture (and then permit) payments that have been accepted as "expenses" under the current law'.[45] Given the criticisms of the language of 'expenses reasonably incurred',[46] and the lack of clarity resulting from this statutory language, this focus on greater detail and expansion beyond the category of 'expenses' appears unsurprising.

Subsequently, chapter 12 expands upon this, stating that the proposals are underpinned by 'four overarching principles':[47] (1) protection against the risks of women being exploited; (2) the surrogate should not be financially worse off as a consequence of the surrogacy; (3) costs involved are costs typically involved in pregnancy or costs that arise due to the surrogacy pregnancy; and (4) the birth of the child 'should not be tainted with criminality'.[48] These are high level principles, and the first two appear to be relatively uncontroversial for any regime regulating payments. However, as the report observes, 'the need to prevent exploitation cannot generally answer the question as to whether particular categories of payment should be permitted'.[49] Therefore, it is not clear that the prevention of exploitation provides much substantive policy content for the determination of which payments should be permitted, and the scale of those permitted payments.[50]

argued 'that the creation of altruistic surrogacy and commercial surrogacy is a fiction of law'.

42 Law Commissions, n1, paras 12.81–12.102, reject the possibility of 'payments for gestational services' and 'compensatory payments'.

43 ibid, para 12.8.

44 ibid, para 12.2 considers the appropriate language, noting the preference of the report for 'payments' and 'costs', rather than 'expenses'.

45 ibid.

46 ibid, paras 1.9 and 1.64.

47 ibid, para 12.9.

48 ibid.

49 ibid, para 12.11.

50 See Natalie Gamble, Chapter 4 of this collection, who argues that it is not only the regulation of payments but the entire structure surrounding surrogacy arrangements that determines whether a regime is ethical. Thus, a 'commercial' regime could be ethical and an 'altruistic' regime unethical.

This appears particularly true given that many historical critics of surrogacy saw the practice as inherently exploitative, regardless of the form and extent of payments.[51] The first principle would be seen by some as a justification for the complete prohibition of surrogacy arrangements, rather than merely justifying restrictions on payments. The third, through its use of the language of 'costs', appears focused upon drawing the boundary of the types of payments that will be allowed restrictively rather than expansively. The fourth overarching principle replicates the language[52] of the Warnock Report[53] concerning surrogacy arrangements.[54] This principle of avoiding the birth of the child being associated with criminal sanction has underpinned the regulation of payments since surrogacy was first regulated by the SAA 1985 and would continue to do so under the proposed system.

Therefore, I argue that these four overarching principles do not suggest any *significant* policy shift from the current law. This is clear from the language of the report, which emphasises: 'Our recommendations seek to ensure that, as under the current law, women who become surrogates are neither left financially worse off nor do they financially benefit'.[55] The use of the phrase 'as under the current law' illustrates the policy continuity between the current approach and the Law Commissions' proposals. Instead, the Law Commissions' focus is on improving outcomes within the existing policy; as the report states: 'We think that our recommendations on permitted payments will provide a degree of clarity that does not exist in the current law'.[56] Chapter 12 is underpinned by 'three key criticisms' of the current law related to payments identified by the law reform project.[57] The first of which is that '[t]here is a lack of certainty as to what payments are permitted as "expenses reasonably incurred" resulting in concerns as to transparency as to what payments are being made for'.[58] These proposals have been designed to address the criticisms of the existing legal regime, in particular the language of 'expenses reasonably incurred', in relation to the clarity

---

51 See Rosemarie Tong, 'The Overdue Death of a Feminist Chameleon: Taking a Stand on Surrogacy Arrangements' (1990) 21 *Journal of Social Philosophy* 40 and Janice G. Raymond, 'Sexual and Reproductive Liberalism' in Dorchen Lediholt and Janice G. Raymond (eds), *The Sexual Liberals and the Attack on Feminism* (Teachers College Press 1990).

52 I previously described this as 'moralistic language': Brown, n10, 100.

53 Warnock Report (n18). The majority of the committee was opposed to surrogacy arrangements, stating, para 8.17: 'Even in compelling medical circumstances the danger of exploitation of one human being by another appears to the majority of us far to outweigh the potential benefits, in almost every case'.

54 ibid, para 8.19.

55 Law Commissions, n1, para 12.15.

56 ibid, para 12.16.

57 ibid, para 12.41.

58 ibid.

provided by the law. The report emphasises that, as a result of this lack of clarity, 'we are unable to say whether payments that are being made are in fact permitted under the law'.[59] Therefore, chapter 12 is premised upon the introduction of greater clarity 'enabl[ing] parties to a surrogacy agreement to understand the types of payments that are and are not permitted'.[60] Promoting clarity is a welcome goal for the legal regime in the context of permissible payments.[61] However, it is somewhat surprising that this focus on clarity was not accompanied by a more fundamental (re)consideration of the underpinning policy relating to payments, as much of the reason for the existing lack of clarity relates to the underlying policy confusion.

More substantively, the report specifies ten categories of permissible payments,[62] which are:

1. costs related to the decision to enter into the surrogacy arrangement;
2. medical, wellbeing and related costs;
3. pregnancy-related items;
4. costs of additional dietary requirements;
5. costs for specified forms of domestic support;
6. travel and 'occasional' overnight accommodation connected to the surrogacy;
7. costs of maintaining contact after birth;
8. the surrogate's lost earnings;
9. two weeks of lost earnings for a person supporting the surrogate;
10. a modest recuperative holiday for the surrogate and her family.[63]

In addition, it provides that 'gifts of a modest nature to the surrogate'[64] would be permitted, as would payments for insurance and certain costs relating to 'screening and safeguarding requirements'.[65] The report describes this as 'a granular approach to the types of costs that intended parents should be able to pay to the surrogate',[66] and it is difficult to disagree with this

[59] ibid.

[60] ibid, para 12.16.

[61] See Brown, n10, 106–108. The report would appear to address some of my previous criticisms of the consultation paper concerning clarity and certainty.

[62] Notably, the Draft Surrogacy Bill (n2) divides these categories into 'permitted costs' (clause 40) and 'permitted discretionary payments' (clause 42), a further distinction between categories of permitted payments.

[63] Law Commissions, n1, para 12.19.

[64] ibid, para 12.20. It is not immediately clear why such gifts are not simply listed as the 11th category of permitted payments.

[65] ibid, para 12.21.

[66] ibid, para 12.117.

description.[67] However, there is no suggestion that maximum values of permissible payments would be specified for any category.[68] This approach appears intended to provide a comprehensive list of the types of payments that will be allowed, drawing a contrast with the current 'expenses reasonably incurred' approach, with the Law Commissions stating: 'No other payments will be permitted to be made'.[69] Despite this seeming clarity, immediately thereafter the report mentions four categories of payment that are not permitted: (1) payments for 'gestational services'; (2) 'compensatory payments for any pain and inconvenience'; (3) payment for 'the handing over of the child'; and (4) payments relating to the surrogate's 'general costs of living'.[70] Given the unambiguous statement that no other payments are permitted, it would appear unnecessary to specify any categories of payments that are not permitted. While this can be understood through the aim of providing greater clarity, it is unclear what benefit exists to mentioning some categories of excluded payments, but not others.[71] This has the potential to introduce unnecessary confusion into what is intended to be a clear statement of what types of payment are permitted, with all others prohibited. However, the report notes: 'Those [categories] that we discuss here are not, therefore, an exhaustive list of prohibited payments, but are categories of payment that have given rise to particular policy considerations during our project'.[72] This approach may potentially *introduce* a lack of clarity, making the situation regarding payments less clear than currently, and some IPs more fearful of making payments that are not permitted, the exact opposite of what is intended.[73]

In addition, chapter 12 makes proposals to reform other aspects of the regulatory regime concerning payments. First, the report states: 'It is essential that there is an effective mechanism to ensure enforcement of the payments scheme that we recommend'.[74] To provide this 'effective mechanism', the report proposes that IPs who have made payments beyond what the new

[67] See Natalie Gamble, Chapter 4, this volume, who argues that the granular approach risks being too prescriptive and having the unintended effect of discouraging some IPs from utilising domestic surrogacy.

[68] Law Commissions, n1, para 12.169, states: 'Where a type of payment is permitted, it is not intended that any statutory cap will be placed on the amount of money that the intended parents can pay the surrogate'. See further paras 12.170–12.176.

[69] ibid, para 12.22.

[70] ibid.

[71] The Draft Surrogacy Bill (n2) does not include reference to any specific categories of payments that are not permitted.

[72] Law Commissions, n1, para 12.80.

[73] I thank Kirsty Horsey for raising this point.

[74] Law Commissions, n1, para 12.225.

regime permits could face civil financial penalties.[75] While it does not specify the level at which these penalties should be set, it does state that 'the amount of the penalty should be linked to the amount of the prohibited payment'.[76] This is explicitly connected to preventing 'a situation where wealthy intended parents see the civil penalty as another cost that is incurred as part of the surrogacy journey'.[77] This proposal is significantly more punitive than the options available within the existing legal regime. However, this approach does not relate impermissible payments to the granting of legal parenthood for IPs, and the report explicitly refers to 'our policy of separating issues of payment from legal parental status'.[78] Perhaps this separation is inevitable given the centrality of the 'welfare test' to determinations of legal parenthood after surrogacy,[79] as the report acknowledges when it states: 'Given the paramount importance of the welfare of the child, we see no other realistic option'.[80] However, the 'welfare test' itself is a creature of statute, not a natural law,[81] and most determinations of parental status (in other contexts) are *not* made on the basis of the child's best interests.[82]

At the same time, the report recommends that (a version of) the existing system of court authorisation for 'payments that go beyond what is otherwise permitted by law or which are excessive, while falling within permitted categories'[83] be retained.[84] This would leave in place a mechanism that has been extensively criticised by academic commentators, and routinely circumvented by the judiciary. This represents another context where the Law Commissions retain the policy of the existing legal framework

---

75 ibid, para 12.52 and paras 12.263–12.284. Such penalties would only apply to domestic surrogacy arrangements, not to international surrogacy arrangements.

76 ibid, para 12.276.

77 ibid, para 12.279.

78 ibid, para 12.251.

79 However, it is clearly arguable that requiring new parents to pay a civil penalty, with potentially significant consequences for the family's economic position is unlikely to serve the best interests of the child. I thank Kirsty Horsey for raising this point.

80 Law Commissions, n1, para 12.51.

81 Given the insertion of the 'welfare test' by the 2010 Regulations, set out in n24, the welfare of the child has been the paramount consideration in judicial determinations of parental orders for less than half of the existence of the order, since it was created in HFE Act 1990, s30.

82 In cases involving 'natural reproduction' (that is, reproduction involving sexual intercourse), the legal rules and presumptions operate without any reference to the welfare of the child, which is instead addressed through determinations of 'parental responsibilities' under the Children Act 1989.

83 Law Commissions, n1, para 12.51.

84 Such authorisation would only be possible under the (retained) parental order process because surrogacy arrangements would not be able to follow the 'new pathway' if they involved such payments. See further ibid, paras 2.29–2.35.

without necessarily justifying (or even fully exploring) that policy. Retaining retrospective judicial authorisation continues the problematic distinction in treatment between domestic and international surrogacy arrangements that is another of the 'three key criticisms' of the current law.[85] I previously described the approach of the joint consultation paper to this criticism as 'disappointing',[86] and the report has not addressed my concerns.[87] Second, while the report reasserts the position that '[s]urrogacy agreements themselves remain unenforceable',[88] this is accompanied by the recommendations that both the surrogate[89] and (in some contexts) the IPs[90] will be allowed to recover payments, representing another significant shift. This allows for the possibility of private enforcement of payments by the parties in the event of disputes, or the breakdown of a relationship between the surrogate and IPs. These proposals, both civil penalties and recovery, are clearly intended to address the criticisms of the current's law approach to enforcement, or the apparent lack of such enforcement,[91] by providing a stronger range of enforcement options.[92] This represents another context (alongside the categories of permitted payments) where the proposals seek to address criticisms of the legal regime while leaving in place the existing policy – in this case the separation of legal parenthood from enforcement of payments and the general unenforceability of surrogacy agreements. Therefore, the lack of clarity of the current law does not appear to be fully addressed by the proposals regarding enforcement.

Despite the proposals concerning payments having been designed to offer more clarity as to the types of payments that are permitted and to strengthen the enforcement mechanisms when payments are made beyond those that are permitted, the proposals do not significantly alter the underlying (relatively restrictive) policy basis on which payments are currently regulated. The extent to which this approach *can* successfully resolve the issues of the current legal regime rests upon whether those issues are based upon the judicial interpretation of the HFE Act 2008, rather than the lack of clear policy underpinning the regime. I have previously argued: '[T]he fundamental point of any proposed reform must be to address [the] ambiguous position

85 ibid, para 12.41.

86 Brown, n10, 110.

87 ibid, 109–110.

88 Law Commissions, n1, para 12.215.

89 ibid, paras 12.213–12.218.

90 ibid, paras 12.219–12.220.

91 ibid, 12.41.

92 See Brown, n10, 108–109. The proposals, particularly in terms of civil penalties and recovery of payments, appear to address some of my criticisms about the consultation paper's approach to enforcement.

[of payments] and set out the principled basis upon which payments are permitted within domestic surrogacy arrangements so as to remove this uncertainty for intended parents and surrogates'.[93] The report itself is premised upon seeking to provide greater certainty for surrogates and IPs,[94] and academic criticism of the law has consistently focused upon the lack of clarity about what payments are permitted. Thus, it would be disappointing if the law was reformed in a manner that changed the substantive rules without addressing these underlying criticisms. Providing this 'principled basis' is fundamental to effectively addressing criticisms of the existing legal regime.

I have also previously argued that 'the issue of whether or not the legal regime permits and facilitates the payment of a surrogate for her services as a surrogate (rather than payments only for "expenses") is more fundamental to the framing of the regime regulating payments than the consultation paper's approach allows'.[95] In its rejection of the significant policy change of allowing 'payments for gestational services', the report notes: 'We consider that such a change would be appropriate only if it was widely supported, and the consultation responses demonstrated that that is not the case'.[96] Given the number of consultation responses received from surrogates themselves, the report is clearly significantly influenced by the views of those most likely to be affected by any changes in the law.[97] Perhaps this pragmatic explanation is reasonable, given the specific role of the Law Commissions in developing the law, but it does not address the underlying questions of policy rationale. Indeed, as the report acknowledges, 'there is, nevertheless, a tension in this situation. The policy considerations that led to limitations being put in place are undermined if surrogacy agreements are simply "exported" to countries and jurisdictions where commercial payments are permitted'.[98] Thus, the criticisms of the current law relating to the distinction in treatment of domestic surrogacy and international surrogacy are largely unaddressed by the proposals.[99]

Overall, while the report contains proposals that appear to represent significant changes from the current regime, particularly potential

93 ibid, 111.

94 Law Commissions, n1, para 1.9.

95 Brown, n10, 98.

96 Law Commissions, n1, para 12.81.

97 See Kirsty Horsey, 'Surrogacy in the UK: Myth Busting and Reform: Report of the Surrogacy UK Working Group on Surrogacy Law Reform' (Surrogacy UK, November 2015), 19–29, for more detail on the views of surrogates regarding payments.

98 Law Commissions, n1, para 12.94.

99 ibid, para 12.95 notes that the 'new pathway' to parenthood is intended to be an 'incentive to intended parents to enter into a surrogacy agreement in the UK rather than going overseas'.

enforcement mechanisms, some much-criticised aspects are retained – for example, retrospective judicial authorisation of payments exceeding those permitted. Thus, despite the laudable focus on providing greater clarity and strengthening enforcement mechanisms, the underlying policy of the current legal regime appears to be left largely intact by these proposals. Therefore, the 'principled basis' of regulation is not set out, and the conceptual uncertainties and ambiguities regarding the position of payments – whether they are to be encouraged or discouraged, whether commercial surrogacy should be prohibited, tolerated, or promoted – remain. In the next section, I move beyond criticism of the proposals and seek to offer some potential solutions to the regulation of payments. Within this, two distinct (but related) questions are foregrounded: (1) What are the different rationales for the regulation of payments within surrogacy arrangements? (2) Are such ambiguities inherent to *any* attempt by a single domestic legal regime to regulate payments in the contemporary, globalised world?

Potential policy rationales for the regulation of payments

There are various policy rationales that *could* underpin the legal regulation of payments. Broadly speaking, these can be distinguished based on relative restrictiveness or permissiveness. Therefore, which rationale *should* be adopted becomes a matter of judgement underpinned by a regulatory regime's policy aims. I have previously described some of the options for the 'principled basis' on which such payments could be regulated, as follows:

1. a clarification and strengthening of the current approach based upon 'altruism' and a resulting model in which only clearly defined 'expenses' can be paid to the surrogate;
2. a model of payments based upon providing 'compensation' for the surrogate for various costs incurred as a result of the surrogacy;
3. a model which clearly and explicitly accepts that the surrogate can be paid for her services as a surrogate.[100]

The first represents a policy approach based upon improving the existing statutory language ('expenses reasonably incurred') and framework, combined with some form of stricter enforcement mechanisms. In the UK context, a policy approach allowing for only clearly defined expenses to be paid would likely result in smaller amounts being permitted to be paid

[100] Brown, n10, 111. In this context, I further noted, 'whether or not that acceptance is accompanied by any other aspects of a fully marketised regime of "commercial surrogacy"'.

than occur under current practice.[101] This assumes that such expenses would be defined restrictively, as opposed to the permissive approach currently adopted. In contrast, the second and third approaches would both involve sanctioning payments beyond those that currently appear permissible. As the Law Commissions noted: 'Compensatory payments for a range of events are paid under the current law'.[102] This practice does not reflect the statutory language, nor the apparent policy, of the legal regime, but rather the manner in which the provisions have been interpreted judicially. However, none of these options were adopted in the report, which rejects the language of 'expenses'[103] (as in the first option), while also rejecting the possibility of 'compensatory payments'[104] (the second option) and 'payments for gestational services'[105] (the third option) being payable to the surrogate. Instead, the report did not set out any clear rationale for its regulation of payments.

However, taking a wider perspective, these three suggested bases can be understood as ranging from the most restrictive ('expenses only') to the most expansive ('payment for services as a surrogate'). Indeed, it would also be possible to adopt a fourth policy approach that is significantly more restrictive than the current law, which would result in a model where *all* payments to the surrogate are prohibited domestically.[106] This provides the full spectrum of potential 'principled bases' for a regulatory rationale. It would also be possible, and likely, for the policy rationale of any legal regime to incorporate more than one of these bases. An approach based upon allowing payments for services as a surrogate (the most expansive potential basis) would likely allow payments that were permitted under the first ('expenses') and second ('compensation') basis, given that these represent more limited bases for permitting payments. It would be somewhat paradoxical for payments

[101] Law Commissions, n1, paras 12.27–12.34, provides some (incomplete) data on payments currently made to surrogates. This includes a review of 52 court files that showed that, 'the median payment made by the intended parents to surrogates in domestic surrogacy arrangements was £14,795.54. The mean payment was £13,535.18'. See also Horsey, Chapter 3, and Gamble, Chapter 4, this volume.

[102] ibid, para 12.97.

[103] ibid, para 12.2 and 12.8.

[104] ibid, para 12.99, the report notes: 'We are persuaded by the views of consultees that provision for compensation is difficult to separate from paying the surrogate for her gestational services'.

[105] ibid, paras 12.82–12.83.

[106] Separately, it would be possible to adopt a model where surrogacy was entirely prohibited domestically (as in France or Italy), but this would not solely relate to the regulation of payments, but access to fertility treatment and an absence of mechanism for transferring legal parenthood to IPs. It would also be possible to have criminal sanctions on engaging in surrogacy (either domestically or internationally) as have recently been enacted by the Italian government.

for being a surrogate to be allowed without compensatory payments and expenses being allowed, unless compensatory payments and expenses are understood as being inherently contained within payments for gestational services.[107] There is further complexity regarding the form of regulation, because there are a range of different legislative regimes that could be designed and implemented within each overarching 'principled basis'. This reflects both the practicalities of statutory language, other aspects of the regulatory regime,[108] and that, as Horsey has previously put it: 'There are many different permutations of surrogacy'.[109] However, despite this, my (relatively simple) argument is that regardless of which overarching option was chosen, the underlying policy for the regulation of payments would be clearly articulated and understood, and the specific legal rules would reflect and give effect to that policy. Undoubtedly, any of these options would address the criticisms of the current law relating to certainty and clarity. Choosing any of these policy bases should assist in addressing the criticisms in relation to enforcement, because it would be easier to design and implement effective enforcement mechanisms for a legal regime where the policy rationale has been clearly provided.

However, where the adoption of a clear regulatory rationale may not address the criticism of the current legal approach, or the proposed approach of the Law Commissions, is in relation to the potential disparity between payments permitted in domestic surrogacy arrangements and payments retrospectively authorised by the court in international surrogacy arrangements.[110] This leads to the second question regarding potential regulatory regimes, the extent to which the ambiguities regarding the position of payments are inherent to *any* attempt to domestically regulate surrogacy arrangements. This becomes the fundamental question, given that different jurisdictions adopt (and will continue to adopt) different approaches to permissible payments for domestic surrogacy, and IPs are likely to continue to travel to undertake surrogacy arrangements in those jurisdictions with more permissive regimes. Unless a legal regime adopts the most expansive option for payments domestically then, regardless of the policy of the regime, the question will arise of what

[107] Similarly, the second basis ('compensation') would likely allow for expenses to be paid for the same reasons.

[108] For example, the approach adopted to enforcement of any limitations on permitted payments, the processes for recognising the legal parenthood of the IPs, and the relationship between such enforcement and legal parenthood.

[109] Horsey, n38, 19. She suggests that there are 'three interlinked aspects' that can be used when describing surrogacy as either altruistic or commercial – 'Types of Payments', 'Service Model', and 'Contractual Frameworks' – with each aspect containing different options. This typography is helpful in illustrating the complexity within each overarching model.

[110] Law Commissions, n1, para 12.41.

approach should be taken towards children born through international surrogacy arrangements involving payments that were permitted under the legal framework of that foreign jurisdiction that would not have been permitted under the domestic framework. The same problem that currently arises for courts when deciding whether to authorise payments in international commercial surrogacy arrangements and grant parental orders under s54 HFE Act 2008 would continue to arise *in some form*.

I have previously argued that 'if the regulatory approach accepts a difference in the scale of payments permitted in domestic surrogacy arrangements and those sanctioned in international surrogacy arrangements then this acceptance should be explicit, rather than implied'.[111] Nevertheless, in answering the questions posed above, whether or not this acceptance is explicit there would remain divergence between payments that were effectively permitted; even if that permission was tacit and/or retrospective for international surrogacy. This divergence would mean that ambiguity about the position of payments within the legal regime would remain, alongside ambiguity regarding the justification for the distinction between the treatment of payments within domestic and international surrogacy arrangements.[112]

I have also previously argued that 'when international commercial surrogacy is being considered judicially, it is compliance with the underlying regulatory regime in the foreign jurisdiction that is effectively being scrutinised by the court'.[113] I reiterate the argument in favour of making explicit that this compliance within the requirements of the jurisdiction in which the surrogacy arrangement takes place is what the domestic regime is examining when considering whether to grant legal parenthood to the IPs. However, reforming the basis on which determinations about legal parenthood after international surrogacy arrangements are made does not change the underlying position that the existence of different legal regimes in different jurisdictions results in some level of ambiguity about the legal approach to payments, if payments that are not permitted domestically can be made in international surrogacy without this affecting legal parenthood. This issue could be addressed through stricter legal rules regarding the access to legal parenthood for those IPs that use international commercial surrogacy.[114] However, this would require a different conceptualisation of the role of 'the child's welfare' in the determination of legal parenthood after

[111] Brown, n10, 112.

[112] Law Commissions, n1, paras 12.91–12.95 seeks to justify this dichotomy.

[113] Brown, n10, 112.

[114] The creation of the 'new pathway' will create a distinction between (some) domestic surrogacy arrangements and international surrogacy arrangements in terms of the attribution of legal parenthood, but the proposals do not provide any additional restrictions on the parental order process for international arrangements.

surrogacy,[115] which (to say the least) appears a very unlikely prospect. This suggests that some ambiguity is inherent to *any* potential legal regulation of payments from the IPs to the surrogate that does not allow payments for being a surrogate to be made domestically, because it is not possible to strictly enforce the boundaries of the domestic legal regime when IPs travel abroad and comply with (more permissive) rules in another jurisdiction. Resultantly, while there are benefits to adopting a clear regulatory rationale this (in and of itself) will not necessarily remove all ambiguities regarding payments.

Conclusion

This chapter has considered the legal regulation of payments from the IPs to the surrogate – critiquing both the current legal approach and the Law Commissions' proposals for reform – before exploring potential policy rationales that could have been adopted to underpin a reformed approach to payments. While it is accepted that the proposals represent an improvement on certain aspects of the current law, particularly regarding clarity and enforcement mechanisms, the proposals do not represent a significant shift in the underlying ambiguous policy basis on which payments are regulated. I explored whether providing a clearly articulated 'principled basis' for the regulation of payments would address this ambiguous position. Ultimately, it is suggested that ambiguity concerning payments is inevitable in any legal regime that includes both restrictions on permissible payments domestically and potential recognition of legal parenthood after international commercial surrogacy. Therefore, while some criticisms of both the current law and its proposed replacement would undoubtedly be addressed through clearly establishing the underlying policy basis on which payments are to be regulated, merely setting out a 'principled basis' for regulation does not necessarily remove the ambiguous position of payments. Instead, removing this ambiguity is only possible through adopting a permissive substantive policy basis for the regulation of payments, which may not be supported for a variety of other reasons.[116] Therefore, it is concluded that due to the globalised nature of surrogacy arrangements and the impossibility of preventing IPs from travelling across borders, any domestic legal regime regulating payments can either be restrictive and ambiguous or permissive and unambiguous, but it cannot be both restrictive and unambiguous.

[115] However, see the approach of the European Court of Human Rights in *Mennesson v France* App no 65192/11 (26 June 2014) and *Labassee v France* App no 65941/11 (26 June 2014), to the issue of legal regimes seeking to enforce strict limitations on legal parenthood after international surrogacy, in jurisdictions where the domestic rules are restrictive.

[116] It is not my intention to make a substantive argument in favour of any one policy approach for the regulation of payments. Although clearly the logic of my argument regarding the problems caused by ambiguity appears to favour a permissive approach.

7

The Creation of the Surrogacy Register: A New Dawn for Children's Rights in Relation to Origin Information?

Katherine Wade

Introduction

Chapter 13 of the joint final report of the Law Commission of England and Wales and the Scottish Law Commission proposes the establishment of a surrogacy register (SR) to regulate storage of and access to origin information for children born through surrogacy.[1] This was proposed because the existing framework for accessing genetic and gestational information for those born through surrogacy is considered unfit for purpose. The Law Commissions recommend that the SR include identifying information about surrogates, intended parents (IPs) and gamete donors for all surrogacy agreements; this includes domestic and international, gestational and traditional arrangements, including those on the 'new pathway' and those following the parental order process. The recommended new pathway proposes a system for domestic arrangements, overseen by a regulated surrogacy organisation (RSO),[2] where legal parenthood would be conferred on IPs upon the child's birth.[3] Parental orders, which transfer legal parenthood from the surrogate and her spouse/

---

1 Law Commission and Scottish Law Commission, *Building Families Through Surrogacy: a New Law: Volume II: Full Report* (Law Com No 411, Scot Law Com No 262, 29 March 2023).

2 Organisations that would be licensed by the Human Fertilisation and Embryology Authority (HFEA) to supervise surrogacy arrangements entering and proceeding on the new pathway.

3 Law Commissions, n1, chapter 2.

civil partner (if relevant), to the IP(s), would be retained for arrangements that do not meet proposed eligibility requirements for the pathway and for international arrangements.[4]

This chapter analyses the proposed SR framework, including the information proposed to be recorded, the suggestions regarding the age at which access to information would be granted, and recommendations regarding birth certificate notification of surrogacy. It also considers the extent to which the current framework is in line with a children's rights-based approach. Arguably, while the proposed SR is a major step forward for the protection of the identity and autonomy rights of those born through surrogacy, some key recommendations lack clarity. In particular, the lack of congruence with the law on access to information about gamete donors would need to be addressed if the SR were introduced. In addition, the recommendations regarding arrangements involving anonymous surrogates/gametes could have sought to implement measures to work towards parity in the enjoyment of children's rights regarding access to origin information in assisted reproduction for all children born through surrogacy.

Origin information

This chapter concerns surrogate-born people's rights in relation to preservation of and access to 'origin information'. This term is not used in the Law Commissions' report or their preceding consultation.[5] It is used here to cover three types of information: that regarding genetic, gestational, and intention-based origins.

Genetic origins

Legal recognition of a person's interest in knowing their genetic origins has been developing for some time.[6] For example, the Children Act 1989

---

4 ibid, chapter 10.

5 Law Commission and Scottish Law Commission, Joint Consultation Paper, *Building Families Through Surrogacy: a New Law* (Law Com Consultation Paper No 244, Scot Law Com Discussion Paper No 167, 6 June 2019).

6 See Katherine Wade, 'Reconceptualising the Interest in Knowing One's Origins: a Case for Mandatory Disclosure' (2020) 28(4) *Medical Law Review* 731, Vardit Ravitsky, 'Autonomous Choice and the Right to Know One's Genetic Origins' (2012) 44(2) *HCR* 36, 37 and Mhairi Cowden, '"No Harm, No Foul": a Child's Right to Know Their Genetic Parents' (2012) 26(1) *International Journal of Law Policy and the Family* 102.

amended the Adoption Act 1976 to establish an adoption contact register, enabling contact between adopted people and genetic relatives.[7] A right to know one's genetic identity has also been recognised in cases involving the establishment of parentage, where there is a clear trend in favour of ensuring that children have accurate information about their genetic parentage.[8] In 2004, the UK prospectively abolished gamete donor anonymity, allowing donor-conceived people to access identifying information about their donor at age 18.[9] The right to know one's genetic origins has also been recognised by the European Court of Human Rights (ECtHR). In *Mikulić v Croatia*,[10] a violation of the applicant's Article 8 right to private life was found because Croatia's system of paternity testing had, due to serious delays, left her in a 'state of prolonged uncertainty as to her personal identity'.[11] It was stated that '[p]rivate life, in the Court's view, includes a person's physical and psychological integrity'[12] and that respect for 'private life' must also comprise to a certain degree the right to establish relationships with other human beings.[13]

Gestational origins

The term 'gestational origins' appeared in the consultation paper. It was defined as knowing about 'the fact that one was carried by a surrogate, and the identity of the surrogate'.[14] It was argued that gestational origins should be treated no differently from genetic origins, based on Article 7 of the United Nations Convention on the Rights of the Child 1989 (UNCRC), which protects a child's right to birth registration, name,

---

7 Now governed by ss56–65, 80 and Schedule 1 of the Adoption and Children Act 2002 and the Disclosure of Adoption Information (Post-Commencement Adoptions) Regulations 2005. See Andrew Bainham and Stephen Gilmore, *Children: the Modern Law* (4th edn, Jordan Publishing 2013) 700–704.

8 See, *Re H (A Minor) (Blood Test: Parental Rights)* [1997] Fam 89; *Re T (Paternity: Ordering Blood Tests)* [2001] 2 FLR 1190; *Re D (A Child) (Paternity)* [2006] EWHC 3545 (Fam); *Re F (Paternity: Jurisdiction)* [2007] EWCA Civ 873; *Re R (Parental Responsibility)* [2011] EWHC 1535 (Fam), *AB v CD* [2019] EWHC 1695 (Fam).

9 Human Fertilisation and Embryology Authority (Disclosure of Donor Information) Regulations 2004. From the coming into force of the Act in 2005, donors could not be anonymous, although anonymous gametes in storage were used after this date. Donor-conceived people who turned 18 from October 2023 have been able to access donor information.

10 App no 53176/99 (7 February 2002).

11 ibid, para 66.

12 ibid.

13 ibid, para 53.

14 Law Commissions, n5, para 3.86.

nationality and the 'right to know and be cared for by one's parents' as well as Article 8 UNCRC, which protects the child's right to 'preserve his or her identity, including nationality, name and family relations'.[15] Empirical evidence regarding the impact of the foetal environment on the child's development and genes was cited in the final report.[16] It is clear that such information is not just important due to its *genetic* relevance and states that research about 'conception and gestation can contribute positively to the quality of relationships and psychological wellbeing within the family'.[17] Including gestational origins as a category of potentially important information for a person's identity is a welcome development, as it recognises that broad categories of information can be relevant for a person's identity, and that such information is not confined to genetic connections.

Intention-based origins

The term 'intention-based origins' is used in neither the consultation paper nor final report and is a newer development in the surrogacy context. This information concerns IPs who initiated the reproductive process, but who do not have a genetic link with the child. In the UK context, such individuals typically engage in surrogacy with another person (for example, a partner) who has a genetic link with the child conceived, since there must be a genetic link with at least one IP for a parental order to be granted.[18] In considering whether such information should be recorded in the SR, the report reflects the broad approach to the potential relevance of information to a person's identity, referring to such individuals as having 'played a role in the formation of the agreement which led to the surrogacy agreement' and as part of the 'narrative of the surrogacy agreement'.[19]

---

[15] ibid, para 10.78.

[16] Law Commissions, n1, para 13.4 citing Edith Heard and Robert Martienssen, 'Transgenerational Epigenetic Inheritance: Myths and Mechanisms' (2014) 157 *Cell* 95 and Ian Cowell, 'Epigenetics – it's not just genes that make us' British Society for Cell Biology, available at https://bscb.org/learning-resources/softcell-e-learning/epigenetics-its-not-just-genes-that-make-us/ (last accessed 26 October 2023). On gestational origins, see Andrea Mulligan, 'Protecting Identity in Collaborative Assisted Reproduction: the Right to Know One's Gestational Surrogate' (2020) 24 *International Journal of Law, Policy and the Family* 20.

[17] Law Commissions, ibid.

[18] s54(1) HFE Act 2008. Applicants must be married, civil partners or 'living as partners in an enduring family relationship and … not within prohibited degrees of relationship to each other'. A platonic relationship was found to satisfy the meaning of 'enduring family relationship' in *W v Y* [2021] EWFC 119.

[19] Law Commissions, n1, para 13.104.

Current law on access to origin information

Genetic origins

Since 1 April 2005, where donated eggs or sperm are used in licensed clinics, individuals conceived this way may, when they turn 18, apply to a register held by the HFEA for the donor's name, date and town of birth, appearance, and last-known address.[20] Thus, surrogate-born individuals may access identifiable information about any gamete donors involved in their conception at age 18, assuming they are aware of their ability to apply. A question that arises is: can surrogate-born individuals find out identifiable information about IPs who contributed gametes? Such a question would only be relevant where an IP is not known to the child, because they did not apply for a parental order or the child remained with the surrogate, without contact with the IPs. The answer to this is not clear in the law, and it seems that the Law Commissions consulted on this point. The report states that currently, where IPs use their own gametes, their information 'will be recorded on the HFEA Register [...] as a donor', although, since 2013, with the prefix 'IP' added 'to show that they are the intended parent, rather than a true donor'.[21] The report states: 'Because they are "not treated as a donor", information about them is not subject to the disclosure provisions'.[22] The point of placing them on the register, the aim of which is collection of information for future disclosure, is not clear; information about them would not be accessible by offspring born through surrogacy. Moreover, it is arguable that IPs are not donors in any sense, since they intend to raise the child born from the use of their gamete in conception.[23]

Another question is to what extent information about genetic origins is accessible by offspring when the surrogate contributes her egg.[24] This

[20] Art 2(3) Human Fertilisation and Embryology Authority (Disclosure of Donor Information) Regulations 2004. They can access non-identifying information at age 16 (Art 2(2)).

[21] Law Commissions, n1, para 13.32. IPs and surrogates do not fall within Sch3, para 5(1) HFE Act 1990, but rather para 5(3), which states: 'This paragraph does not apply to the use of a person's gametes for the purpose of that person, or that person and another together, receiving treatment services'.

[22] ibid. This is because they did not give the necessary consent to be treated as a donor for the purposes of s31ZD(1) HFE Act 1990.

[23] The report makes this point at para 13.32: 'The HFEA does not regard intended parents who provide gametes as donors in the way that they would a "true" sperm or egg donor; that is, someone who simply donates gametes with no expectation that he or she will have an ongoing role in the life of a child conceived with those gametes'. But the report seems to suggest they are, at least, *recorded*, as such.

[24] If the surrogacy takes places in a clinic licensed by the HFEA, surrogates are registered as a patient. This information is not accessible to offspring.

could occur in traditional surrogacy, which the report defines as 'typically, result[ing] from the artificial insemination of a surrogate with the intended father's sperm'.[25] It could also occur where a surrogate's egg is fertilised *in vitro* with the intended father's sperm. The report states: 'The HFEA told us where the surrogate's eggs were used, she would meet the definition of a donor in the 2004 Regulations and therefore it would be possible to identify a traditional surrogate using the provisions'.[26] However, later it states: 'Currently [...] a traditional surrogate would not be recorded as a donor on the HFEA Register'.[27] To decipher the root of this contradiction, it is useful to compare the consultation paper and the report. The former describes a tentative stance from the HFEA, stating:

> The Authority told us that *it thought that*, where the surrogate's eggs were used, it was *arguable* that she might meet the definition of a donor in the Human Fertilisation and Embryology Authority (Disclosure of Donor Information) Regulations 2004 and therefore that, theoretically, it *might be possible* to identify a traditional surrogate using the provisions. However, in practice, such identification would be unlikely to be possible, as the clinic would not have treated the surrogate as a donor, and she would not have given the necessary consent to disclosure of information.[28]

It is unclear from the report whether, in the time period between the consultation and the report, the HFEA clearly stated that a traditional surrogate is treated as a donor.[29] It is also possible that different clinics have different practices.[30] In addition, the report does not explain what occurs where a surrogate's egg is fertilised by the intended father's sperm using IVF, as opposed to through artificial insemination. Therefore, while there is a framework in place to record genetic origins in donor conception, a similar framework does not exist for surrogacy, demonstrating a lack of consistency for children in accessing this form of origin information in different contexts.

25 Law Commissions, n1, para 1.99.

26 ibid, para 13.33.

27 ibid, para 13.175.

28 Law Commissions, n5, para 10.60. Emphasis added.

29 Alan Brown and Katherine Wade, 'Reform of the Legal Framework for Origin Information in Assisted Reproduction' in Charlotte Bendall and Rehana Parveen (eds), *Family Law Reform Now: Proposals and Critique* (Bloomsbury 2024).

30 In conversations I had with two surrogates, one stated that they were not recorded as a donor for either a traditional surrogacy arrangement or an arrangement involving IVF with her own egg and one stated that she was registered as a donor for the surrogacy that involved IVF with her own egg.

Gestational origins

When a child is born through surrogacy, the surrogate is the legal mother.[31] Therefore, the surrogate is named on the long birth certificate and recorded in the register of live births (in England and Wales) or the register of births (Scotland). However, it appears that some children born through surrogacy would not be able to access this birth certificate. Following the granting of a parental order in England and Wales, it is not possible for the General Register Office to provide linking information that would allow a child born through surrogacy to obtain their original birth certificate.[32] This could and did occur before the Human Fertilisation and Embryology (Parental Order) Regulations 2010, and the report notes that it appears to be an oversight that this is no longer possible.[33] In Scotland, after a parental order is granted, access to the original birth certificate is possible.[34] The report is clear that this framework is inadequate, stating: 'None of the current methods for accessing information about one's origins were originally designed for use by people born as a result of surrogacy. As a result, there are gaps in the framework for surrogate-born people, and no clear route specifically for this group to access information'.[35] However, it should be noted that this situation is perhaps unlikely to cause difficulties, at least in domestic surrogacy, as it is more likely that surrogates are known to the IPs and the child.[36] This is due to the altruistic model of UK surrogacy, which emphasises the development of a relationship between surrogate and IPs, and their respective families.[37]

[31] s33 HFE Act 2008.

[32] Law Commissions, n1, para 13.19.

[33] ibid.

[34] ibid, para 13.14.

[35] ibid, para 13.5.

[36] ibid, para 13.165 citing consultation with Natalie Gamble Associates and Brilliant Beginnings. See also Kirsty Horsey, 'Surrogacy in the UK: Myth busting and reform' Report of the Surrogacy UK Working Group on Surrogacy Law Reform (Surrogacy UK, November 2015) at 22: 83 (94.3%) of the 111 surrogates who had completed a surrogacy cycle maintain contact with the children/IPs. 96 (87.3%) said that they knew the IPs they had worked with had told or intended to tell their child they were born through surrogacy. In a 2022 study, 30 of the 31 surrogates who gave birth remain in touch with IPs, with 22 reporting contact 'more than eight times per year' (Kirsty Horsey et al, 'UK Surrogates' Characteristics, Experiences, and Views on Surrogacy Law Reform' (2022) 36(1) *International Journal of Law, Policy and the Family* 1 at 9).

[37] The executive summary of 'Surrogacy in the UK: Myth Busting and Reform' (ibid) emphasises: 'We must guard the principle of altruistic surrogacy in the UK – surrogacy as a relationship not a transaction'. See also the 'friendship first' model of SurrogacyUK, available at https://surrogacyuk.org/2023/09/02/understanding-the-motivations-of-surrogates-in-the-uk/ (last accessed 2 July 2024).

Intention-based origins

As noted above, intention-based origins relate to information about people who initiated the reproductive process, but who do not have gestational or genetic links to the child. It is possible that some intention-based origin information is collected and is accessible. In England and Wales, a surrogate-born person can apply for court records at the age of 18.[38] This allows access to the parental order application form, the order, any other orders, the transcript, and the report from the parental order reporter (a court-appointed reporter from CAFCASS who interviews the surrogate and IPs).[39] In Scotland, at age 16, a person can access court proceedings regarding the parental order.[40] However, it appears that information would not be recorded about intention-based origins in the following circumstances: (1) one IP was not party to the order (due to a breakup or change of mind, for example) and no information was recorded about them;[41] (2) if an order was not applied for and the child remained with the surrogate and her partner (if applicable), was placed in care,[42] or adopted;[43] and (3) where a child remains with IP/s who do not apply for an order. These scenarios would likely be very rare but, nonetheless, information would not be accessible to surrogate-born children.[44]

The proposed surrogacy register

Scope and procedure

The Law Commissions recommend the SR record information for both gestational and traditional surrogacy agreements on both the new pathway or following a parental order, whether that be from domestic or international agreements.[45] Their report sets out the procedure for placing information on the SR. As a prerequisite for entering the new pathway, 'required identity information' would be provided to the RSO, for inclusion on a regulated surrogacy statement (RSS),[46] which would be sent to the SR after the birth

---

38 Law Commissions, n1, para 13.20.

39 ibid. This would presumably include information about the surrogate, and possibly information about whether she was traditional or gestational, as an alternative route for children to find out gestational origins.

40 ibid, para 13.22.

41 ibid, para 13.36

42 ibid.

43 Adoption records would record the surrogate and her partner (if applicable) as the birth parents.

44 Law Commissions, n1, para 13.36.

45 ibid, para 13.70.

46 This refers to a signed agreement regarding legal parenthood of IP(s) and a statement that statutory checks have been carried out.

of the child.[47] Where an application for a parental order (England and Wales)/ petition to the court (Scotland) is made, the report recommends that the information should be sent from the court to the SR, whether or not the order is granted.[48]

It is important to note that the report takes a clear children's rights-based approach. Chapter 13 opens by stating that '[w]e think it important that children learn about both their genetic and gestational origins', citing children's identity rights under Articles 7 and 8 UNCRC, interests children have in accessing information for establishing contact and for health reasons, and research on the value of openness and identity formation.[49]

Recorded information

Recommendation 61 sets out what the Commissions suggest should be recorded in the SR, stating 'the SR should record identifying and non-identifying information about surrogates, intended parents, and gamete donors involved in surrogacy agreements, with the exception of information about gamete donors other than the intended parents, which should continue to be recorded in the HFEA Register'.[50] From this, it is clear that identifying and non-identifying information about surrogates and IPs should be recorded. The next part of the recommendation, however, is unclear. It states that 'gamete donors involved in surrogacy agreements, *with the exception of* information about gamete donors *other than* the intended parents' should also be recorded.[51] There are several issues with this wording. First, it seems to suggest that IPs contributing a gamete should be categorised as 'gamete donors'. This implication is contradicted elsewhere in the report. In chapter 10, it states '[b]y "donor" we mean individuals other than the surrogate and intended parents who provide gametes used in a surrogacy arrangement'.[52] This latter approach seems more appropriate; IPs are unlikely to see themselves as 'gamete donors', since that terminology is used for those who donate gametes without the intention to raise the child. Moreover, designating IPs 'gamete donors' appears contradictory to the proposed new pathway, which allows for IPs to be legal parents at birth, which is never the case for a donor.

Second, it is unclear what individuals are being referred to in this group of 'gamete donors': IPs and identity release donors are excluded. It also

[47] Law Commissions, n1, para 8.190.
[48] ibid, para 13.77.
[49] ibid, para 13.4.
[50] ibid, para 13.88.
[51] Emphasis added.
[52] Law Commissions, n1, para 10.147.

cannot refer to 'known donors', which are donors who are known to the IP/s. When such donors are used in a clinic setting (which they must be for the new pathway)[53] then they will be treated as identity release donors, with their information placed on the HFEA register, meaning they are also not captured in the category the Law Commissions refer to. The only group it could possibly refer to are gamete donors from other jurisdictions, where identifying and non-identifying information is available. However, this is not clear.

Third, the recommendation does not clarify whether the fact that the surrogate used her own egg should be recorded, unless such surrogates are seen as 'gamete donors'.[54] There should be parity between children born through gamete donation and surrogacy; if those born from gamete donation can access identifying information about their donor, children born through surrogacy should have access to information about whether the surrogate used her own gamete. In addition, later recommendations relate to contact between people born of the same surrogate. If the SR does not record whether the surrogate used her own egg or not, these individuals will not know if they are genetically related, which would create a different system from the one used for donor-conceived individuals via the Donor Sibling Link.[55]

Other parts of the report provide some guidance about what the SR should record. For example, recommendation 39 sets out what should be included in the RSS, which must be sent to the SR by the RSO under the new pathway as follows:

(6) identifying details of those involved in the surrogacy agreement: the intended parents and the surrogate, and the Regulated Surrogacy Organisation;
(7) details of whose genetic material is being used in conception:
  (a) identity in the case of the surrogate, intended parents, and known donors;
  (b) details of how to access information regarding identity-release donors via the HFEA Register of gamete donors; and
(8) prescribed non-identifying information regarding the intended parents, surrogate and any known donors.[56]

[53] ibid, para 8.18(5): any donor gametes/embryo used must be screened by the licensed clinic in line with standard procedures.

[54] However, note the comma between surrogate, intended parents and gamete donors, suggesting all three are separate categories.

[55] Donor Sibling Link is run by the HFEA and allows people who share the same donor to exchange contact details with one another. See www.hfea.gov.uk/donation/finding-out-about-your-donor/donor-sibling-link-dsl/ (last accessed 26 October 2023).

[56] Law Commissions, n1, para 8.190.

This is a clearer iteration of the information that should be recorded in the SR. The lack of clarity about recording whether the surrogate used her own egg is cleared up by this separate recommendation. However, it should be noted that known donors will be placed in the HFEA register of gamete donors, and therefore the above proposal that their identity should be recorded on the SR would circumvent current requirements for donors.

Recommendation 48 concerns the information that must be supplied to the court and provided to the SR as a prerequisite for making a parental order, and therefore gives further guidance as to the information that should be recorded. This refers to

> information identifying:
> (1) the surrogate;
> (2) those who contributed gametes, where those are known (intended parents, surrogate, gamete donor, as appropriate); and
> (3) how to access such details (identity-release donor via the HFEA register, or other source of information).

Notably, this recommendation deals with collecting identifying information about gamete donors. Presumably, for the parental order pathway, this would include known donors used in the UK outside of a clinic or known donors used in another country.[57] Since the parental order pathway includes international surrogacy arrangements, the reference to 'other source of information' refers to ways to access information about gamete donors in other countries. There are some issues with this recommendation. First, IPs are not listed as a separate category to be included; they are included only if they provided a gamete. This must be an unintended omission, as para 4.258 states 'in all scenarios, the surrogate's name would be recorded in the Surrogacy Register, as would the intended parents'. Further, recommendation 62 recommends the inclusion of a *former* IP, who is not party to the order, in the SR.[58]

From a reading of the above three recommendations, a lack of clarity exists regarding the information to be recorded on the SR. Therefore, I suggest this wording:

> The following information should be recorded in the Surrogacy Register for arrangements on the new pathway and arrangements which involve a parental order application:

[57] Gamete donors and known donors used in UK licensed clinics will be on the HFEA register.

[58] See Law Commissions, n1, paras 13.103–13.107.

1. Identifying and non-identifying information about the:
   (a) surrogate;
   (b) intended parent/s (including former IPs who do not apply for a parental order);[59]
   (c) known gamete donors (used outside of UK licensed clinics).[60]
2. It should be recorded if the surrogate and/or intended parent/s contributed their own gametes.
3. Those who contributed gametes who are not surrogates, intended parents or known gamete donors (used outside of UK licensed clinics) are registered in the HFEA Register, and not in the Surrogacy Register.
4. Where identity release donors are used, this fact[61] should be recorded in the Surrogacy Register, with details of how to access information via the HFEA Register of gamete donors or through other means.[62]

This wording makes it clear that, in all cases, information about IPs (unlike recommendation 48), and surrogates should be collected. If the surrogate contributed her egg (via intra-uterine insemination or IVF), this should be recorded (unlike recommendation 61). It uses the terminology of 'gamete contribution' for surrogates and IPs who contribute gametes (not used in recommendation 61 but used in recommendations 48 and 39) and maintains the word 'donors' for known or identity-release donors. It is also clear that the fact that donors were used should be recorded, with a cross-reference to the HFEA register/other means of access (not included in recommendation 61 and included in recommendations 48 and 39).[63]

[59] The report recommends that a former IP who is no longer a party to an order should be recorded (ibid, para 13.104).

[60] Those used within a clinic are placed on the HFEA register.

[61] See Law Commissions, n1, para 8.187: 'We recommend that the details of donors – individuals other than the surrogate and intended parents who provide gametes used in a surrogacy agreement – continue to be recorded on the existing HFEA Register. *The fact of the record on that register would be noted in the SR* so that a person born of a surrogacy agreement seeking that information would know to check the HFEA Register'. Emphasis added.

[62] 'Through other means' refers to applying for information in other jurisdictions.

[63] It could also be recommended that it should be possible to register information on the SR for arrangements that occur before any proposed legal changes. While it might be unlikely that parents would register information on the SR that they would not disclose to their children, it could be relevant for information sharing between children who were born of the same surrogate, the surrogate's own children and the children she gave birth to through surrogacy and to enable individuals born through surrogacy to check if a partner was born of the same surrogate.

Failure or inability to provide information

One issue that could arise is that parties do not or cannot provide information for inclusion in the SR. The report is clear that the use of anonymous gametes would make an arrangement ineligible for the new pathway.[64] However, since anonymous gametes could be used in international arrangements, the report gives some guidance as to what should be done if information is not provided on the application for a parental order. It states: '[T]he court will have the ability to dispense with the identification of the surrogate and those who contributed gametes and allow instead the fact that the surrogate could not be identified, or that anonymously donated gametes were used, to be recorded in the Surrogacy Register'.[65] The Law Commissions do not recommend that a parental order should be refused on the basis that information about the surrogate or gamete donors is not available for inclusion in the SR.[66] This approach would create a lack of parity between the requirements for the collection of identity information for children born through new pathway arrangements and those where parental orders are awarded. This is particularly problematic, because, in comparison to domestic arrangements, where contact between the surrogate and her family and the IP and the child is common,[67] the SR is more likely to be relevant for children born from international arrangements, where such contact may be less likely. The approach is problematic from a children's rights perspective, which requires the equal enjoyment by all children of their UNCRC rights under Article 2.

One way to justify this approach is to concede that the non-provision of information for the SR does not adequately protect children's rights under Article 7 and 8, but to argue that seeking to disincentivise this practice through barring IPs from parental order applications, if they do not provide information for the SR, is a disproportionate measure. This is because the alternative to a parental order is an adoption application, which would not recognise the true nature of the surrogacy arrangement, and therefore would not adequately capture the manner of a child's conception and birth (another aspect of their identity).[68] Permitting parental order applications

---

64 Law Commissions, n1, para 8.236. The report states at para 8.227: 'The main argument in favour of excluding these agreements from the new pathway comes from respecting children's rights. Under the UNCRC, children have the right to know their genetic origins'.

65 ibid, para 10.164.

66 ibid, para 10.158.

67 See n36.

68 See *Re A (A Child)* [2015] EWHC 911 (Fam), where Russell J (at [64]) stated: 'Parental orders will provide [the children] with a registration and documentation which designates a "whole of life" identity as members of the Applicants' family [...] In contraposition adoption certificates imply a change of family and wrongly suggest that the children have

arguably better ensures the lifelong welfare of the child, which would remain the 'paramount consideration' of the court in deciding whether or not to grant an order.[69]

Nonetheless, a system of civil penalties could have been considered, whereby parents are fined if they fail to provide origin information for the SR. This would mirror the recommendations for commercial surrogacy, whereby the Law Commissions recommend that while courts should be able to approve payments in granting parental orders, they can also refer any 'prohibited payments' in either domestic or international surrogacy to a state enforcing authority which could enforce civil penalties, such as fines.[70] This is an approach that recognises the importance of compliance with the proposed requirements, while adhering to the welfare of the child principle. This is because it separates the issue of disincentivising payments from the determination of legal parenthood of the child.[71] It would enable the court to grant a parental order, while also being able to separately address parents' non-compliance with domestic rules. In addition, the government could draw up a comprehensive guide for IPs considering international surrogacy, which should include information and research on the importance of children having access to origin information.[72] Proceeds from the fines could be used to promote the dissemination of these guides in hardcopy and online format for clinics, online forums and support groups. Therefore, I would add the following paragraph to my proposed wording earlier in this chapter:

> 5. In the circumstances, where parties are unable to provide any of the above information, as much information as possible must be given.

Age of access to information in the surrogacy register

The report makes recommendations regarding the age at which surrogacy-born people should be able to access information contained in the SR. It recommends that in England and Wales a surrogate-born person should be able to access non-identifying information at 16, and identifying information at 18.[73] In Scotland, access to identifying and non-identifying information

had a disrupted rather than continuously secure identity within their family, the only family they have ever known'.

[69] Law Commissions, n1, para 10.40.

[70] ibid, para 12.176.

[71] ibid, para 12.175.

[72] See ibid, para 16.211, where the Law Commissions suggest guidance regarding nationality and immigration consequences of international surrogacy. Inclusion of information on origin information was discussed at para 16.202 citing Wade and PRCGAR.

[73] ibid, para 13.156.

should be permitted at 16.[74] Acknowledging the inconsistency, the Law Commissions justify this distinction based on the different law on capacity in the two jurisdictions.[75]

The report recommends that in England and Wales, children aged 16 and 17 should be able to access identifying information unless they lack capacity in relation to the decision under the Mental Capacity Act 2005.[76] It also recommends that children under 16 should be able to access identifying and non-identifying information where they are '*Gillick* competent', that is, when they 'achieve a sufficient understanding and intelligence to enable [them] to understand fully what is proposed'.[77] It also recommends access to the same information below the age of 16 in Scotland where children meet the statutory test for legal capacity. In all cases, the Law Commissions recommend that children must have 'been given a suitable opportunity to receive counselling about the implications of accessing the information contained in the Surrogacy Register'.[78] Unlike the current law on access to donor information, this approach would allow children to access identifying origin information before the age of 18. This recognises that a child's autonomy develops throughout childhood, and that they may reach a stage where access to information about their origins is appropriate, even in the absence of parental consent.[79] This also recognises a child's right to participate in decisions affecting them and their evolving capacities, as protected by Articles 12 and 5 UNCRC respectively.[80] Although it is not explicit, the above proposals suggest that access without concurrent parental consent is envisaged, given that this is the traditional use of the *Gillick*/capacity test. However, accessing information about a donor without parental consent or knowledge could carry risks. If children contacted the donor and the donor did not wish to have contact or the meeting did not go well, lack of parental support could exacerbate the potential for psychological harm. Therefore, an alternative approach would be to allow access to origin information through a dual application with consent from a parent and consent or assent

[74] ibid. This difference is due to the age of legal capacity being 16 in Scotland (Age of Legal Capacity (Scotland) Act 1991).

[75] ibid, para 13.146.

[76] ibid, para 13.156.

[77] ibid, para 13.156. The report recommends adapting the test of legal capacity from s2(4ZA) Age of Legal Capacity (Scotland) Act (which deals with medical treatment) to allow children under 16 to access information where they can demonstrate that they are 'capable of understanding the nature and possible consequences' of the decision.

[78] ibid, para 13.156.

[79] See Wade, n6, 738–742.

[80] ibid.

from the child,[81] and to allow for sole applications from those with *Gillick* competency, without parental consent in more exceptional circumstances, where it is considered that not having access to the information is not in the child's best interests. One point to add, however, is that it is important that those who assess children's competence/capacity have the expertise to do so.[82] Allowing access without parental knowledge to origin information is a significant decision and professionals who conduct these assessments will need to understand the implications of disclosure and be able to assess whether children also understand these.[83] In addition, if the above approach to surrogacy was introduced, the law on access to gamete donors should be brought into line with this.[84]

Additional aspects of disclosure

For arrangements on the new pathway, the report recommends children have access to the RSS, with the same rules relating to age of access as applied for the SR, after being offered appropriate counselling.[85] This would include the origin information discussed above, confirmation that the welfare of the child assessment was undertaken, evidence that the eligibility, screening and procedural requirements were met, and a statement about legal parenthood and living arrangements for the child.[86] The report also proposes that a surrogate-born person who was the subject of a parental

81 By consent, I mean the consent of a *Gillick* competent child. By assent, I mean the agreement of a child who does not have *Gillick* competence. Allowing children of younger ages to have access to information through assent would be relevant for children who are curious about this information, have expressed a wish to access it and have their parents' support.

82 Law Commissions, n1, para 13.147.

83 ibid.

84 The HFEA has recommended a different approach in relation to gamete donation, that is, to allow parents to have access to identifying information about donors after the child's birth by request. I do not propose this, as it does not allow for children to be involved in accessing their origin information and means parents can have access without their child's knowledge: HFEA, *Modernising Fertility Law: Recommendations from the HFEA for Changes to the Human Fertilisation and Embryology Act 1990 (as amended)* (HFEA, November 2023), available at www.hfea.gov.uk/about-us/modernising-the-regulation-of-fertility-treatment-and-research-involving-human-embryos/modernising-fertility-law/ (last accessed 26 January 2024).

85 Law Commissions, n1, para 13.253–13.255. I would argue for the same approach as above, namely, allowing access below 16 without parental consent in exceptional circumstances.

86 ibid, para 9.15.

order should have access to the full court file.[87] For arrangements that start on the new pathway and move to the parental order pathway where a surrogate withdraws her consent,[88] such court files would presumably involve details of her reasons, as well as her and the IPs' arguments for an order to be granted in their favour. The report does not suggest redacting information about incapacity of the parties, surrogacy breakdown, or money being exchanged.[89] The Law Commissions argue that even if information in a court file might be distressing in the rare circumstances of a breakdown, this consideration is outweighed by the need to ensure surrogate-born people can access information.[90] In relation to information about expenses to surrogates, they argue: 'If the surrogate-born person was made aware that information was being withheld, without knowing what it was, this could be as psychologically and emotionally damaging to them as the information itself. We think openness and honesty should underpin our approach to surrogacy and to access to information'.[91] They also note that, as is currently the case, counselling should be offered before access to the file is granted.[92] This is a holistic approach to the collection and disclosure of origin information, and arguably broadens the type of information that is available to include the 'circumstances of their conception and birth'.[93]

The report considers the broader network arising through surrogacy; it recommends that two surrogate-born people with the same surrogate should be able to identify each other with the consent of both[94] and that surrogate-born people and the surrogate's own child(ren) should be able

[87] ibid, paras 13.245–13.246. The same recommendations regarding age of access as above apply. Access to court files is currently permitted at 18 in England and Wales and at 16 in Scotland (see paras 13.20–13.22).

[88] Under the proposed new pathway, a surrogate could withdraw consent to the arrangement either before birth or up to six weeks after birth, which may result in the IPs or surrogate applying for a parental order. See ibid, para 4.106 and paras 4.124–4.127.

[89] ibid, para 13.243.

[90] ibid, para 13.243(3). This is likely also the reason for the requirement for counselling, to seek to ameliorate any negative effects.

[91] ibid, para 13.243(2). The report also cites preliminary findings from the Children's Voices in Surrogacy Law (CVSL) project, which stated that only one out of five children born through surrogacy voiced concerns about knowing their surrogate had been paid. In the final CVSL report, five out of seven did not think that payment would negatively affect children born through surrogacy, whereas two voiced some concerns (Katherine Wade, Kirsty Horsey and Zaina Mahmoud, 'Children's Voices in Surrogacy Law: Phase One Preliminary Report' (January 2023), available at https://childrensvoices.bristol.ac.uk/).

[92] Law Commissions, n1, para 13.243(4). See Family Procedure Rules 2010, r13.16(2).

[93] The report does not recognise a new category of information but refers to providing children with a 'breadth of information so that they can understand their origins' (ibid, para 13.248).

[94] ibid, para 13.189.

to identify each other with the consent of both.[95] The same proposed rules regarding age of access as above apply. These recommendations apply regardless of whether there is a genetic link between the individuals. The Law Commissions based this on the argument that, while some people may have no interest in meeting others born to the same surrogate, others might have an interest in meeting someone with whom they share a 'gestational link'. The report states: 'Throughout the project, we have tried not to overemphasise the significance of genetics, and we think that surrogate-born people should be able to decide for themselves how important it is that they are gestationally and perhaps genetically related to someone else'.[96] This reasoning reflects a positive step towards recognising the autonomy of those born through surrogacy, as well as the children of surrogates, since these recommendations leave it to these individuals to decide the importance of genetic and gestational links for themselves. In a similar vein, the Law Commissions recommend that a surrogate-born person should be able to find out, through the register, if a person they are intending to marry, enter into a civil partnership with, or have a sexual relationship with, was carried by the same surrogate, irrespective of whether they are genetically related.[97] The Law Commissions are of the view that, in cases where is no genetic link, it is for individuals to decide the significance of sharing a gestational link with a potential partner.[98]

Disclosure of the fact of surrogacy

The above sections concern recording and accessing origin information. Another issue is whether children should be notified that they were born through surrogacy and that information is available about their origins. It should be noted that it is more likely that children born through surrogacy will know about this and, at least in domestic arrangements, know their surrogate, since parents are more open about surrogacy than gamete donation.[99] For example, a 2012 study involving children born through surrogacy found that, at age 10, all children born through traditional surrogacy had been

95 ibid, para 13.209.

96 ibid, para 13.187.

97 ibid, paras 13.171 and 13.189.

98 ibid, para 13.168.

99 See Susan Golombok, *Modern Families: Parents and Children in New Family Forms* (Cambridge University Press 2015), 132 and Fiona MacCallum, Emma Lycett, Clare Murray, Vasanti Jadva and Susan Golombok, 'Surrogacy: the Experience of Commissioning Couples' (2003) 18(6) *Human Reproduction* 1334. In the latter study, 100% of the 42 couples interviewed who had a one-year-old surrogate-born child planned to tell their child about the surrogacy.

told about the surrogacy arrangement.[100] Where the surrogacy involves a same-sex male couple or a single father,[101] the use of surrogacy will become apparent to children born through such arrangements. Currently, a person would know they were born through surrogacy from being told or from the parental order certificate.[102] When a parental order is made, the court sends a copy of the certificate to the General Register Office and this replaces the child's birth certificate.[103] As noted above, a person can access their birth certificate (both long and short) at age 18 in England and Wales and 16 in Scotland. In England and Wales, since 2010, following a parental order, a certificate is produced that states: 'Certified to be a true copy of an entry in the Parental Order Register'; this replaces the original birth certificate.[104] In Scotland, the top of the full extract states: 'This is an extract of an entry from a register held by the Registrar General for Scotland'.[105] Therefore, the Law Commissions argue that, for those who access their birth certificate, it will be clear that an order was made. However, there are several issues with the current system. As discussed earlier, following a parental order in England and Wales, it is no longer possible for the General Register Office to provide the linking information that would allow a child born of surrogacy to obtain their original birth certificate.[106] All parental order certificates issued before 2010 will not indicate that an order has been made, meaning that a surrogate-born person may not know that they were born through surrogacy.[107] The report also notes that short birth certificates/abbreviated extracts do not make it clear that it is a copy of the parental order register entry, and therefore a situation where the child does not know that they were born through surrogacy is more likely under the current law (at least for the child of an opposite-sex couple).[108]

---

[100] Vasanti Jadva, Lucy Blake, Polly Casey and Susan Golombok, 'Surrogacy Families 10 Years On: Relationship with the Surrogate, Decisions over Disclosure and Children's Understanding of their Surrogacy Origins' (2012) 27 *Human Reproduction* 3008, 3011. However, only 58% had been told about the use of the surrogate's egg.

[101] In such circumstances, surrogacy will be necessary, outside of cases where a transgender man can carry a pregnancy. See *R (on the application of McConnell & Anor) v The Registrar General for England and Wales* [2020] EWCA Civ 559.

[102] Law Commissions, n1, para 13.215.

[103] ibid, para 13.213.

[104] ibid.

[105] ibid, para 13.18.

[106] ibid, para 13.19.

[107] ibid, para 13.18.

[108] ibid, para 13.36. Neither short birth certificates (England and Wales) nor abbreviated extracts (Scotland) refer to parental orders. See para 13.215 citing Births and Deaths Registration Act 1953, s33(2); Registration of Births, Deaths and Marriages (Scotland) Act 1965, s 9E(5)(a) as applied and modified by the 2018 Regulations, reg 5 and Sch 4, para 3.

The Law Commissions make recommendations regarding notification of the fact of surrogacy, setting out a 'preferred model for birth registration'. On the new pathway, if the surrogate did not object to the IPs having legal parenthood, the IPs would be registered as 'parents' on the birth certificate, which would be marked to reflect the fact that the birth was a result of surrogacy.[109] If the surrogate withdraws her consent before birth, she would be recorded on the birth certificate.[110] IPs could then apply for a parental order and, if it is made in their favour, the certificate replaces the original certificate.[111] The report states that a parental order certificate is clear that the birth is a result of surrogacy.[112] However, it is not clear whether the original birth certificate would show that the birth was a result of surrogacy, if an order was *not* made in the IPs' favour. If a surrogate withdraws her consent after birth, the IPs would be on the birth certificate, which would presumably be marked (as above) to show the birth was a result of surrogacy.[113] However, if she applied for a parental order and it was made in her favour, a certificate would be issued, naming her as the parent, and replacing the original birth certificate.[114]

However, because their primary proposed model does not comply with the government's current stance on birth registration, which requires that the person who gives birth is registered as the mother,[115] the Law Commissions propose an alternative. On the new pathway, the surrogate would be placed on the original birth certificate, and, if she did not object, this would be automatically replaced by a parental order certificate after six weeks.[116] If the surrogate were to withdraw her consent, a certificate would still be automatically issued to the IPs after six weeks and she would have to apply for a parental order.[117] If the order was not granted, the certificate would remain unchanged.[118] If her application were successful, then (1) the surrogate could

[109] ibid, para 4.252.

[110] ibid, para 4.257.

[111] ibid, para 4.257.

[112] ibid, para 13.216.

[113] ibid, paras 4.254–4.25.

[114] ibid, paras 4.256(1)

[115] ibid, para 4.244. See *R (on the application of McConnell & Anor) v The Registrar General for England and Wales* [2020] EWCA Civ 559. Freddy McConnell, a trans man who gave birth to his child, lost the argument that there was an unjustified interference with his Article 8 ECHR rights resulting from the requirement that he be registered as the 'mother' of the child on the birth certificate. This was because maintaining birth certificate coherence served a legitimate aim.

[116] Law Commissions, n1, para 4.261. The surrogate is given six weeks to withdraw consent. The report suggests that both IPs and the surrogate could be named in the relevant statutes as permitted informants who can register the birth (para 4.249).

[117] ibid.

[118] ibid.

be issued with a parental order certificate to replace the original certificate, or (2) the initial entry into the parental order register could be removed and replaced with the original birth certificate with the surrogate's name.[119] In the last scenario mentioned, however, where an original parental order issued to the IPs is removed, it is unclear whether a surrogate-born person would be notified about the parental order application and the nature of the birth through surrogacy on their birth certificate. Should this approach fail to notify the surrogate-born person of this information, it would be inconsistent with the other recommendations above, which seek to ensure children know about the nature of their birth.

In addition to the lack of clarity in some of the above recommendations, additional points must be addressed to ensure the effectiveness of these proposals. First, the report does not address how surrogate-born people should be notified of the fact of their birth through surrogacy. It suggests that it is 'clear from the face' of a parental order certificate (which replaces the original) that a person is born through surrogacy,[120] since it states: 'Certified to be a true copy of an entry in the Parental Order Register'.[121] Arguably, this language is not child-friendly and knowledge of the legal framework for surrogacy would be needed to understand that a parental order refers to a transfer of legal parenthood in surrogacy arrangements. However, the report is explicit that the aim of these recommendations is about *children's* rights in relation to origin information. It states: '[W]e are not persuaded by the concerns of those who consider that the intended parents should be left to decide whether to tell their child of the surrogacy; this is a matter that the child has a right to know'.[122] Clear and child-friendly language should be used for both parental order certificates and birth certificate notifications, to fulfil the aim of notifying children about the nature of their birth.[123] Additionally, the report is not clear whether the birth certificate should also notify a surrogate-born person that origin information is available from the SR, which would be useful in protecting the 'right of the child to know'[124] origin information. Notably, the Law Commissions do not propose to mark short birth certificates/abbreviated extracts with information about surrogacy,

[119] ibid.

[120] ibid, para 13.216.

[121] Certificates in Scotland state: 'This is an extract of an entry from a register held by the Registrar General for Scotland'.

[122] Law Commissions, n1, para 13.228.

[123] On birth certificate annotation regarding donor conception, see Assisted Reproductive Treatment Act 2008 in Victoria. Also, Eric Blyth et al, 'The Role of Birth Certificates in Relation to Access to Biographical and Genetic History in Donor Conception' (2009) 17 *International Journal of Children's Rights* 207.

[124] Law Commissions, n1, para 13.228.

because these certificates may be used as a means of providing identification to government bodies and other organisations.[125] They argue that people should not (in effect) be forced to disclose personal information about their origins whenever identification is required to government bodies and other organisations.[126] While this is reasonable, it means that if a person only ever sees their short birth certificate, they will not know about the fact of their birth through surrogacy. Alternatively, all birth certificates could be marked with the following: 'Further information about your birth is contained in the long birth certificate/full extract. This could include information about surrogacy and/or gamete donation'.[127] This would mean that *all* short birth certificates/abbreviated extracts would include notification as to the availability of further information, without the inclusion of individual information about surrogacy or donor conception.

However, if birth certificate annotation were introduced for surrogacy-born people and the law on gamete donation were not reformed, disparities would arise. Under the current law, it is not evident from the long birth certificates/full extracts of donor-conceived people that they are born through gamete donation, nor is there cross-reference to the HFEA register.[128] This would mean that, in the seemingly rare circumstances where surrogacy-born children are not told of their birth through surrogacy,[129] they would be more likely to find out about the manner of their conception than donor-conceived people. In addition, a person born through surrogacy *involving* gamete donation would be able to find out from the SR (below the age of 18 in Scotland, and in some circumstances in England and Wales) that they were born through gamete donation and that donor information is available from the HFEA register, while children born through gamete donation alone have no such notification system. Therefore, child-friendly notification of the fact of surrogacy and donor conception on long birth certificates/full extracts would be required.

Conclusion

The Law Commissions' report deals with a significant range of issues regarding origin information in relation to surrogate-born people. Due

125 ibid, para 17.15(5).

126 ibid, para 13.231.

127 The inclusion of the second sentence could guard against people glossing over the first, as it provides more details about what such information could include.

128 An amendment to the HFE Act 1990 was considered that would involve annotation of birth certificates to indicate use of donor conception. See *Hansard* HL Deb, vol 515, cols 1308–1310, 13 February 1990.

129 See n36.

to its complex nature, however, some areas lack clarity and gaps emerge. This is particularly the case for recommendation 61, which sets out what information should be recorded. It should be clear that the aim is to collect all information (identifying and non-identifying) about all parties involved in the surrogacy (IPs, surrogates, donors) in all arrangements (domestic and international) and it should also be clear who contributed gametes. In addition, long birth certificates/full extracts and parental order certificates should record the fact of surrogacy in a child-friendly way, with all short certificates/abbreviated extracts signalling the potential availability of additional information on the long certificate/full extract. Though the proposed ages for access to information are a positive development, those who assess capacity/competence of children require appropriate expertise.

Chapter 13 refers to Articles 7 and 8 UNCRC, which are the relevant rights for protection of children's identity.[130] There is also reference to 'enhancing children's autonomy', to justify lowering the age at which access to information is permitted.[131] The use of children's rights principles has meant a shift away from a welfare-based approach. Arguments are not based on unsubstantiated claims about the welfare of the child and, instead, are justified by reference to empirical research and consultation about children's welfare and their views.[132] This is in line with a participatory approach to policy development, as encouraged by the Committee on the Rights of the Child.[133] For example, the report cites the Children's Voices in Surrogacy Law project, which collected children's views about law reform on surrogacy,[134] studies on children's psychological development,[135] and consultation with organisations that have experience of disclosure of origin information to children.[136]

However, as the report notes, Article 2 UNCRC provides that states parties shall ensure the enjoyment by each child of their rights without discrimination.[137] One problematic issue is that those who embark in

130 For Article 7, see Law Commissions, n1, paras 3.50–3.54, 4.248, 8.212, 8.227, 13.4, 13.133. For Article 8, see paras 8.227, 13.4, 13.133 and 13.208.

131 ibid, para 13.133.

132 See further, John Eekelaar and John Tobin, 'Article 3: the Best Interest of the Child' in John Tobin (ed.), *The UN Convention on the Rights of the Child: a Commentary* (OUP 2019) 95.

133 Committee on the Rights of the Child, General Comment No 12 (2009), The Right of the Child to be Heard (CRC/C/GC12), para 12.

134 Law Commissions, n1, paras 13.4 and 13.243.

135 ibid, para 13.4 citing Susan Golombok, *We Are Family* (Scribe 2022) 260–264; 274–280.

136 ibid, 13.133. For example, the report does not propose access to origin information below the age of 18 (as a matter of course), due to advice from the Donor Conception Network that this may be distressing, based on their extensive experience of disclosure.

137 ibid, para 3.45.

international surrogacy could use anonymous donors and surrogates. The report does not place any impediments on IPs being granted a parental order in such circumstances and proposes that, where no identifying information is available, as much information as possible should be recorded in the SR. This could result in a group of children for whom the SR does not provide meaningful origin information, meaning that their rights under Articles 7 and 8 UNCRC are not protected. The recommendations could have done more to seek to disincentivise such practices and require a fine, for example. I also suggest the development of a list of ethical principles for international surrogacy, which would include the use of known or identifiable donors and surrogates, and that efforts should be made to disseminate this to prospective IPs.

The children's rights-based ethos of the report is welcome. The report seeks to protect the interests of children, and the adults they become, in having access to a broad range of origin information and being told about the availability of that information. This represents a shift away from an adult-centric approach that shapes the regulation of access to information about gamete donors.[138] It is hoped that, if these proposals were adopted, the law on access to information about gamete donors would also change, to bring the legal frameworks into line with one another.[139] With some clarification and amendments, as detailed above, the proposals in the Law Commissions' report could not only signal a new law, but a 'new dawn' for people born through assisted reproduction.

[138] Wade, n6, 738–742.

[139] Alternatively, a central register for all types of origin information could be developed, which is beyond the scope of the Law Commissions' proposals and this chapter. See Brown and Wade, n29.

PART III

International Impacts and Perspectives

8

Comparing Surrogates' Healthcare Provision in the UK and California

Zaina Mahmoud

Introduction

Surrogacy remains a niche facet of healthcare, with research on surrogates' health remaining 'woefully sparse'.[1] Until recently, the impact of regulatory frameworks for surrogacy was understudied.[2] This chapter argues that surrogates' experiences highlight broader issues within (maternity) healthcare across jurisdictions,[3] drawing on original empirical research comparing the impact of the legal and health regulatory frameworks on surrogates' lived

[1] Natalie Fixmer-Oraiz, 'Speaking of Solidarity: Transnational Gestational Surrogacy and the Rhetorics of Reproductive (In)Justice' (2013) 34(3) *Frontiers: A Journal of Women Studies* 126, 150; Viveca Söderström-Anttila et al, 'Surrogacy: Outcomes for Surrogate Mothers, Children and the Resulting Families – A Systematic Review (2016) 22(2) *Human Reproduction Update* 260, 272.

[2] Zaina Mahmoud, 'Surrogates Across the Atlantic: Comparing the Impact of Legal and Health Regulatory Frameworks on Surrogates' Autonomy, Health, and Wellbeing' (unpublished PhD, University of Exeter 2023).

[3] While 'maternity' is an inappropriate word, first, because surrogates do not see themselves as mothers and, secondly, because such terminology presumes the decision to sustain the pregnancy, give birth, and raise the child as a mother, 'obstetrics' is arguably more inappropriate. Obstetrics as a field of medicine finds its origins in experiments on enslaved Black women during the antebellum period – see Dorothy E Roberts, *Killing the Black Body: Race, Reproduction, and the Meaning of Liberty* (Pantheon Books 1997) ch 1; Rochelle Maurice, 'We Bawl So We Are Heard: the Stories We Must Tell About Obstetric Racism' (2023) 31 *Sexual and Reproductive Health Matters* 1, 3. Additionally, in the UK, the term refers to physician-assisted care received while pregnant and giving birth, and as will be shown, most births are midwife-led.

experiences in the UK and California.[4] In the UK, an idealised ideology of motherhood upheld by the law permeates some healthcare providers' treatment of surrogates, casting shame and judgement on their decisions to act as surrogates when they do not act as mothers. By comparison, in California, some surrogates' experiences accessing postpartum healthcare reveal how the current healthcare insurance model can detrimentally impact on health and wellbeing.

The chapter begins by outlining relevant aspects of the two jurisdictions' regulatory frameworks. The law in the UK ensures the surrogate's status as the legal mother of the resulting child,[5] and this is reflected to a certain extent within relevant health policy. California's approach to gestational surrogacy[6] recognises surrogates as gestational service providers, responsible for their own healthcare insurance covering the pregnancy and eight weeks following delivery.[7] The second section starts by contextualising the empirical data used in this chapter. From here, the section provides a comparative discussion on surrogates' experiences with maternity healthcare provision in both jurisdictions, revealing how surrogates experienced their treatment by healthcare providers and what this tells us about the regulatory systems. Finally, the chapter proposes regulatory reforms to address the issues highlighted by the empirical data.

The law

Until relatively recently, there was a lack of scholarly discussion regarding the allocation of legal motherhood. The basic rule for legal motherhood had been the old Roman aphorism, *mater semper certa est* (it is always certain who the mother is). As the concept of legal parenthood emerged from 'natural' heterosexual reproduction, relying on biological or 'natural' ties legitimated through marriage, only one mother was ever possible: the person who carried the pregnancy and gave birth. The issue was seemingly so clear-cut, in most jurisdictions, the rule had not even been explicitly formulated, but

---

4 Mahmoud, n2.

5 Human Fertilisation and Embryology (HFE) Act 2008, s33 defines the 'Meaning of "mother"' as 'The woman who is carrying or has carried a child as a result of the placing in her of an embryo or of sperm and eggs, and no other woman'.

6 Following *Re Marriage of Moschetta* 30 Cal Rptr 2d 893, 25 Cal App 4th 1218 (1994) at 1223, California differentiates between traditional and gestational surrogacy, with the former judged akin to adoption, and enforcement of traditional surrogacy contracts found incompatible with parentage and adoption statutes. For more information, see Mahmoud, n2, chapter 2.

7 American Bar Association, *Model Act Governing Assisted Reproduction* (2019) §702.

rather assumed.[8] In this way, *mater semper certa est* merely reflected what were assumed to be plainly clear facts.[9]

Surrogacy, by its nature, bifurcates gestation and social motherhood, challenging the *mater est* principle. While the UK and California responded to this challenge differently, both jurisdictions' legislative arrangements were fuelled by the same goal: protecting the nuclear family. However, as this section shows, the two jurisdictions framed the practice of surrogacy differently. The UK paradoxically viewed surrogates as 'original' mothers who were later replaced by the intended mother/parent. California understood surrogates to be delegated gestational service providers, realising the intended parents' (IPs') intellectual property interest in their genes.

The UK regulatory framework

The emergence and rapid expansion of reproductive medicine posed a threat to the valued institution of the nuclear family,[10] and prompted the establishment of the Committee of Inquiry into Human Fertilisation and Embryology (the Warnock Committee) in 1982.[11] Two years later, the Warnock Report was published, recommending government policy for recent and potential developments in human fertilisation and embryology based on an assumed 'common moral position' on the importance of the nuclear family and an idealisation of motherhood.[12] The Warnock Committee differentiated families formed following surrogacy from those formed through donor conception, holding a surrogate's contribution to be 'greater, more intimate and personal than the contribution of a semen donor'.[13] The Warnock Committee's commitment to idealised motherhood was present throughout the report, describing motherhood as 'closely allied to the undeniably natural process of biological reproduction'.[14] The report reflected an insistent focus on the maternal relationship, seen in the committee's belief that 'the deliberate creation of a child for a woman who is not a partner in such a relationship [was] morally wrong'.[15] That a person

8 Harry Willekens, 'Motherhood as a Legal Institution: a Historical-Sociological Introduction' in Harry Willekens et al (eds), *Motherhood and the Law* (Göttinger Juristische Schriften 2019) 29.

9 *Ampthill Peerage Case* [1977] AC 547; Andrea E Stumpf, 'Redefining Mother: a Legal Matrix for New Reproductive Technologies' (1986) 96(1) *Yale Law Journal* 187, 94.

10 Committee of Inquiry into Human Fertilisation and Embryology, Report Cmnd 9314 (1984) (HMSO), para 2.02 ('Warnock Report').

11 For more on the history and purpose of this Committee, see Chapter 1, this volume.

12 Warnock Report, n10, 3.

13 ibid, para 8.10.

14 ibid, para 2.09.

15 ibid.

'after giving birth, might make a rational decision *not* to become a mother'[16] had not been contemplated, as this was contrary to the idealised ideology of motherhood – wherein the capacity to carry a pregnancy evidenced an innate instinctive parenting ability.[17] The person giving birth was deemed not 'a deputy or substitute mother, but [the] genuine and authentic mother to the child she bears'[18] and, to ensure their legal recognition as mothers, codification of the *mater est* principle was recommended by the Warnock Committee, fuelled by its desire to maintain the nuclear family, viewed as 'the bedrock of traditional values and common sense'.[19] Under the heading 'status', s27(1) of the Human Fertilisation and Embryology (HFE) Act 1990 preserved the traditional understanding of 'mother' in law: 'the woman who is carrying or has carried a child as a result of the placing in her of an embryo or of sperm and eggs, and *no other woman*'.[20] Interestingly, s33(1) of the HFE Act 2008 kept the text the same but changed the section heading to 'meaning of "mother"'. This deliberate change ensured that the 'legal standard' remained conveyed, but no further information was provided.[21] 'Legal mother' is the legal label given to the person who carries a pregnancy and gives birth.[22] Recording the person who gives birth as the legal mother enabled a clear and coherent birth registration scheme, a goal deemed more important than reflecting lived reality.[23] By recognising the surrogate as the legal mother even though she has no wish to be, the law has failed to cater for surrogacy. This outcome was a deliberate measure designed to discourage people from entering surrogacy arrangements.[24]

The law recognises those who carry pregnancies and give birth as mothers, prior to the birth even occurring. In doing so, the law reinforces a perceived (potential) social role (as a mother), rather than that individual's current role.

16 Katherine O'Donovan, 'Enfants Trouvés, Anonymous Mothers and Children's Identity Rights' in Katherine O'Donovan and Gerry Rubin (eds), *Human Rights and Legal History: Essays in Honour of Brian Simpson* (OUP 2000) 66, 77 (emphasis added).

17 Linda Gordon, *Woman's Body, Woman's Right: a Social History of Birth Control In America* (Grossman 1976) 31; Eileen Fegan, '"Ideology" After "Discourse": a Reconceptualization for Feminist Analyses of Law' (1996) 23(2) *J L & Soc* 173, 179.

18 Bernard M Dickens, 'Legal Aspects of Surrogate Motherhood: Practices and Proposals' (UK National Committee of Comparative Law Colloquium, 'Legal Regulation of Reproductive Medicine', Cambridge, 15–17 September 1987).

19 Katherine O'Donovan, *Family Law Matters* (Pluto Press 1993) 39.

20 HFE Act 1990, s27(1) (emphasis added); Warnock Report, n10, para 6.08.

21 *Hansard* HC Deb, vol 475, col 1161, 12 May 2008.

22 *Ampthill Peerage Case* [1977] AC 547, 577; *Re G (Children)* [2006] UKHL 43; *In the matter of TT and YY* [2019] EWHC 645 [54], [133].

23 *In the matter of TT and YY* [2019] EWHC 645 at [234], [243], [244].

24 Gillian Douglas, 'The Intention to be a Parent and the Making of Mothers' (1994) 57 *Modern Law Review* 636, 637.

As described elsewhere, prematurely referring to pregnant people as mothers is presumptuous and impacts on healthcare provision.[25] This second point is discussed in the next section, where discussion of surrogates' experiences demonstrates how the UK legal framework's insistence on surrogates' recognition as legal mothers impacted on their healthcare, to the hindrance of their health in various ways within different contexts. As discussed later, in the UK, the healthcare framework compounds the socio-cultural beliefs underlying maternity care, heightening expectations of 'appropriate' maternal behaviour in pregnancy.

The Californian regulatory framework

As in the UK, traditionally in California the person who gave birth was recognised as the legal mother, regardless of their intentions following birth, and legal fatherhood was allocated to the individual married to the legal mother.[26] DNA testing resulted in the 'geneticisation' of legal fatherhood, prioritising a genetic connection, and this was extended to motherhood, through California's 1975 adoption of the Uniform Parentage Act (UPA) into the Family Code.[27] The UPA allowed parenthood to be established beyond the boundaries of marriage, defining parent–child relationships as 'the legal relationship existing between a child and his natural or adoptive parents incident to which the law confers or imposes rights, privileges, duties, and obligations'.[28] While this rendered legal fatherhood a negotiated relationship arising from the putative father's explicit intention to parent the resulting child,[29] it was not until the first reported American gestational surrogacy dispute, *Johnson v Calvert*,[30] that legal motherhood was also understood as similarly negotiable. This case allowed the California judiciary to redefine 'natural' maternity and view parenthood following gestational surrogacy

25 Zaina Mahmoud and Elizabeth Chloe Romanis, 'On Gestation and Motherhood' (2023) 31(1) *Medical Law Review* 109.

26 *Glona v American Guarantee & Liability Insurance Co* 391 US 73 (1968) at [75]–[76]; *Stanley v Illinois* 405 US 645 (1972); *Lehr v Robertson* 463 US 248 (1983) 260; US Congress Office of Technology Assessment, *Infertility: Medical and Social Choices* (OTA-BA-358, 1988) 282; Janet L. Dolgin, 'Status and Contract in Surrogate Motherhood: an Illumination of the Surrogacy Debate' (1990) 38 *Buffalo Law Review* 515, 526.

27 Uniform Parentage Act (Unif Law Comm'n 1973); SB 347 (1975); Civ Code (West 1983) §§ 7003–7004 (a)–(c), 7600–7730.

28 Unif. Parentage Act (1973), §§ 4-6.

29 ibid §5; Yehezkel Margalit, 'Artificial Insemination from Donor (AID) – From Status to Contract and Back Again' (2015) 21(1) *Boston University Journal of Science & Technology Law* 69, 73.

30 *Johnson v Calvert* 9 Cal Rptr 2d 494, 5 Cal 4th 84, 851 P2d 776 (1993).

through an intellectual property lens, with parental intention privileged over biology.

In this case, Anna Johnson entered a surrogacy contract with the Calverts but, as the pregnancy progressed, the relationship between her and the IPs deteriorated. After birth, Anna sought to retain custody, citing the maternal–foetal bond that had developed.[31] At the lowest level court, Judge Parslow enforced the surrogacy contract and found in favour of the Calverts, basing parenthood on their genetic contribution: 'a unit anchored in shared substance'.[32] The District Court of Appeal concurred, as there could only be one natural mother.[33] The Supreme Court reviewed the case, and concluded genetics superseded gestation, distinguishing between 'the ruling "head" and the labouring "body"'.[34] Judge Panelli's opinion concluded that 'it was not the role of the judiciary to inhibit the use of reproductive technology when the Legislature [had] not seen fit to do so'.[35] To resolve this impasse, the California Supreme Court turned to the parties' intentions, viewing surrogacy as a private arrangement.

Both the surrogate, Anna Johnson, and the intended mother, Crispina Calvert, could adduce evidence of natural motherhood under the UPA, through gestation and genetics respectively. However, the judiciary would recognise only one natural, and hence legal, mother. While all three levels of the California courts concluded Crispina was the natural – and hence legal – mother, their rationales were underpinned by different considerations. The trial court adopted a genetic essentialist approach: the Calverts had parental rights arising out of the property interest in their genes and keeping the Calverts 'delineated as a unit anchored in shared substance' was in the child's best interests.[36] At the next level, the Appellate Court's analysis determined the language used in the UPA was susceptible to more than one reasonable interpretation, presupposing a theory of parenthood based on property, with the Calverts' parental rights rising out of the interest in their genes. As a result, pregnancy was *one* way 'for the "natural mother" to establish a parent and child relationship [...] The statute is silent on whether the woman who gives birth is automatically the "natural mother"'.[37] However, it was not

---

[31] ibid.

[32] Janet L Dolgin, 'Just a Gene: Judicial Assumptions About Parenthood' (1993) 40 *UCLA Law Review* 637, 685.

[33] *Anna J v Mark C* 12 Cal App 4th 977, 286 Cal Rptr 369 (1991); Randy Frances Kandel, 'Which Came First: the Mother or the Egg – A Kinship Solution to Gestational Surrogacy' (1994) 37 *Rutgers Law Review* 165, 175.

[34] *Johnson v Calvert* (n30) at 782; Laura Anne Doyle, *Bordering on the Body: the Racial Matrix of Modern Fiction and Culture* (Oxford University Press 1995) 21.

[35] *Johnson v Calvert*, ibid, at 793.

[36] Dolgin, n32, 685.

[37] *Anna J*, n33, at 377.

the *only* way to establish legal motherhood. If legal fatherhood could be displaced through genetics, so could legal motherhood: Anna Johnson was not the mother, as she did not share a genetic connection with the baby. The California Supreme Court agreed with this interpretation: '"May" indicates that proof of having given birth is a permitted method of establishing a mother and child relationship, although perhaps not *the exclusive one*. The disjunctive "or" indicates that blood test evidence, as prescribed in the [UPA], constitutes an alternative to proof of having given birth'.[38] The court turned to the IPs' intentions and viewed surrogacy as a private arrangement, an exercise of individual autonomy. This intent-based approach similarly implicitly invoked property law as a basis for parental rights and applied an intellectual property paradigm to legal motherhood. The Calverts' intentions to exercise their fundamental and constitutionally protected right to procreate was expressed in the surrogacy contract, and this intention was embodied in the creation of the baby, akin to 'the mental element at the root of intellectual property protection'.[39] In this way, Crispina Calvert, as the one 'who intended to procreate the child – that is, she who intended to bring about the birth of a child that she intended to raise as her own – is the natural mother'.[40]

Consequently, *Johnson v Calvert* shaped the social understanding of gestational surrogacy, with the lack of shared genetic connection between Anna Johnson and the baby diminishing any potential maternal claim she might have. Surrogates' wombs were viewed as 'a rentable space with an underdetermined relationship to motherhood, and little impact on a child's physical and personality traits'.[41] This view was directly influenced by the prevalence of neoliberalism, considered the ideology defining this era,[42] with its central tenets being individualism, profit, market competition, and freedom of choice. Neoliberal rhetoric is accompanied by an expectation that people should be responsible and self-reliant, autonomous from social support, and able to care for themselves without state intervention. People are encouraged to view themselves as 'entrepreneurs of the self', with their value dependent on their economic worth.[43]

---

38 *Johnson v Calvert*, n30, 92 (emphasis added).

39 ibid, 99; Stumpf, n9, 195.

40 *Johnson v Calvert*, ibid, 782.

41 Jaya Keaney, 'The Racializing Womb: Surrogacy and Epigenetic Kinship' (2022) 47(6) *Science Technology & Human Values* 1157, 1162

42 Angela McRobbie, 'Feminism, the Family and the New "Mediated" Maternalism' (2013) 80–81 *New Form* 119.

43 Lois McNay, 'Self as Enterprise: Dilemmas of Control and Resistance in Foucault's The Birth of Biopolitics' (2009) 26(6) *Theory Culture and Society* 55, 65; Paul Du Gay, 'Organizing Identity: Entrepreneurial Governance and Public Management' in Stuart Hall and Paul Du Gay (eds), *Questions of Cultural Identity* (SAGE 2011) 156.

Surrogates were seen as 'entrepreneurs of their own productive, and indeed reproductive, capacity',[44] assumed to participate in arrangements 'primarily because the fee [provided] a better economic opportunity than alternative occupations'.[45] With surrogacy framed as an exercise of autonomy, following *Johnson v Calvert*, gestational surrogacy arrangements were organised through contracts. By nature, surrogacy arrangements are inherently risky and, to mitigate this ineliminable risk, surrogates and IPs in California engage in formal contracting.

These contracts have served as reference points for surrogates (and IPs), anchoring expectations for the relationship and arrangement.[46] However, it is hard – if not impossible – to draft a contract accounting for every possible contingency that could emerge during surrogacy. The substance of these contracts has been governed by various model Acts, chiefly the Uniform Parentage Act 2017 (UPA 2017) and the American Bar Association Model Act Governing Assisted Reproductive Technology (ABA Model Act).[47] Surrogacy contracts contain terms related to, inter alia, medical procedures that may/may not be necessary during pregnancy, expectations about the surrogate's behaviour, expectations about the post-birth relationship and, importantly, healthcare insurance.

The UPA outlines a substantive requirement for health insurance covering the pregnancy and the period of eight weeks postpartum (paid for by the IPs).[48] Importantly, unlike British healthcare, within the American context healthcare is regulated by a patchwork of local, state and federal laws, policies and regulations without centralised governance,[49] heavily emphasising neoliberalism and technological innovation. With a strong cultural emphasis on individual freedom, health is viewed as a personal moral responsibility, requiring monitoring and intervention. Commercial and market interests, rather than healthcare providers, drive medicalisation, with a shift in

44 Melinda Cooper and Catherine Waldby, *Clinical Labor: Tissue Donors and Research Subjects in the Global Bioeconomy* (Duke University Press 2014) 15.

45 John A Robertson, 'Surrogate Mothers: Not So Novel After All' (1983) 13(5) *Hastings Center Report* 28, 29; Laura Lange, 'La Gestation pour Autrui: Quelles Représentions du Corps et de la Volonté?' [2014] *Études* 43, 44.

46 Oliver Hart and John Moore, 'Contracts as Reference Points' (2008) 123 *The Quarterly Journal of Economics* 1.

47 Model Acts are drafted by advocacy groups or, more commonly, the National Conference of Commissioners on Uniform State Laws. These Acts provide specific statutory language that can be introduced verbatim or customized to fit the needs of a specific state. For more information, see Mary Whisner, 'There Oughta Be a Law – A Model Law' (2014) 106(1) *Law Library Journal* 125.

48 *ABA Model Act Assisted Reprod* §702.

49 Thomas Rice et al, 'United States of America: Health System Review' (2013) 15(3) *Health Systems in Transition* 1, 26.

responsibility to individuals. Mainstream American culture amplifies the message that health depends on responsible personal lifestyle choices, while simultaneously and paradoxically emphasising that freedom of choice – including the freedom to engage in unhealthy and risky behaviours – should be maximised.[50] Focusing attention on personal responsibility draws attention away from the role of social environments in shaping health. When looking at surrogacy, this becomes exceptionally important, as surrogates' bodies are constantly monitored, administered and managed before conception even occurs. Their pregnancies are 'even more filled with the trappings of American technobirths' than other women's.[51]

As an uncomplicated pregnancy is estimated to cost around $18,865,[52] and complications can result in costs of well over $250,000,[53] surrogacy agencies require surrogates to have health insurance specifically covering surrogate pregnancy-related costs, or IPs to enrol in an insurance programme.[54] Before surrogacy was as widespread, the rarity of the practice allowed surrogates to claim the costs of surrogacy from their insurance provider without questions. Increasingly, insurance providers listed 'surrogacy' as an exclusion, without further explanation regarding whether this applied to those using a surrogate or acting as a surrogate; in fact, the four largest healthcare insurance providers routinely deny coverage in either case.[55] In 2015, medical providers became more specific with their insurance codes, including the introduction of sub-code Z33.3 specifying 'pregnant state, gestational carrier'.[56] Prior to Z33.3, unless the insurance company, administrator or employer had seen the patient's medical records, it was unlikely that the insurer would have known the pregnancy was related to a surrogacy arrangement. Now, some

---

50 Cayce J Hook and Hazel Rose Markus, 'Health in the United States: Are Appeals to Choice and Personal Responsibility Making Americans Sick?' (2020) 15(3) *Perspectives on Psychological Science* 643, 645.

51 Elizabeth FS Roberts, '"Native" Narratives of Connectedness: Surrogate Motherhood and Technology' in Robbie Davis-Floyd and Joseph Dumit (eds), *Cyborg Babies: From Techno-Sex to Techno-Tots* (Routledge 1998) 198.

52 Elizabeth Rivelli and Les Masteron, 'How Much Does It Cost To Have A Baby? 2024 Averages' *Forbes Advisor* 3 January 2024, availble at www.forbes.com/advisor/health-insurance/average-childbirth-cost/ (last accessed 10 January 2024).

53 Jing Hao et al, 'Maternal and Infant Health Care Costs Related to Preeclampsia' (2019) 134(6) *Obstetrics & Gynecology* 1227, 1230.

54 Personal communication with Centre for Surrogate Parenting, based in Los Angeles (19 January 2019; 11 March 2020).

55 House of Representatives, *HR Rep No. 111-706 (2010)* (2010).

56 World Health Organization, *The Icd-10 Classification of Mental and Behavioural Disorders* (Version: 2015, 2015); Centers for Disease Control and Prevention, 'International Classification of Diseases, (ICD-10-CM/PCS) Transition - Background' (6 November 2015), available at www.cdc.gov/nchs/icd/icd10cm_pcs_background.htm (last accessed 28 May 2022); *Moon v Tall Tree Administrators, LLC* 814 F App'x 371 (10th Cir 2020).

insurance providers retain the right to demand that compensated surrogates reimburse the cost of their maternity care,[57] or reserve the right to deduct any compensation received from a surrogate's insurance coverage.[58] Additionally, insurance providers use loopholes, allowing them to delay coverage for pre-existing conditions for 6–12 months.[59]

Where surrogates are not covered by their own insurance, IPs are responsible for the surrogate's (high) medical costs, and they have two insurance plan options. IPs may purchase a separate insurance plan, as agencies and fertility clinics offer bespoke surrogacy policies that cover the cost of IVF, antenatal and postpartum care, and disability and death.[60] Such policies have ranged in cost from $10,000 to $26,000.[61] Alternatively, IPs may purchase a 'surrogacy maternity contractual liability insurance' plan to cover medical expenses. However, this option is only available for singleton or twin pregnancies and costs $25,000–$28,350 or $42,000–$43,350.[62]

The UK and California's divergent regulatory responses to surrogacy emerged out of different understandings of the practice. The British approach responded to the threat posed to the nuclear family through codification of the *mater est* principle, ensuring surrogates' recognition as legal mothers: surrogates are seen as *replacement* mothers rather than *cures*. Additionally, surrogacy was not viewed as something that could be contracted for or that should be commercial in nature. In contrast, California's neoliberal approach precipitates the IPs' recognition as legal parents, due to their intellectual property interest in their genes, with gestation *delegated* to surrogates as gestational service providers. The next section delves into the impact of the described regulatory frameworks on surrogates.

57 Kaiser Permanente, *2019 Individual Plan Combined Membership Agreement, Disclosure Form, and Evidence of Coverage for Kaiser Permanente for Individuals and Families* (2019), 68.

58 TRICARE, *TRICARE Reimbursement Manual 6010.55-M* (2019) Chapter 4, Section 4, XIV.

59 Meghan Boone, 'It's Only Covered If You Keep It: the Legality of Surrogate Pregnancy Exclusions in Health Insurance Policies' (2013) 14 *Georgetown Journal of Gender & the Law* 677, 688.

60 Summer James et al, 'Avoiding Legal Pitfalls in Surrogacy Arrangements' (2010) 21 *Reproductive BioMedicine Online* 862, 864.

61 Circle Surrogacy, 'Circle Surrogacy IVF and Insurance Costs', available at www.circlesurrogacy.com/parents/how-it-works/programs-costs/ivf-financing (last accessed 28 October 2019); West Coast Surrogacy Inc., 'Surrogate Mother Costs' (2019), available at www.westcoastsurrogacy.com/surrogate-program-for-intended-parents/surrogate-mother-cost (last accessed 28 October 2019).

62 Universal Family Insurance, 'Surrogate Maternity Liability Insurance Plan' *Universal Family Insurance*, available at www.universalfamily.com/surrogate-maternity (last accessed 11 March 2021).

Comparative empirical data

In this section, the data are comparatively analysed to reveal the extent to which the regulatory frameworks in each jurisdiction impacted surrogates' experiences when accessing healthcare while pregnant and giving birth. The sample size aimed to provide a snapshot of surrogacy healthcare in Britain and in California, rather than provide inclusive representation of all surrogates. Qualitative data were analysed through framework analysis, an approach utilised in applied policy research to provide targeted answers about the impact of various policies on populations.[63]

Between July 2019 and January 2021, in-depth semi-structured interviews were conducted with 14 British surrogates and 10 Californian surrogates. The British surrogates had undertaken their journeys between January 2014 and May 2019, and the Californian surrogates had undertaken their journeys between January 2015 and December 2020. The UK government (Department of Health and Social Care (DHSC)) issued its first official guidance on surrogacy, with one document for IPs and surrogates, and another for healthcare providers, in February 2018, after working with, among others, three non-profit surrogacy organisations (Childlessness Overcome Through Surrogacy (COTS), SurrogacyUK, and Brilliant Beginnings).[64] This was a significant moment, demonstrating for the first time the UK government's acknowledgement of surrogacy as a positive practice. The guidance acknowledged that:

> Surrogacy is increasingly becoming an option for starting a family for people who are unable to conceive a child themselves. This guidance is intended to give the reader key information about surrogacy and the relevant legal process in the UK. The Government supports surrogacy as part of the range of assisted conception options.[65]

This guidance, updated twice since 2018, sets out best practice for healthcare providers, aiming to 'normalise surrogacy among healthcare professionals,

---

63 Jane Ritchie and Liz Spencer, 'Qualitative Data Analysis for Applied Policy Research' in A Bryman and RG Burgess (eds), *Analysing Qualitative Data* (Routledge 1994); Liz Spencer et al, 'Analysis in Practice' in Jane Ritchie et al (eds), *Qualitative Research Practice: a Guide for Social Science Students & Researchers* (2nd edn, SAGE Publishing 2014).

64 DHSC, 'Having a Child Through Surrogacy' 28 February 2018 (updated April 2024), all documents available at www.gov.uk/government/publications/having-a-child-through-surrogacy (last accessed 2 July 2024). For more detail, see Pott and White, Chapter 2, this volume.

65 DHSC, 'Care in Surrogacy: Guidance for the Care of Surrogates and Intended Parents in Surrogate Births in England and Wales' (2018, updated 25 April 2024).

and to avoid the embarrassments that sometimes occur when healthcare professionals do not understand these arrangements'.[66] Cognisant that some surrogates interviewed had undertaken surrogacy prior to its publication, the discussion in this section discusses the need for guidance, while noting how DHSC guidance had not been fully incorporated at that point, impacting significantly on surrogates' healthcare provision. However, surrogates' experiences in the empirical research suggested significant gaps in its implementation. Many NHS trusts had not updated their surrogacy guidance in over a decade, and others simply had no policies relevant to surrogacy,[67] with this impacting those who completed their surrogacy journeys prior to the DHSC guidance being published. The interview data revealed how, on occasion, surrogates felt pressure to act as mothers and make certain healthcare decisions accordingly. In particular, surrogates' experiences revealed how the UK legal framework's insistence on surrogates' recognition as legal mothers came into play when surrogates accessed healthcare, to the hindrance of their health in various ways within different contexts. As will be shown, in the UK the healthcare framework compounds the socio-cultural beliefs underlying maternity care, heightening expectations of 'appropriate' maternal behaviour in pregnancy.

Across both jurisdictions, the surrogates interviewed described their decision to become surrogates as *explicitly* to help IPs realize their dream of parenthood.[68] They had not framed their relationship to the foetus/baby as maternal and instead reinforced the IPs' connection with the foetus. Surrogates had not created the embryos; their wombs merely provided the necessary environment for the embryos' development into babies. Surrogates displayed continued detachment and distancing, thereby contradicting ideas of maternal–foetal bonding and social and legal meanings ascribed to motherhood. They never saw the babies they carried as theirs, and did not consider themselves to be mothers. This was especially important in the UK, as their feelings contradicted the law's insistence that pregnancy and motherhood are necessarily intertwined.[69] However, this was not an issue in California, as the doctrine of intention-based parenthood results in gestational surrogates explicitly not being recognised as the mothers of babies born through surrogacy arrangements. Instead, for Californian surrogates, their treatment as gestational service providers is heightened by the neoliberal backdrop within which surrogacy is practised, with the uncontrollable

[66] *Hansard* HC Deb, vol 670, col 69WH, 21 January 2020.

[67] Mahmoud, n2.

[68] Zsuzsa Berend and Corinna Sabrina Guerzoni, 'Reshaping Relatedness: the Case of US Surrogacy' (2019) 6(2) *Antropologia* 83, 87–90.

[69] Mahmoud and Romanis, n25.

nature of pregnancy forgotten. As this section reveals, a pressing issue for Californian surrogates related to gaps present within the current approach to healthcare insurance provision.

Pregnancy and birth are significant events. In the UK, guidelines provided by the National Institute for Health and Clinical Excellence (NICE) highlight the importance of birth plans, with a plan's creation seen as a critical moment of interaction between pregnant people and healthcare systems. They serve as tools outlining expectations and providing information about a pregnant person's preferences to healthcare providers to support the provision of individualised care.

In the UK, all the surrogates interviewed expressed how they insisted that healthcare providers use their names rather than 'mum' or other maternal language during their appointments. Nevertheless, surrogates spoke about being consistently described in maternal terms such as 'mum' or 'the mother' during their healthcare interactions despite their proactive approaches:[70]

> [The consultant] was very keen on referring to me as the mother, and despite me, sort of, very politely saying 'I'm not the mum', that made no difference. (Bella)

> When you're in hospital, everybody calls you 'mum', 'cause that's the assumption, even though you are not. If you look at your medical notes, you know, you're anything and everything except what you really are. (Barbara)

Surrogates identified the lack of continuity of maternity care provision as contributing to their inappropriately designated maternal identities during surrogacy: when there were handovers between various healthcare professionals, some important details, such as those related to personal preferences, were not necessarily transferred, and surrogates found themselves repeating their situation over and over. Healthcare providers' use of maternal language went beyond presupposing their intentions and evidenced a lack of respect for surrogates' autonomy and choices entirely. Surrogates described this maternal terminology as inappropriate and 'patronising', though demonstrated an awareness that *legally* nothing could be done to limit it:

[70] This is not unique to surrogacy, and is noted in clinical settings overall, see: Monica J Casper, 'At the Margins of Humanity: Fetal Positions in Science and Medicine' (1994) 19(3) *Science, Technology & Human Values* 308, 312–13; Richard P Horgan et al, 'Ascertaining Women's Choice of Title During Pregnancy and Childbirth' (2005) 98(2) *Irish Medical Journal* 55, 56. All quotes used in this chapter are allocated to surrogates via a pseudonym.

> Surrogates go into the hospitals, you know, for scans and things, and midwives naturally [go] 'Mum, take a seat.' [*grimaces*] Obviously, I don't think that it should be the law that they don't say it, it makes that awkward situation a lot more awkward. (Bianca)

Along with the use of this maternal terminology, surrogates revealed how they felt an increased expectation to act as 'good mothers' during their pregnancies, birth and the immediate postnatal period. It is not uncommon for pregnant people to not always feel in control of their decisions and to feel pressured by healthcare providers to conform to various societal and legal perpetuations of medicalised birth as normal. As almost all the surrogates in this sample had previously given birth, they understood the importance of birth plans, detailing preferences for, inter alia, the location of the birth, who will be in attendance, what medical intervention(s) would be acceptable, labour management, pain relief, and immediate postnatal care:[71] 'We'd got a copy of it, this birth plan of who was cutting the cord, who was doing this, who was doing, all, literally like, you name it, it was on this birth plan' (Bianca).

Despite creating these birth plans alongside and with the IPs, surrogates' descriptions of their experiences revealed how they felt (m)othered by the healthcare system. While elsewhere, more extreme examples of the impact of denying surrogates' decisions have been described,[72] here the focus is on more common issues, such as over-medicalisation, postpartum care, and handing over the baby.

The over-medicalisation of obstetric healthcare for pregnant people is a noted issue, extending beyond surrogacy.[73] However, surrogates' narratives in their interviews indicated that healthcare providers adopted more conservative protocols with regards to their obstetric care than expected. Almost all the surrogates indicated a preference for natural vaginal deliveries, yet few were able to have this choice realised. Two surrogates described how they were pressured by their healthcare providers to opt for an induced delivery to accommodate the perceived preferences of IPs,

---

71 Rebecca Webb et al, 'When Birth Is not as Expected: a Systematic Review of the Impact of a Mismatch between Expectations and Experiences' (2021) 21 *BMC Pregnancy and Childbirth* 475, 476.

72 Zaina Mahmoud, 'Mandatory (M)othering: an Exploration of British Surrogates' Healthcare Experiences' in Rebecca Brione, Samantha Halliday and Jacqueline Nichols (eds), *Reproduction, Narratives of Consent and Invisible Women* (Routledge forthcoming).

73 Ibone Olza et al, 'Women's Psychological Experiences of Physiological Childbirth: a Metasynthesis' (2018) 8 *BMJ Open* 1, 2.

rather than because of medical indications. One surrogate described how, during her first appointment, the consultant presented her with a 'choice' of an elective Caesarean section or an induction at 38 weeks, explaining how this would allow the IPs to plan for the birth. After discussions with the IPs and the healthcare provider, she opted for an induction at 40 weeks; however, this resulted in a harder delivery and significant postpartum hæmorrhaging.

> From the initial appointment, the consultant said, 'So would you prefer a C-section?' [*pauses*] To someone who had had a natural birth, with no risk factors, normal BMI within the range, you know. I wasn't old – I was fit and healthy. So, to be honest, a C-section or 'We'll induce you at 38 weeks.' I just thought, that's really strange. But I think where the consultant was coming from was to try and give reassurance to the [IPs], you know? […] When asked, I guess, we all decided that I would opt for induction. Um, and in hindsight, maybe, I think, I probably would have liked to hold on a bit [longer]. (Beverley)

Many surrogates described how they were made to perform as mothers in the post-birth period: in some cases, babies stayed in the recovery room with the surrogates in the immediate post-natal period, despite their birth plans indicating a different preference.

> I told them it was surrogacy, probably on about three or four occasions. It was well-documented in my notes, and they were like 'OK, we understand'. […] The staff didn't really acknowledge that these weren't my family members, and I had to stay there like that for a long time, and it was just a little bit embarrassing, and awkward. I didn't have any proper recovery time. (Bethany)

> So [the intended mother] couldn't take the baby out, because legally the baby is mine, so she was outside, and I didn't realise until about 20 minutes the baby was crying, I thought 'God, why is she in here?' Like you know, I can't … I'm, you know, laid down, still being stitched up, I can't get to her obviously! (Bree)

In another example of how surrogates felt (m)othered by the healthcare system, Brandy described how the matron on the ward that she was on refused to acknowledge that she was a surrogate who had given birth to twins, and told her 'you're not going anywhere till I've seen you feed those babies and bond with them'. She continued to describe how this matron would pass by the room periodically: 'She'd come in and she'd say, "I assume this is your husband as he's holding your babies," and she knew full well that wasn't my husband. Yeah, she just made it really, really difficult'. Brandy's negative experiences were a direct consequence of health policies that were not fit for purpose and had not been kept up to date, as her delivery occurred following publication of the previously mentioned DHSC guidance.

Some surrogates were informed by hospital staff that the IPs would not be allowed to leave with the baby. Others described how they were made to hand over the baby to the IPs in hospital car parks. Unfortunately, this was a relatively common practice due to healthcare providers' fear they would be implicated in legal disputes should the exchange occur on hospital premises.[74] Notwithstanding the DHSC guidance specifically outlining how this handover should occur 'in an appropriate place on the hospital premises [...] the parties should not be forced to leave the premises in order to complete this transfer',[75] many surrogates were made to go through this process, feeling judged and shamed as a result: 'I was made to feel like I was doing something secret, that I had to smuggle this baby out' (Bethany).

Surrogates understood the lack of recognition of their choice to become surrogates as impacting on their healthcare experiences. Their experiences revealed how the concept/idea of legal motherhood operated within healthcare contexts in ways that hindered their autonomy, due to healthcare providers' lack of awareness or knowledge regarding medico-legal aspects of surrogacy,[76] outdated policies, and gaps in implementation of the DHSC guidance. These factors contributed to the surrogates feeling that healthcare providers disregarded their decision to become surrogates and, consequently, they felt pressured to prioritise the baby over their own health, in line with expected behaviour of good mothers.[77]

---

[74] See Siobhan Fenton, 'NHS Hospitals Forcing Surrogate Families to Hand Over Newborn Babies in Car Parks Due to "Dire and Outdated" Laws' *The Indpendent* 9 October 2016; Andrew Percy MP, *Report on Understandings of the Law and Practice of Surrogacy* (All-Party Parliamentary Group on Surrogacy, 2020).

[75] DHSC, n65.

[76] Heather Sharon Hodgson, Abigail Nye and Fiona Finlay, 'Consent for Babies Born Following Surrogate Pregnancies' (2021) 106 *Archives of Disease in Childhood* 186. Training provided by the Royal College of Obstetricians and Gynaecologists is also exceptionally minimal: Antony Hollingworth and Maggie Thomson, *Ethical and Legal Issues e-Learning* (Royal College of Obstetricians and Gynaecologists 2016), available at https://elearning.rcog.org.uk/ethical-and-legal-issues/ (last accessed 10 May 2021).

[77] Mahmoud and Romanis, n25.

Pregnancy can be experienced as empowering, especially when the healthcare provided is individualised, reassuring and supportive. Effective communication and engagement among healthcare providers and pregnant people are essential in ensuring that care is responsive to their needs and preferences.[78] Pregnant people, including surrogates, should be referred to by their names in healthcare settings, as a means of promoting their autonomy and 'reinforcing their status as individuals rather than their perceived (potential) social role'.[79] 'I just find it really patronising. And I'm not just mum, I'm me, and the main thing for me is that I'm me' (Bonnie).

Unlike the UK, in California, surrogates' issues were not related to healthcare providers' treatment of surrogates as mothers, as IPs involved in Californian surrogacy arrangements are recognised at birth as the legal parents of the baby, by virtue of a pre-birth parentage order; this order requires the relevant documents to be filed with the court during the first trimester of the pregnancy, as processing them can take up to nine weeks. As the legal parents, the IPs are imbued with responsibility over the baby, including care and medical treatment. Almost all the surrogates interviewed in California had the pre-birth parentage order paperwork completed prior to birth, so the IPs had been immediately legally recognised as the babies' parents. In Celeste's case, as she had a preterm birth, she was the legal parent for the first four days postpartum; in her case the parentage paperwork had yet to be filed with the court. She was, however, adamant that the IPs be the first to interact with the babies; the IPs' lack of legal parental status was difficult for her to reconcile with her role as a surrogate: 'That I was giving them permission to see their own children made me feel, you know, heartbroken for them' (Celeste).

As expected, the Californian cohort's experiences reflect a heightened version of the usual technocratic and individualistic model of healthcare focusing on the 'perfect baby'. The surrogates in the cohort underwent a high level of prenatal testing and invasive diagnostic testing during pregnancy, mostly accepted by the surrogates because they understood themselves to be providing a gestational *service* for the IPs that they were paid for. However, given the risks involved, surrogates were clear that they would only undergo diagnostic testing when it was medically necessary. All the surrogates saw an obstetrician/gynaecologist (OB/GYN) very regularly: at least monthly in the first trimester, bi-weekly in the second trimester, and weekly in the

78 World Health Organization, *WHO Recommendations: Intrapartum Care for a Positive Childbirth Experience* (Geneva 2018) 19.

79 Mahmoud and Romanis, n25.

last month of the pregnancy. Since surrogacy is an established practice in California, the surrogates interviewed were satisfied with their OB/GYNs' understanding of surrogacy and felt sufficiently involved in directing their own care.

As mentioned earlier, healthcare insurance specifically covering surrogate pregnancy-related costs is exceptionally rare, with many providers specifically excluding surrogacy – notwithstanding maternity care coverage. All the interviewed surrogates were covered by healthcare insurance, as the surrogacy agencies they worked with required that they not be enrolled in Medicaid, the federal healthcare insurance programme that covers low-income Americans. As described above, insurers often denied claims on the basis that surrogacy was different from 'regular' pregnancies. Even the biggest insurer in California retained the right to demand reimbursement from compensated surrogates for the maternity healthcare costs.[80]

A feature of American healthcare is the narrow networks limiting healthcare service provision to a restricted set of healthcare providers and hospitals, as gatekeepers to healthcare are health maintenance organisations, which provide healthcare services through a prepaid network of healthcare providers and preferred provider organisations, who contract with healthcare provider networks but pay physicians on a fee-for-service basis.[81] The breadth of a healthcare provider network dictates how healthcare is accessed. California has some of the narrowest and most exclusive networks in the US, meaning that there is limited choice of healthcare providers; narrow networks raise concerns regarding accessing healthcare services.[82] When healthcare is accessed out-of-network, patients are generally responsible for higher co-payments or co-insurance compared to using an in-network provider. Issues arise when there are emergencies, as patients simply go to the nearest hospital. However, if this hospital is not within-network, patients are billed for their out-of-network ambulance fees and any emergency healthcare that they access. Alternatively, the use of specialists within in-network hospital settings results in the provision of out-of-network care. Out-of-network healthcare providers often charge more than insurers are willing to reimburse. Furthermore, some out-of-network healthcare providers do not accept payment offered by the insurers, will not negotiate on price, or, even if they do accept payment, they will

[80] *Kaiser Permanente*, n57, 68.

[81] Rice et al, n49, 91.

[82] Simon F Haeder, David Weimer and Dana B Mukamel, 'A Consumer-Centric Approach to Network Adequacy: Access to Four Specialties in California's Marketplace' (2019) 38 *Health Affairs (Millwood)* 1918.

not pursue unpaid bills for out-of-network care, and instead write them off as bad debt.[83]

Many surrogates had to deal with insurance-related issues, for example certain healthcare choices being unavailable due to network coverage. Only one surrogate experienced healthcare insurance issues at birth, when she went into preterm labour. The other surrogates experienced healthcare insurance-related issues in the postpartum period. Part of these issues stemmed from the fact that their healthcare insurance coverage was only valid for six weeks, with just one surrogate's coverage extending up until a year postpartum. For some surrogates interviewed, intrapartum complications required medical intervention and recovery beyond the agreed-upon time limit for insurance coverage, resulting a variety of difficulties, with some healthcare costs needing to be covered out-of-pocket by the IPs. If the IPs decided not to pay, leave the country, or if the IPs' attorneys closed escrow[84] following the birth, the surrogates remained responsible for any outstanding medical bills. For example, Cassie's healthcare insurance provider requested payment even though she had not yet given birth:

> Even now, I still am dealing with the insurance, my insurance company wanting money, because they know I'm getting paid. So they want a piece of it – it's called a lien – they put a lien on my policy. So I saw I saw the doctor for the surrogacy once through my insurance, and they want the lien, even though I didn't deliver [yet]. They want money for that one appointment, and I'm still dealing with it. (Cassie)

Some surrogates explained how they received medical bills in their names, leading to difficulties with insurance companies. One surrogate shared that at the time of interviewing she was still dealing with medical bills totalling over $132,000, almost a year and a half following the surrogacy. Currently, with surrogates seen as gestational service providers, their insurance coverage paid for by the IPs expires 60 days' postpartum – the standard for maternity care, as this is when their 'service provision' concludes. One surrogate unusually described having an entire year of postpartum insurance coverage as part of her surrogacy arrangement. However, she developed a chronic

[83] Kelly A Kyanko and Susan H Busch, 'The Out-of-Network Benefit: Problems and Policy Solutions' (2012) 49 *Inquiry* 352, 352–354.

[84] An escrow fund is used manage all the money held for the purposes of the surrogacy arrangement. Payment to the surrogate proceeds according to pre-determined dates as the journey moves along until birth. Usually, surrogacy agencies require the fund to include some contingency funds but, if unused, this reverts to the IPs.

condition following the surrogacy, and this impacted her medical coverage and bills going forward.

> I was very fortunate that our agency's contracts … I forget the wording, but it's basically, like, all surrogacy or pregnancy-related medical things up to one year postpartum are covered as well. So the hospitalisation and like both surgeries, and then all the medication for the first year was covered. So, it basically like, you know, covers all the problems and everything, the immediate treatment afterwards. But, now moving forward, I have to remain on blood thinners, and that is covered by me now. (Clementine)

These surrogates' experiences reveal a particular issue in the American context related to gaps in healthcare insurance. Such gaps in coverage before and after pregnancy were common. Coverage generally extended to 60 days postpartum, despite research showing that many pregnancy-related deaths and complications occur beyond 60 days postpartum.[85] Within the sample of interviewees, many surrogates described the months of physical recovery required after giving birth, and many developed medical conditions well beyond two months postpartum, and were correspondingly responsible for their own healthcare expenses:

> It took me a solid five months to physically recover [from the birth]. I had to continue going to physical therapy, because I had excruciating back pain … everyone just said it was because the twins shifted stuff […] I developed diastasis recti.[86] Insurance won't cover that […] it's gonna cost me another 15-20 grand. (Chloe)

Surrogates described their lack of comprehensive, continuous healthcare insurance coverage during pregnancy and the year following the pregnancy.[87] Their experiences revealed how the current approach to maternity healthcare insurance is not fit for purpose, failing to account for the inherent nature of pregnancy and its potential impact on health. Research reveals that more comprehensive health insurance coverage is likely associated with

---

85 Susanna Trost et al, *Pregnancy-related Deaths: Data from Maternal Mortality Review Committees in 36 US States, 2017–2019* (Centers for Disease Control and Prevention; 18 September 2022, 2022).

86 Diastasis recti is a postpartum complication where when the left and right abdominals separate during pregnancy.

87 This was a common complaint, beyond surrogacy, and was addressed in federal policy; see Biden–Harris Administration, *White House Blueprint for Addressing the Maternal Health Crisis* (June 2022) 4, 9.

greater attendance at postpartum visits.[88] Surrogates' healthcare experiences highlight several issues with inadequate or inappropriate healthcare insurance coverage, stemming from a categorisation of pregnancy as a discrete event ending at birth. In reality, the impact of pregnancy on health and wellbeing often extends far beyond birth. Even where pregnancies are uncomplicated, there is still a risk of chronic health conditions emerging in the postpartum period. As previously mentioned, surrogacy agencies require that surrogates be covered by private healthcare insurance, rather than Medicaid. However, since conducting the empirical research discussed in this chapter, in 2022 the Biden–Harris administration introduced an extension to maternity healthcare coverage provided by the state-funded insurance programme, from six weeks to 12 months postpartum.[89] This policy emerged out of a desire to reduce disparities in women's health outcomes and improve their overall experience during and after pregnancy. It was an especially welcome policy to address the maternal health crisis faced by the US, with a comprehensive assessment of physical recovery from birth, of reproductive and sexual health needs. Without access to consistent, comprehensive health insurance coverage following pregnancy, many women may face challenges obtaining the care they need to support their own health. It is unclear whether private healthcare insurance providers will follow suit, and indeed whether such an approach would extend to surrogacy, given the exclusions described above. Additionally, given the relative rarity of surrogacy, and the increased potential health risks, bespoke healthcare insurance plans, such as the surrogacy maternity contractual liability insurance plans described above, should ensure postpartum coverage of at least one year, in line with the change to Medicaid.

Future directions in healthcare provision

Over 20 years ago, Blyth and Potter noted that 'government preoccupations for health care [were] far removed from surrogacy arrangements'.[90] The empirical data discussed in this chapter reveal an unanticipated, yet common, frustration shared by surrogates in the UK: the use of maternal terminology when accessing healthcare during their surrogacy journeys. In clinical settings, healthcare practitioners frequently refer to pregnant people as 'mum'

[88] I.J. Saldanha et al, 'Health Insurance Coverage and Postpartum Outcomes in the US: a Systematic Review' (2023) 6 *JAMA Network Open* e2316536.

[89] Biden–Harris Administration, n87.

[90] Eric Blyth and Claire Potter, 'Paying For It? Surrogacy, Market Forces and Assisted Conception' in Rachel Cook, Shelley Day Sclater and Felicity Kaganas (eds), *Surrogate Motherhood: International Perspectives* (Hart Publishing 2003) 239.

or 'mother' by default.[91] In doing so, there is a presumption that the decision to sustain a pregnancy and keep and rear the resulting baby has been made, which is clearly not the case with surrogates.

Within the UK context, the issues experienced by surrogates emerged from (mis)recognising surrogates as mothers and the fact that healthcare providers are provided with limited legal and professional guidance regarding surrogacy. In late February 2024, the Royal College of Midwives hosted a webinar to ensure its members' awareness of the current framework around surrogacy in the UK, and the changes proposed by the Law Commissions in 2023,[92] and to enable them to provide appropriate care and support.[93] In March 2024, My Surrogacy Journey, one of the UK's non-profit surrogacy organisations, ran surrogacy-specific training for midwives.[94] Such programmes will ideally result in more personalised healthcare provision for surrogates – provision that does not presume their motherhood status.

This idealised ideology of motherhood permeated healthcare providers' treatment of surrogates, sometimes casting shame and judgement on their decisions. The empirical data discussed in this chapter revealed how surrogates were made to hand over the baby to IPs in hospital car parks, resulting in their descriptions of feeling judged, despite DHSC guidance specifically outlining that this should not happen in this way.[95]

More often than not, surrogates were required to take on a more assertive role in healthcare provision, ensuring that they were not pressured by healthcare providers to conform to societal perpetuations of medicalised birth as 'routine' and 'perform' as mothers, beyond the usual permeation of notions of 'good' motherhood in birth decision-making.[96] This pressure was exacerbated by the technological nature of the pregnancy and the need to account for the IPs' preferences. Surrogates' experiences revealed a lack of personalised maternity healthcare provision, revealing the extent to which various NHS trusts' surrogacy guidelines for practice had failed to incorporate DHSC guidance into the day-to-day provision of maternity healthcare at the time of interviews. Some surrogates interviewed had uneventful births, whereas others experienced the handover in the car

---

91 Casper, n70, 312–313.

92 Law Commission and Scottish Law Commission, *Building Families Through Surrogacy: a New Law: Volume II: Full Report* (Law Com No 411, Scot Law Com No 262, 29 March 2023.

93 'Surrogacy: What do Midwives Need to Know?'

94 All4Maternity, 'Understanding Surrogacy; Strengthening Maternity Services' (27 June 2023) www.all4maternity.com/understanding-surrogacy-strengthening-maternity-services/.

95 DHSC, n65.

96 Mahmoud, n72.

park, as described above, and others still dealt with healthcare providers confusing adoption and surrogacy, as described elsewhere.[97] These inconsistencies in healthcare provision were due, in part, to the various guidance documents published by individual NHS trusts[98] – not all of which reflect appropriate or contemporary DHSC policy guidelines. In tandem with various legal reforms, changes to health policies and surrogacy-specific training for reproductive consultants or midwives are necessary.

Policy changes may be on the horizon, following the publication of the Women's Health Strategy. The Women's Health Strategy makes it clear that 'personalised maternity care so that women are empowered to make purposeful choices during pregnancy and childbirth' is a fundamental priority.[99] This is a welcome step, as it will ideally ensure that surrogates receive personalised care as well. In fact, evidence of how policies emerging from the Women's Health Strategy have already positively impacted surrogates is seen in their inclusion within the newly introduced baby loss certificate scheme.[100] Ideally this trend will continue, especially when the relevant Law Commissions' law reform proposals are taken forward.

Recalling the earlier discussion, in California, the doctrine of intention-based parenthood results in gestational surrogates explicitly not being recognised as mothers of the babies born through surrogacy arrangements. Instead, by virtue of a pre-birth parentage order, IPs involved in California surrogacy arrangements are recognised at birth as the legal parents of the baby in Californian law. None of these issues were experienced by the Californian cohort of surrogates interviewed, as they were explicitly not recognised as mothers. However, their recognition as gestational service providers, within the unique American healthcare context, meant that surrogates' main issue related to healthcare insurance.

In California, a potential solution to the issues surrounding healthcare insurance that impacted on surrogates' health, specifically related to the postpartum complications that became surrogates' responsibility (for example, surgery for diastasis recti, blood thinners), would be prohibiting insurers from denying certain coverage for maternity care where the insured person is acting as a surrogate. Currently, there are only two US states where insurers

97 ibid.

98 For a detailed discussion, see Mahmoud, n2, chapter 3.

99 Women's Health Strategy for England, available at www.gov.uk/government/publications/womens-health-strategy-for-england/womens-health-strategy-for-england (last accessed 14 March 2024). Notably, however, the policy contained in the Women's Health Strategy only applies to England.

100 Surrogates are explicitly mentioned as eligible to apply. See www.gov.uk/request-baby-loss-certificate (last accessed 14 March 2024).

cannot exclude coverage for surrogates' medical expenses – Wisconsin and Nevada.[101] A 2010 Wisconsin Supreme Court ruling held that insurers may not deny coverage for surrogates 'based solely on the insured's reasons for becoming pregnant or the method used to achieve pregnancy'.[102] A similar reform has been adopted in Nevada,[103] simplifying the process for surrogates and reducing the costs for IPs as a result, and adoption thereof could be welcome in California. In addition, the Biden–Harris administration's introduction of extended Medicaid to 12 months postpartum,[104] ideally serving as a model for appropriate maternal healthcare coverage, should be adopted by private healthcare insurance providers. More specifically, within the surrogacy context, agencies should require that IPs obtain healthcare insurance extending beyond the birth for *a minimum of one* year, to alleviate any financial and health-related burdens imposed on surrogates.

Drawing on original empirical research comparing the impact of the legal and health regulatory frameworks on surrogates' lived experiences in the UK and California, this chapter has demonstrated how surrogates' experiences revealed issues with maternity healthcare provision, because of their non-normative reproductive choices. In the UK, surrogates were often treated as 'mothers' by healthcare professionals, even once the situation had been explained, and some felt judged, illustrated in part by the way some healthcare professionals spoke to and about them. Different issues were experienced by surrogates in California, likely explained by the contractual nature of surrogacy there and the idea that the surrogate provides a service for the IPs. By comparison, in California, surrogates' experiences with healthcare insurance coverage postpartum reveals the detrimental impact of treating surrogates as merely gestational service providers.

[101] *Tall Tree*, n56.

[102] *MercyCare Insurance Company and MercyCare HMO v Wisconsin Commissioner of Insurance* 2010 WI 87, 786 NW2d 785.

[103] Assemb 472, 2019 Leg, Reg Sess (Nv 2019).

[104] Biden–Harris Administration, n87.

9

Surrogacy in Europe: The Findings of the ECtHR and the Law Commissions' Reform Proposals

Marianna Iliadou

Introduction

In many contracting states of the European Convention on Human Rights (hereinafter ECHR or the Convention), surrogacy is not a lawful practice.[1] However, this does not stop European citizens from seeking surrogacy services abroad in surrogacy-friendly destinations.[2] This in turn can cause problems when parents return to their home country with their surrogate-born children, as domestic authorities are reluctant to recognise the 'parent–child relationship' created abroad[3] and, as a consequence, the parents cannot pass on their citizenship to the children. If the state does not recognise any other link between the child and the state (for example, residence), the children cannot acquire the state's citizenship.[4] Families affected may turn

---

1 Some examples are France, Germany, Italy and Spain. For more discussion on different countries' approaches, see Jens M Scherpe, Claire Fenton-Glynn and Terry Kaan (eds), *Eastern and Western Perspectives on Surrogacy* (Intersentia 2019).

2 See further, Gamble, Chapter 4, this volume.

3 This is the preferred term used by the European Court of Human Rights (ECtHR) in its case law, used interchangeably in this chapter with the term legal parenthood. Parentage is only used to indicate the genetic link between children and parents. See Andrew Bainham, 'Parentage, Parenthood and Parental Responsibility: Subtle, Elusive Yet Important Distinctions' in Andrew Bainham, Shelley Day Sclater and Martin Richards (eds), *What is a Parent? A Socio-Legal Analysis* (Hart 1999).

4 This can lead to the children's statelessness if the state they were born in does not award citizenship based on *ius soli*. For more, see Marianna Iliadou, 'International Surrogacy and

to the ECtHR, arguing a violation of their Article 8 ECHR right to respect for private and family life.

This chapter explores ECtHR case law on surrogacy, identifying two emerging themes: protection of the child's right to respect for private life when there is genetic relatedness between the child and (at least one of) the intended parents (IPs),[5] and the concomitant requirement that parenthood under these circumstances must be established promptly and effectively. Other than a clear preference for genetic connection in recognising the parent–child relationship established through surrogacy abroad, the themes also illuminate a vague application of the child's best interests, with a narrow understanding of the child's identity. These themes create the impression of a common European standard shaped by the ECtHR, which can then serve as basis to assess the compatibility of recent UK reform proposals with the Convention.

This chapter highlights the significance of the Convention for domestic regulation and practices, in an attempt to assess and inform the reform proposals stemming from the Law Commission of England and Wales and the Scottish Law Commission.[6] Given the themes identified above, the main proposals addressed here are the retention of a requirement for a genetic link to establish legal parenthood following surrogacy, and the proposed new 'pathway' to legal parenthood. It is argued that the current European standard, if considered a standard applicable to the UK, is very low, because surrogacy is unlawful in the states that were thus far brought before the court. The ECtHR has yet to receive an application against a state where surrogacy is lawful.[7] It is, therefore, argued that appreciating the context of the current case law demonstrates a potentially very different application of Convention rights in terms of both establishing legal parenthood and the genetic link requirement.

This chapter first addresses the ECHR framework, essentially Article 8 ECHR, on which surrogacy families rely for their claim, and key doctrines

Stateless Children: Article 7 UNCRC and the Harmful Effects of Statelessness' (2024) 5(3) *Amicus Curiae* 474.

5 Intended parents (at times termed as intended father(s) and/or intended mother(s)) is the term used for those who enter a surrogacy arrangement with a woman (surrogate) where she carries and gives birth to a child they will raise.

6 Law Commission and Scottish Law Commission, *Building Families Through Surrogacy: a New Law. Volume II: Full Report* (Law Com No 411, Scot Law Com No 262, 29 March 2023). While the Northern Ireland Law Commission has been non-operational in the past couple of years, the Law Commissions hope that any change they are proposing would extend to Northern Ireland: para 1.91.

7 *H v UK* App no 32185/20 (ECtHR, 31 May 2022) is discussed later, as although it is not on legal parenthood itself, it does address birth certificates when a surrogacy arrangement is in place.

used by the ECtHR, such as margin of appreciation and European consensus. It then identifies the themes generated by ECtHR case law, which leads to a somewhat developed standard as to when a non-recognition of the parent–child relationship constitutes a violation of Article 8. It finally addresses the impact of this low standard on UK reform proposals in relation to establishing legal parenthood and the genetic link requirement

The emerging themes

Many European states deem domestic surrogacy unlawful, which leads some IPs to go abroad to seek surrogacy. These families face problems when they return home with the surrogate-born children, as domestic authorities refuse to register the parent–child relationship, which also raises concerns about the children's citizenship, as explained earlier. Therefore, an increasing number of surrogacy cases are brought to the ECtHR. This section identifies some emerging themes, focusing on establishing legal parenthood and the requirement of genetic link between (at least one of) the IPs and the surrogate-born child.

There are two emerging themes: protection of the child's right to respect for private life when there is genetic relatedness between the child and (at least one of) the IPs, and the concomitant requirement that parenthood under these circumstances must be established promptly and effectively. The themes illustrate a clear preference for genetic relatedness and a vague application of the child's best interests, where the child's identity is construed in a rather narrow way. The analysis relies on cases of cross-border surrogacy brought before the ECtHR against states where surrogacy is unlawful.[8] There are European states where surrogacy is lawful, such as the UK, but IPs may still

[8] The cases are: *Mennesson v France* App no 65192/11 (ECtHR, 26 June 2014); *Labassee v France* App no 65941/11 (ECtHR, 26 June 2014); *D and Others v Belgium* App no 29176/13 (ECtHR, 8 July 2014); *Foulon and Bouvet v France* App nos 9063/14 and 10410/14 (ECtHR, 21 July 2016); *Laborie v France* App no 44024/13 (ECtHR, 19 January 2017); *Paradiso and Campanelli v Italy* App no 25358/12, (ECtHR, 24 January 2017); *C and E v France* App nos 1462/18 and 17348/18 (ECtHR, 19 November 2019); *D v France* App no 11288/18 (ECtHR, 16 July 2020); *Valdís Fjölnisdóttir and Others v Iceland* App no 71552/17 (ECtHR, 18 May 2021); *S.-H. v Poland* App nos 56846/15 and 56849/15 (ECtHR, 16 November 2021); *A.M. v Norway* App no 30254/18 (ECtHR, 24 March 2022); *D.B. and Others v Switzerland* App nos 58817/15 and 58252/15 (ECtHR, 22 November 2022); *K.K. and Others v Denmark* App no 25212/21 (ECtHR, 6 December 2022); *Bonzano and Others v Italy* App no 10810/20 (ECtHR, 30 May 2023); *C v Italy* App no 47196/21 (ECtHR, 31 August 2023). Although not a decision, the advisory opinion concerning the recognition in domestic law of a legal parent–child relationship between a child born through a gestational surrogacy arrangement abroad and the intended mother (ECtHR, 10 April 2019) is also considered due to its critical value as guidance.

go abroad.[9] Only one case where surrogacy was lawful has been brought before the Strasbourg court, *H v UK*.[10] Though this was not a case on surrogacy as such, it addresses birth certificates for surrogacy arrangements, testing the applicability of the ECtHR's findings in the UK, and will be addressed later in the chapter.

Preliminary remarks

Before looking at the emerging themes, it is worth making some preliminary remarks on the ECHR framework. These remarks cover Article 8 ECHR, on which surrogacy families rely for their claim, and key doctrines used by the ECtHR, such as margin of appreciation and European consensus. While some of the ECtHR cases argue a violation of Article 8 in conjunction with Article 14, the prohibition of discrimination, the ECtHR has so far never found discrimination in the context of surrogacy and, therefore, exploration of Article 14 ECHR goes beyond the scope of this chapter.[11]

Article 8 enshrines the right to respect for private and family life, shielding several personal interests under its protective umbrella, varying from gender identity to environmental issues.[12] Two closely intertwined aspects of Article 8 are its nature as a qualified right and the use of the doctrine of margin of appreciation. Article 8 does not offer absolute protection: Article 8(2) stipulates that state interference with private and family life may be justified if it is in accordance with the law, serves a legitimate aim, and is necessary in a democratic society. This express limitation enables the use of the 'margin of appreciation' doctrine, according to which the ECtHR considers domestic authorities better placed to assess their internal matters, giving them certain leeway as to how they interfere with certain aspects of private and family life.[13] The ECtHR, therefore, decides whether the state has overstepped this margin of appreciation, which can be either wide or narrow.

9 Emily Jackson, 'UK Law and International Commercial Surrogacy: "The Very Antithesis of Sensible"' (2016) 4(3) *Journal of Medical Law and Ethics* 197; see also Gamble, Chapter 4, this volume.

10 *H v UK*, n7.

11 On this, see Marianna Iliadou, 'Medically Assisted Reproduction and the ECtHR: the Evolving Case Law in an Evolving Field' in Philip Czech, Lisa Heschl, Karin Lukas, Manfred Nowak and Gerd Oberleitner (eds), *European Yearbook on Human Rights 2024* (Brill, forthcoming).

12 David Harris et al, *Harris, O'Boyle, and Warbrick: Law of the European Convention on Human Rights* (5th edn, OUP 2023) 508.

13 Dimitrios Tsarapatsanis, 'The Margin of Appreciation Doctrine: a Low-level Institutional View' (2015) 35(4) *Legal Studies* 675.

From several factors determining the scope of this deference,[14] two main considerations for surrogacy are the nature of the matter in dispute and the existence of European consensus. For the former, in cases that raise sensitive moral and ethical matters, such as surrogacy,[15] the margin of appreciation is wide.[16] For the latter, European consensus scrutinises whether contracting states offer a similar protection to the interest at hand, limiting the scope of the state's leeway; alternatively, disparity in the way a matter is regulated/protected among the different states permits a wide leeway.[17] The ECtHR has found no European consensus on surrogacy. In April 2019, a survey carried out on 43 states parties to the Convention showed that nine permitted and ten tolerated surrogacy, with 24 overtly or covertly prohibiting the practice.[18] Thirty-one states permitted recognition of the parent–child relationship with the genetic father, with 19 states permitting the same for the intended mother not genetically linked to the surrogate-born child.[19] Based on the combination of the sensitive ethical issues evoked by surrogacy and the absence of European consensus, the ECtHR appears to grant a wide margin of appreciation to states interfering with surrogacy. However, as elaborated below, the ECtHR attaches great significance to genetic parentage, and it restricts the margin of appreciation regarding the child's private life due to identity considerations.[20]

With Article 8 in mind, the following examines the themes emerging from ECtHR case law. These emerging themes are addressed to 'decipher' the likely protection offered to IPs and surrogate-born children in Europe, revealing when the non-recognition of the parent–child relationship constitutes a violation of the Convention. It is noted that this court-offered protection, arising as a somewhat 'European' standard, should not be conflated with the concept of European consensus. The latter refers to the similarity of protection/regulation of surrogacy across the contracting states, while the former brings together the protection thus far offered to IPs and surrogate-born children by the ECtHR. This ECtHR protection of

[14] Koen Lemmens, 'The Margin of Appreciation in the ECtHR's Case Law' (2018) 20(2–3) *European Journal of Law Reform* 78, 92.

[15] For example, *Mennesson*, n8, para 79.

[16] Janneke Gerards, *General Principles of the European Convention on Human Rights* (2nd edn, CUP 2023) 177.

[17] Nikos Vogiatzis, 'The Relationship Between European Consensus, the Margin of Appreciation and the Legitimacy of the Strasbourg Court' (2019) 25 *European Public Law* 445, 452–453.

[18] Advisory Opinion, n8, paras 22–24.

[19] ibid.

[20] *Mennesson*, n8, para 80.

the parent–child relationship leads to an apparent European standard, later used to evaluate some current reform proposals by the Law Commissions.

Recognition of legal parenthood for children with genetic link

There are certain similarities in cross-border surrogacy cases brought before the ECtHR. While IPs and surrogate-born children live together in their home state without the authorities interrupting their cohabitation,[21] there is no recognition of legal parenthood.[22] As a consequence, IPs and surrogate-born children complain that the failure to recognise the parent–child relationship established through surrogacy abroad is a violation of Article 8. States refuse to recognise parenthood, when surrogacy is unlawful domestically and they argue that, by not recognising the parent–child relationship, they prevent their citizens from circumventing domestic law.[23]

The ECtHR accepts there is interference with the applicants' private and family life in cases of non-recognition of legal parenthood,[24] but addresses private life and family life separately.[25] Interference with family life has so far been justified as 'necessary in a democratic society'.[26] This has been the court's consistent position since the first case brought before the ECtHR, *Mennesson v France*, where a different-sex couple from France undertook surrogacy in the US and the authorities refused to register their children upon return to France.[27] States argue that, by making surrogacy unlawful, they aim to protect women from exploitation and commercialisation of their bodies, and children from 'being reduced' to the 'object' of a contract.[28] These interests fall under the 'protection of health' and 'the protection of the rights and freedoms of others' of Article 8(2). The ECtHR accepts that, notwithstanding the difficulties faced with regard to the enjoyment of family life (for example, registering the children with social security, enrolling them in different activities, travelling together as a family, and so on[29]), these families are still able

---

21 For a worrying exception, see *Paradiso*, n8.

22 *Mennesson*, n8.

23 ibid, para 72.

24 ibid, paras 48–50.

25 ibid, para 86.

26 To assess this requirement, the court usually addresses whether the state interference corresponded to a pressing social need, whether it was proportionate to the legitimate aim sought and whether relevant and sufficient reasons were provided by national authorities as a justification for the interference, considering the state's margin of appreciation: Gerards, n16, 333–334.

27 *Mennesson*, n8.

28 ibid, para 60.

29 ibid, paras 87–89.

to enjoy family life with no evidence that they could not surpass these obstacles/difficulties.[30] Therefore, states, acting within their margin of appreciation, strike a fair balance between the interests of the applicants and states' interests in banning surrogacy and prevent their citizens from circumventing the law.[31]

The ECtHR does not always consider the IPs' private life[32] but, when it does, it observes that IPs opted to have children contrary to the state's laws and public policy, and it is within the state's margin of appreciation to refuse legal recognition of their parenthood towards their children.[33] The ECtHR emphasises the knowledge and clarity of the consequences for the IPs undertaking cross-border surrogacy, as in the existing case law IPs have not argued the law was unclear or unknown to them.[34] This leads the ECtHR to consider that a fair balance is struck between the IPs' interests and the interests posited by the state, as elaborated above. Consequently, the ECtHR has not found a violation of IPs' rights for non-recognition of legal parenthood.[35]

Nevertheless, the court takes a different approach to the *children's* right to private life. In *Mennesson*, the intended father was genetically linked to the surrogate-born children.[36] The ECtHR held that respect for one's private life 'implies that everyone must be able to establish the substance of their identity, including the legal parent–child relationship'.[37] Both parenthood and citizenship were deemed aspects of children's identity, while inheritance was also considered 'a component of their identity in relation to their parentage', of which they were deprived, as without legal recognition of the parent–child relationship they were unable to inherit from their parents under the same terms as other children.[38] These serious restrictions on the children's identity meant that the state exceeded its margin of appreciation by preventing the recognition of the parent–child relationship with their genetic fathers, which breached the children's right

30 ibid, paras 92–93.

31 ibid, para 94.

32 ibid.

33 For example, *D.B. and Others*, n8, paras 92–94.

34 *A.M. v Norway*, n8, para 129.

35 An outlier is *A.L. v France* App no 13344/20 (ECtHR, 7 April 2022), where the violation of the genetic intended father's right under Article 8 was not based on the refusal to recognise his paternity, but on the fact that the court proceedings for his claim took an extremely long time, at which point (six years afterwards) it was not possible to acknowledge his paternity, as it would be contrary to the child's best interests.

36 *Mennesson*, n8.

37 ibid, para 99.

38 ibid, paras 96–98.

to private life.[39] This applies irrespective of the sexual orientation of the genetic father.[40]

In *Mennesson*, the existence of a genetic link with the intended father was considered a special dimension;[41] later, only genetic parentage afforded protection via recognition of legal parenthood. In *Valdis Fjölnisdóttir and Others v Iceland*, the ECtHR found no violation of the child's private life where authorities refused to recognise the legal parenthood established by surrogacy abroad and, instead, made foster care arrangements for the IPs.[42] In Iceland, surrogacy is prohibited by law,[43] aiming to protect women from the potential pressure of entering into a surrogacy arrangement and the right of children 'to know their natural parents'.[44] Given the balancing exercise under Article 8(2), the ECtHR accepted that making foster care arrangements instead of recognising legal parenthood was justified as the applicants did not face real, practical hurdles in enjoying their family life.[45] In this case, however, there was no genetic relatedness between the intended mothers (female same-sex couple) and the child. The ECtHR did not address the child's private life at all, simply mentioning that the protection of private life did not merit separate consideration.[46] Nonetheless, this approach is inconsistent with the distinction between issues relevant to family life and private life in *Mennesson*, where legal parenthood was considered separately as part of private life due to its importance to the child's identity.[47] Overlooking the child's private life and the identity concerns raised by the non-recognition of legal parenthood demonstrates a very narrow understanding of the child's identity, confined solely to genetics.

The failure to consider the child's identity in cases where there is no genetic relatedness between IPs and surrogate-born children demonstrates a vague application of the child's best interests. As Judge Lemmens mentioned in his concurring opinion, the non-recognition of legal parenthood has the same effect on a child's private life, irrespective of genetic relatedness to their IPs.[48] The child's best interests require a broader consideration of the consequences when their parenthood is not legally established. The lack of depth of the best interests assessment is evident in *Valdis*, where the

39 ibid, para 100.

40 *Foulon and Bouvet*, n8, as discussed in Lydia Bracken, 'The ECtHR's First Advisory Opinion: Implications for Cross-Border Surrogacy Involving Male Intended Parents' (2021) 21(1) *Medical Law International* 3, 15.

41 *Mennesson*, n8, para 100.

42 *Valdis*, n8.

43 ibid, para 64.

44 ibid, para 65.

45 ibid, para 75.

46 ibid, para 76.

47 *Mennesson*, n8, paras 96–98.

48 *Valdis*, n8, Concurring Opinion of Judge Lemmens, para 4.

refusal to award legal parenthood left the child effectively parentless, and the ECtHR did not even address the implications for the child's identity, or overall protection. Addressing this inconsistency between the court's analysis in *Mennesson* and in *Valdis*, Bracken rightly notes that this casts doubt on the seeming commitment of the ECtHR to the child's best interests, which it otherwise calls a paramount consideration.[49]

The fixation on genetics seems consistent with the ECtHR's case law on identity, which, at times, has forcefully sought to protect a right to know one's genetic origins.[50] As Mulligan notes, within the identity case law, the concept of identity is limited to 'simple and biological fact',[51] but at the same time knowledge of genetic heritage is almost exclusively understood in light of self-formation and self-development, and does not include practical concerns, such as medical interests and inheritance.[52] Under these terms of self-formation and self-development, Mulligan urges for a more comprehensive understanding of the child's identity that goes beyond genetic heritage and, while genetic and gestational information are important to a child's identity, the importance of intention should also be recognised; it is the IPs who caused the child's birth, which would also be central to the child's identity.[53] This would move the ECtHR away from only valuing genetic parentage in the context of surrogacy, and uphold more fully children's rights, without genetics encroaching upon other dimensions of identity.[54]

The ECtHR's approach is even more puzzling when considering the position regarding the non-genetic IP, when they are registered on the foreign birth certificate together with the genetic IP. When considering whether refusing to recognise the non-genetic IP's legal parenthood overstepped the state's margin of appreciation, the ECtHR considered the potential detrimental effects on the child.[55] This includes the denial of the non-genetic IP's citizenship, adverse effects on the child's immigration status, inheritance, lack of protection of the parent–child relation in case of parental separation

[49] Lydia Bracken, 'Cross-Border Surrogacy before the European Court of Human Rights: Analysis of *Valdís Fjölnisdóttir and Others v Iceland*' (2022) 29(2) *European Journal of Health Law* 194, 215.

[50] Levy observes a seeming obligation to know one's genetic heritage and to legally recognise genetic parentage in *Mandet v France*: Melanie Levy, 'Surrogacy and Parenthood: a European Saga of Genetic Essentialism and Gender Discrimination' (2022) 29(1) *Michigan Journal of Gender & Law* 121, 162.

[51] Andrea Mulligan, 'Identity Rights and Sensitive Ethical Questions: the European Convention on Human Rights and the Regulation of Surrogacy Arrangements' (2018) 26(3) *Medical Law Review* 449, 471.

[52] ibid.

[53] ibid, 472.

[54] ibid.

[55] Advisory Opinion, n8, para 40.

or death of the genetic intended father, and lack of protective measures in case of parental neglect.[56] On this basis, it held that domestic law should offer the possibility of recognising the legal parenthood of the non-genetic intended mother when she appears as the 'legal mother' on a foreign birth certificate.[57] This was later extended to same-sex couples and the non-genetic intended father[58] and, while the finding relies on the existence of one IP with a genetic link,[59] it nonetheless demonstrates an acknowledgment of a much broader understanding of the child's best interests. It is unclear why this broad understanding that applies to the non-genetic parent should cease to apply solely on the basis of lack of an additional genetic parent, as the consequences of refusing to recognise the parent–child relationship will be the same.

Despite the above criticism, the ECtHR is consistent in protecting genetic parentage.[60] It restricts states' margin of appreciation in cases of genetic parentage and demands recognition of legal parenthood, notwithstanding domestic unlawfulness of surrogacy. It is not far-fetched to argue that the ECtHR uses the genetic link to validate or legitimise the parent–child relationship in cross-border surrogacy cases. The genetic link requirement is perceived to 'make surrogacy a more socially acceptable practice'.[61] By contrast, in the absence of genetic relatedness with an IP, the legal limbo in which surrogate-born children are placed seems to be accepted based on the IPs' unlawful conduct (domestically), or prevailing moral views of the society.[62] In the absence of genetic relatedness with at least one IP, the focus on the unlawfulness of surrogacy takes precedence over the child's welfare.[63]

Means of establishing legal parenthood

Another theme arising from the ECtHR case law on surrogacy relates to the means of establishing the parent–child relationship. The previous section illustrated that states must recognise legal parenthood of genetic IPs, and

56 ibid.

57 ibid, para 46.

58 *D.B. and Others*, n8, para 85.

59 So far, there has been no case where it is only the intended mother who is genetically linked to the child.

60 This was reaffirmed in the latest ECtHR case, *C v Italy* (n8).

61 Lydia Bracken, 'Surrogacy and the Genetic Link' (2020) 32(3) *Child and Family Law Quarterly* 303, 307.

62 Similarly, *Valdis*, n8, Concurring Opinion of Judge Lemmens, para 4.

63 Lydia Bracken, 'Assessing the Best Interests of the Child in Cases of Cross-border Surrogacy: Inconsistency in the Strasbourg Approach?' (2017) 39(3) *Journal of Social Welfare and Family Law* 368, 376.

even of non-genetic IPs who appear on the birth certificate together with the genetic IP.[64] Refusal to do so constitutes a violation of the child's private life under Article 8 ECHR. With regard to establishing this parent–child relationship, the ECtHR has provided guidelines, without specifying a preferred method of establishing legal parenthood. Nonetheless, as elaborated below, it has held that where legal parenthood should be recognised, it must be established promptly and effectively.

When the *Mennesson* court held that the state should recognise the legal parenthood of the children in relation to their genetic intended father, it did not specify the means of recognition. The Article 8 violation was based on the inability of the children to have their genetic parentage acknowledged by *any* means, with the ECtHR explicitly mentioning the registration of their foreign birth certificate, declaration of paternity, adoption, or even *de facto* enjoyment of civil status.[65] Given the ECtHR's initial findings, any of these methods would appear adequate for establishing the surrogate-born child's legal parenthood. However, as a response, French authorities registered the foreign birth certificate partially: only for the genetic intended father.

Subsequently, the ECtHR engaged with the specific means needed to recognise the parent–child relationship in the context of cross-border surrogacy via the advisory opinion mechanism.[66] The Advisory Opinion on Surrogacy was brought by French courts asking whether requiring the intended mother in the *Mennesson* case to adopt her surrogate-born children was compatible with Article 8.[67] The ECtHR held the state's margin of appreciation was narrow in relation to the recognition of legal parenthood for the child's private life, but deference was rather wide in relation to means of recognition.[68] This became a contentious issue in practice. For cross-border surrogacy cases, states permitted partial registration of the foreign birth certificates for the intended genetic father, requiring adoption for the other IP, even in the case of a genetically related intended mother.[69] The ECtHR clarified that registration of the foreign birth certificate need not be the method chosen by the state; upholding the child's right to private

64 However, no violation was found in *A.M. v Norway*, n8, where the genetic IP refused to consent to the legal recognition (via adoption) of the non-genetic IP, who was also registered on the foreign birth certificate.

65 *Mennesson*, n8, para 100.

66 This is a mechanism by which the highest courts and tribunals of the contracting states can request an advisory opinion on 'questions of principle relating to the interpretation or application' of the ECHR or its protocols: Article 1, para 1 Protocol No 16 to the Convention.

67 Advisory Opinion, n8.

68 ibid, paras 44 and 51.

69 *D v France*, n8.

life requires neither the registration of the foreign birth certificate for the genetic intended father, nor that of the genetic intended mother.[70]

However, the ECtHR's guidelines are that the means to establish legal parenthood in cross-border surrogacy cases must have similar effects to the registration of the foreign birth certificate, and the procedure must be implemented 'promptly and effectively'.[71] Relatedly, and to uphold the child's best interests, it held that uncertainty around the child's parental status should be as short term as possible and, while legal parenthood need not be recognised *ab initio*, it should be 'at the latest when it has become a practical reality'.[72]

Nonetheless, the terms 'promptly and effectively' in relation to the timeframe of the procedure are not elaborated. There is no guidance as to when the parent–child relationship should be considered a practical reality. The failure to define this key point of time when recognition of the parent–child relationship must be provided equips states with wide discretion.[73] When interpreting the requirement for prompt and effective recognition in later cases, the court found four months to decide on an adoption procedure satisfied these criteria,[74] while a total of seven years from the child's birth until the adoption by the non-genetic IP was considered excessive.[75] However, there is plenty of scope between four months and seven years, such that the lack of clarity of 'prompt and effective', or when a relationship is a practical reality, arguably persists.

Impact on reform proposals

Thus far, this chapter has identified two emerging themes in ECtHR cross-border surrogacy case law. States must establish legal parenthood for children who are genetically related to (at least one of) the IPs. Legal recognition should involve a procedure implemented promptly and effectively, carried out at the latest when the parent–child relationship has become a practical reality. The themes create the impression of a common European standard shaped by the ECtHR, serving as a basis to assess the compatibility of the UK reform proposals with the ECHR. Therefore, it is pertinent to consider the impact of the ECtHR's findings on British surrogacy regulation. This

[70] ibid, para 51.

[71] Advisory Opinion, n8, para 55.

[72] ibid, paras 49, 52.

[73] Elena Brodeala and Marie-Hélène Peter-Spiess, 'Surrogacy and Same-Sex Parenthood before the European Court of Human Rights: Reflections in Light of Cases against Switzerland' (2022) 32(3) *Swiss Review of International & European Law* 397, 412.

[74] *C and E v France*, n8, para 43.

[75] *D.B. and Others*, n8, para 89.

section addresses the compatibility of the current reform proposals with the two themes identified. It is ultimately argued the low standard created by the ECtHR should not be applicable to the UK, given the lawfulness of surrogacy in the UK and the context-specific assessment employed by the ECtHR.

It is noted at the outset that compatibility of domestic law with the ECHR is key. Since the enactment of the Human Rights Act 1998, the ECHR's direct enforceability by domestic courts has been particularly significant for surrogacy. Domestic courts rely extensively on the Convention and, particularly, Article 8 to purposively interpret or 'read down' domestic surrogacy law,[76] to make rights 'practical and effective' and not 'theoretical and illusory',[77] following a longstanding principle of the ECtHR.[78] Similarly, protecting ECHR rights has led to legislative changes in surrogacy law.[79] The ECHR has been a drive for change in domestic law without the need for the court to find a violation against the UK. In addition, the ECtHR's interpretation of Article 8 affects its interpretation by domestic courts;[80] accordingly, the cross-border surrogacy cases may directly influence the protection of surrogacy offered at domestic level. It is, therefore, pertinent to assess the reform proposals considering ECtHR case law.

Compatibility of the Law Commissions' proposals

The two emerging themes from the ECtHR's case law correspond to two principal changes to UK regulation of surrogacy suggested by the Law Commissions. For the purposes of this chapter, therefore, two main areas of the Law Commissions' reform proposals are of particular importance: attribution of legal parenthood and the genetic link requirement. To address the compatibility of the Law Commissions' reform proposals, this subsection first gives a brief overview of the current law and each suggested change, followed by an assessment of its compatibility with ECtHR surrogacy case law.

Surrogacy in the UK is lawful, but any agreement is unenforceable.[81] The surrogate is the legal mother and, if she has a spouse/partner, they are the legal

[76] Kirsty Horsey, 'Fraying at the Edges: UK Surrogacy Law in 2015' (2016) 24(4) *Medical Law Review* 608, 619.

[77] *Re X (A Child) (Surrogacy: Time limit)* [2014] EWHC 3135 (Fam) at [58].

[78] *Airey v Ireland* (1979) 2 EHRR 305, para 24.

[79] In *Re Z (A Child) (No 2)* [2016] EWHC 1191 (Fam), Munby P declared that the requirement to have two IPs as applicants for transfer of legal parenthood was incompatible with the Convention. The declaration of incompatibility triggered a remedial order, which led to a new provision (s54A) added to the HFE Act 2008.

[80] Lewis Graham, 'The Modern Mirror Principle' (2021) (3) *Public Law* 523.

[81] Surrogacy Arrangements Act (SAA) 1985, s1A.

father/second legal parent of the child.[82] Legal parenthood can be transferred to the IPs via a parental order, under criteria found in ss54–54A Human Fertilisation and Embryology Act (HFE Act) 2008. A relevant criterion for this chapter is the existence of a genetic link between the surrogate-born child and at least one of the IPs.[83] If the criteria are not fulfilled, the other option is transfer of legal parenthood through adoption. In practice, some criteria are almost impossible to meet, with the six-month time limit of bringing the parental order application counting from the child's birth a prominent example.[84]

For the attribution of legal parenthood, the Law Commissions suggest the creation of a new pathway to legal parenthood, attributing legal parenthood to IPs from birth.[85] This would be a rigorous administrative process, involving a regulator for surrogacy, which would oversee clinics and surrogacy organisations involved in surrogacy arrangements, whose core functions are matching and facilitation services.[86] The new pathway is envisaged as a (more appropriate) way of establishing legal parenthood following surrogacy; however, if its requirements are not fulfilled, including for all overseas surrogacy arrangements, the IPs would have to apply for a parental order.[87]

This is a very welcome proposal that corresponds to the views of surrogates and IPs.[88] The new pathway better reflects the lived experiences of those involved in surrogacy arrangements, endorsing the key element for parental claims in surrogacy and assisted reproduction more generally: intention.[89] When addressing the compatibility of this new pathway with the ECtHR's findings, it becomes evident that it entails a procedure operated promptly

82 HFE Act 2008, ss33, 35–36 and 42–43. For a comprehensive account of the medico-legal conflation of gestation and mothering, and why it is problematic, see Zaina Mahmoud and Elizabeth Chloe Romanis, 'On Gestation and Motherhood' (2023) 31(1) *Medical Law Review* 109.

83 HFE Act 2008, ss54–54A.

84 Amel Alghrani and Danielle Griffiths, 'The Regulation of Surrogacy in the United Kingdom: the Case for Reform?' (2017) 29(2) *Child and Family Law Quarterly* 165, 176–177.

85 Law Commissions, n6, paras 2.15–2.16.

86 ibid, paras 7.10, 7.24.

87 ibid, para 2.13.

88 Kirsty Horsey et al, 'UK Surrogates' Characteristics, Experiences, and Views on Surrogacy Law Reform' (2022) 36(1) *International Journal of Law, Policy and the Family* 1, 13, and Kirsty Horsey et al, 'UK Intended Parents' Characteristics, Experiences, and Views on Surrogacy Law Reform' (2023) 37(1) *International Journal of Law, Policy and the Family* 1, 14.

89 Kirsty Horsey, 'Challenging Presumptions: Legal Parenthood and Surrogacy Arrangements' (2010) 22(4) *Child and Family Law Quarterly* 449.

and effectively, establishing legal parenthood from the moment of birth, and definitely by the time the parent–child relationship has become a practical reality. For the remaining parental order route, it would depend on the length of the entire procedure, from birth to the transfer of legal parenthood. Parental orders for domestic surrogacy cases with no complications have typically one celebration hearing before magistrates and, therefore, are not as lengthy as the cases that go to the High Court (domestic cases that are not straightforward, or cases of cross-border surrogacy), where the procedure may last between four to 12 months or even more.[90] Nevertheless, as explained earlier, the understanding of when a procedure is implemented promptly and effectively, or when the parent–child relationship has become a practical reality, can be quite broad, leaving contracting states with significant discretion and, thus, presumably compatible with the ECHR.

Although adoption has been considered an adequate means of recognising the parent–child relationship by the ECtHR, the domestic paradigm is strikingly different. In domestic law, adoption is not usually considered an adequate form of establishing legal parenthood for surrogacy, as 'adoption certificates imply a change of family and wrongly suggest that the children have had a disrupted rather than continuously secure identity within their family, the only family they have ever known'.[91] Though adoption's adequacy for the ECtHR standard depends on whether the procedure is prompt and effective, in practice this is not usually an avenue followed by IPs in the UK.[92]

When considering the genetic link requirement for granting a parental order, initially the Law Commissions suggested its potential removal in cases of medical necessity for both new pathway and domestic surrogacy arrangements following the parental order route.[93] In their final report they reverted to the current position. Although the Law Commissions accept that genetic relatedness is not a prerequisite for forming loving parent–child relationships, and the disproportionate impact on single women,[94]

[90] 'Parental orders (surrogacy law)' (NGA Law), available at www.ngalaw.co.uk/knowledge-centre/parental-orders-surogacy-law/ (last accessed 5 February 2024). For a rare case that reached the Court of Appeal, see Zaina Mahmoud, 'Mother Today, Stranger Tomorrow?' (2023) *Journal of Social Welfare and Family Law* 1.

[91] *A & B (Children) (Surrogacy: Parental orders: time limits)* [2015] EWHC 911 (Fam) at [64].

[92] For an exception, see *Re H (Surrogacy: Step-parent adoption)* [2023] EWFC 214, where adoption was preferred to a parental order so as to secure the child's eligibility for Italian citizenship. In Italy, surrogacy is unlawful and a parental order would not be registered, but adoption potentially would, which would create the necessary link between the child and the (non-genetic) IP who holds the Italian citizenship.

[93] See Park-Morton, Chapter 5, this volume.

[94] Law Commissions, n6, para 6.119.

preserving the genetic link requirement relates to the difficulty in defining medical necessity and in adopting a test to check whether this requirement is fulfilled.[95] As the Commissions only consulted on medical necessity, they felt unable to make a suggestion on double donation.[96]

It is disappointing that the Law Commissions did not go through with their double donation reform proposals for technical reasons. Nonetheless, this requirement is in line with the ECtHR's findings. The ECtHR places utmost significance on the genetic link, with the protection offered to children born through cross-border surrogacy essentially reliant upon the existence of a genetic father. As mentioned previously, it uses genetic relatedness as a legitimising factor, a trait that makes surrogacy more socially acceptable.

Unsurprisingly, not only are the domestic framework and the proposals in line with the ECtHR's findings, but the reform proposals in terms of establishing legal parenthood go further in terms of protecting children and IPs. Surrogacy in the UK is lawful, while the cases brought before the ECtHR are cross-border cases in states where surrogacy is unlawful. This has led to the development of principles that are applicable in the specific context of surrogacy being unlawful. The standards discerned from the ECtHR's case law are low, and could be considered the bare minimum. As to whether this bare minimum should apply to the UK, it is submitted next that the Convention's rights should be applied differently to the UK, given the domestic context of surrogacy. This bare minimum would be inadequate given the specific circumstances of the state.

Applicability to the UK

In this section, it is argued that the low standard identified through the ECtHR's surrogacy case law should not apply to the UK. Should a case be brought against the UK, or should domestic courts deal with surrogacy matters, they should not apply merely the bare minimum protection identified above. Instead, given the lawfulness of surrogacy in the UK, any state interference with attributing legal parenthood and requiring genetic relatedness should receive stricter scrutiny. The ECtHR's case law was developed around cross-border cases in states where surrogacy is unlawful. The sentiment in those states is that surrogacy is an unacceptable practice and should not be the base of forming family relationships.[97] In the UK, the reality is very different: surrogacy is a supported form of assisted

[95] ibid, paras 6.138–6.140.

[96] ibid, para 6.141.

[97] For example, *Mennesson*, n8, para 60.

conception,[98] an invaluable method of family formation with a noticeable growth over time.[99]

The different context in which surrogacy operates in the UK is very significant. The ECtHR addresses questions in the concrete circumstances rather than in abstract.[100] To assess the democratic necessity requirement under Article 8(2) for state interference, the ECtHR frequently starts by examining whether, given the particular facts of each case and the conditions prevailing in the specific state at the specific time, the interference corresponds to a pressing social need, assessed in light of the state discretion.[101] It is not uncommon for the ECtHR to hold states accountable based on their domestic context instead of giving them wide leeway based on the absence of European consensus. Any comparison made is with states demonstrating some similarity on the protection offered to the relevant interest.

For example, in *Vallianatos v Greece* due consideration was given to the fact that Greece had enacted legislation introducing a system of registered partnership,[102] as an alternative to marriage, and, therefore, excluding same-sex couples from its scope constituted a violation of the ECHR.[103] At the time, there was no European consensus on providing an alternative to marriage, or on recognising same-sex relationships in general. This would appear to leave a wide scope of deference. However, the ECtHR assessed the specific circumstances of Greece, where registered partnerships were lawful, comparing Greece only to those states where registered partnerships were available. The court observed that out of 19 states that provided some type of registered partnership, only Lithuania and Greece reserved it exclusively to different-sex couples,[104] thus finding a violation.

If a case against the UK were to reach the ECtHR on issues related to recognition of legal parenthood in surrogacy cases or the genetic link

---

[98] DHSC, 'Having a Child Through Surrogacy' (2018, updated April 2024), all documents available at www.gov.uk/government/publications/having-a-child-through-surrogacy (last accessed 2 July 2024).

[99] Kirsty Horsey, 'Surrogacy in the UK: Further Evidence for Reform: Second Report of the Surrogacy UK Working Group on Surrogacy Law Reform' (December 2018), 22.

[100] However, at times it offers both concrete and abstract review, given its double role of providing individual and general justice, that is, individual redress and general interpretations potentially relevant to future cases: Janneke Gerards, 'Abstract and Concrete Reasonableness Review by the European Court of Human Rights' (2020) 1(2) *European Convention on Human Rights Law Review* 218.

[101] *Animal Defenders International v UK* (2013) 57 EHRR 21, para 100.

[102] This is the term used by the court, with some of its alternatives being 'civil unions' or 'civil partnerships'.

[103] *Vallianatos and Others v Greece* App nos 29381/09 and 32684/09 (ECtHR, 7 November 2013).

[104] ibid, para 91.

requirement, the court would look at states where surrogacy is lawful, and not the existing emerging themes. For example, while there are few European states where surrogacy is lawful, and not simply tolerated,[105] some award legal parenthood to IPs from birth,[106] or do not require a genetic link.[107] A thorough analysis would be required to find a potential trend there, but it is argued that it would be the standards found in states where surrogacy is lawful against which the UK would need to be assessed; it would not be the bare minimum protection emerging from case law on cross-border surrogacy in states where surrogacy is unlawful.

An indication leading to the opposite direction appears to be *H v UK*, where the applicant child complained of an Article 8 violation, as her genetic father was not registered on her birth certificate.[108] The ECtHR found the claim inadmissible, as birth certificates do not necessarily reflect genetic parentage, and there is no European consensus favouring the recognition of the genetic father on the birth certificate.[109] In doing so, it did consider its previous findings on the means of establishing legal parenthood, holding that, according to this cross-border surrogacy case law, the requirement is that 'domestic law provide a possibility of recognition of the legal relationship between him and the child'.[110] Nevertheless, the ECtHR was careful to note that, in this case, the complaint was not against the existing mechanism for obtaining legal parenthood, that is, parental orders,[111] as the disputed provisions (ss35 and 38 HFE Act 2008) apply to assisted reproduction rather than to surrogacy *per se*.[112] Any uncertainty claimed arises from the lack of automatic recognition of her genetic father as her legal father, interference found to be very limited by the ECtHR.[113] While this case partially affirms the ECtHR findings, there is a significant caveat that it addressed the contentious issue of birth certificates rather than legal parenthood following surrogacy.

Regarding the genetic link requirement, it is worth highlighting that the identity emphasis at ECHR level is not equivalent to the domestic context.

---

[105] In 2019, there were nine states according to the Advisory Opinion (n8). As Russia is no longer a contracting state, this number would be reduced to eight states.

[106] For example, Cyprus, Georgia, Greece, Ukraine: Committee on Bioethics, *Surrogacy: Addendum to the Replies to questionnaire on access to medically assisted procreation (MAP), on right to know about their origin for children born after MAP* (DH-BIO/INF (2016) 4 Addendum, 2021).

[107] ibid, Cyprus, Georgia, Greece.

[108] *H v UK*, n7.

[109] ibid, para 50.

[110] ibid, para 56.

[111] ibid, para 57.

[112] ibid, para 50.

[113] ibid, para 48.

As Park-Morton observes, emphasis on the child's identity in domestic case law on granting parental orders does not distinguish between IPs on the basis of genetic relatedness: domestic courts acknowledge the formative role of non-genetic IPs in commissioning the child's conception and their intention to become parents, linking this to the child's identity.[114] Therefore, domestic understanding of identity diverts from the ECtHR's findings on identity and surrogacy, where intention is not given weight.[115] Brown and Wade go a step further, arguing that at domestic level the use of identity to determine legal parenthood is inconsistent, because it retains an adult-centric approach; thus, they call for an engagement with different models of parenthood instead, where the justification for granting legal parenthood should be a 'more truly holistic analysis of the welfare of the child'.[116] The above reinforce the idea that the ECtHR's findings on using genetic identity to establish legal parenthood on surrogacy should not be followed at domestic level.

It is also important to keep in mind the nature of the ECHR. The Convention offers a minimum protection to the rights and freedoms it enshrines, and the court finds a violation when states fall below this;[117] States can go above this to provide more comprehensive protection. Keeping in mind that the ECtHR is effectively attempting to protect surrogate-born children by using the genetic link as a factor legitimising the cross-border surrogacy arrangement, it is apparent that this context is missing in the UK, where surrogacy is lawful. As the Law Commissions went above the minimum protection offered by the ECtHR on the means of establishing legal parenthood, it is suggested that any reform of the current regulation should remove the genetic link requirement as well. Removing this requirement (for domestic arrangements)[118] appears more consistent with the

[114] Lottie Park-Morton, 'The Role of Non-Genetic Parents in a Surrogate-Born Child's Identity: an Argument for Removal of the Genetic Link Requirement' (2024) 32(1) *Medical Law Review* 61, 71–72. See also Park-Morton, Chapter 6, this volume.

[115] ibid.

[116] Alan Brown and Katherine Wade, 'The Incoherent Role of the Child's Identity in the Construction and Allocation of Legal Parenthood' (2023) 43(1) *Legal Studies* 29, 45.

[117] Janneke Gerards, 'Article 53 ECHR and Minimum Protection by the European Court of Human Rights' (2022) 3(4) *European Convention on Human Rights Law Review* 451.

[118] Domestic case law highlights the dangers of international surrogacy, which in the past has left children 'marooned stateless and parentless' at a different jurisdiction and unable to remain there or return home: *Re X and Y (Foreign Surrogacy)* [2008] EWHC 3030 (Fam) [10]. Furthermore, one of the main aims of the current reform proposals is to encourage domestic surrogacy and dissuade IPs from going abroad, as stated in the Law Commissions' report (n6), for example, para 12.95. Given the above, and considering the importance of domestic context, this chapter addresses the genetic link requirement for domestic arrangements.

domestic context of surrogacy, for at least three reasons, the context being crucial for the Convention's application, as elaborated above.

First, removing the requirement for genetic relatedness to attribute legal parenthood would bring surrogacy in line with domestic law on assisted reproduction. A genetic link is not required to undertake other means of assisted reproduction, as double donation is otherwise permissible.[119] Removing the genetic link requirement would ensure consistency, as intention-based parenthood would be central to all forms of assisted reproduction.[120] Second, as already mentioned, in parental order cases, domestic courts do not differentiate between IPs on the basis of genetic relatedness. Removing this requirement, therefore, seems consistent with domestic courts' understanding that genetic parenthood does not prevail over intentional parenthood.[121] Finally, the Law Commissions did not take forward their initial proposal to remove the genetic link requirement based on the difficulty of tying double donation to medical necessity. They did not oppose the removal of genetic relatedness as such; on the contrary, they urged the UK government to consider the permissibility of double donation, which suggests they recognise the value of arguments in favour of removing the genetic link requirement.[122]

Conclusion

Surrogacy is a means of assisted reproduction, subject of reform efforts both domestically and internationally. In Europe, the ECtHR receives more and more applications from citizens undertaking cross-border surrogacy and facing problems when they return home with their surrogate-born children. This chapter explored two emerging themes from ECtHR case law on surrogacy, notably protection of the child's right to respect for private life when there is genetic relatedness between the child and (at least one of) the IPs, and the concomitant requirement that parenthood under these circumstances must be established promptly and effectively. These themes show a clear and flawed preference for genetic connection, leading to a vague application of the child's best interests, while key terms, such as prompt and effective procedure, lack clarity and permit significant deference.

Nonetheless, this apparent European standard, derived from the ECtHR's findings, was used to assess the compatibility of the UK Law Commissions'

119 There is no provision in the HFE Act 2008 stopping double donation other than ss54–54A's parental order criteria. See further discussion in Park-Morton, Chapter 6, this volume.

120 Horsey, n89.

121 Park-Morton, n114.

122 ibid, 77. Some of these arguments included its potential for discriminatory impact, particularly on single women: Law Commissions, n6, para 6.142.

reform proposals with the ECHR. Given this low standard, the two relevant reform proposals, that is, establishing legal parenthood through the new pathway, together with the parental order route, and the genetic link requirement, pass this ECHR compatibility assessment. However, due to surrogacy being unlawful in the states referred to the ECtHR, this should not be the standard applicable to the UK. Instead, a different application of the Convention's rights should be applied, one considering the lawfulness of surrogacy in the domestic context, bringing the UK into a comparable situation with other states where surrogacy is lawful. In particular, removing the genetic link requirement for domestic arrangements would be more appropriate given its consistency with other areas of assisted reproduction, the non-differentiation of IPs based on genetics in domestic case law, and the absence of opposition to remove this requirement by the Law Commissions.

10

Ireland's Irreconcilable Approaches to Domestic and International Surrogacy?

Brian Tobin

Introduction

In Ireland, the Health (Assisted Human Reproduction) Act 2024 (hereafter '2024 Act'), which regulates surrogacy arrangements (both domestic and international), was enacted on 2 July 2024.[1] This chapter examines Parts 7 and 8 of the 2024 Act; the former contains provisions regulating domestic surrogacy, and the latter contains provisions regulating international surrogacy, based on recommendations contained in the Final Report of the Oireachtas Joint Committee on International Surrogacy (hereafter 'Oireachtas Final Report').[2] The chapter assesses whether the provisions of Parts 7 and 8 are capable of equitably balancing the needs of intended parents (IPs), surrogates and surrogate-born children, while respecting international law, and international surrogacy-related best practice as suggested by the 'Verona Principles'.[3]

---

1 In Ireland, a Bill passed by both Houses of the Oireachtas only becomes an Act once it is signed into law by the President of Ireland: see Article 25.4.1, Constitution of Ireland. The Act is available at https://data.oireachtas.ie/ie/oireachtas/act/2022/18/eng/enacted/a1824.pdf (last accessed 26 July 2024).

2 Joint Committee on International Surrogacy, 'Final Report of the Joint Committee on International Surrogacy' (Dublin, Houses of the Oireachtas, 2022). Oireachtas is the word for 'Parliament' in the Irish language.

3 In 2016, the International Social Service (ISS) launched an initiative to draw up a set of principles that could be agreed on globally to guide policy and legislation in the context of international surrogacy arrangements. The core group of experts that drafted what ultimately became known as the 'Verona Principles' consulted with a broad range of

The chapter begins by outlining the rather tortuous journey towards establishing a statutory regime for the regulation of surrogacy in Ireland, before examining the reluctance to legislate for traditional surrogacy arrangements. It then critiques the proposed complex administrative–judicial 'hybrid model' for regulating prospective domestic gestational surrogacy arrangements, before exploring alternative, fully administrative models for regulating such arrangements, as recently recommended by the New Zealand Law Commission,[4] and by the Law Commission of England and Wales and the Scottish Law Commission (hereafter 'Law Commissions').[5] The compatibility of these alternative models with the requirements of international law and best practice is then explored. At the time of writing, the 2024 Act was very new, so the chapter will briefly discuss the situation under Irish law for IPs who have been availing of international surrogacy arrangements to date. It will then critique the approach to prospectively regulating international arrangements in Part 8 of the 2024 Act, before assessing whether, in the absence of an international convention on surrogacy, there is any alternative means of regulating complex cross-border situations under Irish law.

A surrogacy framework for Ireland – the long and winding road

Statutory regulation of surrogacy arrangements was first recommended by Ireland's Commission on Assisted Human Reproduction (CAHR) in its report in 2005.[6] At the time, the CAHR noted that no Irish fertility clinic appeared to be providing surrogacy treatment.[7] The CAHR favoured the

experts representing all regions of the world. The lived experience of donor-conceived and surrogate-born persons was also incorporated. The principles were published in 2021 and are designed to provide guidance on legislative, policy and practical reforms to protect the rights of children born through surrogacy arrangements: 'Principles for the Protection of the Rights of the Child born through Surrogacy (Verona Principles)', available at https://bettercarenetwork.org/sites/default/files/2021-03/VeronaPrinciples_25February2021.pdf.

4 New Zealand Law Commission, *Review of Surrogacy* (NZLC R146, 2022). Proposed reforms in New Zealand are discussed by Debra Wilson, Chapter 11, this volume.

5 Law Commission and Scottish Law Commission, *Building Families Through Surrogacy: a New Law: Volume II: Full Report* (Law Com No 411, Scot Law Com No 262, 29 March 2023).

6 The CAHR was established in March 2000 by then Minister for Health and Children Micheál Martin. Its role was to examine how assisted human reproduction, including surrogacy, might be regulated in Ireland. Its recommendations were published in the 'Report of the Commission on Assisted Human Reproduction' (Dublin, Department of Health, 2005). Among the 40 recommendations was a proposal that assisted human reproduction, including surrogacy, should be regulated by a regulatory body established by the Oireachtas.

7 CAHR, ibid, 52.

regulation of surrogacy in Ireland, but concluded that a surrogate should only be entitled to receive reimbursement of expenses 'directly related' to participation as a surrogate. It strongly opposed 'commercialisation of the practice'.[8] However, it took a further eight years before the political will to regulate surrogacy arrangements gained any impetus. In February 2013, then Minister for Justice and Equality Alan Shatter stated that he was 'reviewing existing legislation worldwide addressing the issues of parentage, assisted human reproduction and surrogacy and considering the recommendations contained in the Report of the Commission on Assisted Human Reproduction'.[9] Less than a year later, on 30 January 2014, the minister published the General Scheme of the Children and Family Relationships Bill, which included proposals to place the regulation of domestic, altruistic, gestational surrogacy *and* 'pre-commencement' international surrogacy arrangements on a statutory footing.[10] However, Ireland's first surrogacy proposals were met with heavy criticism and were never enacted.[11] Indeed, by the time a revised version of the Bill was published in September 2014, the surrogacy provisions had been deleted in their entirety.[12] A new Minister for Justice and Equality, Frances Fitzgerald, had by then succeeded Alan Shatter, and she stated that the surrogacy provisions had been removed because the Supreme Court's decision in the 'surrogacy case' of *MR and Another v An tArd Chláraitheoir*[13] was pending and because there were critical issues relating to the rights of children born through surrogacy.[14] The minister acknowledged

8 ibid, 54.

9 *Report on Hearings in Relation to the Scheme of the Children and Family Relationships Bill* (Dublin, Joint Committee on Justice, Defence and Equality, 2014), 3.1.

10 The proposals would have tightly regulated international surrogacy arrangements carried out prior to the date of commencement of the ultimate legislation, but the proposals were later removed from the Bill and not enacted.

11 See Brian Tobin, 'The Revised General Scheme of the Children and Family Relationships Bill 2014: Cognisant of the Donor-conceived Child's Constitutional Rights?' (2014) 52 *Irish Jurist* 153; see also comments from Professor Deirdre Madden, School of Law, University College Cork, in the *Report on Hearings in Relation to the Scheme of the Children and Family Relationships Bill* (n9).

12 When signed into law by the president on 6 April 2015, Parts 2 and 3 of the Children and Family Relationships Act 2015 purported to regulate, inter alia, legal parentage in cases of clinical donor-assisted human reproduction (DAHR) *other than surrogacy*.

13 *MR and Another v An tArd Chláraitheoir* [2013] IEHC 91. This case involved a challenge to Ireland's birth registration laws by IPs who wished to have the intended (genetic) mother, rather than the surrogate, registered as 'mother' on their twins' birth certificates. The High Court ruled in their favour, but this was reversed by the Supreme Court, which said that the regulation of surrogacy is a matter for the Oireachtas.

14 Department of Justice and Equality, 'Minister Fitzgerald publishes General Scheme of Children and Family Relationships Bill' (Dublin, Department of Justice and Equality, 2014), available at www.justice.ie/en/JELR/Pages/PR14000257 (last accessed 31 January 2024).

that the proposed legislation was 'very complex' and raised 'many questions of balancing constitutional rights'.[15]

As I have stressed elsewhere, it is ironic that the minister showed such deference to the Supreme Court's pending decision in *MR* because, in its decision, released in November 2014, the Supreme Court largely deferred to the Oireachtas as regards the regulation of surrogacy, and invited it to take 'urgent action'.[16] Subsequently, on 17 February 2015, the then Fine Gael/Labour coalition government approved the drafting by the Department of Health of the General Scheme of a Bill on Assisted Human Reproduction. The government decided that surrogacy should be included in this scheme. The General Scheme of the Assisted Human Reproduction Bill 2017 (hereafter 'General Scheme') was approved by the subsequent Fine Gael/Fianna Fáil minority government on 3 October 2017 and, despite languishing in development hell for almost five years, was finally succeeded in March 2022 by the Health (Assisted Human Reproduction) Bill 2022 (hereafter '2022 Bill'). As already discussed, the Bill has now been enacted, and the 2024 Act regulates many matters pertaining to assisted human reproduction, including gamete and embryo donation and embryo and stem cell research. Further, it provides for the establishment of a regulatory body known as the Assisted Human Reproduction Regulatory Authority (AHRRA). As stated earlier, Part 7 of the 2024 Act regulates domestic surrogacy arrangements, with international surrogacy arrangements provided for in Part 8.

The failure of the 2022 Bill, as initiated, to propose a mechanism for regulating international surrogacy arrangements under Irish law led to the establishment of the Oireachtas Joint Committee on International Surrogacy (hereafter the 'Joint Committee'). The Joint Committee was tasked with expeditiously making recommendations, over a three-month period, on measures to address issues arising from international surrogacy. It carried out its work between April and July 2022 by, inter alia, holding 11 public meetings in which it engaged extensively with academics, legal and medical experts and other relevant stakeholders such as surrogacy families to form an evidence base for its ultimate recommendations. The Joint Committee's Final Report was published in July 2022 and contains a series of detailed recommendations as to how international surrogacy arrangements might best

[15] ibid.

[16] The Supreme Court did not give the Oireachtas free reign in relation to the regulation of surrogacy because in his judgment Clarke J frequently referred to 'constitutionally permissible' legislation: see *MR v An tArd Chláraitheoir* [2014] IESC 60, [8.7]. See, further, Brian Tobin, 'Forging a Surrogacy Framework for Ireland: the Constitutionality of the Post-birth Parental Order and Pre-birth Judicial Approval Models of Regulation' (2017) 29(2) *Child and Family Law Quarterly* 133, 142.

be dealt with by Irish law.[17] Such recommendations were largely incorporated into what became Part 8 of the 2022 Bill.[18] The 2022 Bill was passed by both Houses of the Oireachtas, the Dáil and the Seanad, and signed into law by President of Ireland Michael D. Higgins, on 2 July 2024.

Traditional surrogacy – excluded from the ambit of the Irish legislation

In Ireland, a moral reluctance to regulate traditional surrogacy has existed since the first proposed legislation in the area. The explanatory notes accompanying the original General Scheme of the Children and Family Relationships Bill 2014 stated that there were 'compelling public policy reasons' for excluding traditional surrogacy arrangements from the ambit of the scheme's provisions, yet there was no attempt by policy makers to articulate what exactly these public policy reasons were.[19] Only one justification was given, which was because 'the effect would be to allow the woman to "contract out" of her parental responsibility for a child which is clearly hers both by genetics and by birth', which is somewhat indicative of a moral reluctance to legislate for surrogacies where the surrogate is a genetic and gestational progenitor.[20]

Ireland is not alone in viewing traditional surrogacy differently from gestational surrogacy. Internationally, statutory regulation of traditional surrogacy arrangements is most uncommon, and it is largely gestational surrogacy that has been expressly legislated for in most jurisdictions where regulation is in place. The most surrogacy-friendly states in the US – California, Nevada, New Hampshire, Nevada, Connecticut, Delaware and Maine – have all legislated for gestational surrogacy arrangements.[21] Indeed, traditional surrogacy is estimated to account for only 5% of all surrogacies in the US.[22] Further, in the few jurisdictions where traditional surrogacy is expressly legislated for,[23] the (traditional) surrogate's genetic relationship with the child holds more legal weight than that of a gestational surrogate, because she is provided with a 'cooling-off period' during which she can repudiate the arrangement. In South Africa, where both gestational and

17 Joint Committee, n2.

18 See comments made by the Minister for Health, Stephen Donnelly TD, Dáil debate, 27 April 2023, available at www.oireachtas.ie/en/debates/debate/dail/2023-04-27/43/.

19 See General Scheme of the Children and Family Relationships Bill 2014, head 2 (Notes).

20 ibid.

21 See Tobin, n16.

22 Diane S. Hinson and Maureen McBrien, 'Surrogacy Across America' (2011) 34(2) *Family Advocate* 32, 33.

23 Therefore, not including the UK, where traditional surrogacy is permitted but treated the same under the law as gestational surrogacy.

traditional surrogacy are permitted, a traditional surrogate can seek to terminate the surrogacy agreement for up to 60 days after the birth of the child, an option that is unavailable to a gestational surrogate.[24] Although Greece only permits gestational surrogacy, legislation there provides that, if it is proven that the fertilised ovum was that of the surrogate, she can bring a claim challenging the intended mother's legal motherhood within six months of the birth and, if successful, she becomes the legal mother of the child.[25] In Florida, traditional surrogacy is referred to as 'pre-planned adoption' and the traditional surrogate has a 'cooling-off' period for up to 48 hours after the child's birth.[26]

It has been argued that an intention-based parental status model applies equally to both traditional and gestational surrogacy arrangements.[27] Arguably, it does not apply as neatly in the former context if viewed from an ethical perspective. A traditional surrogate forms an intention to conceive, carry, give birth to and relinquish to IPs a child that is genetically related to her, whereas a gestational surrogate forms an intention to undergo embryo implantation, act as a 'carrier' and give birth to a child formed entirely from the genetic material of other persons. While each of these surrogates might never intend to be a parent of the child, gestational surrogacy can more clearly be viewed as a woman providing 'reproductive labour' to assist IPs by carrying and giving birth to a child who is genetically unrelated to her, whereas traditional surrogacy can be viewed as a woman wilfully creating and then treating her genetically related child as a commodity by allowing other adults to acquire him or her, sometimes for notable financial gain.[28]

Indeed, in the UK, despite operating an allegedly altruistic domestic surrogacy regime that allows for traditional surrogacy arrangements, evidence suggests that, in practice, surrogacy is not always of the truly altruistic variety. The law allows for the very broad and undefined payment of 'expenses reasonably incurred' to the surrogate and, as Fenton-Glynn and Scherpe observe, 'payment for services of surrogates is being hidden behind the

[24] Julia Sloth Nielsen, 'South Africa' in Jens M. Scherpe, Claire Fenton-Glynn and Terry Kaan (eds), *Eastern and Western Perspectives on Surrogacy* (Intersentia 2019) 186.

[25] Eleni Zervogianni, 'Greece' in Jens M. Scherpe, Claire Fenton-Glynn and Terry Kaan (eds), *Eastern and Western Perspectives on Surrogacy* (Intersentia 2019) 147, 152.

[26] See Ch.63.213.FL Stat., available at www.leg.state.fl.us/statutes/index.cfm?App_mode=Display_Statute&Search_String=&URL=0000-0099/0063/Sections/0063.213.html (last accessed 15 February 2024)

[27] See Kirsty Horsey, 'Challenging Presumptions: Legal Parenthood and Surrogacy Arrangements' (2010) 22(4) *Child and Family Law Quarterly* 449.

[28] See Tobin, n17, 137.

shield of undefined and unmonitored "expenses"'.[29] As far back as 1998, the Brazier Report pointed out that, in the UK, 'in many cases a component of the amount paid to the surrogate mother is a direct payment for services rendered rather than the reimbursement of actual expenses'.[30] Fenton-Glynn observes that in parental order applications that have come before the English courts 'a very clear picture emerges of a permissive approach to payments beyond reasonable expenses'.[31] Indeed, she notes that no application for a parental order has been refused by the English courts on the grounds of payments going beyond reasonable expenses.[32] If traditional surrogacy was regulated in Ireland and a similar judicial approach to reasonable expenses emerged over time in practice, then a woman's intention to conceive and, once born, abdicate responsibility for a genetically related child for financial gain would be permissible. One can only surmise that for Irish policy makers the possibility of this occurring was perhaps too close to the notion of 'baby selling' that has been associated with surrogacy.[33]

Globally, and despite ongoing efforts, there is as yet a dearth of information about how most adults born via surrogacy arrangements feel about the circumstances of their conception and birth.[34] Golombok observes that it is not yet known 'crucially, how children born through surrogacy will feel

[29] Jens M. Scherpe and Claire Fenton-Glynn, 'Surrogacy in a Globalised World: Comparative Analysis and Thoughts on Regulation' in Jens M. Scherpe, Claire Fenton-Glynn and Terry Kaan (eds), *Eastern and Western Perspectives on Surrogacy* (Intersentia 2019) 515, 580.

[30] In 1997, the Labour government asked Professor Margaret Brazier to chair a group that would review surrogacy laws. This resulted in the publication of the Brazier Report in 1998 (Margaret Brazier, Alastair Campbell and Susan Golombok, 'Surrogacy: Review for Health Ministers of Current Arrangements for Payments and Regulation – Report of the Review Team' (HMSO 1998) 43).

[31] Claire Fenton-Glynn, 'The Regulation and Recognition of Surrogacy under English Law: an Overview of the Case Law' (2015) 27(1) *Child and Family Law Quarterly* 83, 87.

[32] ibid. Emily Jackson has argued that because of this, 'the UK's prohibition on commercial surrogacy is, therefore, completely ineffective': see Emily Jackson, 'Assisted Conception and Surrogacy in the United Kingdom' in John Eekelaar and Rob George (eds), *Routledge Handbook of Family Law and Policy* (Routledge 2014) 189, 198. See also Gamble, Chapter 3, this volume.

[33] Dominique Ladomato, 'Protecting Traditional Surrogacy Contracting through Fee Payment Regulation' (2012) 23 *Hastings Women's Law Journal* 245, 250; William J. Winslade, 'Surrogate Mothers: Private Right or Public Wrong?' (1981) 7(3) *Journal of Medical Ethics* 153.

[34] The UK Longitudinal Study of Assisted Reproduction Families is the only investigation to have followed up children born through surrogacy since their birth. The most recent findings relate to 15 surrogate-born children who are now young adults, with a mean age of 20: Vasanti Jadva et al, '"I know it's not normal but it's normal to me, and that's all that matters": Experiences of Young Adults Conceived Through Egg Donation, Sperm Donation, and Surrogacy' (2023) 38(5) *Human Reproduction* 908.

about their origins later in their lives'.[35] It is possible that, for some surrogate-born adults, being conceived by and born to a genetically related traditional surrogate and then transferred to IPs may be a complicating factor as regards their sense of identity over time. Horsey points out that 'though we know that children born from surrogacy fare well in a psychological development sense, it would be interesting to glean the views of children who experience surrogacy, either by being born through surrogacy or as the existing child of a surrogate, especially on the law'.[36] Indeed, the views of children and adults born to traditional surrogates as to how UK law regulates traditional surrogacy arrangements would be insightful, and should be pursued.[37] Thus, the question whether traditional surrogacy is ethically sound from a child-centric perspective should not be lightly dismissed at present. Traditional surrogacy raises significant issues, and it appears legitimate for states like Ireland to choose not to regulate the practice. However, despite only regulating gestational surrogacy, it will be demonstrated below that, upon the birth of the child, the 2024 Act nonetheless designates the surrogate as the 'mother' of the child, and grants her remarkable latitude in determining the post-birth legal parentage of the child.[38]

Part 7 of the Health (Assisted Human Reproduction) Act 2024 and the 'hybrid model'

Part 7 of the 2024 Act establishes a 'hybrid model' for the regulation of altruistic, gestational surrogacy agreements that take place in Ireland. The proposed regulatory model contains elements of both the 'pre-conception state approval' and 'post-birth parental order' models.[39] In Part 9, the Act provides for the establishment of the AHRRA, a state body that must, among its many functions, approve a surrogacy agreement prior to treatment. This pre-surrogacy regulatory oversight is similar to that which exists in other jurisdictions, such as Greece, South Africa, Israel, New Zealand, and the Australian states of Victoria and Western Australia, which require a court or a regulatory body to 'pre-authorise' surrogacy agreements before treatment commences. This state oversight might assuage the fears of those who are uncomfortable with surrogacy being practised in Ireland.

35 Susan Golombok, *Modern Families* (CUP 2015) 137.

36 Kirsty Horsey et al, 'UK Surrogates' Characteristics, Experiences, and Views on Surrogacy Law Reform' (2022) 36(1) *International Journal of Law, Policy and the Family* ebad004.

37 However, see the ongoing project, *Children's Voices in Surrogacy Law*, available at https://childrensvoices.bristol.ac.uk.

38 See Health (Assisted Human Reproduction) Act 2024, ss15(2)(a) and 56.

39 For a discussion of these models see generally Brian Tobin, n16.

In Ireland, the AHRRA's 'pre-authorisation' of surrogacy agreements between the IPs[40] and the surrogate will be limited to the approval of treatment, *not legal parentage of the surrogate-born child*. Part 7 does not propose to sanction any 'pre-conception state approval' of legal parentage. Instead, the gestational surrogate will be the legal mother and guardian at birth and the IPs must go through a 'post-birth parental order' process in court to establish their parental status.[41]

The 2024 Act's approach to legal parentage is remarkable for a variety of reasons. First, according to s55, before the surrogacy agreement can be submitted to the AHRRA for the proposed 'pre-authorisation' process, the surrogate must be 'assessed and approved as suitable to act as a surrogate by a registered medical practitioner'. This process should help to ensure that, inter alia, the surrogate has the legal capacity to consent to the surrogacy agreement. Further, to ensure that her consent is free and fully informed, the surrogate is required to receive legal advice, which is separate and independent from that received by the IPs, and she must also receive 'AHR counselling'.[42] If the medical assessment is sound, the surrogate has received the requisite independent legal advice and AHR counselling, and is content to proceed with the arrangement, she should not be patronised but should instead be deemed capable of consenting to a clause in the surrogacy agreement that stipulates that, immediately upon the birth of the child, legal parentage rests with the IP(s) by operation of law. In other words, given the significant pre-surrogacy safeguards contained in the Act, the gestational surrogate should be able to consent to, and Part 7 of the Act should enable the AHRRA to approve, as part of the 'pre-conception state approval' process, legal parenthood arising in favour of the IPs by operation of law *at birth*.[43]

Second, unlike the UK, which also regulates traditional surrogacy where, as discussed, a surrogate might more justifiably be afforded a strong legal

[40] The IPs are the couple that initiates the surrogacy arrangement. Section 56 of the 2024 Act also allows for single IPs in domestic surrogacy arrangements, which demonstrates that the Oireachtas wishes to comply with any potential obligations under Articles 8 and 14 of the ECHR. The ECHR was granted some domestic effect in Ireland under the European Convention on Human Rights Act 2003.

[41] However, following the birth, the surrogate will be able to make a statutory declaration agreeing to the appointment of the IPs as guardians of the child: see s227 of the 2024 Act, which proposes to insert ss6BA and 6BB into the Guardianship of Infants Act 1964.

[42] See ss61 and 18 of the 2024 Act. These sections also require the IPs to receive independent legal advice and AHR counselling, respectively.

[43] However, as discussed later in this chapter, this would be subject to the surrogate's right to withdraw her consent within a defined period after birth, which appears to be required by international law. A similar proposal is included in the Law Commission of England and Wales and Scottish Law Commissions' final recommendations.

position in relation to the child at birth due to the genetic connection, Part 7 of the 2024 Act only regulates gestational surrogacy in Ireland.[44] This is where the surrogate does not use her own ovum in the arrangement but instead carries an embryo formed entirely from the gametes of others. Having had the benefit of medical assessments, independent legal advice and counselling, a surrogate is likely to fully understand, and agree to, her role as a 'carrier'.[45] In the UK, where the surrogate is regarded as the legal mother at birth under existing law (whether the surrogacy is gestational or traditional), the Law Commissions published a joint consultation paper on surrogacy law reform in 2019, in which they pointed out that the view expressed to them by surrogates is that:

> [B]y making them the legal mother at birth, the current law goes directly against their wishes. They do not consider themselves to be the mother of the child they have gestated for the intended parents, and do not want to be held legally responsible for a child whom they have never considered to be theirs.[46]

Indeed, *intention-based status* is a fundamental aspect of all surrogacy arrangements.[47] In Ireland, a gestational surrogate should not be viewed as the legal mother at birth, not merely because she is genetically unrelated to the child, but because, in a well-regulated surrogacy system, this clearly reflects her free and informed intention, as well as that of the IPs. The intention of the parties is also what justifies according legal parentage at birth to IPs,

44 An in-depth discussion of traditional versus gestational surrogacy is beyond the scope and the intention of this chapter, which is designed to focus on and pragmatically critique future directions in surrogacy law in Ireland. Part 8 of the 2024 Act only regulates international gestational surrogacy. Past domestic and international gestational surrogacy is regulated under Part 12. Traditional surrogacy is not regulated by any Part of the Act.

45 A traditional surrogate can also form the intention to act as a carrier, but the reality is that she will conceive, carry and give birth to a genetically related child, irrespective of intention.

46 Law Commission and Scottish Law Commission: Joint Consultation Paper, *Building Families Through Surrogacy: a New Law* (Law Com Consultation Paper No 244, Scot Law Com Discussion Paper No 167, 6 June 2019).

47 Horsey has long-since advocated that the notion of '"intention" should operate as the pre-birth determinant in "awarding" parental status when a child is born following (traditional or gestational) surrogacy or assisted conception' as this 'would more precisely reflect the expected outcome for *all* parties concerned' (Kirsty Horsey, n27, 455 and 472). However, as discussed earlier, in most jurisdictions that regulate traditional surrogacy, where the intention-based parental status model clashes with the genetic bond between the surrogate and the child, the law accords weight to this genetic relationship and dictates that the former gives way to the latter for a certain period of time after the child's birth.

genetically related and otherwise.[48] As noted by the Law Commissions in 2019, 'the intention of all the parties to the arrangement that the surrogate will have a child which the intended parents will then raise as their own is the very core of what a surrogacy arrangement is'.[49] Thus, it is unclear as to why Part 7 does not propose to settle the issue of legal parenthood in favour of the IP(s) at the 'pre-conception state approval' stage, especially when one considers that, in addition to the intentions of the parties, according to s56(3), at least one of the IPs is required to contribute a gamete to the formation of the embryo. Thus, in all domestic, gestational surrogacies, *unlike the surrogate*, one of the IPs will always be genetically related to the child. Indeed, in practice, it appears that in gestational surrogacy arrangements, it is not unusual for both IPs who are of the opposite sex to contribute their genetic material to the formation of the embryo(s).[50]

The surrogate's consent to a post-birth parental order

The requirement in Part 7 of the 2024 Act that, at birth, the surrogate will be the child's legal mother, is not unusual – it is replicated in, inter alia, the UK, New Zealand, Portugal, and the Australian states of Victoria and Western Australia. However, despite the rather selfless, admirable role she undertakes, a gestational surrogate has no genetic connection to the child, and designating her the child's legal parent at birth does not accord with her intention.[51] Nonetheless, akin to the existing position in the UK,[52] Part 7 provides that IPs must pursue a 'post-birth parental order' process to establish their parentage. The IPs must apply to the court for a parental

48 See Vasanti Jadva, 'Surrogacy: Issues, Concerns and Complexities' in Susan Golombok et al (eds), *Regulating Reproductive Donation* (Cambridge University Press 2016) 126, 128.

49 Law Commissions, n46, 25. Indeed, Douglas argues that a law that makes a gestational surrogate the legal mother of the child at birth when she has no wish to be is 'a deliberate measure designed to discourage people from entering into surrogacy arrangements': see Gillian Douglas, 'The Intention to be a Parent and the Making of Mothers' (1994) 57(4) *Modern Law Review* 636, 637.

50 See Marilyn Crawshaw, Eric Blyth and Olga van den Akker, 'The Changing Profile of Surrogacy in the UK – Implications for National and International Policy and Practice' (2012) 34(3) *Journal of Social Welfare and Family Law* 267; Carol Coulter, 'Why Surrogacy Has Nothing to Do With Same-Sex Marriage' *Irish Times* 2015, available at www.irishtimes.com/opinion/why-surrogacy-has-nothing-to-do-with-same-sex-marriage-1.2189717.

51 See Law Commissions, n46, 182.

52 See ss54 and 54A Human Fertilisation and Embryology (HFE) Act 2008. Note, however, that the Law Commissions' current proposals are to create a new 'pathway to parenthood' allowing IPs to have legal parenthood at birth, with the parental order model being reserved for 'non-pathway' arrangements (including international arrangements).

order transferring legal parenthood from the surrogate to them a minimum of 28 days after the birth of the child, and the surrogate must consent to the granting of the order.[53]

Mirroring existing UK legislation, Part 7 affords remarkable post-birth leeway to the surrogate, which arguably makes more sense in the UK context where traditional surrogacy is permitted and the surrogate can be genetically related to the child, but makes little sense in an Irish context where only the regulation of gestational surrogacy is proposed.[54] Significantly, Part 7 also mirrors the current UK law surrounding the surrogate's consent to a parental order, such that this can only be dispensed with by the court where she is either deceased or cannot be located after reasonable efforts have been made to find her.[55] This is a significant retrograde step when compared to the draft legislation from which the 2024 Act emanated, the General Scheme, published in 2017. At least there was a provision in the General Scheme that provided some potential relief for IPs should the surrogate refuse her consent to an order. The General Scheme enabled the court to waive the requirement for the surrogate's consent in a wider variety of circumstances, including where she is deceased; lacks the capacity to provide consent; cannot be located after reasonable efforts have been made to find her; or, importantly, 'for any other reason the court considers to be relevant'.[56]

This would have offered a potential remedy to IPs in this particular predicament and might, in practice, prevent the kind of outcome that occurred in the case of *Re AB (Surrogacy: Consent)*[57] in the UK. Indeed,

---

53 See ss65(5) and 66(1)(a)(iii) of the 2024 Act.

54 I have discussed elsewhere that, despite the Supreme Court clarifying that the Oireachtas has the freedom to depart from it in a surrogacy context, the Department of Health has interpreted the principle *mater semper certa est* as meaning that, even in the context of gestational surrogacy, the woman who gives birth is the 'mother': see Brian Tobin, 'An Appraisal of Ireland's Current Legislative Proposals for Regulating Domestic Surrogacy Arrangements' (2019) *Journal of Social Welfare and Family Law* 205. See also *MR v An tArd Chláraitheoir* [2014] IESC 60, [88].

55 See s66(2)(b). The equivalent provision in the UK is s54(7) HFE Act 2008, which provides that the surrogate's consent to a parental order is not required *only* when she cannot be found or is incapable of giving agreement. There is no opportunity for the court to otherwise dispense with the surrogate's consent, as observed by Theis J in *Re AB (Surrogacy: Consent)* [2016] EWHC 2643 (Fam).

56 See head 48 of the General Scheme 2017. Indeed, elsewhere I have questioned 'whether this provision was intentionally removed from the Bill to make domestic surrogacy as perilous an undertaking as possible for Irish intended parents': see Brian Tobin, 'Proposed Laws Discourage Surrogacy Arrangements Here' *Irish Examiner* 16 March 2022, 11.

57 [2016] EWHC 2643 (Fam). In this case the surrogate and her husband refused to consent to a parental order and there was no possibility for the court to waive their consent as the HFE Act 2008 makes no provision for this. For an analysis of this case, see Brian Tobin, 'A Critique of *Re AB (Surrogacy: Consent)*: Can Ireland learn from the UK Experience?'

in 2018, during oral evidence sessions at Westminster to consider reform of the law on surrogacy in the UK, the All-Party Parliamentary Group (APPG) on Surrogacy was impressed that in Ireland the General Scheme was 'responding to some of the thorny issues that have arisen in the English courts, by planning to remove the aspect of the law that means the surrogate's consent could not be dispensed with if unreasonably withheld'.[58] Nonetheless, Part 7 of the 2024 Act has reverted to a provision identical to that contained in Ireland's first legislative proposals on surrogacy, which were scrapped back in 2014. In Part 3 of the General Scheme of the Children and Family Relationships Bill 2014, head 13(12) only allowed for the surrogate's consent to a parental order to be waived by the court if she was deceased or could not be located after reasonable efforts had been made to locate her.

Given that children's rights are expressly protected in Article 42A of the Irish Constitution, the 2024 Act should be amended to grant the court the ability to dispense with the surrogate's consent if it is unreasonably withheld and where the resulting situation would be contrary to the best interests of the child.[59] I have suggested elsewhere that a provision equivalent to that contained in s31 Adoption Act 2010, as amended by s14 Adoption (Amendment) Act 2017 would be a worthwhile addition to any legislation designed to regulate domestic surrogacy.[60] In the context of an adoption, s31 of the 2010 Act allows the High Court to dispense with the need for the mother's consent where she fails, neglects or refuses to give her consent to the making of an

(2017) 20(1) *Irish Journal of Family Law* 3. See also Gillian Douglas, 'Case Report: *Re AB (Surrogacy: Consent)* [2016] EWHC 2643 Fam' (2017) *Family Law* 57.

58 All-Party Parliamentary Group on Surrogacy, *Report on Understandings of the Law and Practice of Surrogacy* (APPG on Surrogacy, 2021), 13.

59 In Article 42A of the Constitution of Ireland: 'The State recognises and affirms the natural and imprescriptible rights of all children and shall, as far as practicable, by its laws protect and vindicate those rights' and the concept of 'best interests' is expressly referred to in Article 42A as 'the paramount consideration' in the resolution of child protection proceedings brought by the state, and guardianship, custody and access proceedings. This does not mean that the 'best interests' concept should only be incorporated by the Oireachtas into legislation concerning these specific types of proceedings. In addition, Article 42A was drafted in 2012, when the very idea of parental order proceedings for surrogacy was alien in an Irish context.

60 See Tobin, n54, 209. O'Mahony also appears to be in favour of this approach to consent: see Conor O'Mahony, *A Review of Children's Rights and Best Interests in the Context of Donor-Assisted Human Reproduction and Surrogacy in Irish Law* (Department, of Children, Equality, Disability, Integration and Youth 2021) 24, available at www.gov.ie/en/publication/3e601-a-review-of-childrens-rights-and-best-interests-in-the-context-of-donorassisted-human-reproa-review-of-childrens-rights-and-best-interests-in-the-context-of-donor-assisted-human-reproduction-and-surrogacy-in-irish-law-duction-and-surrogacy-in-irish-law/ (last accessed 30 January 2024).

adoption order. However, before doing so, the High Court must have regard to 'the rights, whether under the Constitution or otherwise, of the persons concerned (including the natural and imprescriptible rights of the child)'.[61]

Indeed, in the UK, the Law Commissions recommended in their report, *Building Families Through Surrogacy: A New Law*, that, as regards the existing criteria for making parental orders under UK domestic law, a court should be able to dispense with the requirement that the surrogate must consent to a parental order being made, in circumstances where the welfare of the child requires it.[62] The Law Commissions stated that the test for dispensing with the surrogate's consent to a parental order should be the same as that which applies in adoption proceedings.[63] Thus, if the Oireachtas chooses to proceed with the current model for regulating domestic surrogacy, it should reconsider its approach to the surrogate's consent to a parental order in light of the observations above and the recent recommendation of the Law Commissions regarding similar legal provisions in the UK.

Restrictive domestic surrogacy laws – promoting international commercial surrogacy?

As the restrictive 'post-birth parental order' model in Part 7 of the 2024 Act has become law, IPs may continue to look to international surrogacy. A domestic model where the surrogate will be the legal mother at birth and can arbitrarily refuse to consent to a parental order, with no possibility for the court to resolve the parentage situation in favour of IPs if she does so, will discourage IPs from undertaking surrogacy in Ireland. Where there is uncertainty regarding legal parentage under a domestic surrogacy regime, IPs are inclined to go abroad. This has been highlighted in recent literature from both New Zealand and the UK. As the New Zealand Law Commission (NZLC) clearly emphasised in its Review of Surrogacy:

> *While disputes over legal parenthood are rare, their potential and the lack of any process to resolve disputes can 'create an atmosphere of fear and mistrust' in surrogacy arrangements.* This may deter some intended parents from pursuing a domestic surrogacy arrangement in favour of an international

[61] Section 31(4)(a)(iv) of the Adoption Act 2010, as amended.

[62] Law Commissions, n5, 47–48.

[63] The Law Commissions previously suggested that UK law could be amended to enable a court to dispense with the need for the surrogate to consent to a parental order, *but only* in situations where the surrogate has consented to the child living with the IPs, or where a court determines that the child's primary residence should be with the IPs, and the child's welfare should be the paramount consideration for the court (Law Commissions, n46, 266–267).

surrogacy arrangement in a jurisdiction where they have clearer legal rights and responsibilities in relation to the child.[64]

The NZLC observed that, when preparing its review, 'several intended parents we spoke with told us that the legal uncertainty in Aotearoa New Zealand was a factor in them deciding to pursue surrogacy offshore'.[65] In the UK, a survey of international surrogacy arrangements published by the Cambridge Family Law Centre reveals that, for IPs, 'legal considerations were key to their decision-making process' and 'the existence of pre-birth orders in some jurisdictions was seen as a significant benefit'.[66] However, in Ireland, the same 'post-birth parental order' model for domestic surrogacy arrangements in Part 7 must also be complied with for international surrogacy arrangements in Part 8, and identical provisions surrounding the surrogate's consent to a parental order are contained therein, such that, where it is refused, a foreign surrogate's consent can only be dispensed with by a court if she is deceased, cannot be located, or lacks capacity to make a decision on consent.[67] The 2024 Act makes international surrogacy no more attractive to IPs than domestic surrogacy.

The 2024 Act and international law

The 2024 Act discourages IPs from pursuing surrogacy arrangements, prevents the surrogate-born child from having its IPs recognised as its legal parents at birth, and is even paternalistic toward surrogates. However, the great irony is that the Act is in compliance with international law obligations. In 2018, the then UN Special Rapporteur on the Sale and Sexual Exploitation of Children (hereafter the 'UN Special Rapporteur') published a report that stated that, under the UN Optional Protocol to the Convention on the Rights of the Child on the Sale of Children, Child Prostitution and Child Pornography, surrogacy arrangements constitute the sale of children whenever the surrogate receives 'remuneration or any other consideration' in exchange for the legal and physical transfer of a child.[68]

64 New Zealand Law Commission, *Review of Surrogacy* (NZLC IP47, 2021) [7.34] (emphasis added).

65 ibid, [7.35].

66 Claire Fenton-Glynn, *International Surrogacy Arrangements: a Survey* (Cambridge Family Law 2022) 8. There were 168 participants involved in this survey. See also, Vasanti Jadva, Helen Prosser and Natalie Gamble, 'Cross-border and Domestic Surrogacy in the UK Context: an Exploration of Practical and Legal Decision-making' (2021) 24 (2) *Human Fertility* 93; Kirsty Horsey, *Surrogacy in the UK: Further Evidence for Reform: Second Report of the Surrogacy UK Working Group on Surrogacy Law Reform* (Surrogacy UK, December 2018).

67 Section 103(2)(c) in Part 8 of the 2024 Act.

68 See UNHRC, *Report of the Special Rapporteur on the Sale and Sexual Exploitation of Children* (UNHRC 2018), 12.

In order that a surrogacy arrangement does not constitute sale of children, the UN Special Rapporteur stated that the surrogate must be accorded legal motherhood at birth, and she must be under no legal obligation to transfer the child to the IPs. All payments must be made to the surrogate prior to the post-birth transfer of the child, and all such remuneration must be non-refundable. On this analysis, the surrogate would be viewed as having been remunerated for the acts of gestation and childbirth and would have satisfied any legal and contractual obligations in that regard *at the time of the child's birth*. Therefore, her choice after the birth to legally and physically transfer the child to the IP(s) would be a gratuitous act, based on her own post-birth intentions, rather than on any legal or contractual obligation to make the transfer.[69] This ensures that there is no 'sale' of a child. Thus, by making the surrogate the legal mother at birth (in domestic or international arrangements) and ensuring that her consent to a parental order can only be dispensed with by a court in the most limited, unusual circumstances, the 2024 Act is entirely consistent with the UN Special Rapporteur's interpretation of the Optional Protocol.[70]

One might counter-argue that the UN Special Rapporteur's interpretation of the Optional Protocol holds less relevance in a jurisdiction like Ireland, because the 2024 Act establishes an *altruistic* surrogacy regime. However, the UN Special Rapporteur was aware that altruistic surrogacy regimes do not always operate as such in practice, and she emphasised that 'labelling surrogacy arrangements or surrogacy systems as "altruistic" does not automatically avoid the reach of the Optional Protocol' because altruistic surrogacy arrangements can in practice involve substantial reimbursements to surrogates that exceed reasonable expenses, thus blurring the lines between commercial and altruistic surrogacy.[71] The UN Special Rapporteur cautioned nations that

[69] ibid, 17–18.

[70] Akin to the UN Special Rapporteur's interpretation of the Optional Protocol, the Verona Principles (Principle 10) also contemplate that states can choose to make the surrogate the legal mother at birth. However, Principle 10.4.b provides that if the surrogate wishes to retain legal parentage or parental responsibility, then a court or other competent authority should expeditiously conduct a post-birth best interests of the child determination. Therefore, by allowing the surrogate to arbitrarily refuse to consent to the making of a parental order and thus allowing applications for parental orders to come to a 'juddering halt' (in the words of Theis J in *Re AB (Surrogacy: Consent)* [2016] EWHC 2643 Fam), section 66 of the 2024 Act (and the equivalent provision in the UK, s54(7) HFE Act 2008) do not appear to be aligned with the far more child-centred process that is envisaged by Principle 10.4.b of the Verona Principles.

[71] UNHRC, n68, 17–18. For a discussion of how some 'altruistic' surrogacy systems would appear to be operating as commercial surrogacy systems in practice, see Brian Tobin, *The Legal Recognition of Same-Sex Relationships: Emerging Families in Ireland and Beyond* (Hart 2023) 104–106. Additionally, the terms 'commercial' and 'altruistic' are not binary opposites, because as the Law Commissions note, 'describing surrogacy as altruistic does

'to prevent the sale of children in the context of altruistic surrogacy' the surrogate must, *as in the context of commercial surrogacy arrangements*, 'retain parentage and parental responsibility at birth'.[72]

One might also point out, as the Law Commissions have done, that the UN Special Rapporteur's report merely provides 'guidance' on the reach of the Optional Protocol 'rather than being a definitive or binding interpretation'.[73] Nonetheless, as Fenton-Glynn and Scherpe observe, the UN Special Rapporteur's interpretation of the Optional Protocol is certainly a 'powerful argument from an influential source, and cannot be dismissed lightly'.[74] Another argument is that whatever its reach, the Optional Protocol is non-binding in Ireland as it has not yet been ratified by the state.[75]

The Verona Principles – international best practice

In her 2018 report, the UN Special Rapporteur also urged the international community to 'support the work of the International Social Service in developing international principles and standards governing surrogacy arrangements'.[76] In 2021 the Verona Principles, a set of non-binding international guidelines that, in the words of the UN Committee on the Rights of the Child, are designed to contribute 'to developing normative guidance for the protection of the rights of children born through surrogacy' and 'may serve as an important tool that will help identify appropriate legislative responses to the new challenge related to the protection of children's rights in the context of surrogacy'[77] were published by the International Social Service (ISS). The Principles envisage and provide guidance in situations where the surrogate is the legal mother at birth *and,* alternatively, where the IPs are the legal parents at birth.[78] In the former scenario, a court or 'other competent authority' should determine the post-birth wishes of the surrogate after an appropriate reflection period, and if she chooses to transfer legal parenthood then she should be provided with an expeditious legal mechanism to do so. If she chooses to retain legal

not, itself, preclude the payment of some expenses, nor does it identify the types of payments that should be permitted': see Law Commissions, n5, 304.

72 UNHRC, n68, 19.

73 Law Commissions, n46, 77.

74 Jens M Scherpe and Claire Fenton-Glynn, n29, 585.

75 Ireland ratified the UN Convention on the Rights of the Child in 1992, but this international human rights instrument has not yet been incorporated into domestic law. The *Optional Protocol on the Sale of Children, Child Prostitution and Child Pornography* has not yet been ratified by Ireland.

76 UNHRC, n68, 20.

77 Verona Principles, n3, 3.

78 ibid, Principle 10, 18.

parenthood, then a court or 'other competent authority' should expeditiously conduct a best interests of the child determination.

However, the Verona Principles also contemplate that states can provide IPs with exclusive legal parentage by operation of law at birth, but only where the following two conditions are met – the surrogate must freely confirm her consent to this post-birth, and a post-birth best interests of the child determination must not otherwise be required by the Principles.[79] According to the Principles, the main reasons why a post-birth best interests of the child determination might be deemed necessary are where there 'have not been adequate pre-surrogacy arrangements' or 'if the surrogate mother either revokes consent or fails to confirm consent', or where the surrogacy arrangement is an international one. Thus, it would appear that 'pre-conception' authorisations of domestic surrogacy arrangements *and* legal parenthood with built-in pre-surrogacy safeguards for the parties, coupled with a process that facilitates the surrogate's post-birth right and autonomy to *freely* confirm (or object to) the earlier determination of parentage, would be in compliance with the Verona Principles, and such a regulatory model could have been introduced in Ireland.

Alternative models of regulation for Ireland: looking to New Zealand and the UK

Possible administrative models for regulating domestic surrogacy arrangements have recently been proposed in New Zealand and the UK. Both offer an alternative to the Irish model and, while neither is without its shortcomings, it is submitted that the New Zealand model is the preferable of the two because of its stricter adherence to possible international law obligations, and international best practice under the Verona Principles.[80]

New Zealand

In 2022, the NZLC recommended that legal parentage in domestic surrogacy should be determined by a fully administrative process overseen by the Ethics Committee on Assisted Reproductive Technology (ECART, a body similar in

---

[79] The Verona Principles seem to envisage that states can provide for the surrogate to either expressly confirm consent after birth, akin to what is proposed in New Zealand, or tacitly confirm consent after birth by not exercising her right to withdraw consent within a specified time period, akin to what is proposed in the UK. However, where the surrogate is not a legal parent at birth, she must be able to 'freely' confirm/withdraw her consent (UNHRC, n3, Principles 10.5 and 10.6).

[80] The *Optional Protocol on the Sale of Children, Child Prostitution and Child Pornography* has not yet been ratified by Ireland.

function to Ireland's (yet-to-be-established) AHRRA).[81] ECART 'comprises of members with expertise in assisted reproductive procedures, human reproductive research, ethics and law, as well as members with the ability to articulate issues from a consumer perspective and a disability perspective', and is responsible for pre-authorisation of surrogacy agreements.[82] Under the NZLC's proposals, for domestic surrogacy arrangements that have been ECART-approved, the surrogate would be the legal mother at birth, and the IPs would be additional legal guardians of the child until such time as the surrogate consents to the transfer of parentage by completing a standard form statutory declaration.[83] The surrogate cannot consent until the child is at least seven days old, and her consent must be witnessed by her lawyer, who would be required to certify on the standard form that they have explained the effect and implications of the statutory declaration to the surrogate.[84] Once the surrogate provides valid consent, the transfer of parenthood to the IPs by operation of law would be complete, and there would be no need for the parties to apply to the court seeking a post-birth parental order. The NZLC emphasises that 'if consent is not given, the intended parents would need to seek a parentage order' in the courts.[85]

The NZLC favours a streamlined administrative route to legal parentage in domestic surrogacy arrangements that is likely to be attractive to IPs because it avoids the need for a post-birth parental order court process once the surrogate consents to a transfer of legal parenthood. Nonetheless, by proposing that the surrogate will be a legal parent and guardian at birth and must confirm her consent to the transfer of parenthood, the NZLC's proposals might still deter some IPs from choosing domestic surrogacy, as it places the onus on them to seek a parental order if she does not consent. However, with its proposals, the NZLC appears to be erring very much on the side of caution as regards compliance with international law and best practice. After all, the surrogate would be the legal mother at birth, her lawyer would qualify as an 'other competent authority' and the statutory declaration as 'an expeditious post-birth legal and safe mechanism' under the Verona Principles for the surrogate to transfer legal parentage, and the seven-day minimum timeframe before she can engage in such a transfer could be viewed as 'an appropriate reflection period'. This straightforward,

[81] NZLC, n4, 194–195. The NZLC had previously published an issues paper on surrogacy in 2021: see New Zealand Law Commission, *Review of Surrogacy* (NZLC IP47, 2021).

[82] ibid, 69.

[83] In New Zealand, the parties are required to have received counselling and independent legal advice before ECART can approve their gestational surrogacy arrangement: see NZLC, n4, 99–100; also Debra Wilson, Chapter 11, this volume.

[84] ibid, 194–195. See further Verona Principles, n3, Principle 10.4.

[85] NZLC, n4, 202

balanced, cost-effective and thoughtful regulatory model for domestic surrogacy arrangements could work equally as effectively in Ireland.

UK

The Law Commissions jointly propose a 'new pathway' to parenthood involving the 'pre-authorisation' of domestic surrogacy agreements by a regulatory body prior to conception.[86] The parties would have to comply with certain pre-surrogacy safeguards, including implications counselling, independent legal advice and criminal record checks.[87] Following 'pre-authorisation' of their agreement, by operation of law the IPs would be the legal parents of the child *at birth*.[88] Akin to New Zealand's proposed model, this would also establish a fully administrative route to legal parenthood for IPs in the UK. However, this would be subject to the surrogate's right to withdraw her consent up to six weeks after birth.[89] If the surrogate withdraws her consent *after* birth, the IPs remain legal parents, but the surrogate would be able to apply to the court for a parental order that could recognise her as the legal parent instead.[90]

From the IPs' and surrogate-born child's perspective, the Law Commissions' recommendations have much to commend them. The recommendations provide IPs with a strong incentive to choose a domestic surrogacy pathway over international surrogacy, as their parental status in relation to the surrogate-born child would not only be secured at birth, but fixed under the law *in their own country*. Thus, there would be no need to wait for or worry about any time-consuming, costly, post-birth court application and a parental order being made strictly subject to the surrogate's consent.[91] From the surrogate-born child's perspective, their intended (opposite-sex, same-sex or single parent) family structure would be recognised by domestic

[86] It is envisaged that such a body would be a new branch of the existing Human Fertilisation and Embryology Authority (HFEA), which already regulates the provision of licensed fertility treatment.

[87] See generally, Law Commissions, n5, chapter 2.

[88] ibid. It is proposed that the post-birth parental order route would remain for those in domestic arrangements who cannot, or choose not to, follow the Law Commissions' recommended 'new pathway'. For example, if the surrogate withdraws consent prior to the birth the surrogacy arrangement falls off the 'new pathway' and onto the post-birth parental order route. Then, the surrogate would be the legal mother at birth and the IPs would need to apply for a parental order: see Law Commissions, n5, 18.

[89] ibid.

[90] ibid, 36.

[91] See *Re C (Surrogacy: Consent)* [2023] EWCA Civ 16; also *H v United Kingdom*, App no 32185/20 (ECtHR, 31 May 2022).

law *at birth*.[92] The child would only ever have one legal mother, parent, or set of legal parents and again there would be no need for post-birth court proceedings to transfer legal parenthood from the surrogate. From the surrogate's perspective, however, the Law Commissions' recommendations would appear to be somewhat at odds with international law, and best practice under the Verona Principles. In fact, the Law Commissions' interpretation of the Verona Principles is dubious, given the onus that their recommendations place on the surrogate:

> The Verona Principles say that if the surrogate revokes her consent, then a court should conduct a determination of the child's best interests. This is the same as our recommendation that if the surrogate withdraws her consent, a decision about legal parental status would be taken by the court following a parental order application.[93]

The two are not 'the same', albeit that part of the problem is the Verona Principles' silence on where legal parenthood should lie if the surrogate revokes consent in a surrogacy system where she is not a legal parent of the child at birth, and *who* should be responsible for initiating a court action in such cases of conflict. While the surrogate would have a right to withdraw consent by giving recorded notice to the IPs and the regulatory body, the practical effect of this recommendation by the Law Commissions is rather meaningless. The IPs' parenthood remains fixed, and the onus is on the surrogate, usually the financially weaker party to the arrangement, to initiate costly court proceedings *and* (if she can even overcome this financial hurdle) she must then demonstrate in court that she should be recognised as the child's legal parent.[94]

The Verona Principles clearly stipulate that 'where the surrogate mother is not a legal parent by operation of law at birth', she must be able to 'freely' confirm or revoke her consent to the IPs having exclusive legal parentage after the birth of the child.[95] However, it cannot be said that a surrogate's

92 See further, Kirsty Horsey and Emily Jackson, 'The Human Fertilisation and Embryology Act 1990 and Non-Traditional Families' (2023) 86(6) *Modern Law Review* 1472.

93 Law Commissions, n5, 80–81.

94 A recent survey of surrogates in the UK revealed that 55% of respondents (25 of 44 surrogates) had an annual household income of £40,000 or less, with 25% of those respondents having an annual household income of below £29,900: see Kirsty Horsey et al, 'UK Surrogates' Characteristics, Experiences, and Views on Surrogacy Law Reform' (2022) 36(1) *International Journal of Law, Policy and the Family* ebac030. The fee for a parental order application is £260 and it is most likely this cost would be substantially added to because to attempt to successfully overturn the fixed legal parenthood of the IP(s) the surrogate may choose to hire lawyers.

95 Verona Principles, n3, Principle 10.5.

inaction during the six-week period after birth is a freely given, tacit confirmation of consent when she knows that issuing a recorded withdrawal of consent to the regulatory body would do nothing to change the legal situation regarding parenthood, and she does not have the financial means to initiate a court application for a parental order that would alter this in her favour.[96] The practical effect of the Law Commissions' suggested approach to pre-authorisation in the UK would mean that most surrogates will be 'locked in' to the determination of legal parenthood at birth. This outcome would be of particular concern in a country like the UK, where traditional surrogacy is permitted and the surrogate might also be the genetic mother of the child,[97] and it would not appear to be in keeping with the spirit of either the UN Special Rapporteur's recommendations or the Verona Principles, both of which appear to envisage the surrogate having greater autonomy in the post-birth decision-making concerning the child's parenthood.

The best way forward for Ireland?

For domestic arrangements, Ireland should have adopted a combination of the fully administrative routes to legal parenthood suggested by the law reform bodies in New Zealand and the UK. Where the pre-surrogacy legislative safeguards set out above have been fully complied with, the AHRRA would be the appropriate body to carry out the pre-authorisation of surrogacy arrangements in tandem with pre-authorisation of the child's exclusive legal parenthood being fixed with the IPs at birth by operation of law.[98] However, to comply with international law, as set out in the UN Optional Protocol, and best practice, as reflected in the Verona Principles, a surrogate should be able to freely exercise her right to withdraw consent to the exclusive allocation of parenthood within a certain period after the birth simply by writing to the AHRRA, whereupon she should share legal parenthood with the IPs. If this situation should arise, the AHRRA should notify the IPs of the surrogate's withdrawal of consent and its legal effect,

[96] Thus, the surrogate's 'right' to withdraw her consent may be of no tangible, practical legal significance to her.

[97] In contrast, in South Africa, where traditional surrogacy is also permitted, the surrogate has a 'cooling-off' period up to 60 days after the birth of the child, during which she has the right to terminate the surrogacy agreement with the IPs and keep the child: see Melodie Slabbert and Christa Roodt, 'South Africa' in Katarina Trimmings and Paul Beaumont (eds), *International Surrogacy Arrangements: Legal Regulation at the International Level* (Bloomsbury 2013) 325–345. See also, J Sloth Nielsen, 'South Africa' in Jens M Scherpe, Claire Fenton-Glynn and Terry Kaan (eds), *Eastern and Western Perspectives on Surrogacy* (Intersentia 2019) 186 and 191.

[98] See earlier discussion under 'Part 7 of the Health (Assisted Human Reproduction) Act 2024 and the "hybrid model"'.

and they in turn should be required to apply for a court order confirming their exclusive, pre-authorised legal parenthood, with an expeditious process in place. The application should be on notice to the surrogate, who may challenge it in court. Options available to the court should include an order confirming the IPs' exclusive legal parenthood and extinguishing the surrogate's shared parenthood, or one transferring exclusive legal parenthood to the surrogate, with the best interests of the child being the paramount consideration for the court, just as it is in relation to guardianship, custody, access, and adoption under Irish law.

This approach should not discourage domestic surrogacy arrangements because the IPs would acquire exclusive legal parentage at birth and, in the event that the surrogate might exercise her post-birth right to withdraw consent to this, they would remain legal parents, but share parenthood with the surrogate. Further, this would only be for a short time until a court either confirms their exclusive legal parenthood or makes another determination in the best interests of the child. This approach actually enables the surrogate to 'freely' withdraw her consent should she wish to, makes such withdrawal of practical legal significance for the surrogate and IPs in that it leads to shared parenthood and necessitates that the IPs seek a best interests determination from a court that either confirms or removes their exclusive parenthood. This balanced approach is more likely to be compliant with the tenor of the UN Special Rapporteur's recommendations and the Verona Principles.

International surrogacy – a 'novel' Irish approach to a global dilemma

Most Irish couples who need to have a child through surrogacy access services internationally in countries such as the US, Canada and Ukraine. However, for those IPs who have gone, and may continue to go, abroad for surrogacy, the Bill which ultimately became the 2024 Act did not initially purport to establish any legal mechanism whereby an intended mother or, in a same-sex relationship, a non-genetic intended father, could establish parental status in relation to the child upon returning to Ireland.[99] This would have meant that the current status quo would prevail, with Irish law continuing to recognise the surrogate as the child's legal mother.[100] An intended father could be

[99] However, Part 8 of the 2024 Act now prospectively regulates parentage in international surrogacy arrangements, and Part 12 retrospectively regulates parentage in 'past' international and domestic surrogacy arrangements. Given the proximity of the time of writing the final version of this chapter to the addition of these new Parts to, and the enactment of, the 2024 Act, a detailed analysis of Part 12 is unfortunately beyond the scope of this chapter.

[100] *MR v An t-Ard Chláraitheoir* [2014] IESC 60.

recognised as a parent and guardian following a successful court application, but only where he is the genetic father of the child.[101] A child born through international surrogacy was unable to have their intended mother recognised as their legal mother under Irish law, even where she had contributed her ovum to the creation of the embryo(s) carried by the surrogate. Similarly, a non-genetic intended father could not be recognised as a parent of a child born via international surrogacy. The intended mother or non-genetic intended father could only apply to be appointed as a guardian of the surrogate-born child by a court a minimum of two years after the child's birth. Such an IP must either be married to, in a civil partnership with, or cohabiting with the genetic parent of the child, and have shared responsibility with that parent for the child's day-to-day care for a minimum of two years. However, unlike legal parenthood, guardianship rights end when the child reaches the age of 18.[102]

In its Final Report, the Oireachtas Joint Committee on International Surrogacy recommended incorporating prospective international surrogacy arrangements within the type of 'hybrid model' contained in Part 7 of the (now) 2024 Act.[103] Essentially, the Joint Committee proposed that 'intending parents resident in Ireland should be obliged to engage with the AHRRA prior to engaging in an international surrogacy agreement'.[104] The Joint Committee proposed that, prior to conception, IPs should submit evidence to the AHRRA of, inter alia, the country in which the surrogacy is to take place, evidence that the IPs and the surrogate have complied with the same pre-surrogacy safeguards required in domestic surrogacy arrangements (independent legal advice, AHR counselling, safety checks), details of any clinic or surrogacy agency involved, and a copy of the parties' detailed, written surrogacy agreement.

---

[101] See s35 of the Status of Children Act 1987, and s6A of the Guardianship of Infants Act 1964, as inserted by s11 of the Status of Children Act 1987.

[102] I have suggested elsewhere that the lengthy waiting period before such an IP can apply for guardianship of their surrogate-born child under Irish law may be contrary to the surrogate-born child's right to respect for private life under Article 8 of the ECHR: see Brian Tobin, *The Legal Recognition of Same-Sex Relationships: Emerging Families in Ireland and Beyond* (Hart 2023) 116. Guardianship is the equivalent of parental responsibility under Irish law.

[103] The Joint Committee also proposed that 'in cases where international surrogacy arrangements have taken place before the introduction of legislation regulating them, intended parents should be able to apply for parental orders' and that 'the requirements for granting a parental order for an international surrogacy arrangement retrospectively should be less onerous than those for future surrogacy arrangements' and also that 'the court should carry out a 'best interests test' as part of the parental order application': see Joint Committee on International Surrogacy, n2, 21–23.

[104] ibid, n2, 19.

Provided that the surrogacy arrangement is legal[105] in the country in which it is to take place, and the pre-surrogacy safeguards have been complied with, it is envisaged that the AHRRA would issue the IPs with a 'pre-authorisation certificate' certifying this.[106] However, following the birth of the child, the IPs would still have to obtain a parental order from an Irish court in order to establish their legal parenthood.[107] The Joint Committee's recommendations have largely been replicated in Part 8 of the 2024 Act. It suggested that 'international surrogacy arrangements should be fairly and ethically compensated', and Part 8 seems to allow for this, because a surrogate's reasonable expenses can, inter alia, stretch to a loss of income for 'a period of not more than 6 months during which the birth happened or was expected to happen' and 'any other period during the pregnancy or thereafter, not exceeding 12 months in total, when the surrogate mother was unable to work on medical grounds related to pregnancy or birth'.[108] However, Part 8 precludes the AHRRA from approving any prospective commercial surrogacy arrangements.[109]

The Joint Committee – discouraging the legally and ethically questionable

The approach taken by the Joint Committee in its Final Report appeared to place a considerable onus on the AHRRA, and envisaged IPs being 'pre-authorised' by this state body to commence a surrogacy arrangement in countries where the regulation of surrogacy is neither closely aligned with what was proposed for domestic surrogacy under Part 7 of the (then)

---

[105] Part 8 requires that, for the AHRRA to approve a surrogacy jurisdiction, the surrogacy must be well regulated by the law of the jurisdiction. The AHRRA will scrutinise, inter alia, the protections afforded under the law of the jurisdiction to children that may be born as a result of AHR treatment in the event of them not receiving adequate care and protection, as well as the law relating to intermediaries in the jurisdiction, and medical professionals undertaking surrogacy in the jurisdiction, in particular whether there is a regulatory authority exercising oversight of such intermediaries/medical professionals and the nature and degree of such oversight: see s81 of the 2024 Act.

[106] Joint Committee, n2, 20.

[107] ibid, 14.

[108] ibid, 17. See s94(3)(c) of the 2024 Act.

[109] See s89(1)(e) of the 2024 Act. Zervogianni observes that 'in many countries there is a correlation between exploitation of women and commercial surrogacy. This has been the case in Thailand and India, and both ended up prohibiting international surrogacy agreements': see Eleni Zervogianni, 'Lessons Drawn from the Regulation of Surrogacy in Greece, Cyprus and Portugal, or a Plea for the Regulation of Commercial Gestational Surrogacy' (2019) 33(2) *International Journal of Law, Policy and the Family* 160, 164. In 2015, Golombok noted that 'Indian surrogates often live in "surrogacy houses" away from their family during the pregnancy': see Susan Golombok, *Modern Families* (CUP 2015) 121.

2022 Bill, nor in compliance with the requirements of international law and suggested international best practice.

As demonstrated, international best practice, as highlighted in the Verona Principles, requires that the surrogate must retain an autonomous legal decision-making role in relation to the child's legal parenthood after birth. This poses problems when one recognises that international surrogacy destinations popular with Irish intended parents strip the surrogate of legal rights early in the surrogacy process. In 2018, a survey by Growing Families estimated that up to 68% of surrogacies for Irish IPs were taking place in Ukraine.[110] This commercial surrogacy destination remains popular with Irish IPs, despite the ongoing conflict in the region.[111] Twenty-five babies born through surrogacy arrangements in Ukraine were expected to arrive in Ireland by the summer of 2023.[112]

The Ukrainian Family Code provides that, when an embryo conceived by the IPs is implanted in the gestational surrogate, the IPs are regarded as the legal parents of the child when he or she is born.[113] Thus, the surrogate is stripped of legal parentage as she has no post-birth right to object to the exclusive allocation of legal parentage. While these types of commercial surrogacy arrangements are legal in Ukraine, they clearly fly in the face of the approach to domestic surrogacy arrangements as envisaged by Part 7 of the 2024 Act, as well as the UN Special Rapporteur's interpretation of international law, and even international best practice as suggested by the Verona Principles.

Surrogacy in Ukraine can only be accessed by Irish opposite-sex, married IPs, but the legal situation is similar in California, the surrogacy destination of choice for some Irish same-sex IPs. The Family Code of California allows commercial surrogacy contracts to be fully enforced by the parties and for a court order that 'shall terminate any parental rights of the surrogate' to be

[110] See Tobin, n102, 120.

[111] Paul Hosford, 'Irish Families Still Travelling to Ukraine for Surrogacy Despite Government Pleas Not to Do So' *Irish Examiner* 14 August 2023, available at www.irishexaminer.com/news/arid-41204845.html.

[112] See Paul Hosford, 'Government Worried About Those Still Using Ukrainian Surrogates' *Irish Examiner* 15 May 2023, available at www.irishexaminer.com/news/arid-41139544.html. However, Part 8 clarifies that the Ukraine will not be approved by the AHRRA for prospective international surrogacy arrangements, not just because it is a commercial surrogacy destination, but because in deciding whether or not to approve a jurisdiction, the AHRRA shall have regard to 'any civil or military activities…that may present a potential significant risk of harm to any person participating, in any capacity, in an international surrogacy undertaken in the jurisdiction': see s81(2)(d) of the 2024 Act.

[113] Article 123(2), Family Code of Ukraine. Even before the war, the Law Commissions noted that there had been some concerning reports about the treatment of surrogates in Ukraine (Law Commissions, n46, 35–36).

made in favour of the IPs prior to the birth of the child. Indeed, Fenton-Glynn and Scherpe have observed that, in California, 'the obligation to hand over the child is unconditionally enforceable'.[114] Consequently, it would not appear ethical for the AHRRA to 'pre-authorise' *any* prospective surrogacy arrangement scheduled to take place in these jurisdictions, given how the law in both fully extinguishes the surrogate's legal parental rights in a manner contrary to international law and best practice. Such jurisdictions also operate in a manner contrary to the model for regulating domestic surrogacy in Ireland under Part 7.

In any event, Part 8 clarifies that the AHRRA will not pre-approve *any* commercial surrogacy destinations, so that appears to rule out Ukraine and California on that ground alone.[115] However, that begs the question as to which surrogacy destinations will actually be eligible for 'pre-authorisation' by the AHRRA once it commences its work? Emerging surrogacy destinations such as Mexico and Georgia engage in ethically questionable practices, such as permitting the use of anonymous donor eggs in surrogacy arrangements, thus completely frustrating the child's right to knowledge of their genetic identity, as required by the Verona Principles, which set out that 'States have a duty to ensure that every child born through surrogacy has the opportunity to access information concerning their identity'.[116]

The Joint Committee's attempt to incorporate international surrogacy arrangements within the type of 'hybrid model' proposed for domestic, altruistic surrogacy arrangements is notable for trying to tightly regulate (and discourage) such arrangements by requiring pre-surrogacy engagement with the AHRRA, compliance with numerous significant pre-surrogacy safeguards, and a post-birth application to an Irish court for a parental order determining legal parenthood. This approach has been elaborated upon in Part 8 of the 2024 Act, which not only precludes commercial surrogacy abroad, but also rules out many popular surrogacy destinations that engage in legally and ethically questionable practices. Part 8 requires the AHRRA to consider 'the rights of pregnant women, including surrogate mothers, as regards their health, privacy and bodily autonomy' before pre-approving a surrogacy destination.[117] Further, in order to be a 'permitted international surrogacy', the parties' surrogacy arrangement must comply with the requirement that all of the child's origin information (details of the IPs,

[114] Claire Fenton-Glynn and Jens M Scherpe, n29, 526.

[115] s89(1)(e) of the 2024 Act.

[116] Verona Principles, n3, Principle 11.2. Note Georgia was intended to be 'closed' to foreign intended parents from 1 January 2024.

[117] s81(2)(g) of the 2024 Act.

surrogate, and any donor(s)) is both recorded and provided to the AHRRA for entry into the National Surrogacy Register.[118] Thus, on the basis of this latter requirement, it appears that emerging surrogacy destinations like Mexico or Georgia cannot be approved by the AHRRA either.

However, what if some Irish IPs fail to engage with the AHRRA before pursuing their international surrogacy arrangement? Evidence shows that some IPs will continue to use a warzone for surrogacy and flagrantly ignore official advice not to do so.[119] Thus, it is not unreasonable to suggest that some Irish IPs will simply choose whatever jurisdiction they desire for surrogacy, irrespective of that jurisdiction's treatment of surrogates or its scant regard for the identity rights of any surrogate-born children. Nonetheless, if they do so, it appears that the court will be unable to grant them a parental order.[120]

The unenviable task of legislating to regulate international surrogacy arrangements

Ireland is not alone in grappling with how best to regulate international surrogacy. No remarkable recommendations for dealing with this phenomenon have come from the law reform processes in New Zealand or the UK either. Both ultimately recommended that international arrangements should be dealt with by a post-birth application to a domestic court for a parental order and a judicial best interests of the child determination.[121] This approach is consistent with the Verona Principles. International surrogacy poses difficulties for states because, in the absence of an international treaty or convention that specifically deals with surrogacy and legal parenthood, states must decide how best to regulate these complex cross-border arrangements under their domestic laws.

The best way to discourage international arrangements is to legislate for the most viable model possible to regulate domestic surrogacy. In that regard, it is regrettable that, prior to enactment, Ireland did not abandon the approach to domestic surrogacy contained in Part 7 of the 2024 Act, and take heed of the recommendations from New Zealand (and, to a lesser extent, the UK), and adopt its own, fully administrative route to legal parenthood for IPs, that errs on the side of caution as regards the requirements of international law and best practice. A streamlined, fully administrative model would facilitate domestic surrogacy arrangements when compared

118 ss89(1)(f), 99 and 105 of the 2024 Act.

119 Hosford, n111. Generally, see Anika König, 'Reproductive Entanglements in Times of War: Transnational Gestational Surrogacy in Ukraine and Beyond' (2023) 42(5) *Medical Anthropology* 479–492.

120 s103 of the 2024 Act.

121 NZLC, n4, *Executive Summary* 14–15; Law Commissions, n5, recommendation 49.

to the hybrid model provided under Part 7 of the 2024 Act. Instead, the 2024 Act arguably encourages neither domestic nor international surrogacy arrangements through the provisions of Parts 7 and 8.

Conclusion

The 2024 Act establishes a complex, hybrid legislative model for the regulation of surrogacy arrangements that involves both administrative *and* judicial processes and unduly favours the position of the gestational surrogate over all other parties. This chapter proposes an alternative, fully administrative means of regulating domestic arrangements, one that realises the potential of the AHRRA and is influenced by proposals emanating from law reform bodies elsewhere. The proposal is also cognisant of recent developments in international law and best practice, in particular the requirement that the surrogate must be able to 'freely' exercise her post-birth right to confirm or withdraw her consent to the IPs having exclusive legal parenthood, and that such right must have legal and practical effect, and not be merely illusory.

The recognition of international surrogacy agreements poses a more complex dilemma for policy makers in the absence of an international treaty or convention setting out some minimum global standards for regulation. Finding a means of regulating international surrogacy in a manner that would alleviate the legal and ethical concerns associated with surrogacies carried out abroad while also respecting the right of the child to have its intended family structure recognised under Irish law was a difficult, unenviable task for the Oireachtas. However, Part 8 of the 2024 Act represents a noble attempt by the Oireachtas to (very) tightly regulate international surrogacies that is largely in line with the considered recommendations contained in the Final Report of the Joint Committee. Arguably, Part 8 is so restrictive that it does nothing whatsoever to promote international surrogacy over domestic surrogacy as a viable option for Irish IPs. Nonetheless, after a lengthy and meandering legislative process that commenced over a decade ago, Ireland now has legislation in place to regulate both domestic and international surrogacy arrangements. Only time will tell how the provisions of that legislation are operating in practice.

11

Regulating Ethics: Potential Lessons from New Zealand

Debra Wilson

Introduction

New Zealand is one of three jurisdictions that requires domestic surrogacy arrangements involving fertility clinics to be individually considered and pre-approved by an ethics committee.[1] This ethics approval process is detailed and thorough, requiring the intended parent(s) (IPs) and the surrogate (and her partner, if any) to go through medical checks, joint and individual fertility counselling, and receive surrogacy-specific legal advice. If any of the parties already have children these children are often involved in the counselling process (depending on age and understanding), and the views of the wider families, and of any egg or embryo donors, are also considered.

The Ethics Committee on Assisted Reproductive Technology (ECART) considers any specific medical, ethical, cultural, or societal implications raised by these requirements, before deciding whether to approve a surrogacy arrangement. Minutes of its meetings are anonymised and published, allowing insight into the matters considered. This ethics process can be described as best practice for surrogacy arrangements. It ensures that any medical and other issues are identified and discussed, that the views of all relevant people are understood, and that difficult conversations in relation to surrogacy are discussed early. A recent New Zealand Law Commission (NZLC) review of domestic surrogacy noted the clear benefits of the process and recommended not only that it continue, but that the role of ECART be expanded.[2] This

1 The others are Israel and the Australian state of Victoria. New Zealand is the only jurisdiction that publishes the minutes of its meetings.

2 NZLC, *Review of Surrogacy* (Report 146, 2022).

raises the interesting question of whether other jurisdictions should follow New Zealand's lead and introduce a similar process. This chapter describes the role of ECART and analyses the data reported in the minutes of its meetings to provide an understanding of the issues discussed in relation to individual applications. It will briefly discuss the recent NZLC conclusions as to the effectiveness of the process, the issues that have arisen with it, and recommendations for reform, before turning to consider whether other jurisdictions should adopt a similar approach.

Surrogacy laws and guidelines in New Zealand

Early surrogacy regulation in New Zealand

Prior to 2004, surrogacy was not specifically regulated in New Zealand.[3] The first reported surrogacy case was *Re P (Adoption: Surrogacy)*[4] in 1990. This was a 'natural conception' surrogacy, utilising a surrogacy arrangement. The genetic father and his wife then applied to adopt the child.[5] The second case, *Re G,*[6] occurred through private artificial insemination and involved an application to adopt. In 1997, the first application to the National Ethics Committee on Assisted Human Reproduction (NECAHR) for approval to undertake surrogacy was made by a fertility clinic and that same year, legal regulation of surrogacy was introduced into Parliament as part of the Assisted Human Reproductive Technology Bill. While this Bill did not become law, its surrogacy provisions were copied into the next Bill considered by Parliament, the Human Assisted Reproductive Technology Bill.

The Human Assisted Reproductive Technology Act 2004 and other relevant laws[7]

There are only two provisions in the Human Assisted Reproductive Technology (HART) Act 2004 explicitly referring to surrogacy. Section

---

3 For a general discussion, see D. Wilson, 'New Zealand' in J. Scherpe, C. Fenton-Glynn and T. Kann (eds), *Eastern and Western Perspectives on Surrogacy* (Intersentia 2019).

4 *Re P (Adoption: Surrogacy)* [1990] NZFLR 385.

5 While the term 'natural conception' is not specifically explained in the reported judgment, the language used suggests that there was a written agreement in which the genetic father would have sexual intercourse with the woman and that the child born as a result would be adopted and raised by the genetic father and his wife. The woman consented to the adoption application.

6 *Re G* DC Invercargill Adopt 6/92 (3 February 1993).

7 See Debra Wilson, 'Avoiding the Public Policy and Human Rights Conflict in Regulating Surrogacy: the Potential Role of Ethics Committees in Determining Surrogacy Applications' (2017) 7(3) *UC Irvine Law Review* 653.

14 states that surrogacy arrangements are not in themselves illegal but are not legally enforceable, but that commercial surrogacy arrangements are illegal (although reasonable and necessary expenses in relation to medical, counselling or legal costs can be paid directly to the providers). Section 15 prohibits advertising in relation to surrogacy arrangements in newspapers or periodicals printed, published or distributed in New Zealand. These provisions have received very little attention from the courts.[8]

These two provisions are not the extent of surrogacy regulation, as might be first thought. The HART Act creates an overall regime where all human assisted reproductive technologies performed by fertility clinics are placed into one of three categories:

1. *established procedures*, which must be declared as such by the Governor-General through an order in Council. These can be performed by any fertility clinic without the need for prior approval;[9]
2. *prohibited actions*, found in Schedule 1 HART Act. These cannot be performed by a fertility clinic under any circumstances;
3. *assisted reproductive procedures,* which are all other assisted reproductive technologies. These are generally known as 'regulated procedures', and under s16 cannot be carried out by a fertility clinic unless the clinic has the written approval of the 'ethics committee'.

The HART Act established two committees: the Advisory Committee on Assisted Reproductive Technology (ACART), which devises guidelines for the use of regulated procedures following public consultation, and ECART, which decides the individual applications from fertility clinics using ACART's guidelines. The composition of ACART and ECART, and the relevant guidelines, are discussed in the next section.

8 The only cases in which s14 has been mentioned or discussed are: *Re Application by BWS* [2011] NZFLR 621, *Re SCR* [2012] NZFC 5466, and *Re Kennedy* [2014] NZFC 2526. All three involved international surrogacy arrangements, and in none of the applications for adoption did the payment for the surrogacy affect the outcome. For discussion of issues relating to commercial surrogacy in New Zealand, see R. Powell and A. Masselot (eds), *Perspectives on Commercial Surrogacy in New Zealand: Ethics, Law, Policy and Rights* (Centre for Commercial and Corporate Law Inc, University of Canterbury 2019) and D. Wilson and J. Carrington, 'Commercializing Reproduction: in Search of a Logical Distinction Between Commercial, Compensated and Paid Surrogacy Arrangements' (2015) 21 *New Zealand Business Law Quarterly* 178–190. For results of empirical work examining judicial perspectives in relation to surrogacy adoption cases, see D. Wilson, 'Understanding the Experience and Perceptions of Surrogacy Through Empirical Research: Judges Survey' (Te Whare Wānanga o Waitaha | University of Canterbury May 2020).

9 Human Assisted Reproductive Technology Order 2005.

There are two clear gaps in the HART Act. First, it has no extra-territorial effect, meaning international surrogacy is not subject to the Act (and therefore not regulated in New Zealand).[10] Second, it imposes liability on fertility clinics for gestational surrogacies only. Traditional surrogacies remain unregulated, even if they are carried out with the assistance of a fertility clinic.[11] It is also notable that ECART's role ends with the granting of approval to the fertility clinics to carry out the procedure. While it will often make recommendations and require consideration of events after this (for example in relation to birth plans, what the child is told, and so on), these are in no way enforceable.

The other relevant pieces of legislation are the Status of Children Act 1969 and the Adoption Act 1955. The 1969 Act confirms that for children born as a result of assisted reproduction, the 'mother' is the woman who becomes pregnant (that is, the surrogate) and the other parent is her partner (of any gender), if they have consented to the procedure.[12] Gamete or embryo donors are not the legal parents of the child, nor are the IPs whether or not they are genetically related to the child.[13] Transfer of parentage to the IPs can currently only occur through adoption, under the Adoption Act 1955.[14]

[10] This lack of regulation of international surrogacy reflected international trends at the time the Act was drafted, which were to focus on prohibiting commercial surrogacy and addressing parentage. For further discussion of international surrogacy in a New Zealand context, see Debra Wilson, 'International Surrogacy and the Adoption (Intercountry) Act: Defining Habitual Residence' (2016) *New Zealand Family Law Journal* 217. The NZLC has recently recommended that the HART Act be amended to recognise New Zealand IPs' legal parentage following international surrogacy through a special protocol for applying for adoption in the Family Court: see NZLC, n2, recommendations 52–57. Similar consideration of the regulation of international surrogacy appears in the Law Commission of England and Wales and Scottish Law Commission, *Building Families Through Surrogacy: a New Law: Volume II: Full Report* (Law Com No 411, Scot Law Com No 262, 29 March 2023). Regulation of international surrogacy was also recommended in Ireland by the Oireachtas Joint Committee on International Surrogacy, Final Report (2022), recommendation 32, and was subsequently incorporated in the Health (Assisted Human Reproduction) Act 2024. For discussion, see Brian Tobin, Chapter 10, this volume.

[11] Under the HART Act, traditional surrogacies are effectively treated as IVF or artificial insemination, which are established procedures and therefore do not require ECART approval, whereas gestational surrogacies are treated as regulated procedures and require approval.

[12] Status of Children Act 1969, ss7–18.

[13] ibid, ss19–22.

[14] The use of the adoption process for transfer of legal parentage reflected the international position at the time the New Zealand law was enacted, but subsequent heavy criticism of the adoption route by IPs and judges led to the NZLC recommending the introduction of an administrative post-birth pathway: NZLC, n2, ch 6 and recommendations 17–19. A post-birth administrative pathway is also included in the Irish Health (Assisted Human

The ACART guidelines

The composition of ACART and ECART

Under the HART Act, ACART is required to have 8–12 members, with at least one member with expertise in each of the following: assisted reproductive procedures, human reproductive research, ethics, and law.[15] Further, one member must be 'Māori [...] with expertise in Māori customary values and practice and the ability to articulate issues from a Māori perspective', one member must be able to 'articulate the interests of children', and one must be able to 'articulate issues from a consumer perspective'. At least half of the members must be lay people.[16] ECART is also required to have 8–12 members, and while s27 HART Act requires only one member with expertise in assisted reproductive procedures and one with expertise in human reproductive research, its terms of reference require a similar make-up to ACART.[17]

The relevant guidelines

Since its formation, ACART has produced three versions of guidelines to inform ECART's decision-making function in relation to surrogacy.[18] The current guidelines are governed by the principles outlined in section 4 of the HART Act, which state:

> All persons exercising powers or performing functions under this Act must be guided by each of the following principles that is relevant to the particular power or function:

Reproduction) Act 2024. In contrast, the UK Law Commissions recommended a change where, if stipulated safeguards are met, *some* IPs would become legal parents at birth via an administrative process, rather than following the existing post-birth judicial system, n10, chapters 2 and 4).

15 ss32–35.

16 A 'lay person' is defined as a person who is not a health practitioner, involved in health research, or employed by a health provider.

17 With the addition of a member to articulate the disability perspective, and the requirement for two Māori members (ECART, 'Terms of Reference', available at https://ecart.health.govt.nz/about-us/terms-of-reference (last accessed 4 July 2024)).

18 Guidelines on IVF Surrogacy (2005), Guidelines on Surrogacy involving Assisted Reproductive Procedures (2013), and ACART Advice and Guidelines for Gamete and Embryo Donation and Surrogacy (2021). The current guidelines are available at https://acart.health.govt.nz/publications-and-resources/guidelines-issued (last accessed 4 July 2024). The previous guidelines are not available online but are on file with the author.

(a) the health and well-being of children born as a result of the performance of an assisted reproductive procedure or an established procedure should be an important consideration in all decisions about that procedure;
(b) the human health, safety, and dignity of present and future generations should be preserved and promoted;
(c) while all persons are affected by assisted reproductive procedures and established procedures, women, more than men, are directly and significantly affected by their application, and the health and well-being of women must be protected in the use of these procedures;
(d) no assisted reproductive procedure should be performed on an individual and no human reproductive research should be conducted on an individual unless the individual has made an informed choice and given informed consent;
(e) donor offspring should be made aware of their genetic origins and be able to access information about those origins;
(f) the needs, values, and beliefs of Māori should be considered and treated with respect;
(g) the different ethical, spiritual, and cultural perspectives in society should be considered and treated with respect.

The 2021 guidelines contain general requirements (applicable to gamete and embryo donation as well as surrogacy) of appropriate counselling for all parties and their families, appropriate legal and health advice, and consent. In addition, the procedure must be the 'best or only opportunity for intending parents to have a child' and must not be for 'social or financial convenience or gain'.

Specific to surrogacy, the guidelines require that:

(1) affected parties have discussed, understood and declared intentions between themselves about the day-to-day care, guardianship and adoption of any resulting child and any ongoing contact;
(2) the risks associated with a surrogacy for the adult parties and any resulting child are justified in the proposal. These risks include risks to the health and wellbeing of:
    (a) the intending surrogate, including risks:
        - associated with pregnancy, childbirth and relinquishment of a resulting child to the intending parent(s);
        - that the intending parent(s) may change their mind about parenting a resulting child;
        - to the surrogate's reproductive capacity in the future;

   (b) the intending parent(s) (and embryo donor if applicable), including risks that the surrogate changes her mind about relinquishing a resulting child;
   (c) a resulting child, including risks that arise where that child becomes the subject of a dispute if the relationship between the surrogate and intending parents breaks down.
(3) the residency status and plans of the surrogate and intending parent(s) safeguard the health and wellbeing of the child, particularly in relation to being born in New Zealand;
(4) all affected parties have received joint and individual counselling;
(5) counselling will be made available to all parties before and after pregnancy is achieved;
(6) in the opinion of the counsellor, the health and wellbeing of the intending surrogate and any resulting offspring are adequately safeguarded;
(7) all affected parties have considered and, in the opinion of the counsellor, have understood:
   (a) each other's needs and plans for continuing contact;
   (b) specific issues that might affect the health and wellbeing of all affected parties.

There have been notable changes to the guidelines over time following public consultations. As examples, the following initial requirements have been amended:

- At least one of the IPs should be the potential child's genetic parent (included in the 2005 and 2013 guidelines, removed in 2021).
- The intended mother (if any) must have a medical condition (or a medical diagnosis of unexplained fertility that has not responded to other treatments) that prevents her from becoming pregnant or makes pregnancy potentially damaging to her or the child (replaced in 2013 and 2021 with the requirement that surrogacy be the 'best or only opportunity for the intending parents to have a child').
- The surrogate be either a family member or close friend of the IPs (replaced in 2013 by the requirement that 'the relationship between the intending parents and the intending surrogate safeguards the wellbeing of all parties and especially any resulting child'). In 2021, the initial language of 'the relationship' became 'any relationship'.
- The prospective surrogate and her partner (if she has one) should have completed their family (replaced in 2021, with a consideration of risks 'to the surrogate's reproductive capacity in the future').

As described earlier, the first surrogacy application to NECAHR was in 1997. From 1998 to 2004, NECAHR heard six to eight applications per year. It approved 29 applications, declined three, and deferred 17 (many of these because more information was required, and the applications were subsequently approved when this was provided).

In mid-2005, NECAHR was replaced by ECART following the enactment of the HART Act. ECART meets five to six times a year to consider applications relating to regulated procedures, and the number of applications considered in a year has grown steadily, from 20 applications in 2005 to 87 in 2022.[19] Figure 11.1 shows a breakdown of applications to ECART per reporting year (July–June).[20] By mid 2023, ECART had approved a total of 353 surrogacy applications (77 of which had conditions attached), declined seven, and deferred 21 to seek further information.[21] It is not clear, however, that these figures represent the total number of people that fertility clinics are seeing in relation to surrogacy each year. ECART can only consider about 12 applications per meeting, and holds six meetings per year. Fertility Associates, the largest fertility clinic in New Zealand, has reported that it submitted a total of 27 applications in 2020, but noted that by March 2021 it had a further 29 applications ready to go. It explained that its practice was to submit a few applications for each ECART meeting deadline, rather than all applications, to avoid overwhelming ECART.[22]

Relevant factors in ECART's decisions

While ECART's meetings are closed to the public and applications are anonymised to preserve the privacy of those involved, ECART does publish the minutes of its meetings.[23] In the beginning, these minutes provided little

19 With the exception being between 2015 and 2018 when it considered over 100 applications each year. The majority of these related to storage of frozen gametes. The HART Act allowed these to be stored for ten years from 2005, and then an application to extend storage was required.

20 Data is taken from ECART annual reports and minutes of meetings, all available at https://ecart.health.govt.nz/.

21 A conditional acceptance (or an acceptance with recommendations) is often used when the issues with the application are considered minor. A deferral is likely to occur if there are multiple small issues, or more information is required to make the decision. A decline tends to occur only if there are serious issues relating to the health of the surrogate or child, or if an application to adopt the child would not be approved. It was more common to see deferred or declined applications in the early years, when ECART, fertility clinics and the parties were getting used to the process. Now, lawyers and fertility clinics have a greater understanding of issues and information required and will generally address them prior to the application being submitted.

22 NZLC, *Te Kopu Whangai: He Arotake | Review of Surrogacy* (Issues Paper 47, 2021) at [5.21].

23 Available at https://ecart.health.govt.nz/meetings (last accessed 3 March 2024).

Figure 11.1: ECART applications

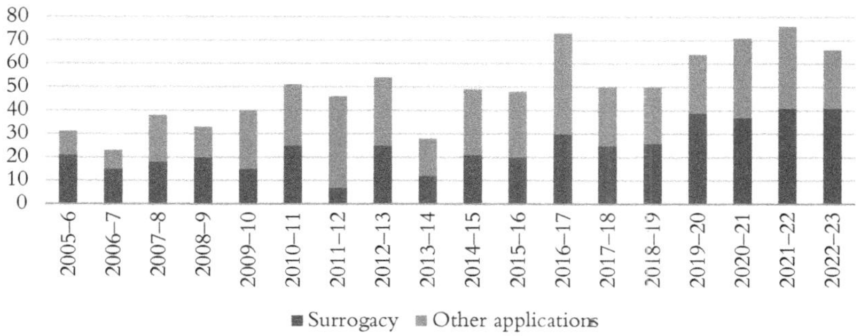

insight into factors considered (due to brevity), but over time more detailed (but still anonymised) information has begun to be provided, enabling some understanding of the decision-making process. Some factors considered by ECART are discussed below.[24]

The relationship between the parties

The 2005 guidelines required the surrogate and an IP to be 'family or close friends'. This was altered in 2013 to a requirement that 'the relationship […] safeguards the wellbeing of all parties and especially any resulting children' and again in 2021 to require that 'any relationships' safeguard wellbeing. Although it is not explicitly stated why this alteration occurred, it does appear to reflect an increasing trend in applications where the parties explained that they had met (or deepened casual friendships) in relation to the surrogacy. Despite the altered language, ECART has continued to consider the nature of the relationship between the parties, as this appears to be a useful starting point for discussions of what might happen should there be an issue with the pregnancy or birth, or for considering some of the other requirements (for example, that consent is free and informed, or that the arrangement is altruistic). While the relevant 'parties' are generally limited to the IPs and

[24] ECART applications are referred to using the abbreviation EXX/YY, with E meaning ECART application, XX being the last two digits of the year of the application and YY being the number of the application for that year. For example, E23/01 is the first ECART application considered in 2023. NECAHR decisions are referred to using the abbreviations XXXX/YY, with X being the year of the application and YY being the number of the application for that year. For example, 2005/01 was the first NECAHR application received in 2005.

the surrogate and her partner, if there is an egg donor or embryo donor, consideration will be given to these relationships as well.[25]

Concerns might arise if the nature of the relationship is not explained,[26] if the parties have only known each other for a short period of time,[27] if they were introduced for the purpose of the surrogacy arrangement,[28] or if they met online.[29] The latter might be particularly problematic if it appears that the surrogacy journey will be publicised.[30] These concerns can be mitigated by evidence that the parties have since developed their relationship,[31] or have a clear plan to do so.[32] In addition, evidence that a 'high level of thought and consideration'[33] has gone into the arrangement will be important.

Where the parties have an existing relationship, ECART might still be concerned if there is evidence that one party might be exerting influence on the other. This could occur where the relationship 'appears unequal'[34] or where there is a possibility of family pressure.[35] Concerns may arise if the existing relationship could be impacted should the arrangement not proceed or not result in a live birth.[36] Again, these concerns can be addressed if the relationship appears 'reciprocal'[37] or 'close',[38] or if counselling reveals no evidence of a problematic relationship.[39] Alternatively, ECART will be satisfied if the counselling reports indicate that all parties have demonstrated

25 E17/24 (egg donor is a 'close friend' of the IPs. They met the surrogate through social media).

26 E05/16, E12/29.

27 E06/11, E12/22.

28 E07/04 and E09/01 (introduced by fertility clinic).

29 E07/10, E09/08, E16/66, E17/24, E17/31, E18/59, E19/53, E19/145, E21/44.

30 E16/94 (IPs intend to publicise for awareness. The application was deferred to allow for discussion of impact on the surrogate and her children).

31 E09/01 (initial introduction by fertility clinic, but built relationship over a year); E15/64 (ECART noted with concern 'how they met', but added that they had developed a 'functional friendship' since); E17/110 (met online but 'genuine and open connection'), E18/135 (met online but 'trusting' relationship), E18/126 (met online but known each other for a couple of years). Compare E13/16 (met online and described as a 'hurried application'. Application deferred to give them time to develop the relationship).

32 E14/05 ('aware are in honeymoon stage of relationship' and intend to work through issues as they arise).

33 E09/13.

34 E09/05 (work relationship); E16/26 (work relationship); E17/62 (family relationship, concern raised 'about power imbalance').

35 E09/13 (surrogate is the adopted cousin of the intended mother).

36 E17/07 (close friends. Concern about implications for friendship if not successful).

37 E09/05.

38 E10/20.

39 E09/09.

an awareness of these potential issues and a willingness to work on these and/or develop their relationships further.[40]

Considerations in relation to the surrogate

The HART Act and the guidelines require consideration of any risks to the surrogate. Principle (c) of the Act states: 'While all persons are affected by assisted reproduction procedures and established procedures, women more than men, are directly and significantly affected by their application and the health and wellbeing of women must be protected in the use of these procedures'. The 2013 guidelines required consideration of the risks associated with pregnancy or childbirth, as well as the risk that the IPs might change their minds. In the 2021 guidelines, concerns about the surrogate's future reproductive capacity were added.

An important consideration for ECART is balancing the surrogate's right to autonomy with the need to protect her from risks. This requires a consideration of what the potential risks are (and often there are multiple medical or other risks identified in an application), and what level of risk is acceptable. In relation to the level of risk, ECART has commented that the test is not limited to whether there is a 'significant risk to life', but is broader than this.[41] Understanding these risks may require ECART to consider detailed medical information on the surrogate, and failure to provide this might result in an application being deferred until this information is provided.[42] Further, if the risk to the surrogate also involves a risk to the child, ECART needs to consider whether the IPs should be made aware of the issue (and therefore consent to the risk).[43]

Where risks have been identified, ECART may approve the application if it is satisfied that the risk can be mitigated by having a care plan in place to address this,[44] or by the surrogate being under specialist care.[45] It might also be sufficient that the surrogate is aware of and accepts the risk.[46] ECART might defer a decision if it feels that a risk is not well understood and requires

---

[40] E16/26; E16/27 (noting that the surrogate 'has clearly stated boundaries').

[41] E19/06 (medical report said that there was no significant risk to life. ECART noted that this is not the only consideration. The application was declined due to the risk to the surrogate and child).

[42] E05/10, E05/16.

[43] The application was deferred for this reason in E17/78, E17/115, E18/31 and E18/91.

[44] E13/05.

[45] E07/15, E21/177.

[46] E12/29 (risk of becoming unwell due to pregnancy history. The surrogate was described as 'well informed and aware of risks'. E12/23 (surrogate was insightful, well-informed and has perspective').

further medical or specialist advice,[47] or it might decline the application if it feels the risk is too high.[48] Given the number of reproductive medicine experts on the committee, it is well placed to identify and evaluate these risks. Some specific risks to the surrogate are discussed below.

Has the surrogate finished her family?

The 2005 and 2013 guidelines required that the surrogate had finished her family as there is always a risk that complications might arise during a pregnancy or birth that might affect future reproductive capacity. In 2021, this was replaced with a requirement that 'risks to the surrogate's reproductive capacity in the future' are considered.

ECART comments that it is not clear whether this language requires that she has had at least one child before becoming a surrogate,[49] although concerns have been raised that the woman might not be emotionally prepared to give up the child if she has never given birth before.[50] It has approved applications where the surrogate was unsure if her family is completed,[51] provided she understood the potential risks and has made an informed decision.[52]

Why does the woman wish to become a surrogate?

Although not directly relevant to the guidelines, the surrogate's motivations can provide some insight into her state of mind. It is not unusual for surrogates to wish to help close friends or family members because of existing relationships. In situations where the surrogate and IPs were not previously known to each other, the surrogate may be motivated by her own fertility struggles (or struggles of someone close to her), or by their own birth stories.[53] This information might, however, raise potential red flags around coercion or undue influence, or underlying mental health

47 E17/62.

48 E11/21.

49 E08/20 (concern raised that there might be unforeseen issues with handing over the child if the surrogate has not given birth before). E08/26 (the surrogate has not had a child, but has consciously decided not to. This was accepted by ECART).

50 E08/20.

51 E09/09.

52 E14/113, E15/42, E18/62, E18/63.

53 E15/45 (motivated by fertility struggle), E18/83 (motivated by own adoption). Motivations of this nature have also been reported by UK surrogates: see Kirsty Horsey, 'Surrogacy in the UK: Further Evidence for Reform: Second Report of the Surrogacy UK Working Group on Surrogacy Law Reform' (Surrogacy UK, 2018) at 3.1 and Horsey, Chapter 3, this volume.

issues (which might suggest an issue with handing over the child) that might require consideration.

The woman's age and general health

The age of the woman may be important, particularly if she is older[54] or post-menopausal and in need of hormonal replacement drugs for the pregnancy to occur.[55] Her weight might be relevant, as a high BMI might affect the ability to become pregnant or carry the pregnancy to term.[56] ECART carefully considers applications where the BMI is above 30–35[57] and might defer applications until the surrogate's BMI is lower (or might approve applications subject to this happening, where it is clear that the surrogate is already taking steps to lose weight).

Medical concerns from previous pregnancies/births

If the surrogate has a medical history related to being pregnant or giving birth, this might signal risks to her during the surrogacy. This might include a history of gestational diabetes[58] or preterm labour.[59] Other issues that have arisen are a previous miscarriage (if potentially due to a condition that might affect another pregnancy),[60] or the risk of pre-eclampsia (high blood pressure during pregnancy)[61] or simply having had a difficult previous birthing history.[62]

---

54 E05/07, E05/02, E06/09.

55 E09/19.

56 While ECART has specifically considered high BMIs, there is also anecdotal evidence to suggest that this is also occurring during the clinical assessment period, when fertility clinics may be addressing significantly high levels of BMI (that is, over 35) with potential surrogates before applications are made to ECART and suggesting to the parties that applications be delayed until steps are taken to reduce the surrogate's BMI. It is interesting to note, however, that there is recent research suggesting that there are similar IVF, live birth, obstetrical and neonatal outcomes among patients with BMIs between 30 and 60, and recommending that IVF not be withheld on this basis alone: J.S. George, S.S. Srouji, S.E. Little, E.S. Ginsburg, A. Lanes, 'The Impact of Increasing Body Mass Index on In Vitro Fertilization Treatment, Obstetric, and Neonatal Outcomes' (2023) *American Journal of Obstetrics and Gynecology* 239.e1–239.e14.

57 E10/32, E13/29, E19/06, E07/06.

58 E06/17, E12/48.

59 E18/91.

60 E08/26, E22/97.

61 E10/10, E19/11.

62 E21/177 (complex birthing history. ECART recommends specialist care and that IPs are informed of the potential risk). E20/39 (surrogate needed blood transfusion during previous birth). E22/89 (surrogate suffered vaginal tears and post birth haemorrhage

Other medical concerns

Other general medical concerns that might result in a risk to the surrogate that have been identified by ECART include having: a high resting heart rate;[63] a familial history of cardiomyopathy;[64] profound anaemia[65] or endometriosis.[66]

Mental health concerns

The guidelines are not just limited to physical risks to the surrogate, but include risks 'associated with pregnancy, childbirth and relinquishment'. ECART will therefore not only consider the physical health of the potential surrogate, but also potential impacts on her mental health. It has acknowledged that, in evaluating this, there are sometimes concerns that not all relevant information is being shared,[67] or that the information given lacks detail,[68] but that this needs to be approached carefully.

Any history of post-natal depression[69] or pregnancy-related depression[70] might need to be considered. In addition, the particular stresses of being a surrogate might exacerbate any non-pregnancy-related mental health issues the surrogate might have. If she has a history of depression[71] it will be important for ECART to know if this has been discussed in counselling[72]

following two previous pregnancies. The application was deferred to receive more information on these. E22/135 (the surrogate's most recent pregnancy was complicated by rhesus disease. Any pregnancy would require frequent monitoring. There was a plan in place, but ECART required more information before approving the application).

63 E10/10.

64 E10/10.

65 E20/39 (surrogate needed blood transfusion during one pregnancy. Declined because of risk to her, taking into account that she has four children).

66 E22/97.

67 E21/180.

68 E09/30.

69 E09/25, E10/13, E11/29 (surrogate suffered post-natal depression after her first child, but this was well controlled with the second).

70 E09/13 (the surrogate's first surrogacy ended in a miscarriage. ECART recommended more counselling to ensure that she is psychologically sound and committed to the surrogacy).

71 E07/10 (concern will not be able to hand over the child), E08/07 (need medical advice that being a surrogate will not expose her to any unnecessary risks or increased emotional stress), E10/06 (surrogate had suffered child abuse, and reported difficulty bonding with her first child. Concern raised that she might be predisposed to vulnerability and blurring of boundaries. ECART also doubted whether she would be able to hand over the child). E14/249 (history of depression. ECART was specifically concerned as she will give birth offshore alone).

72 E07/10 and E21/108 (application deferred as this was not discussed in counselling), E21/180 (some issues were mentioned in one individual counselling report but not in the joint report. ECART raised a concern that not all relevant information was being shared).

and whether there are plans in place to provide assistance if necessary.[73] If the surrogacy might make the depression worse[74] or the depression is somehow linked to the surrogacy[75] this might be a relevant consideration. If the depression is being treated by antidepressants that might impact on the pregnancy, this must also be considered as medications might need to be ceased during the pregnancy.[76]

Birth plan

ECART will also consider any implications for the surrogate and the child of a chosen birth plan. This is most commonly considered where it is identified that the woman will require or choose to have the child by caesarean section.[77] It has been noted that, where a woman has already had two caesarean sections, having a third is not recommended unless there has been consultation with a specialist.[78] If a caesarean section is elected, ECART will look to see if the medical implications of this have been discussed.[79]

Considerations in relation to the surrogate's family

The surrogate's partner

If the surrogate has a partner (of any gender, and whether they are married or in a *de facto* relationship), the partner will be considered the 'other parent' of the child if they have consented to the surrogacy under s18 Status of Children Act. If they have not specifically consented (or do not satisfy the requirements for marriage or a *de facto* relationship) they will not be the legal parent but they will still play an important supporting role in the surrogacy arrangement. It is therefore encouraged that they be involved in counselling and their views on the surrogacy be considered.

In one application, a partner admitted in counselling that he was concerned about the impact of surrogacy on their life together and on his partner's wellbeing. The counsellor's report explained that these concerns had been

---

73 E19/25.

74 E07/10 and E14/113 (work related stress, so unlikely to be affected by surrogacy).

75 E09/30 (concern that she is using pregnancy to treat depression), E18/59 (had previously been a surrogate. Reported sadness and loss after the last surrogacy. Defer for more counselling).

76 E09/19.

77 E06/17, E10/43 E14/04, E12/23 (surrogate chose caesarean section. ECART thinks this is a way for the surrogate to differentiate this birth from the previous births of her own children, and therefore reasonable).

78 E08/22, E10/12, E10/06, E19/79.

79 E05/12, E05/14.

'recognised and dealt with'. The application was approved, subject to the availability of ongoing counselling for the partner.[80] In another application, the partner's history of depression was considered,[81] and in a third, their criminal record was raised.[82] While a criminal record was not specifically relevant to the surrogacy arrangement, the fact that he did not wish this to be revealed to the IPs was of some concern to ECART, which commented that the surrogacy relationship 'requires high trust and confidence' and therefore required disclosure of this information.[83] The application was deferred, the conviction was disclosed to the IPs, and the application subsequently approved.

The surrogate's existing children

If the surrogate has children, her decision to be a surrogate might impact them. If an existing child is young this might be considered by ECART, particularly if the woman is still breastfeeding. In several applications ECART has considered situations where an existing child is aged four months,[84] six months,[85] eight months,[86] or under one year.[87] In the case of the six-month-old, the application was approved, but subject to the condition that the necessary hormonal treatment did not begin until planned breastfeeding was completed. In the case of the eight-month-old, it was noted that it is generally recommended that pregnancies occur one year apart. In another application ECART discussed whether it should require a gap of 18 months between the birth of the surrogate's own child and the surrogate pregnancy.[88] It concluded that there was no medical reason to require this unless the woman was breastfeeding or had previously given birth by caesarean section.

If the surrogate is the main caregiver for their child, this might require consideration of a care plan for the existing child,[89] particularly if the child has a condition that requires additional support.[90] Support will also be important during the later stages of the pregnancy, during recovery from

80 E09/28.
81 E09/36.
82 E22/138.
83 E22/138.
84 E6/10.
85 E05/07.
86 E20/36.
87 E11/50.
88 E21/175.
89 E10/13, E11/50 (surrogate is the single mother to two children, one under the age of one year).
90 E20/08, E19/47 (surrogate has four children, two with special needs).

giving birth,[91] or should hospitalisation be required.[92] In one application it was noted that a planned elective caesarean section would mean that the surrogate could not drive for six weeks, and that this would impact on her existing children.[93]

Even if the children are older, their interests should still be considered. In one application the surrogate was the daughter of the intended mother.[94] While it was felt that the surrogate had made her choice free from any undue influence, ECART noted the importance of discussing this with the intended mother's other adult children, due to a potential blurring of generational lines.

The process of being a surrogate and then handing the child to the IPs might be confusing for the surrogate's existing children, and ECART generally recommends that they receive counselling.[95] On occasion, an application will note that existing children will be informed only if the application is approved,[96] or if a pregnancy occurs.[97] While this plan is generally accepted by ECART, it has noted its concern at times, along with a 'strong recommendation'[98] or 'encourage[ment]'[99] that counselling occurs prior to this.[100] In one application, it was noted that the children had had the surrogacy explained to them, but had received no counselling. ECART noted that it 'expect[ed]' counselling if the pregnancy occurred.[101]

---

[91] E15/42 (noting that the surrogate was electing a caesarean section, and that there would be recovery time).

[92] E18/125 (application declined for this reason), E20/39 (potential surrogate was profoundly anaemic, and concern was raised that if she was hospitalised, there would be no one to look after her children).

[93] E10/43. While it might be thought that alternative transport might be a reasonable expense of the surrogacy, the law in New Zealand is unclear as to whether reasonable expenses can be paid. Section 14(3) HART Act prohibits the payment of 'valuable consideration' to the surrogate. Section 14(4) provides an exception for reasonable expenses paid directly to medical and legal practitioners. This suggests that a surrogate cannot receive reasonable expenses from the IPs. ECART has been asked for clarification on this from fertility clinics (E12/18) and Children, Young Persons and Their Families (now Oranga Tamariki - Ministry for Children) (Minutes, 27 September 2012 at [14 Correspondence])) and ECART has admitted uncertainty about the language of s14. The NZLC has recommended that the rules be clarified, and further recommended including a list of permitted expenses: NZLC, n2, para 8.20.

[94] E09/19. See also E14/254 (the surrogate was the intended mother's adopted daughter, and the adult children were not aware that their adopted sibling would be the surrogate).

[95] E05/05, E05/06, E10/35.

[96] E18/12.

[97] E05/02, E12/18, E12/27, E15/10.

[98] E12/18.

[99] E12/27, E08/01, E08/02.

[100] E12/18, E15/108.

[101] E18/58.

Where the children are too young to understand, a statement that the children will be told at an age-appropriate time is generally accepted.[102] In one application, it was explained that counselling would occur through school counsellors rather than through a fertility clinic. It was noted that the school counsellor would be able to talk to the children in an age-appropriate manner.[103] Where counselling occurs, ECART will look to ensure that the children understand what will happen, and that they are comfortable with the arrangement. In one application, ECART raised a concern that the surrogate's children had originally objected to the surrogacy and had then changed their minds without explanation. The application was deferred for this to be explored.[104] In another application, the woman had previously been an egg donor.[105] Her child had described having issues with this, because of the genetic connection. The child had no such issues with surrogacy as the resultant child would not be genetically related to them.

Considerations in relation to the intended mother (if applicable)

Medical reasons preventing successful pregnancy

The 2005 guidelines required that the 'intended mother' have a medical condition that would prevent her from becoming pregnant or that would make being pregnant potentially damaging to her or the foetus. The 2013 guidelines adopted the 'best or only opportunity to have a child' test and, while gender-neutral language is used, most of the examples provided in the guidelines related to a woman having a medical condition that would affect this. An example permitting psychological reasons to be considered was also included. The guidelines also require that the surrogacy not be for 'personal or social convenience'.[106] The 2021 guidelines repeat the gender-neutral 'best or only opportunity' requirement (although the examples are deleted), and also require that the surrogacy not be for 'social or financial convenience or gain'. In interpreting 'best or only opportunity' ECART looks for a medical or psychological reason why a female IP cannot carry the child. If this reason is not provided, the application will be deferred until it is. In some applications, satisfying this criterion might require 'exhaust[ing] all procedural possibilities',[107] including using an egg donor.[108]

---

102 E15/05, E15/11.

103 E09/37.

104 E05/10.

105 E15/82.

106 E05/14, E17/96, E18/126, E19/29.

107 E11/50.

108 E14/06.

Genetic considerations

In the 2005 and 2013 guidelines there was a requirement of a genetic link between the child and at least one IP. This was removed in 2021, allowing for an application for the use of embryo donation combined with surrogacy.[109] Embryo donation has been subsequently considered in two applications.[110] In the first, a same-sex male couple preferred embryo donation over the use of an egg donor, explaining that, with embryo donation, the child would not be genetically related to only one of them, and that they preferred this outcome. In the second, there was a difficulty in finding an egg donor, yet a donor embryo was available. In both applications it was noted that the wait time for an egg donor was approximately two years, and that therefore the 'best or only opportunity' test could permit the use of embryo donation.

If an IP has a condition that might be hereditary and is to provide genetic material, the risk of passing this on to the child should be considered.[111]

Other medical considerations

As the health and wellbeing of the future child is a consideration for ECART, it might be a relevant consideration that one of the IPs has a medical condition that will hinder or prevent them raising the child. This might include a physical condition like multiple sclerosis,[112] or a disability[113] or long-term medical condition[114] that might affect the ability to care for the child. It might alternatively include a condition that is exacerbated by stress.[115] In one application, an intended mother had suffered mental health issues following a previous pregnancy. ECART deferred the application in order to receive more information on whether the issues were hormone related, or were related to raising the child. If it was the latter, there was a concern that this might still arise following a surrogacy arrangement.[116]

A condition like cancer might also be a relevant consideration.[117] In this case, ECART will look at the likelihood of the cancer recurring. In one

[109] For a discussion, see Debra Wilson, 'The Importance of a Genetic Link in Surrogacy Arrangements: Law, Public Opinion and Reconciling Conflict' in R. Shaw, *Reproductive Citizenship* (Springer 2002) 203. See also Park-Morton, Chapter 5, this volume.

[110] E21/178, E22/62.

[111] E12/16, E22/55, E22/60.

[112] 2005/04.

[113] E18/125.

[114] E20/83.

[115] E10/46.

[116] E13/09.

[117] E05/16, E07/12.

application, a 5% chance of cancer recurring in the next year was seen as a 'reasonably high risk'. The application was approved, subject to waiting for two years after the cancer treatment had been completed. In another, the IP was cancer-free for three years at the time of the application, but ECART deferred the application in order to receive a five-year prognosis.[118] In a third, the decision was deferred as it was felt that the application was made too soon after the cancer treatment and loss of fertility, and that time to reflect was needed.[119]

Mental health conditions

If one or both IPs is suffering, or has suffered, from grief or depression because of their fertility issues, this should also be given consideration,[120] particularly if the surrogacy might retrigger these issues.[121]

Gender considerations

The 2005 guidelines used the phrase 'intended mother' and, while their partner (if there was one) was phrased in the gender-neutral language of 'intended parent', the fact that the Adoption Act 1955 required either a single applicant or two married applicants suggested that the 'intended parent' needed to be male.[122] The 2013 and 2021 guidelines are more gender-neutral in terms of their use of 'intended parent' instead of 'intended mother' and given the broadening of the adoption legislation, the gender of the intended parent(s) is no longer an issue.[123]

In 2022, an application was made by a trans woman (who had stored sperm before transitioning) and her non-binary partner. While the non-binary person could physically carry a pregnancy, it was noted that this would 'threaten their mental stability'. This was considered sufficient for the 'best or only opportunity' test to be met.

---

[118] E18/14.

[119] E07/12.

[120] E10/09 (grief over infertility issues).

[121] E14/117 (mourning death of two babies. Concern about depression after IVF if worried that there won't be a pregnancy, or post-natal depression after child is born).

[122] Same-sex marriage was not legalised in New Zealand until the Marriage Amendment Act 2013.

[123] As a comparison, the UK's Human Fertilisation and Embryology (HFE) Act 2008 still uses the wording 'husband and wife' in s54 and requires the surrogate to be a woman. For a discussion of the gendered language in the HFE Act, see Kirsty Horsey and Emily Jackson, 'The Human Fertilisation and Embryology Act 1990 and Non-Traditional Families' (2023) 86(6) *Modern Law Review* 1472.

Considerations for wider intended family

Just as with the surrogate's family, if the IPs have existing children they should be involved in counselling.[124] It is also important that the wider family is told, particularly if the surrogate or an egg donor is part of the family.[125] In one application, ECART noted its concern that the wider family had contributed to 'fertility treatment' without being informed that the money would be used for surrogacy.[126]

Considerations relating to donors

Egg donors

If there is an egg donor involved, they should also be part of the process. ECART considers it important that counselling takes place.[127] If this is a second or subsequent surrogacy, the egg donor should be made aware of this.[128] If the egg donor has not completed their family, this should be discussed, as the process of donation might affect future fertility.[129] It is important that an egg donor understands her legal rights, for example when her consent to her eggs being used may be withdrawn,[130] and how many couples she can donate eggs to.[131] If the egg donor has a health issue,[132]

---

124 E06/11.

125 E22/188 (egg donor is the cousin of an intended parent). This focus on the involvement of the wider family reflects the traditional Māori values of whanaungatanga (the importance of relationships and family connections) and whakapapa (the ability to trace genealogy and connect to people). While the practice of surrogacy is not specifically seen as problematic from a Māori perspective (particularly given the tradition of whāngai, or informal cultural adoptions) it is considered of highest importance that a Māori person understand their place in their wider family and in society and that the family understands its relationship to that person. These values have been adopted into the HART Act and other family law legislation through requirements of openness and transparency in relation to genetic relationships, and are incorporated into the terms of reference of both ECART and ACART.

126 E12/38.

127 E09/29, E09/07.

128 E17/99, E19/32.

129 E10/27, E14/241.

130 E10/27.

131 E17/80. While there is no legal limit in New Zealand for the number of couples that a gamete donor can donate to, fertility clinics unofficially apply a five-family donation rule. There is, however, a rule in relation to embryo donation that allows full genetic siblings to be born into two families only: ACART, 'Guidelines for Family Gamete Donation, Embryo Donation, The Use of Donated Eggs with Donated Sperm and Clinic Assisted Surrogacy' (2020).

132 E19/47 (psychiatric history), E19/142 (history of depression) E21/66 (post-natal depression).

particularly if genetic in nature,[133] any risks to the pregnancy and birth, or to the resulting child should be discussed and the IPs should be aware of these risks. Finally, the egg donor's views on termination of pregnancy might be a relevant consideration.[134]

Embryo donors

The requirement in the 2005 and 2013 guidelines that at least one IP should have a genetic link to the child prevented the use of embryo donation for surrogacy. This requirement was removed in the 2021 guidelines. This clearly allows for embryo donation, particularly since an additional 'risk' consideration was added to the guidelines: the risk that the IPs refuse to take the child. In the few applications where ECART has discussed embryo donation, there have not been any issues raised with the donation,[135] although it can be assumed that the same issues discussed in relation to egg donation are applicable.

Considerations relating to resulting children

Principle (a) of the HART Act states: 'The health and wellbeing of children born as a result of the performance of an assisted reproductive procedure or an established procedure should be an important consideration in all decisions about that procedure'. The 2013 and 2021 Guidelines referred to health and wellbeing risks for the resulting child, which specifically included becoming the subject of a dispute if the relationship between the surrogate and intended parents breaks down.

The language of 'should be an important consideration' has been criticised as 'no longer align[ing] with the international consensus that confirms the paramountcy of this child's best interests'.[136] The wording appears to have been chosen at first to reflect the fact that, while the wellbeing of the child is an important consideration, 'other factors may need to be taken into account where parenthood laws are concerned'.[137] The NZLC has noted that other New Zealand child-focussed legislation, like the Care of Children

[133] E10/42, E12/43, E20/12.

[134] E14/06 (the egg donor and her partner both had concerns about termination, but these were worked through in counselling).

[135] E19/49, E21/178, E21/181.

[136] NZLC, n2, at 5.3.

[137] NZLC, *New Issues in Legal Parenthood* (Report 88, 2005) at [1.19], and NZLC, *Te Kopu Whangai: He Arotake | Review of Surrogacy* (Issues Paper 47, 2021), at 3.9.

Act 2004 and the Oranga Tamariki Act 1989, make the best interest of the child 'the first and paramount consideration', and has recommended that this language be reconsidered.

When will the child be told?

Principle (e) of the HART Act states that donor offspring should be made aware of their genetic origins and be able to access information about those origins. While the Act does not provide any indication of when parents should share this information with their children, Part 3 of the Act requires information about donor offspring to be collected and stored by relevant agencies, and then made available on request once the child reaches the age of 18. Research suggests that best practice is for parents to introduce this information to the child as early as possible, in an age-appropriate way.[138] In a longitudinal study of UK families, Golombok et al found that introducing this information to children by the age of seven resulted in less negative relationships with their mothers in young adulthood, as well as lower levels of anxiety and depression for the mothers.[139]

As part of its decision-making process, ECART considers whether there has been a discussion about when the child will be told about their birth story, and what agreements have been made. The committee acknowledges that it has no control over whether or not this actually occurs in reality (as its jurisdiction ends once pregnancy occurs) but has noted that 'openness is encouraged'.[140] In one application the IPs 'expressed initial shock' at the idea that they should be sharing this information with the child, but it was reported that they 'came around to this idea' in counselling.[141]

Genetic conditions

In one application, ECART noted there was a 'moral issue' with knowingly having a child with a genetic condition.[142] If one of the donors has a

---

[138] See Marilyn Crawshaw and Ken Daniels 'Revisiting the Use of 'Counselling' as a Means of Preparing Prospective Parents to Meet the Emerging Psychosocial Needs of Families that Have Used Gamete Donation' (2019) 8 *Families, Relationships and Societies* 395 at 402.

[139] S. Golombok, C. Jones, P. Hall, S. Foley, S. Imrie and V. Jadva, 'A Longitudinal Study of Families Formed Through Third-Party Assisted Reproduction: Mother–Child Relationships and Child Adjustment from Infancy to Adulthood' (2023) 59(6) *Developmental Psychology* 1059.

[140] E07/05.

[141] E18/83.

[142] E13/03. This might include future generations: see E16/96 where an IP had a genetic condition that would not manifest in their children, but might in their grandchildren.

potentially inheritable condition that can be tested for,[143] ECART might defer an application so that appropriate counselling for, and consideration of, genetic conditions can be discussed.[144] If the risk is considered small, this might not be required.[145]

Issues relating to termination of pregnancy

In New Zealand, the decision about termination of the pregnancy is legally made by the surrogate. However, it is common for this to be discussed in counselling, as the surrogate may feel the decision is for the IPs to make. It goes without saying that any decision to terminate must be made in accordance with New Zealand law.[146] ECART looks for evidence that termination was discussed in relation to situations where there is a risk to the surrogate's life, where the resulting child will not survive, and where the child may be born with a disability.[147] As the decision is for the surrogate to make, ECART will defer the application if it is not clear that the surrogate understands this.[148] Further, given the unique nature of the surrogacy relationship (and in an attempt to avoid later conflict), ECART will defer for further counselling if it appears that any of the parties (surrogate, her partner, IPs, egg donor) are not in full agreement.[149]

Legal considerations

ECART must be satisfied that parties received detailed[150] and independent[151] legal advice. Lawyers must fill out a form certifying that certain information was discussed.[152]

---

143 See E15/63 where there was a chance that the child could inherit the intended mother's condition, but preimplantation genetic diagnosis was not available.

144 E10/42.

145 E12/43. In E22/12 a 1/58 chance of inheriting the condition was deferred for counselling.

146 Contraception, Sterilisation and Abortion Act 1977.

147 E05/12 (no discussion of termination for disability), E16/68 (no discussion in joint counselling), E17/25 (surrogate will not terminate for Down's. This was not discussed in joint counselling).

148 E07/06 (surrogate 'heavily guided' by intended mother's wishes), E10/20 (surrogate 'uncomfortable' with termination but will do what intended mother wishes), E14/151 (surrogate believes intended parents will decide), E18/15 (surrogate 'reluctant to terminate but will abide by intended parents' wishes').

149 E10/13 and E15/63 (inconsistent views between surrogate and intended mother), E14/06 (surrogate and intended mother in agreement on when termination might occur, but egg donor uncomfortable with termination).

150 E05/16 and E06/09 (sparse legal information provided).

151 E06/01 and E16/85 (same law firm advised both surrogate and intended parents).

152 For the results of empirical work analysing the perspectives of lawyers in relation to surrogacy arrangements, see Debra Wilson, 'Reflecting on Surrogacy: Perspectives

Surrogacy arrangements

Under s14 HART Act, surrogacy arrangements are not illegal, but are not enforceable. Lawyers often use written arrangements to record parties' expectations and facilitate discussions, but ECART looks to ensure that parties are aware that these are not binding.[153]

Payments

As mentioned earlier, s14 HART Act prohibits the payment of valuable consideration to the surrogate, and it is unclear whether reasonable expenses are permitted. While any payments to the surrogate might be considered in breach of s14 (resulting in a conviction and a penalty of imprisonment for a term not exceeding one year, or a fine not exceeding $100,000, or both), they might also be an issue under s25 Adoption Act, which prohibits 'any payment or reward in consideration of the adoption or proposed adoption of a child' (with the consequence that the adoption cannot be granted unless the court consents to the payment).

Types of payments acceptable under s14 HART Act posed issues in earlier applications,[154] though lawyers are increasingly familiar with potential issues and ECART accepts lawyers' reports that s14 HART Act on accepted payments has been explained to the parties. Increasingly, ECART is asked to consider whether payment of life insurance[155] and income protection insurance[156] are permitted. While it accepts the former, and often encourages parties to consider this, it is less clear whether the latter is acceptable under the HART Act. To address this uncertainty, the NZLC has recommended that the rules be clarified, further recommending a list of permitted expenses, but not permitting a 'fee'.[157]

Birth certificate and adoption

It is important that parties are aware that the surrogate and her partner (if they have consented) are the legal parents and will therefore be named on

---

of Family Lawyers' (2018) *New Zealand Family Law Journal* 9, and Debra Wilson, 'Understanding the Experience and Perceptions of Surrogacy Through Empirical Research: Lawyers Survey' (Te Whare Wānanga o Waitaha | University of Canterbury, May 2020).

153 E15/74, E17/06.

154 E05/05, E05/12.

155 E07/09, E07/12, E09/01, E09/07.

156 E15/62, E15/108, E16/41.

157 NZLC, n2, recommendation 46.

the initial birth certificate.[158] Transfer of parentage is required to remove legal parenthood from these people and vest it in the IPs, and then the birth certificate can be changed. As the only way to transfer legal parentage in New Zealand is through adoption, generally, ECART requires evidence the parties meet the adoption criteria,[159] and that the ministry responsible for providing a report to the court in relation to the adoption (currently Oranga Tamariki – Ministry for Children) would 'in principle' approve the adoption.[160] The 2005 guidelines stated that the child 'should be adopted' by the IPs. The 2013 and 2021 guidelines require that the parties have 'discussed, understood and declared intentions about the day-to-day care, guardianship and adoption of any resulting child, and any ongoing contact'.

In Māori culture, whāngai (or informal, cultural, adoptions) are not uncommon. ECART seemingly accepts this as a reason why the parties may not plan a formal adoption, while noting the instability of an informal arrangement,[161] unless there is something to suggest that whāngai is being used because there is a reason why a court would not grant an adoption.[162]

Citizenship and residency

Although international surrogacy is not permitted in New Zealand, some applications involve an international element, where either the IPs or the surrogate live overseas. In this situation, ECART considers the logistics of the application, including where the implantation and birth will take place, whether the child born will have New Zealand citizenship,[163] and how the child will travel to join the IPs.

An early decision of NECAHR in 2005 suggested that the surrogate needed to obtain the status of citizen or permanent resident before approval could be granted.[164] The subsequent 2005 guidelines then introduced a requirement

[158] E06/13, E07/02, E08/22, E10/23, E10/30.

[159] E07/12 (parties not married, which was an adoption requirement at the time), E08/19 (parties not planning to adopt, raised a concern).

[160] E05/02 (previous criminal history might affect adoption, so application declined), E08/108 (intended parent spent time in prison for a violent crime. The ministry responsible for writing the adoption report for the court initially reported that they would not support the adoption for this reason, but agreed to reconsider).

[161] E05/02.

[162] 2005/08.

[163] In New Zealand, a child's citizenship is generally acquired by descent (requiring that at least one of the legal parents is a citizen or permanent resident) or by specific grant by the Minister of Internal Affairs. Prior to 2006, *jus soli* (or being born in New Zealand) also resulted in the child being granted citizenship, but post-2006 this applies only if the child is abandoned and their legal parentage is unknown.

[164] 2005/09.

that the surrogate and her partner be citizens or permanent residents of New Zealand. The 2013 guidelines eased this by requiring a consideration of 'whether the residency of the parties safeguards the wellbeing of all parties and especially any resulting child'. The 2021 guidelines add 'particularly in relation to being born in New Zealand'. While the reasoning behind this requirement is not explained, in one application where the surrogate lived overseas (and it was not clear that she had New Zealand citizenship), ECART noted:[165]

> This raises several issues for the committee: the issue of jurisdiction in the event of a dispute between New Zealand and the birth parents' country, whether there are any immigration issues for the birth parents who are intending to come and live in New Zealand for the third trimester of the pregnancy and the third that of access to medical care in New Zealand.

If the surrogate lives overseas, legal advice in that country will need to be obtained, as well as an understanding of where the birth will take place.[166] If the surrogate is to travel to New Zealand for the birth, the risk that the baby is born overseas must be addressed, as well as medical costs in New Zealand if the surrogate is not a New Zealand citizen or permanent resident, and, therefore, will be required to pay for medical care.[167] If the child is born overseas, this might raise issues with bringing the child to New Zealand.[168]

If the IPs live overseas, this requires consideration of how the implantation will occur in a New Zealand fertility clinic.[169] Their travel plans will also be considered.[170]

Previous surrogacies

In 47 applications, ECART noted that this was the IPs' and/or surrogate's second application, and in six applications it was the third application. Parties' previous experience with surrogacy is taken into consideration. In some applications, previous approval was given, but the pregnancy or live

---

165 E16/71.

166 E14/08, E14/247.

167 E16/71.

168 E20/12 (surrogate is in process of getting residency, so can give birth in New Zealand. Defer until this is complete), E21/67 (concerns about travel impacts of COVID-19 led to plans being altered).

169 E15/02 and E21/73 and E23/26 (embryos to be shipped to New Zealand).

170 E19/52 (intended parents will travel from Ireland for the birth).

birth did not eventuate, and the IPs wished to try again, at times with a new surrogate or egg donor.[171] In other applications, a child was born and the IPs sought a second or third child to complete their family.

If the second or subsequent surrogacy arrangement involves the same surrogate, this might make the approval process easier, as the parties have developed their relationship. However, if a significant time has passed between the surrogacies, ECART might consider whether anything significant (particularly in relation to the surrogate's health) has changed.[172] If the second or subsequent surrogacy arrangement involves a new surrogate, ECART is often interested in the reason for the change. This might be because the first surrogate was unavailable, or it might suggest difficulties in the relationship. In one application, it was noted that, if there was a previous surrogate, ECART would like to hear from them about their experiences.[173] In another application, ECART raised concerns that the current surrogate was not aware of previous attempts.[174]

ECART has also noted that it is useful to know if the surrogate has acted as a surrogate before for another family, and how that experience had gone.[175] This may indicate that the surrogate has a deeper, learned, understanding of the implications of being a surrogate. If the surrogate had any issues or concerns in the previous relationship, it might be important that these are addressed in the new relationship. It might also provide a deeper understanding of her motivations for wanting to be a surrogate. In one application, ECART noted that the surrogate was 'taking a semi-professional approach' to surrogacy, which was of concern given the prohibition on commercial surrogacy, but accepted that she was not being paid and her reasons for engaging in the surrogacy were altruistic.[176]

Social media use

An emerging issue is the use of social media to bring public attention to issues around surrogacy or to document the journey. Given that a significant

[171] E13/13, E22/188, E22/198 (new attempt, this time using an egg donor), E14/08 (new attempt, this time using a younger surrogate), E15/72 (new surrogate), E17/60 and E18/16 (ECART approved the application, but surrogate changed mind due to risk).

[172] E10/48 (had been a 'natural' surrogate before, now a gestational surrogate), E12/28 (noting a three-year gap between surrogacies).

[173] E08/23 (first surrogate has moved to Australia), E13/07 and E17/79 (first surrogate included a letter suggesting a positive experience). E17/99 (first surrogate not available but had spoken to new surrogate about experiences). See E10/42 where there was a concern raised as to why the first surrogacy had not gone ahead after approval. Conflicting information was given in counselling and in the surrogate's letter to ECART.

[174] E08/18.

[175] E15/82, E17/10, E22/185.

[176] E14/01.

number of parties now meet on social media, documenting their journey in this way might not be considered unusual. If it has been mentioned that this might occur, ECART will look to ensure that all parties have reached a mutual understanding as to what will be posted[177] and that the privacy of the other parties will be maintained.[178] If the aim is to publicise surrogacy to help others, ECART will mention that the express consent of all parties should be sought.[179] If existing children are old enough to engage with social media, this should extend to them.[180]

The effectiveness of the ethics committee process

New Zealand has undergone some major societal shifts since the HART Act was enacted in 2004. Surrogacy, once considered so unusual that it was not included in the initial government Bill, has become more popular and more socially acceptable,[181] and now occupies a large proportion of ECART's meetings. While the HART Act 2004 and the Adoption Act 1955 have not been amended to reflect these changes, other legislation has been enacted to legalise same-sex marriage and the courts have interpreted the Adoption Act requirement of two spouses broadly enough to encompass same-sex spouses and heterosexual and same-sex *de facto* couples. ACART has responded to societal shifts by updating its 2005 surrogacy guidelines in 2013 and in 2021 by removing the gender-based requirement of 'intended mother' and the requirement of a genetic link with one IP. These amendments open up the availability of surrogacy to more people, notably LGBTQ+ IPs.

ACART guidelines require ECART to consider the impact of the surrogacy from multiple perspectives. While recognising that assisted reproduction has the strongest impact on all women involved and on the children born as a result, the guidelines take a broad approach to requiring consideration of the impact of surrogacy on all parties. This includes surrogates and IPs, and surrogates' partners and surrogates' and IPs' existing

177 E18/131.

178 E22/57.

179 E21/106.

180 E22/09 (surrogate's children agree to keep the story off social media).

181 See the discussion of this in NZLC, n2, 'New Zealanders' changing attitudes to surrogacy' at 2.29–2.36, particularly at 2.32 where it notes: 'A survey of public attitudes on surrogacy conducted by Te Whare Wānanga o Waitaha | University of Canterbury in 2017–2018 (Debra Wilson, 'Understanding the Experience and Perceptions of Surrogacy Through Empirical Research: Public Perceptions Survey' (Te Whare Wānanga o Waitaha | University of Canterbury, May 2020) reveals how, since the enactment of the HART Act, surrogacy has become embedded in New Zealand society as a legitimate method of family formation'.

children and wider families, where applicable. Where egg donors or embryo donors are involved, they are also included in the counselling process and their opinions on matters like termination of pregnancy are discussed. By the time ECART considers an application, the parties have been through fertility clinic counselling (individually and jointly) and medical examinations (if necessary). They have had legal advice and received a positive report from Oranga Tamariki-Ministry for Children that they are 'fit and proper persons to adopt' (required for the adoption process under the Adoption Act). ECART uses this information, as well as its expertise in reproductive medicine, law, and ethics, and perspectives from its cultural, disability and children's rights members, to decide whether the application can proceed. Analysis of the ECART minutes in the previous section provides interesting insights into the broad range of matters considered.

Statistics suggest that ECART's processes are effective. Of the approximately 360 applications for surrogacy made to ECART, only seven were declined due to serious medical risks, or advice that the IPs would be unable to adopt the child. While approximately 20 applications were deferred to receive further information, they were generally approved when considered again. Of the 353 applications approved, 77 were subject to conditions, like the provision of further information, or reassurances that additional steps will be taken.[182] Another indicator of success is that there are very few examples of surrogacy arrangements ending badly between the parties. This is likely due to the requirements of counselling and legal and medical advice, allowing the parties time to develop their relationships, and discuss and reflect on difficult issues involved in surrogacy. The NZLC talked to fertility clinic professionals, lawyers, surrogates and IPs as part of its 2020–2022 review, discussed below, and identified only one example of an ECART-approved arrangement ending in 'controversy or dispute'.[183]

The process is not without its problems. The requirements of individual and joint counselling, medical checks, and legal advice add significant

[182] If ECART requires further information before it can be satisfied that the surrogacy can proceed, it has two options. First, it can defer the decision if it feels that the application might need further discussion following provision of this information before it can be approved or, second, it can approve the decision subject to a condition if it feels that the completion of the additional condition does not warrant further consideration. The additional condition might require sign-off by ECART (for example a letter from Oranga Tamariki that it will support the adoption) or it might require the fertility clinic to provide further advice (for example advice about a medical or counselling concern identified by ECART) or to wait before beginning the treatment (for example if the surrogate is still breastfeeding her own child). The completion or otherwise of these conditions is not generally reported in the minutes or annual reports unless they raise further issues.

[183] The surrogate suffered pre-natal depression and terminated the pregnancy without advising the IPs: NZLC, *Te Kopu Whangai: He Arotake | Review of Surrogacy* (Issues Paper 47,

expense to the process. Given that these are listed as acceptable payments in s14 HART Act, these costs fall to the IPs. The process is also time-consuming: it takes significant time to complete all the requirements, and the applicants must wait for ECART to hear their application. The increasing popularity of surrogacy in particular, and ART in general, has led to an increasing workload for ECART and consequential delays in the outcome. Given that it is clear from many applications that surrogacy is the last option in a long journey to have a child, these additional delays can clearly be frustrating or even prohibitive for hopeful IPs.[184] These issues with the process were identified by the NZLC in its review of surrogacy.

The New Zealand Law Commission Review of Surrogacy

In November 2020, NZLC began its review of surrogacy. Its issues paper, published in July 2021 found that fertility clinics saw the process as 'safe and thorough' and that lawyers noted that 'very few end in controversy or dispute'.[185] Despite overall approval of the process, several issues were identified. First, the process can be slow and complex. One fertility clinic counsellor noted that an ECART surrogacy application took four times the work of other ECART applications and involved many meetings. They added, however, that:[186]

> I think for some people the romantic idea of being a surrogate gets weeded out with all the time and appointments which is actually good for intending parents. It's also good for preparing people for what's going to happen even though sometimes you feel like the doomsday counsel. You have to ask all these hypothetical questions.

2021) at [5.25]. The UK's Law Commissions also noted that, while their consultation had identified some examples of problems with surrogacy arrangements, these were 'rare', and that organisations had procedures in place for managing any difficulties that might arise: Law Commission and Scottish Law Commission: Joint Consultation Paper, *Building Families Through Surrogacy: a New Law* (Law Com Consultation Paper No 244, Scot Law Com Discussion Paper No 167, 6 June 2019), at 3.95–3.98.

184 Many surrogates or egg donors are friends or close family members of the IPs. The lengthy process, particularly if followed by years of trying to conceive naturally and then trying IVF, might well mean that one or both are approaching ages of decreased fertility. There have been 53 applications where the IPs or surrogate have applied to ECART before. It is not unusual in these applications to see IPs reapplying with a younger (or different) surrogate or egg donor, following a lack of success.

185 NZLC, n182, para [5.24].

186 Para [5.29].

The process is described as 'expensive'[187] with all the counselling, legal, and medical appointments required. Some requirements, notably that Oranga Tamariki–Ministry for Children consider the IPs to be 'fit and proper' people to adopt, has been described as 'overly invasive', due to it approaching surrogacy in the same manner as stranger adoption applications.[188] ECART's examination of the 'finer details of the dynamic of the relationships between the parties' has also been described as 'invasive'.[189]

In terms of reforming the current process, the NZLC's preliminary view was that ECART approval should continue to be required. The approval process operated as a 'proactive safeguard'[190] that is consistent with best practice and, crucially, has strong public support. It also considered that ECART, with its wide range of member perspectives, was the appropriate body to decide applications. However, there were clearly aspects of the process that could be improved, including increasing the capacity to consider applications, reconsidering the 'fit and proper' requirement for IPs, requiring surrogacy arrangements to be in writing and signed, and improving cultural aspects of counselling.[191] In addition, the process should be extended to all forms of surrogacy.

The final report released on 27 May 2022 contained 63 recommendations intended 'to establish a new framework for determining legal parenthood in surrogacy arrangements and otherwise improve surrogacy law and practice'.[192] Most recommendations relating to ECART reflected the preliminary views in the issues paper, and two are worth specific mention.

The first is found in recommendations 2 and 3. Recommendation 2 outlines that ECART approval 'should be amended to extend this requirement to all clinic-assisted surrogacy arrangements', as at present it is required for only gestational surrogacies. Recommendation 3 adds that 'the Government should consider ways to encourage parties to traditional surrogacy arrangements

[187] Para [5.35].

[188] Para [5.38].

[189] Para [4.28].

[190] Para [5.50].

[191] s4 HART Act 2004 includes as two of its principles that all persons exercising powers or performing functions under the Act must be guided by '(f) the needs, values, and beliefs of Māori' and '(g) the different ethical, spiritual, and cultural perspectives in society'. For Māori in particular, there are important issues in assisted reproduction around treating human reproductive material with respect. It is also important that genealogical connections are discussed by all parties and that the future child's understanding of their place in 'Te Ao Māori' (the Māori world) is discussed and safeguarded. This is particularly important where not all the parties involved are Māori, or are from different iwi (tribes). These discussions need to take place in a culturally appropriate environment to be effective.

[192] NZLC, n2.

to participate in the approval process, including whether parties should be supported to make applications directly' to ECART. A potential way to 'encourage' the use of the ECART process is found in recommendation 17, which relates to the creation of a post-birth 'administrative pathway' to parenthood as an alternative to the current adoption (court) pathway.[193] To access this pathway, there are two requirements. Requirement one is the written consent of the surrogate (recommendation 18). This consent will not be valid until the child is seven days old (recommendation 20) although the IPs will be deemed additional guardians of the child from the time of birth (recommendation 21). Requirement two is the eligibility criteria. Recommendation 19 states:

> The administrative pathway [...] should apply only if:
>
> a. the surrogacy arrangement was approved by the Ethics Committee on Assisted Reproductive Technology (ECART) and complied with any conditions imposed by ECART;
> b. the intended parents who entered the surrogacy arrangement that was approved by ECART have taken the child into their care; and
> c. the surrogacy arrangement otherwise complied with any requirements prescribed in regulations.

Accessing a post-birth administrative pathway for transfer of parenthood (and therefore being able to avoid the time, delay and dissatisfaction with the adoption process) might sufficiently incentivise IPs to utilise the ECART process and its recognised benefits. The ECART process has identified issues, which are the subject of other recommendations. These include increasing resourcing to ensure applications are considered in a 'timely manner',[194] reviewing public funding of surrogacy and the ECART process[195] and requiring Oranga Tamariki-Ministry for Children to 'develop a specialist

193 It is interesting to note that the UK has also recommended a new 'administrative pathway' (Law Commissions, n10). The criteria for this are: (1) the surrogate is over the minimum age required for surrogates (21); (2) the IPs are over the minimum age (18); (3) at least one IP has a genetic link to the child; (4) where the IPs are in a couple, they are married, in a civil partnership, or living as partners in an enduring family relationship with each other; and (5) the IPs and surrogate are domiciled or habitually resident in the UK when they sign the regulated surrogacy statement (the document that must be completed for an agreement to proceed on the new pathway) and at the birth of the child, and the assisted reproduction procedure is carried out in the UK. If the criteria are met, the IPs will become the legal parents at birth.

194 NZLC, n2, recommendation 4.

195 ibid, recommendation 62.

framework for preparing surrogacy reports' that would be less 'invasive' than the current approach.[196]

While the Labour government did not respond to the NZLC's report, it is notable that a governmental Bill, the Improving Arrangements for Surrogacy Bill, is currently before the Health Select Committee. An interim report of the committee on 24 August 2023, on advice from the Ministry of Justice, took the approach that the Bill should be reworked to align with the NZLC's recommendations. However, two weeks later, on 8 September 2023, Parliament dissolved in preparation for the 2023 general election. The 54th Parliament sat for the first time on 5 December 2023 and on 6 December the new National–ACT–NZ First coalition government reintroduced all the bills that had lapsed due to the dissolution, including the Improving Arrangements for Surrogacy Bill. The Bill was subsequently redrafted to incorporate recommendations from the NZLC and a public consultation was held on the terms of the new Bill, closing on 18 September 2024.

A model for other jurisdictions?

The ECART process has many commendable aspects. The clear focus on ensuring that IPs and surrogates have reached consensus on important ethical and moral issues, and understand each other's perspectives and feelings around issues relating to the surrogacy, increases the likelihood of either an issue-free surrogacy or, more realistically, develops the parties' relationship to a point where they are able to discuss any arising issues. The inclusion of, or at least consideration of, the wider family and their concerns, intends to address potential issues before they arise, and shows an understanding that surrogacy affects entire families, not just surrogates and IPs. Medical checks of the surrogate and IPs ensure that potential physical, psychological, or mental health risks to surrogates, resulting children, or IPs are identified and discussed early, and the requirement of legal advice ensures that all involved in the arrangement understand their legal rights. The variety of expertise and perspectives of ECART committee members increases the likelihood that other potentially relevant factors are considered. There is little surprise that this process can be described as best practice, and ECART's reported statistics support a conclusion that the process has been successful.

Would this process work as successfully in other jurisdictions? That is less than clear. It must first be noted that the three jurisdictions utilising an ethics committee process are relatively small in terms of population. New Zealand has a population of approximately five million people, Victoria, Australia, approximately six million people, and Israel approximately nine

[196] ibid, recommendation 6.

million people. The population of the UK, by comparison, is approximately 68 million. Even with the small population in New Zealand, a significant issue described in relation to the ethics process is how long it takes. As the number of applications for surrogacy increase yearly, this issue is likely to become more significant. However, it is not an unsolvable problem, with several potential solutions: increase ECART's funding, so it can meet more regularly; increase ECART membership, so it can hear more applications; create a sub-committee of ECART that only considers surrogacy applications; or convert ECART from a national committee to a series of smaller regional committees. These options appear workable to reduce wait times, but clearly require additional governmental funding. The requirements of counselling, medical and legal advice remain time-consuming (for good reason, allowing time for parties to reflect on these sessions). Whether the benefits of the process are outweighed by the detriment of delay will be a matter for relevant authorities to consider.

The second issue raised is that of increased cost for IPs in paying for the counselling, medical, and legal sessions. NZLC recognised that this can be addressed by increased public funding. Again, this appears to be a question of whether the benefits of the process are outweighed by this additional cost.

The final issue raised, the invasiveness of the process, is a result of three factors. First, any judicial model of transfer of parentage requires the court to consider the best interests of the child, which will include information about the living environment and family circumstances of the IPs.[197] Second, New Zealand's archaic 1955 Adoption Act includes the consideration of additional requirements that seem outdated and problematic in today's society.[198] These factors are arguably a consequence of the post-birth judicial transfer of parentage model, which are not specific to the ECART process, and can be avoided under the proposed new administrative pathway (and with the amendment of the Adoption Act, currently under review by the Ministry of Justice).

Third, to be satisfied that the interests of all parties and any resulting child are protected, ECART considers it necessary to understand both the relationships between the parties and any relevant mental or physical health issues of the parties. The final factor is obviously an inherent part of the ECART process and, while ACART and ECART are aware of this,[199] both see a level of invasiveness as necessary to carry out their roles and ensure that all parties are protected. It is interesting to note that of 190 submissions to

[197] This is also the case under the current procedures in the UK, where CAFCASS provides a parental order report to the court.

[198] Most notably the presumption against granting an adoption of a female child by a sole male applicant unless 'special circumstances' exist: s4(2) Adoption Act 1955.

[199] NZLC, n2, 4.28.

the NZLC on the question of whether ECART approval should continue to be required for gestational surrogacy, 78% either agreed (63%) or agreed in part (15%) it should continue.[200] This suggests that, while invasive, there are benefits to the process. In addition, when asked if the ECART process should be extended to include traditional surrogacies[201] 82% of the 188 submissions thought that it should be extended, noting the benefits of the process in safeguarding the wellbeing of the parties and the resulting child.[202]

Two other factors that potentially contributed to the success of the ethics committee model in New Zealand are not necessarily shared by other jurisdictions considering surrogacy reform. First, the ethics committee process was introduced at the same time as the HART Act was enacted. New Zealand IPs accept the process because they have never known anything different. The time, cost, and discomfort with the current procedure are often met with resigned acceptance: this is the process that must be complied with. Imposing this process on another jurisdiction at this stage of surrogacy regulation might not be as successful. Second, New Zealand is geographically isolated. While many IPs engage in international surrogacy, the most common destinations are states in the US, which involve at least a 12-hour flight. Frustrations about cost and time in the ethics process must be balanced against the additional expenses, stresses, and time delays when engaging in international surrogacy from such a distance.

Overall, the ethics committee process might not be as successful in other jurisdictions as it is in New Zealand due to the factors discussed above. However, this does not mean that parts of the process cannot be adopted. The requirements of counselling, medical examinations and legal advice should be standard in any surrogacy arrangement involving a fertility clinic (or perhaps a non-profit surrogacy organisation as in the UK), and the discussion of ECART's considerations above provides valuable guidance as to what should be covered in these sessions.[203] While placing the ultimate decision-making in the hands of an ethics committee might not be considered feasible or desirable, all jurisdictions can learn important lessons from each other as to discussions that need to be had with, and among, those involved in surrogacy and their families. The fact that ECART provides insight into these conversations in the minutes of its meetings is an excellent starting point.

---

200 ibid, 4.31.

201 ECART currently only has jurisdiction over gestational surrogacy arrangements (see n11).

202 NZLC, n2, 4.40–4.41.

203 While it is likely not possible to enforce these requirements in relation to surrogacy arrangements not involving a fertility clinic, the NZLC has suggested that an incentive of eligibility to the proposed administrative pathway for those involved in traditional arrangements that utilise the ECART process could be considered.

12

Epilogue: Future Directions in Surrogacy Law – Law and Policy Reform in the UK and Beyond

Kirsty Horsey, Zaina Mahmoud and Katherine Wade

The chapters contained in this collection provide a timely and thorough examination of surrogacy law in light of the recommendations of the Law Commission of England and Wales and the Scottish Law Commission, and the accompanying draft Surrogacy Bill. The contributions offer a mix of academic, practitioner, and first-hand viewpoints, which contribute to the originality and timeliness of the collection. While much has been written on the legal and ethical issues surrounding surrogacy in the UK, there is less scholarship engaging specifically with issues stemming from law reform.

This book offers a critical interrogation of the most recent UK law reform proposals in a way that advances the current field, offering insights not only on how the law should change but also informing past, wider, and even international debates on key issues within surrogacy. Some of the recommendations under consideration could serve as a model for other jurisdictions considering (re)regulation of surrogacy. We recognise that the current recommendations are not perfect and, in some places, could be informed by good practice and legal developments elsewhere, as some of the chapters here consider.

We remain convinced that effective domestic regulation of surrogacy can foster ethical and safe practice and balance the diverse and often competing interests of all parties involved, including children born through surrogacy, surrogates, and intended parents (IPs). Good regulation has the potential for disincentivising IPs from seeking surrogacy overseas, where practices and safeguards may not be as effective at protecting those involved. The perception that overseas surrogacy is an easy, better, or more certain solution must be challenged.

International regulation or, at least, collaboration regarding surrogacy would be welcome, although we recognise the challenges in doing so, particularly since some counties ban the practice. Surrogacy gives rise to much ethical debate and several jurisdictions are reviewing and creating new surrogacy laws. There is a trend in some Western nations, including New Zealand, Australia, Ireland, Portugal and Denmark, towards more liberal regulation focusing on the best interests of those involved, not least children born through surrogacy. Similarly, there is a softening that is apparent in recent judgments of the European Court of Human Rights (ECtHR), which is leaning towards protecting the citizenship and identity rights of children, even when their parents have acted outside the law. It is likely that, over time, this approach will soften further. Some countries continue to prohibit surrogacy, though this does not prevent IPs entering international arrangements. Attempts to punish those that do, as seen most recently in Italy, for example, have proved ineffective. At the same time, new surrogacy destinations seem continuously to emerge, often concerningly in unregulated spaces, with minimal safeguards for those involved. Past experiences suggest this may give rise to problematic and unethical surrogacy practices. While such 'destinations' may be 'shut down' to IPs from overseas, we also know that shutting down surrogacy in one space just means it 'opens up' elsewhere.

We recognise the strong anti-surrogacy voice emerging among some groups. These are often promoted by anonymous accounts, with links to other causes, and some are related to a resurgence of a Christian-right ideal of the nuclear family. Some groups consider *all* surrogacy to be contrary to human dignity. Often, they take an essentialist view of women and motherhood, inevitably rendering them anti-surrogacy. These groups frequently make such claims without reference to peer-reviewed studies or empirical work, and will not engage with such work when it is presented. Potentially dangerous misinformation is presented about what surrogacy is, who uses it and why, who surrogates are, as well as generalities about surrogates' supposed regret and harm to people born through surrogacy. This results in calls to ban surrogacy, globally and within individual countries (as is argued by such groups in relation to the UK proposals). While we understand – and agree – that *some* surrogacy is highly problematic (usually in unregulated destinations where there is commerciality and/or an already existing imbalance of power and wealth), as stated earlier, we contend that effective domestic regulation is a better solution, alongside national and international attempts to prevent potential harms occurring in some surrogacy destinations. Banning surrogacy will only push it underground and overseas, in nobody's best interests.

Part of developing effective domestic and international frameworks requires an understanding of international developments, awareness of anti-surrogacy sentiment and where it comes from, and engagement with the tricky issues raised by surrogacy. There is a need for more representative narratives of surrogacy in media/culture, potentially gained by better understanding of, and education about, surrogacy and alternative family forms more generally. Understanding of who surrogates are – especially in well-regulated jurisdictions – and who IPs are and their reasons for using surrogacy, as well as better education about the risks of engaging with surrogacy in unregulated places, can help. Similarly, follow-up studies or critical engagement with surrogacy-born children (and adults) should inform the debate.

The UK is often looked to as a model framework in assisted reproduction, with existing legislation on surrogacy since the 1980s and a respected regulatory body and relevant legislation covering assisted reproduction and related research since 1990. Rather than the UK simply being used as a model framework for surrogacy regulation, it is important other jurisdictions use the insight into the challenges of the current framework and envisage alternative strategies to regulate surrogacy, such as those set out by the Law Commissions and by the contributions in this volume. For example, at the time of writing Ireland was the most recent jurisdiction to legislate for surrogacy; however, Ireland's new law largely follows the current UK model, including the post-birth transfer of parentage to IPs. It is important that the issues with the UK framework are known to legislators in other jurisdictions, so problematic aspects of the current legislation are not repeated. The sooner the law is changed in the UK, and the anticipated benefits achieved, the better.

We think it is important, therefore, that the reform recommendations are debated publicly and in parliament. The Law Commissions' project should not have been in vain. There was no time for the recommendations to be considered in the last parliament, but we are hopeful that law and policy makers under the newly elected Labour government will not allow them to gather dust. We hope that the contributions in this volume will influence these long-awaited debates and law reform, to positively shape the future direction of surrogacy law both in the UK and beyond.

Index

References to endnotes show both the page number and the note number (95n1).

P

R

S